The Psychology

There is a rich anthropological literature on the nature and meaning of gifts. There is also an interesting and important sociological literature on the behaviour of rich and poor people, and the social consequences of a large gap between the two. We know a great deal about the psychology of sex, but the psychology of money is one of the most neglected topics in the whole discipline of psychology. This fascinating book looks at why money is even more 'taboo' than sex and death.

Adrian Furnham and **Michael Argyle**, highly respected psychologists and renowned authors, look at such diverse and compelling subjects as: money and power; morality and tax; how wealth affects behaviour and self-esteem; gender differences; what causes one person to become a spend-thrift and another to become a miser; and why some people gain more pleasure from giving away money than from retaining it.

Comprehensive and cross-cultural, *The Psychology of Money* integrates fascinating, scattered literature from many disciplines, and includes the most recent material to date. It will be of interest to psychologists, anthropologists, sociologists and to people interested in business and economics.

Adrian Furnham is Professor of Psychology at University College London. Widely published, his books include *Culture Shock* (with Stephen Bochner, 1986), *The Protestant Work Ethic* (1990), *Complementary Medicine* (1997) and *The Psychology of Behaviour at Work* (1997).

Michael Argyle is Emeritus Professor of Psychology at Oxford Brookes University. He has written more than 25 books, including *The Psychology of Everyday Life* (1992), *The Psychology of Social Class* (1994) and *The Psychology of Religious Behaviour, Belief and Experience* (with Benjamin Beit-Hallahmi, 1997).

The Psychology of Money

Adrian Furnham and Michael Argyle

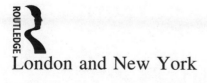

London and New York

First published 1998 by Routledge
11 New Fetter Lane, London EC4P 4EE

Simultaneously published in the USA and Canada
by Routledge
29 West 35th Street, New York, NY 10001

Typeset in Times by
J&L Composition Ltd, Filey, North Yorkshire
Printed and bound in Great Britain by
T.J. International Ltd, Padstow, Cornwall

British Library Cataloguing in Publication Data
A catalogue record for this book is available from the
British Library

Library of Congress Cataloging in Publication Data
Furnham, Adrian.
   The psychology of money/Adrian Furnham and
   Michael Argyle.
   Includes bibliographical references and index.
   1. Money–Psychological aspects.   I. Argyle, Michael.
   II. Title.
HG222.3.F87   1998
332.4'01'9–dc21   97–36974

ISBN 0–415–14605–4 (hbk)
ISBN 0–415–14606–2 (pbk)

For Benedict Adrian Felix and the numerous Argyle grandchildren

Contents

Figures

Tables

Acknowledgements

The authors and publishers gratefully acknowledge the following for permission to reprint previously published material.

Addison Wesley Longman: a figure from E. E. Lawler (1981) *Pay and Organisation Development*, p. 94.

American Psychological Association: a figure from *Journal of Personality and Social Psychology*, 1995, *69*, 851–64.

American Sociological Association: a figure from T. Caplow (1982) *American Sociological Review*, *47*, 383–92.

Cassidy, T.: a figure from T. Cassidy and R. Lynn (1991) *British Journal of Educational Psychology*, *61*, 1–12.

Elsevier Science: two tables from A. Furnham (1995) *Personality and Individual Differences*, *19*, 557–83; a figure from A. Furnham (1984), *Personality and Individual Differences*, *5*, 95–103; Appendix B from W. F. Van Raaig and H. Granolten (1990), *Journal of Economic Psychology*, *11*, 288–90.

Kluwer: two figures from E. Diener, E. Sandvik, L. Seidlitz and M. Diener (1993) *Social Indicators Research*, *28*, 195–223.

Open University: two tables from P. Lunt and S. Livingstone (1992) *Mass Consumption and Personal Identity*.

Oxford University Press: a figure from A. B. Atkinson (1983) *The Economics of Inequality*.

Personnel Psychology: a table from R. A. Guzzo, R. D. Jette and R. A. Katzell (1985) *Personnel Psychology*, *38*, 275–91.

Policy Studies Institute: a table from P. W. Willmott (1976), *Help Given and Received from Kin (USA)*; a table from P. W. Willmott (1987) *Friendship Networks and Social Support*.

Sage: a table from S. W. Hoffman and J. D. Manis in F. I. Nye (1982) *Family Relationships*.

Select Press: a table from N. L. Kamptner (1991) in F. W. Rudmin (ed.), To Have Possessions, special issue of *Journal of Social Behaviour and Personality*, *6*, 209–28.

Transaction: a table from R. Hill (1970) *Family Development in Three Generations*.

University of Wisconsin Press; a table from J. Medina, J. Saegert and A. Gresham (1996), *Journal of Consumer Affairs*, *30*(1).

Wiley: a table from T. Tang (1992) *Journal of Organizational Behaviour*, *13*, 199; two tables from A. Furnham (1996), *Journal of Organizational Behaviour*, *17*, 382, 384.

Winston & Son, Inc.: a table from M. Harris (1995) *Journal of Applied Social Psychology*, *25*(8), 725–44.

Quotations at the beginning of each chapter were derived from the following sources:

Dormann, H. (1987) *The Speaker's Book of Quotations*, New York: Fawcett Columbine.

Manser, M. (1987) *The Chambers Book of Business Quotations*, Edinburgh: W. & R. Chambers.

Weber, E. (1991) *The Book of Business Quotations*, London: Routledge.

White, R. (1987) *Speaker's Digest: Business Quotations*, London: Foulsham.

The authors and publishers have made every effort to contact copyright holders of material published in this book. If a proper acknowledgement has not been made, the copyright holder should contact the publishers.

1 The psychology of money

Money isn't everything: usually it isn't enough.

Anon.

Americans respect people who earn money. Earning proves you have certain qualities. In France as in Italy and Britain, people who have money are better regarded than those who earn it.

Jacques Maisonrouge

Money is a singular thing. It ranks with love as man's greatest source of joy. And with his death as his greatest source of anxiety.

John Kenneth Galbraith

The value of a dollar is social, as it is created by society.

Ralph Waldo Emerson

We Americans worship the mighty dollar! Well, it is a worthier god than Hereditary Privilege.

Mark Twain

Money is as much a reality as the Blessed Trinity.

Monsignor Ralph Brown

Money never remains just coins and pieces of paper. It is constantly changing into the comforts of daily life. Money can be translated into the beauty of living, a support in misfortune, an education, or future security. It can also be translated into a source of bitterness.

Sylvia Porter

Money is like an arm or leg – use it or lose it.

Henry Ford

Poverty is no disgrace to a man, but it is confoundedly inconvenient.

Sydney Smith

The American talks about money because that is the symbol and measure he has at hand for success, intelligence, and

power; but, as to money itself, he makes, loses, spends, and
gives it away with a very light heart.

George Santayana

A NEGLECTED TOPIC

Psychologists have been interested in a bewildering array of human behaviours and endeavours. There are books, papers and reports on topics as diverse as the psychology of Christmas and the psychology of the Chinese. There are a plethora of papers in psychology on depression, death and drawing, but little on the psychology of debt. We know a great deal about the psychology of sex, of selection (of both mates and employees) and even singing but little on the psychology of saving, shopping or spending.

One of the most neglected topics in the whole discipline of psychology, which prides itself in the definition of *the* science of human behaviour, is the psychology of money. Open any psychology textbook and it is very unlikely that the word money will appear in the appendix. This is as true of specialist textbooks on organisational behaviour as it is of general books. Most people would expect a psychology textbook dealing with occupational or organisational behaviour to refer to the power of money as a work motivator or discuss the symbolism of salaries; but few do.

Why have psychologists tended to neglect the topic of money? There is a rich anthropological literature on the nature, meaning and function of gifts. There is also an interesting and important sociological literature on the behaviour of rich and poor people, and the social consequences of a large gap between the two. Sociologists have been interested in the way in which the different social classes spend and save money, and the consequences of the perception of relative deprivation as they compare themselves with others.

It is true, as we shall see, that not all psychologists have ignored the topic of money. Freud directed our attention to the many unconscious symbols money has, which may explain unusually irrational monetary behaviours. Behaviourists have attempted to show how monetary behaviours arise and are maintained. Cognitive psychologists showed how attention, memory and information processing leads to systematic errors in dealing with money. Some *clinical* psychologists have been interested in some of the more pathological behaviours associated with money, such as compulsive savers, spenders and gamblers. *Developmental* psychologists have been interested in when and how children become integrated into the economic world and how they acquire an understanding of money. More recently, *economic* psychologists have taken a serious interest in various aspects of the way people use money, from the reason why they save, to their strategies of tax evasion and avoidance.

Yet it still remains true that the psychology of money has been neglected.

There may be various reasons for this. Money remains a taboo topic. Whereas sex and death have been removed from both the social and the research taboo list in many Western countries, money is still a topic that appears to be impolite to discuss and debate. To some extent psychologists have seen monetary behaviour as either rational (as do economists) or beyond their 'province of concern'. It may even be that the topic was thought of as trivial compared with more other pressing concerns, like understanding brain anatomy and the causes of schizophrenia. Economics has had a great deal to say about money but very little about the behaviour of individuals. Both economists and psychologists have noticed but shied away from the obvious irrationality of everyday monetary behaviour.

Lindgren (1991) has pointed out that psychologists have not studied money-related behaviours as such because they assume that anything involving money lies within the domain of economics. Yet economists have also avoided the subject, and are in fact not interested in money as such, but rather in the way it affects prices, the demand for credit, interest rates and the like. Economists, like sociologists, also study large aggregates of data at the macro level, in their attempts to determine how nations, communities and designated categories of people use, spend and save their money.

It is, of course, impossible to do justice to the range and complexity of economic theories of money in this book. Economists differ from psychologists on two major grounds, though they share the similar goal of trying to understand and predict the way in which money is used. Economists are interested in *aggregated* data at the *macro* level – how classes, groups and countries use, spend and save their money under certain conditions. They are interested in modelling the behaviour of prices, wages, etc., not of people. To this extent economists have more in common with sociologists than with psychologists who are interested in individual and small group differences. Thus, whereas economists might have the goal of modelling or understanding the money supply, demand and movement for a country or continent, psychologists would be more interested in understanding how and why different groups of individuals with different beliefs or different backgrounds use money differently. Whereas individual differences are 'error variance' for the economists, they are the 'stuff' of social psychology. Second, whereas economists attempt to understand monetary usage in terms of rational decisions of people with considerable economic knowledge and understanding, psychologists have not taken for granted the fact that people are logical or rational in any formal or objective sense, though they may be self-consistent. Indeed, it has been the *psychological*, rather than the *logical*, factors that induce people to use money the way they do that has, not unnaturally, fascinated psychologists.

Lea and Webley have written:

We do not need to look far to understand this negligence. Psychologists do not think about money because it is the property of another social science, namely economics. Economists can tell us all there is to know about money; they tell us so themselves. It is possible, they admit, that there are certain small irregularities of behaviour, certain deficiencies in rationality perhaps. This, psychologists can try to understand, if this amuses them. But they are of no importance. As economic psychologists, we disapprove of both the confidence of economist and the pusillanimity of psychologist.

(1981, p. 1)

A number of books have appeared entitled *The Psychology of Money* (e.g. Lindgren, 1991). Most supposedly reveal 'the secrets' of making money, though one left unsaid was the motive for writing that particular kind of book itself! Often those most obsessed with finding the secret formulae, the magic bullet or the 'seven steps' that lead to a fortune are least likely to acquire it. Dogged, single-minded pursuit of money can lead to success though often wealth results serendipitously. It is the peculiar combination of accident/chance but the sagacity in knowing how and, most of all, when to exploit discoveries or insights that seems most frequently to lead to wealth.

Many famous writers have thought and written about monetary-related matters. Marx talked about the fetishism of commodities in capitalistic societies because people produced things that they did not need and endowed them with particular meanings. Veblen believed that certain goods are sought after as status symbols because they are expensive. Yet this demand for the exclusive leads to increase in supply, lowered prices and lessened demand by conspicuous consumers, who turn their attention elsewhere. Galbraith, the celebrated economist, agreed that powerful forces in society have the power to shape the creation of wants, and thus how people spend their money.

This book is an attempt to draw together and make sense of a very diverse, scattered and patchy literature covering many disciplines. It attempts to provide a comprehensive social- and experimental psychological perspective on money and all its associated meanings and behaviours. A theme running through the book is not how cool, logical and rational people are about acquiring, storing and spending of money but the precise opposite.

A central feature of nearly all social-science, especially psychological, research and theorising on money has been a criticism of the economic model of how people behave with respect to money. All sorts of studies, from using experimental games (Vlek, 1973) to simple interviews (Haines, 1986) have attested to the often highly irrational beliefs and behaviours people appear to have with respect to money. Consumer psychologists have shown the relationship between price and quality in consumer markets and show consumers to be behaving irrationally. Indeed, it is not always clear whether consumers operate according to the somewhat 'watered-down' bounded rationality model (Hanf and von Wersebe, 1994). Even some economists have challenged the rationality model, pointing out that it may be quite possible for 'rational' agents to violate some of the foundational axioms of the expected-utility model (Anand, 1993). Equally, Stanley (1994) has pointed out how, for experimental economists, it may be difficult to identify irrationality and, hence, easy to label 'silly' economic behaviour as rational. We shall see that the psychological literature again and again shows people to act in ways quite different from the dispassionate, logical, utility and profit-maximisation model so long held by economists.

Further, we shall move beyond the remit of anthropologists, economists and sociologists, and ask (as well as, we hope, answer) questions such as, does money make people happy? Where their often curious attitudes to money arise, why do some give it all away and why, quite frequently, are most treasured and valued possessions often worth nothing? In short, this book addresses the psychological meanings people give to money, how their beliefs and attitudes to it arise and how they use it as adults.

THE PSYCHOLOGY OF MONEY

The dream of becoming rich is widespread. Many cultures have fairy tales, folk-lores and well-known stories about wealth (Wiseman, 1974). This dream of money has several themes. One is that money brings security; another that it brings freedom. Money can be used to show off one's success as well as to repay those who in the past slighted, rejected or humiliated one. One of the many themes in literature is that wealth renders the powerless powerful and the unloved lovable. Wealth is a great transforming agent, which has the power to cure all. Hence the common desire for wealth and the extreme behaviours sometimes seen in pursuit of extreme wealth.

However, it is true to say that there are probably two rather different fairy tales associated with money. The one is that money and riches are just deserts for a good life. Further, this money should be enjoyed and spent wisely for the betterment of all. The other story is of the ruthless destroyer of others who sacrifices love and happiness for money, and eventually gets it but finds it is of no use to him/her. Hence all they can do is give it away with the same fanaticism with which they first amassed it. Note the moralism in the story, which is often associated with money.

The supposedly fantastic power of money means that the quest for it is a very powerful driving force. Gold-diggers, fortune-hunters, financial wizards, robber barons, pools winners and movie stars are often held up as examples of what money can do. Like the alchemists of old, or the forgers of today, money can actually be *made* (printed, struck or indeed electronically moved). Money through natural resources (oil, gold) can be *discovered* and exploited. Money through patents and products can be *multiplied*. It can also *grow* in successful investments.

Throughout this century there has been mass migration from developing to developed countries and from the country to the cities (Furnham and Bochner, 1996). All have dreamed of a new life with more money. Having no roots or families, people were brought together by money-making. Networking and famous connections were often ultimately business based. Ordinary people in these settings had to become more aware about money: how to prevent being conned and how to exploit opportunities. However, later this century, people became less enchanted with some forms of money-making. Edward Heath, former Conservative prime minister, talked of the 'ugly and unacceptable face of capitalism'.

The acceptability of openly and proudly seeking money and ruthlessly pursuing it at all costs seems to vary at particular historical times. In the 1980s and the 1990s it seemed quite socially acceptable, even desirable, in some circles to talk about wanting money. It was acceptable to talk about greed, power and the 'money game'. But this bullish talk appears only to occur and be socially sanctioned when the stock market is doing well and the economy is thriving. After the various crashes this century, brash pro-money talk is considered vulgar, inappropriate and the manifestation of a lack of social conscience. The particular state of the national economy, however, does not stop individuals from seeking out their personal formula for economic success, though it inevitably influences it.

Money is, in and of itself, inert. But everywhere it becomes empowered with special meanings, imbued with special powers. Psychologists are interested in attitudes towards money, why and how people behave as they do towards and with money, as well as what effect money has on human relations.

Money effectiveness in society now depends on people's expectations of it rather than on its intrinsic or material characteristics. Money is a social convention and hence attitudes to it are partly determined by what they collectively think everyone else's response will be. Thus, when money becomes 'problematic' because of changing or highly uncertain value, exchange becomes more difficult and people may even revert to barter. In these 'revolutionary' times long-established, taken-for-granted beliefs are challenged and many people find themselves articulating and making explicit ideas and assumptions previously only implicitly held.

Carruthers and Babb (1996) looked at post-civil war America when two monetary alternatives were debated: that of the bullionists who favoured gold-based money, and that of the greenbackers, who favoured paper money. In contemporary American society, monetary issues have little of the popular salience they possessed in the greenback era in the last century. Money is once more perceived to be an apolitical, neutral device that facilitates trade. The 'greenback era' with the two alternatives offered a moment of acute, collective and contested reflection on the nature of money. Many people, although not the bullionists, believed that monetary institutions had significant distributional consequences and created distinct groups of winners and losers. The greenback era attested to the fact that when a social institution becomes problematic and is no longer taken for granted, there is great potential for radical change. Indeed, the same may be true today in the European Union, as countries consider giving up their currency (pound, mark, franc) for the new Euro-currency. This change seems to allay anxieties and issues not considered important until this issue arose.

What is money? *The New Oxford (Colour) Thesaurus* defines money thus:

> **money** *n* affluence, arrears, assets, bank-notes, *inf* bread, capital, cash, change, cheque, coin, copper, credit card, credit transfer, currency, damages, debt, dividend, *inf dough*, dowry, earnings, endowment, estate, expenditure, finance, fortune, fund, grant, income, interest, investment, legal tender, loan, *inf* lolly, *old use* lucre, mortgage, *inf* nest-egg, notes, outgoings, patrimony, pay, penny, pension, pocket-money, proceeds, profit, *inf* the ready, remittance, resources, revenue, riches, salary, savings, silver, sterling, takings, tax, traveller's cheque, wage, wealth, *inf* the wherewithal, winnings.

The above definition gives some idea of all the money related issues that will be discussed later in the book. Money not only has many different definitions, but multiple meanings and many uses. Appendix A (pp. 292–300) gives some of the names given to money as well as the idioms used for it. The sheer number of terms attests to the importance of money in society.

There are no grand psychological 'theories' of money although various psychological paradigms or traditions have been applied to the psychology of money. These include psychoanalytic theories, Piagetian development theories, behaviourist learning theory and, more recently, interesting ideas emerging out of economic psychology. *Behaviourist research* has been concerned with how money becomes a conditioned reinforcement and hence a valued and meaningful object. Research in this tradition has been limited to studies on animals in which animals of various sorts (rats, chimpanzees, cats) perform a task in order to get tokens (poker ships, iron balls, cards), which, like money, can be exchanged for desirable objects such as food. Hence, money is valued because it represents or is associated with various desirable objects.

As well as animal studies, there is a vast literature on '*token economies*', which is effectively the application of behaviourist 'monetary' theories to clinical populations such as mental patients (especially schizophrenics), disturbed adolescents and recidivists. A token economy is a self-contained economic system where clients/patients are paid (reinforced) for behaving appropriately (socialising, working), and in which many desirable commodities (food, entertainment, cigarettes) can be purchased. Thus luxuries (indeed, necessities) must be earned (Ayllon and Azrin, 1968).

Numerous studies have shown the benefits of token economies (Ayllon and Roberts, 1974) but have also received various criticisms on clinical grounds. These include the fact that, as there is little comparative research (only a no-treatment control condition), it is difficult to establish whether token economies are better or worse than other conditions; that token economies are often aimed at institutional rather than individual needs; that token economies violate many individual rights in total institutions; but, perhaps most important, that conditioned behaviour does not generalise to new environments where the token economy does not operate (Bellack and Hersen, 1980).

Finally, it should be pointed out that there is a fairly large literature, in the behaviourist tradition, on the effects of monetary incentives on various cognitive tasks (Eysenck and Eysenck, 1982). Most of this work has demonstrated that motivation (through monetary reward) controls attention and hence learning, which in turn affects memory.

Lea *et al.* (1987) have noted that there is an experimental and social psychology of money, as well as numerous important psychometric studies on the topic (see Chapter 2). They argue that we need to move towards a new psychological theory of money which takes cognisance of the symbolic value of money. Finally, they believe psychologists need to move on from arguing and demonstrating that people are clearly irrational or a-rational with regard to money and look at the many institutions and rituals that accept, sanction or even encourage less than rational economic behaviour. Indeed, because social psychologists have always seen it as their task to socialise psychology and individualise sociology, they have found themselves in a strong position to understand the way in which social groups, organisations and institutions can and do have a powerful effect on the monetary beliefs and behaviours of ordinary people.

ECONOMISTS ON MONEY

Most libraries contain hundreds of books with the term 'money' but nearly all are found in economics. There are books on monetary theory; monetary policy; money and capital markets; internal money; money, politics and government policy; and the relationship between money, income and capital. Economists note that money may be analysed according to substance: copper, silver, gold, paper or nothing. The great bulk of money is credited by banks who mobilise securities to circulate money. Further, bank deposits have important merits: they are convenient, entirely homogeneous, and not intrinsically valuable, representing only 'money on paper'.

While there are passionate theoretical debates and policy implications, there is substantial agreement between economists. The following axiomatic points, made by Coulborn (1950), are probably not in dispute: money may be defined as a means of valuation and of payment; as both a unit of account and as a generally acceptable medium of exchange. Money is an abstract unit of account; the 'mathematical apparatus' used to express price. It is a common denominator for precision in calculation. Money does have a legal status but the 'commercial' idea of general acceptability is vital to any definition of money. Money should be portable, durable, divisible and recognisable. The common unit of account should be of suitable size. Money now no longer needs to be intrinsically valuable. In a barter economy ratios of exchange fixed by a rigid custom inhibit economic progress. Money-based systems, unlike barter, generalise purchasing power and make for full satisfaction in exchange. Over time money has imperfections and any durable goods (e.g. gold) may serve as a link between present and future values. Money can mean the loan of money: hence there is a money market where money is borrowed and the price of money refers to the rate of interest at which money is borrowed. There is often a difference between real, nominal and legal capital. *Real* capital refers to actual goods and services (i.e. stocks in a warehouse); *nominal* capital refers to the agreed contemporary values of the real capital; while *legal* capital is the amount on which companies pay fixed interest and dividends.

Various technical terms refers to monetary groups:

1 Legal tender: a lawful form of payment.
2 Currency: coins, notes, and the whole tangible media of exchange.
3 Cash: anything which is customary in payment, synonymous with medium of exchange, especially coins and notes.
4 Commodity money: e.g. gold coins where the metal is equal to the face value (full bodied).
5 Token money: usually base metal coins which were once commodity money.
6 Representative money: notes, which are freely convertible into full-bodied commodity money.
7 Fiat money: money, which the state says shall be legal tender.
8 Bank money: notes and bank deposits issued by individual banks.
9 Substitute money: all deposits, including treasury notes and notes.
10 Credit: a belief in payment or repayment; all bank deposits are therefore credits.
11 Overdrafts: also a form of credit where people are allowed to draw out more than they deposited.

The functions of money are well known. Money is a *medium of exchange*: while paper and plastic money is intrinsically worthless, they are guarantees of value that can be used in exchange for goods and services. Money is also *unit of account*: we can judge the cheapness or dearness of goods by using money. Third, money is a *store of value*: unlike perishable goods money does not rot, but it does change value over time, particularly in times of political instability. Finally, money is a *standard of deferred payment*: buying and selling can take place *before* a commodity actually goes on to the market (as in future trading).

What are the qualities of *good money*? Essentially they are: first, its *portability*, i.e. it is easily carried. Indeed, electronic money or plastic money may be rather too easily moved so eluding proper authorities of the law. Second, good money has *durability*: it stands up to wear and tear. Paper money may last as little as six months because it 'wears out' while coins can last twenty to thirty years, even with problems of inflation. Coins can be made of anything, including plastic, but frequently follow specific symbolism of gold, silver and bronze. Third, good money must ensure *recognisability*: it should be immediately recognisable for its exact worth. Fourth, it needs to be *homogeneous*: one note or coin needs to be as acceptable as any other. Even rare coins, if part of the official currency can serve in acceptable exchange/payment of debt. Fifth, naturally money must be *stable*: the value of money should not vary widely, erratically or unpredictably. Finally, it must also be *limited*: the supply of money needs to be controlled, otherwise if too scarce or too plentiful, it could seriously change stability.

Where does money go? How does it circulate: money is earned for producing 'real worth' – goods and services (wages, salaries). Money is spent on consuming the goods produced, including 'necessities', amusements and savings. Money is invested for future prosperity – investments, stocks, etc. Finally, there is money management – attempts by the government to control the money system and prevent both depression and inflation. Economists are not interested in the everyday monetary behaviour of individuals, but are always interested in aggregated data and building theories to explain it.

THE HISTORY OF MONEY

Earliest human records show evidence of what Adam Smith called 'truck, barter and exchange'. Bartering, which still goes on today for those who have no cash or wish to avoid taxation, has obvious drawbacks. These include: the necessity of the *double coincidence of wants* – both parties in the exchange must want exactly what the other has; barter does not help in establishing the *measurement* of worth; the *relative value* of the changed products – while it may be possible to exchange multiple items of lesser worth for a single item of greater worth, it may be that only one item of less worth is required, i.e. it does not work well if things cannot be divided; barter cannot easily be *deferred* – some items perish and need to be consumed relatively rapidly.

Hence as barter transactions grew more sophisticated, people formed the habit of assessing 'prices' in terms of a standard article, which in turn came to enjoy preferential treatment as a medium of exchange (Morgan, 1969). Thus cattle, slaves, wives, cloth, cereals, shells, oil, wine, as well as gold, silver, lead and bronze have served as a medium of exchange (see Table 1.1). Often, religious objects, ornaments or model/miniature tools served as the medium of exchange. During the post-war period in Germany coffee and cigarettes became the medium of exchange and in the 1980s bottled beer served that function in war-torn Angola. Until the middle of this century (in New Guinea) the cowrie shell (as well as pigs) was a very popular Asian medium of exchange.

Using cattle or oxen in exchange for other goods was a cumbrous system. Traders took time to make a settlement, if they reached an agreement at all. The quality of the animals varied, as did the quality of the goods for which they were exchanged. Cattle and oxen, when used as money, were portable and recognisable, but not durable, divisible or homogeneous.

The next step in the development of money came about when the trading countries around the Mediterranean began to use metal for exchange purposes. The metals were gold, silver and copper: precious enough to be wanted, useful and decorative enough to be generally acceptable, and their quality did not vary with time. Some believe the earliest people to use metal money were the Assyrians of Cappadocia, whose embossed silver ingots date back to 2100 BC. The Assyrians may even have had a primitive

Table 1.1 Unusual items which have been used as money

Object	Where used
Beads	Parts of Africa and Canada
Beer	Current-day Angola
Boars	New Hebrides
Butter	Norway
Cigarettes	Prisoner-of-war camps and in post-war Europe
Cocoa Beans	Mexico
Cowries (shells)	World-wide (South Sea Islands, Africa, America and Ancient Britain)
Fish hooks	Gilbert Islands
Fur of flying fox	New Caledonia
Fur of black marmot	Russia
Grain	India
Hoes and throwing knives	Congo
Iron bars	France
Knives	China
Rats (edible)	Easter Island
Salt	Nigeria
Shells	Solomon Islands, Thailand, New Britain, Paraguay
Skins	Alaska, Canada, Mongolia, Russia, Scandinavia
Stones	South Sea Islands
Tobacco	USA
Whale teeth	Fiji

banking system, including what we now call 'interest': payment for loans and debts.

By the eleventh century BC, bars of gold and electrum were being traded between merchants. Electrum is a naturally occurring mixture of gold and silver. The bars or lumps of electrum were not coins, for they were of differing weights, but they had great advantages over the exchange of goods by barter and over the use of animals as a form of money. Metals do not rot or perish, so deferred payments could be arranged. Yet these metal bars were bulky and did not easily pass from hand to hand. They were difficult to divide. The quality and quantity of the metal in different bars was not the same; the ratio of gold and silver in electrum varied. Traders in different parts of the world often used different weights, so all metal bars had to be weighed before goods could be exchanged.

Because of the need to weigh metals to ensure that they were of the correct value, traders tried to identify their own metal bars by marking them. Smaller pieces of metal, easily handled, were later produced, and marked in the same way as the larger pieces had been, so that they, too, would be recognisable by traders.

At first it was not clear how much metal should be exchanged for cattle. Eventually, the amount of gold, silver or copper was made equal to the local value of an ox. This measure was called by the Greeks a *talanton* or 'talent': a copper talent weighed 60 pounds. The Babylonians used shekels for their weights: 60 shekels equalled one manah, and 60 manahs equalled 1 biltu, which was the average weight of a Greek copper talent.

The process of marking small pieces of metal was probably how the first coins were produced in 700 BC, when the Lydians of Asia Minor gave their electrum pieces the head of a lion on one side and nail marks on the other. From Lydia the use of coins like these spread to other areas such as Aegina, and the states of Athens and Corinth; to Cyrenaica, Persia and Macedon. China, Japan and India were also using coinage about this time.

Some media of exchange were weighed, others counted. Coins eventually compromised between two principles because their characteristics (face, stamp) supposedly guarantee its weight and fineness and hence did not have to be weighed.

Metal discs have been found in both the middle east and China dating back more than ten centuries BC. In the seventh century BC it became possible to stamp coins on both obverse and reverse sides so as to distinguish between different denominations and guarantee quality. As today the coinage of one country could be, indeed had to be, used by others.

Because money could serve as a payment for wages it could bring benefits to a wide section of the community. Even slaves could be paid a ration allowance, rather than being fed, by masters. Precious metal coins have been dated to the Peloponnesian Wars of 407 BC: gold for large transactions, bronze for very small ones. Alexander the Great, who spread the use of money in his empire, was the first to have his face on coins. The

Romans varied the appearance of their coinage for political ends but also manipulated its value to suit the financial needs of the state. Nero, among others, reduced the weight in coins and caused a crisis of confidence in the currency.

Until this century the means of payment in commercial societies were, with rare exceptions, either coins made from precious metals or notes or bank deposits convertible into coin. The inconvertible paper note and the deposit repayable on such notes is a very recent development, which has now displaced the precious metals for internal transactions in all the highly developed economies of the world. So long as they retain public confidence, they have great advantages of convenience, but they are liable to abuse and on many occasions in their short history they have broken down. Banks have gone bankrupt in many Western countries through bad debt, incompetence or financial crisis they could not foresee. Sometimes investors are partly recompensed by government; often they are not! The government which adopts an inconvertible currency, therefore, takes on a heavy responsibility for maintaining its value. Indeed paper money – that is documents rather than actual notes – are now being transferred electronically such that a person might fly 1,000 miles, go into a bank in a foreign country never before visited, and emerge with the notes and coinage of that country.

There are various ways to approach the history of money. Usually one starts with primitive money, followed by the first use of coinage, then goes on to banking, credit and gold/silver standards, and finally on to inconvertible paper and plastic money. Chown (1994) has explained some of the concepts associated with money. It costs money to manufacture coins from silver or gold, and the mint authority charges a turn (usually including a profit) known as '*seignorage*'. Issuers can cheat, and make an extra profit by *debasing* the coinage. If this is detected, as it usually is, the public may value coins '*in specie*' (i.e. by their bullion content) rather than '*in tale*' (i.e. by their official legal value). The purchasing value of coins may change without any debasement; the value in trade of coinage metal itself may change. The monetary system may be threatened by *clipping* and *counterfeiting* and, even if rulers and citizens are scrupulously honest, the coinage has to contend with fair wear and tear.

In medieval and early modern time coins were expected (although in some places and times only by the naive and credulous) to contain the appropriate weight of metal. The use of more than one metal raised problems. These are sometimes referred to collectively as 'tri-metallism', but are more conveniently divided into the two separate problems of 'bi-metallism' (the relationship between silver and gold) and 'small change' (the role of the 'black coins'). The new and more complicated coinages also caused problems by definition – 'ghost money' and 'money of account'. For much of the late medieval period, there would be more than one coinage type in circulation in a country. This creates a serious problem for the modern historian, as it presumably did for the contemporary accountant. 'Ghost money' units consist of accounts which have names based on actual coins which have disappeared from circulation. It arose, of course, from depreciation and the phenomena of bi-metallism and petty coins.

Money is used as a 'unit of account' as well as a medium of exchange and store of value. Some system was needed by which debts could be recorded and settled, and in which merchants could keep their accounts. It was convenient to have a money of account for this purpose. This could be based on a silver and gold standard, or very occasionally on black money. Two systems often existed side by side. The value of actual real coins could fluctuate in terms of the appropriate money of accounts and this was often based on a ghost from the past. Money could be used as cash or stored in a bank.

Cash

Derived from the French word *caisse*, meaning money-box or chest, cash is often known as 'ready or liquid' money. Traditionally it comes in two forms: coins and bank notes.

Coins

Standard coins, where the value of the metal is equal to the face stamped on the coin are rare but used in the collecting world. *Token* coins are more common: here the metal (or indeed plastic) content is worth (far) less than the face value. The Jewish shekel was first a weight of metal, then a specific coin. Monasteries were the first mints because it was thought they would be free of theft.

Wars or political crises often lead to the debasing of a country's currency. Precious metal coins are filed down (shaved), made more impure, or give way to token (non-metallic) coins. But even coins which began as standard could come to a bad end. Unscrupulous kings rubbed off metal from the edge of gold coins, or put quantities of lead into silver coins to gain money to finance wars. In Henry VIII's time the coins issued in 1544 contained one-seventh less silver than those issued in 1543; Henry continued in this way until, by the time coins were issued in 1551, they contained only one-seventh of the original amount of silver.

The idea of a standard coin was that it should be a coin of guaranteed weight and purity of metal. That remained true until coins became tokens in the sense that their intrinsic metal value was not the same as their face value.

Paper

Paper money was primarily introduced because it was much easier to handle large sums. Second, coins could not be produced in sufficient amounts for the vastly increased world trade that developed from the seventeenth century onwards. Third, inevitably, trade demonstrated that there were more profitable uses for metal than as exchange pieces. Finally, it was argued that paper money (cheques, credit cards) reduced the amount of cash in transit and therefore reduced the possibility of theft.

Cash money probably developed from the practice of giving a receipt by a gold or silversmith who held one's precious metal for 'safe-keeping'. In time, this receipt, although it had no real value of its own, became acceptable in payment of debt among the literate. Bank notes, printed by banks, first appeared in the twentieth century. Up until the beginning of the First World War, notes in Britain were called *convertible* paper because they could be exchanged for gold. Alas, now all notes are *inconvertible* paper. Clearly, one of the disadvantages of convertible paper money is that the supply and issue of notes is related to the amount of gold held by the issuing authorities (i.e. government, banks) and not to the supply of goods. Another disadvantage of the old convertible money is that prices depend on the world market not simply on gold supply. A government cannot control its country's prices without taking account of what is going on in other parts of the world. Equally, imprudent governments can literally print (issue) as much money as they wish, with too much money chasing too few goods with a concomitant fall in the value of the money.

China printed money in the Ming Dynasty (1368–1644), while, in 1656, the Swedes were the first Europeans to issue paper money. Notes can have any face value and the variation within and between countries is very wide. They have also varied considerably in shape, size, colour and ornamentation. Provided paper money is immediately acceptable in payment of debt, it fulfils the criteria of being money. Cheques, postal orders, credit cards, electronic transfers, etc., are 'claims to money' sometimes referred to as *near* money.

Banks

Goldsmiths were the first bankers. They soon learnt to become *fractional reserve* banks in that they kept only a proportion of the gold deposits with them and invested the rest. Many failed, as have banks in this century, because they could not immediately pay back deposits on demand when they had not enough reserves or 'liquid money'. The *cash ratios*, or the amount of actual cash, kept by banks is about 6–10 per cent of all the money deposited with them. Another 20–5 per cent of deposits are kept as 'near money', which are investments that can be turned back into cash almost immediately.

The Christian church objected to usury and money lenders, which opened up the profession, particularly to Jews. Islam too disapproves of interest and has been more zealous than Christianity in trying to discourage it. Some Christians later lent money free for a short period, but if the debt was not paid back at the time promised, Church laws appeared to allow the delay to be charged for. The Crusades and the Industrial Revolution were a great impetus to banking because people needed capital. Goldsmiths, rich landowners and prosperous merchants pioneered modern banking by lending to investors and industrialists.

By manipulating the liquidity rate and their preferred patterns of lending, banks are inevitably very powerful institutions. However, they are not the only institutions that lend money. For example, in the UK, building societies make loans to house buyers; finance houses lend money for hire-purchase transactions; and insurance companies have various funds available for borrowers. The relationship of money to income and capital may be summarised as follows. First, money circulates, or passes from hand to hand in payment for: (a) goods and services which form part of the national income; (b) transfers and intermediate payments, which are income from the point of view of the recipients but are not part of the national income; (c)transactions in existing real assets, which are part of the national capital; and (d) transactions in financial claims, which are capital from the point of view of their owners but are not part of the national capital.

Money is also held in stock. Stocks are, however, very different in the time for which they are held, and the intention behind the holding. Money in stock is part of the capital of its owners, but it is not part of the national capital unless it is in a form which is acceptable to foreigners. New money can be created by a net addition to bank lending, and money can be destroyed by a net payment of bank loans. For a closed community, income and expenditure are identical, but for an individual they are not. An individual can spend less than his income and so add to his stock of money or of some other asset, and he can spend more than his income by reducing his stock of money or other assets or by borrowing.

For most people in the UK, the 'high-street bank' is the primary source of money. They borrow from, and lend to, banks which are also seen as major sources of advice. Estimates are that over three-quarters of all UK adults have a current bank account or chequeing account and in the past five years there has been a considerable increase in such accounts as well as those in building societies.

The cheque (or check in US) arose about 300 years ago directly out of the use of exchanged receipts or promissory notes and was illegal to begin with and certainly regarded as highly immoral, but the convenience soon outweighed any moral considerations and the legalities soon followed. Until 1931, there was a national responsibility not to issue more hard currency than could be backed up by gold deposits. So, in effect, until that date if everyone handed in their notes for value, there would have been enough gold to go around. Today, if in Britain we all demanded our face-value gold, the banks and the nation would go bankrupt overnight. There is currently enough gold on deposit in the Bank of England's vaults to cover around one-third of the issued currency. It is no longer possible, in fact, to receive face-value gold.

Until recently, the biggest difference between a bank in the UK and a bank in the US was that in the UK, in order to open a bank account, it used to be necessary not only to have money but also to have friends. A reference provided by a bank-account holder had to be furnished before a new account could be opened. The process took about two weeks. In the US and now in most developed countries anyone can walk into almost any bank and open an account on the spot, receive a cheque book and use it, provided they deposit enough money in the account to cover the cheques. One of the reasons why this is so in New York State is that it is a crime to write a cheque without having funds to back it. In the UK a bouncing cheque will not send you to prison.

In addition, in the US, with some of the competing banks, opening an account and depositing a fixed amount of cash will bring you free gifts. British banks have copied this trend, especially in attempting to lure young people (i.e. students) to open accounts with them.

Banks all over the world lend money to each other. This is called the Interbank lending system and it occurs because the larger banks have more money on deposit than the smaller ones and all banks must balance their accounts each day – so they borrow and lend among themselves. Thus, if you leave a lot of money in your current account each day, even though the banks are not paying you any interest on that money they are making interest on it through the overnight Interbank lending market – about 11 per cent per annum in the UK. In the US almost all money in all accounts earns interest, if only at a low rate, and this system is slowly being taken up in the UK, too, with various different names. No bank is giving anything away with these accounts, they are simply reducing their profits slightly to attract more custom.

Credit cards

Credit cards make more profit than almost any other form of lending, with interest rates of over 25 per cent per annum in many cases. In 1995, Barclaycard, in association with the British Bankers Association, estimated the number of card holders to be nearly 26 million. They were broken down by banks thus:

Barclays	9.0 million
National Westminster	4.4 million
Trustees Savings Bank	3.8 million
Midland	3.3 million
Lloyds	1.3 million
Bank of Scotland	1.3 million
Royal Bank of Scotland	0.9 million

Co-operative Bank	0.9 million
Giro Bank	0.6 million
Halifax	0.4 million

In-house research done by the British banks themselves in the mid-1990s showed that about half of all British adults now hold a debit card. Further, about one-third expect 'debit' cards to be the main payment method in the future. One in six adults surveyed said that the speed and convenience of 'debit' cards actually influenced the way they choose and paid for goods and services. Not surprisingly, one-fifth of all card holders point out that whether a store accepts debit cards affects where and whether they choose to spend their money.

The highest ever growth rate for credit and debit card expenditure in Britain was in September 1996, when £7.3 billion was spent, up 31 per cent on the same month in the year before. In addition, there were probably over 6 million (and growing fast) store cards, used for extended credit, subscription accounts etc., in British stores. There are clearly large numbers of people owing money on credit cards, many at a very high interest. Such loans float in and out of credit all the time and a surprisingly small number of people leave their credit cards unpaid for more than a month. The growth of the use of cards of all sorts has been exponential rather than linear, yet the market does not appear to be saturated.

The latest idea for plastic money development is the economically controlled, personally 'finger-printed', pay-and-store credit card. The card will probably be in general use before the end of the century and will be the size of the modern credit card. It will carry a small liquid-crystal screen on which the carrier can check their credit line, directly linked to their bank account, from which payment is immediately and directly drawn whenever they purchase an item or draw cash from a machine. The card is linked by short-wave transmission to a computer, which keeps the card's accounts and pays the credit company or the store for each use, thus saving a fortune in collection costs. The card is also a calculator, and identity system and a direction finder, and it may be used in a limited way to obtain general information regarding travel and currencies, and local information.

The card would naturally be useless to anyone else as it will only function upon the touch of the owner, through sub-microscopic sensor cells in the surface of the plastic. The whole mechanism will be made up of very low-density material, micro-chips which would contain the transmission, a mini-computer/calculator and the liquid-crystal screen.

Currently, some people do 'home computing' on their personal computer. Certainly, money is moved and spent 'electronically' as never before, necessitating the closure of many redundant bank branches. Automatic tills dispensing money and electronic communication means that fewer and fewer people ever go into banks.

ECONOMIC ANTHROPOLOGY AND PRIMITIVE MONEY

Unlike psychology, anthropology has long been interested in economics and consumption (Douglas and Isherwood, 1979). Economic anthropology is concerned with the economic aspects of the social relations of persons. Indeed, there are standard textbooks on economic anthropology (Thurnwald, 1932; Herskovitz, 1952; Dalton 1971). Although there have been a number of well-established authorities in this field, Polanyi's work is perhaps the best known. Anthropologists have long been aware that nearly all economic concepts, ideas and theories are based on only one type of economy – industrial capitalism. Some have argued that these modern economic concepts (maximising, supply, demand) are equally applicable to primitive societies, while others are not convinced.

One of the major tasks of economic anthropology is to detect economic universals in human society by sampling the many forms in which they are manifest across cultures: for instance, whereas the deferment of wants, through saving and investing, may be considered good for some cultures, most primitive cultures dictate that resources should be expended on food and shelter.

First, it should be pointed out what all economies have in common. Dalton (1971) has noted three features: a structured arrangement with enforced rules for the acquisition or production of material items and services; rules whereby natural resources, human co-operation and technology are combined to provide materials and services in a sustained, repetitive fashion; and the existence of superficially similar institutional practices in the form of marketplaces, monetary objects, accounting devices and external trade. However, he was much more impressed by the differences in economics in terms of their organisation, performance, change, growth and development.

Anthropologists have been concerned with all aspects of economic activity, including barter, the market, distribution of goods and wealth, ownership and property. They note there are similarities between different primitive societies' economic behaviour. Thurnwald (1932) suggested that a characteristic failure of most primitive economies is the absence of any desire to make profits from either production or exchange. Many studies have looked at the symbols of value and stages of the evolution of money, and the diverse number and type of object used as units of barter, including shells, dogs' teeth, salt and copper bracelets. Various distinctions have been made such as objects which are treated as treasure and hoarded as such or as articles of daily use; whether the object is regarded as capital capable of yielding profit; and also whether the object is the potential source of others of its own kind. Certainly, what is interesting about anthropological studies of money is not only the range of objects used as money but the fact that primitive money does not fulfil many of the functions that current money does.

Whereas economists seem concerned with only non-social aspects of money, such as its worth, divisibility, etc., anthropologists look at money which is used in reciprocal and redistributive transactions, in terms of the personal roles and social context of what occurs. The exchange of whatever serves as money – be it armbands, pigs' tusks, shells or stones – as well as its acquisition and disposition is a structured and important event that often has strong moral and legal obligations and implications, and might change various status rights and social roles. Because money is a means of reciprocal and redistributive payment used fairly infrequently to discharge social obligations in primitive societies its portability and divisibility are not very important. The introduction of Western-style money does more than just displace indigenous money; it has inevitable repercussions on the social organisation of a people. This is because Western-style money allows both commercial and non-commercial (traditional) payments to be earned with general-purpose money earned in everyday market transactions. Hence patrons, elders and heads of families and clans lose some control over their clients and juniors who can earn their own cash and dispose of it as they wish.

The essence of the anthropological message is this: money has no essence apart from its uses, which depend on the traditional transactional modes of each culture's economy. Money is what it does and no more. For the anthropologist Douglas (1967), money rituals make visible external signs of internal states. Money also mediates social experience, and provides a standard for measuring worth. Money makes a link between the present and the future. But money can only perform its role of intensifying economic interaction if the public has faith in it. If faith in it is shaken, the currency is useless. Money symbols can only have effect so long as they command confidence. In this sense all money, false or true, depends on a confidence trick. There is no false money except by contrast with another currency which has more total acceptability. So primitive ritual is like good money, not false money, so long as it commands assent.

Thus whereas economists see the origin of money in terms of commercial issues, anthropologists stress non-commercial origins as in bride payments, sacrificial and religious money, status symbols, as well as the payment of fines and taxes. Certainly, money used for non-commercial payments appears to occur before it is used for commercial purposes, suggesting that anthropologists' theories of the origins of money are correct (Lea *et al.,* 1987).

Anthropologists have already emphasised the variety of monies existing in any culture: that is, the number of items that serve as money. Thus great art is now seen as an investment today rather than as purely an aesthetic object. Further, anthropologists have always been sensitive to the symbols of money and the symbolic value of ritual possessions. This observation is always manifest when a country decides to change its currency (coins and notes) even if there is no change in value. Equally, as we see with the introduction of pan-European currency, the symbols on notes and coins (or lack of them) are a source of much passion and speculation.

Because so many things have different types of value – symbolic, sentimental, exchange – anthropologists have enriched our understanding of money. Coins and notes are but one form of money which is widely used in a society ritually and symbolically. Psychologists have recently become more aware of the anthropological insights into money.

THE SOCIOLOGY OF MONEY

The line between economics, political science and sociology is rarely clear. Just as we have the sub-discipline of economic psychology, so there is economic sociology. Early sociologists like Spencer, Durkheim and Weber recognised the sociological implications of the division of labour and how societies try to regulate co-operation and equitable exchange among economic agents by law, customs and codes (Smelser, 1963). Most economic sociology has examined advanced capitalist societies.

Economic sociologists are particularly interested in social organisations, be they formal (business, hospitals), informal (neighbourhoods, gangs) or diffuse (ethnic groups). The roles individuals have within them, the behavioural norms that develop, the values they implicitly or explicitly hold and the structures they impose are all central to the economic sociologists' concepts of institutionalisation.

Sociologists are also interested in monetary and economic ideologies which can be used to morally justify or attack existing arrangements. Money, as such, is of less interest to economic sociologists than the nature of the organisations that are set up to create and control it. They are of course interested in such things as wage differentials and bargaining over wages but nearly always at the level of the social group.

Social theorists and political economists like Adam Smith and Karl Marx are happily claimed by sociologists as one of their own. Marx, along with Darwin and Freud, perhaps one of the most influential thinkers of the modern era, wrote about money. He claimed that money transformed *real human and natural faculties* into mere abstract representations. Further he thought money, appeared as a *disruptive* power for the individual and for social bonds. For it changed fidelity into infidelity, love into hate, hate into love, virtue into vice, vice into virtue, servant into master, stupidity into intelligence, and intelligence into stupidity.

Sociologists are interested in monetary networks and the technological, institutional and social mechanisms that allow them to operate (Dodd, 1994). They research money policies, monetary institutions and the social consequences of economic theories and circumstances.

Sociologists tend to reject materialistic definitions of money, preferring, like anthropologists, to focus on the social relationships that monetary transactions involve. The economic idea that modern money is general purpose, fulfilling all the possible monetary functions, is rejected by sociologists. There exists no form of money which serves all such functions simultaneously. Legal-tender notes are rarely used to store value in practice. Notes and coins represent standard units of value without literally embodying them; indeed, if they did so they would be worth considerably more than their legal-tender equivalents. Cheques, credit cards and bank drafts serve only as means of payment. These different forms of money inevitably fulfil different functions.

Sociologists are interested in control, particularly control of the money supply and attempts to control inflation, deflation and economic depression. They are also interested in monetary networks, which are networks of information. Dodd (1994) notes there are five factors which must be in place for a network to be defined as such. First, the network will contain a standardised accounting system into which each monetary form within the network is divisible, enabling its exchange with anything priced in terms of that system. Second, the network will rely on information from which expectations regarding the future can be derived: money is acceptable as payment almost solely on the assumption that it can be reused later on. Third, the network will depend on information regarding its spatial characteristics: limits placed on the territory in which specific monetary forms may be used will probably derive initially from measures designed to prevent counterfeiting, although they will eventually refer to the institutional framework governing the operation of a payments system. Fourth, the network will be based on legalistic information, usually in the form of rules, concerning the status of contractual relationships which are fleeting and conclusive: to pay with money is literally to pay up. Finally, the operation of the network presupposes knowledge of the behaviour and expectations of others. This is usually derived from experience, but can also be sought out and even paid for. Such information is vital in generating trust in money's abstract properties. Monetary transactions are often impersonal, even secretive and networks need to be able to cope with this. A network is an abstract aggregated concept that reflects the typical sociological level of analysis.

Sociologists agree that the use, perception and understanding of money in any society influences the way money networks work and vice versa. The existence of money within a society serves to alleviate the kinds of uncertainty inherent in a system of barter exchange. Such uncertainties as an imbalance between the supply and demand of particular goods, lack of information regarding future levels of supply and demand, insecurity as to the trustworthiness of others, the authenticity of the goods they bring to an exchange and the contracts they seek to establish are social problems. The responses of different societies to such imperfections is to set up institutions that deal with these problems. The social, political and cultural realities which generate economic uncertainty are the conditions for the very existence of monetary networks in the first instance. It is for this reason that money is the legitimate focus of sociological study. That is, it is the institutions that societies develop to control money that are the primary focus of sociology.

In an excellent, comprehensive paper entitled 'The Social Meaning of Money', Zelizer (1989) rejects the utilitarian concept of money as the ultimate objectifer, homogenising all qualitative distinctions into an abstract quality. She believes that too many sociologists have accepted economists' assumptions that money *per se* and market processes are invulnerable to social influences; free from cultural or social constraints.

Yet all sociologists have argued and demonstrated how cultural and social factors influence the uses, meaning and incidence of money in current society. Zelizer (1989) believes that the extra economic social basis of money remains as powerful in modern economic systems as it was in primitive and anxiety societies. Central to sociological (as well as anthropological and psychological) conceptions of money are the following fundamental points. First, while money does serve as a key rational tool of the modern economic market, it also exists outside the sphere of the market and is profoundly shaped by cultural and social-structural factors. Second there are a plurality of different kinds of monies; each special money is shared by a particular set of cultural and social factors and is thus qualitatively distinct. Third, the classic economic inventory of money's functions and attributes, based on the assumption of a single general-purpose type of money, is thus unsuitably narrow. By focusing exclusively on money as a market phenomenon, the traditional economic view, it fails to capture the very complex range of characteristics of money as a non-market medium. A different, more inclusive understanding is necessary, for certain monies can be indivisible (or divisible but not in mathematically predictable portions), non-portable, deeply subjective, and therefore qualitatively heterogeneous. Fourth, the assumed dichotomy between a utilitarian money and non-pecuniary values is false, for money under certain circumstances may be as singular and unexchangeable as the most personal or unique object. Last, the alleged freedom and unchecked power of money become untenable assumptions. Culture and social structure set inevitable limits to the monetisation process by introducing profound controls and restrictions on the flow and liquidity of money.

Extra economic factors systematically constrain and shape (a) the *uses* of money, earmarking, for instance, certain monies for specified uses; (b) the *users* of money, designating different people to handle specified monies; (c) the *allocation* system of each particular money; (d) the *control* of different monies; and (e) the *sources* of money, linking different sources to specified uses.

In order to demonstrate the sociology of special or modern money, sociologists have examined domestic money: husbands', wives' and children's money, and how changing conceptions of family life and gender relationships affect how family money is used (this will be examined in some detail later). Domestic or family money is clearly a very special kind of currency. Regardless of its source, once money enters the household its allocation (timing as well as amount) and uses are subject to rules quite distinct from the market. Only changes in gender roles and family structure influence the meaning and use of money. Domestic money usage and attitudes show the instrumental, rationalised model of money and the market economy to be wanting. Money in the home is transformed by the structure of social relations and the idiosyncratic system of each family. Equally, institutional, charitable, gift and dirty money all take on unique social meanings.

What sociologists share with anthropologists and psychologists is an interest in the meaning individuals, groups, societies and cultures give to money and how that meaning affects its use. Further, they are particularly interested in how institutions use all forms of money.

A FEMINIST PERSPECTIVE ON MONEY

Both historical and current sex differences in the use of money will be discussed later in the book, as will gender differences in the styles of acquiring, saving and spending money. Recently, feminists have looked quite specifically at women and money. It is a radical, unusual and provocative perspective. Randall (1996) has argued that monetary, not sexual, abuse is 'widespread and damaging enough that we might legitimately call it terrorism of epidemic proportions' (p. 11). She believes that women have been encouraged not to talk about money. Hence they feel shame and guilt about the subject and may lie about how much they earn or the cost of things.

Women, it is argued, have great difficulty saying how much they earn, need, spend, save or have. Money, say the feminists, is the currency of domination. Girls and women are deliberately kept in the dark with respect to household finances – paying bills, filing tax returns, acquiring a bank book. Some feminists believe that until recently a woman's sense of self-worth was directly traceable to how much money there was in her family, how her relationship to it was perceived and handled, and what attitudes she developed around it. Feminists believe that women are particularly exploited at work; that they are much more likely than men to operate out of an ideology of service and caring. There is a great imbalance around job categories, how these are spoken about, and the remuneration they bring. For example, tough jobs like construction, precision tooling, plumbing and other typical male trades are generally well paid, while women-friendly job categories, such as school teaching, remain underpaid.

Feminists believe that salary determines a significant difference, not only in the way society views a woman but in the way that a woman views herself. Job descriptions are important: psychiatrists as compared with psychologists or counsellors, doctors as opposed to physician's assistants or nurses, custodians versus janitors, actors versus entertainers, professors versus teachers, persons in retail versus sales clerks. The first set of titles refers to positions most frequently held by men, while women typically fill the second. This line of argument is rather old hat, recognised to be true for some time and many groups have therefore tried to change these stereotypes.

It is also argued that housewives/home-makers are economically exploited, as are women volunteer workers. The feminisation of poverty is seen to be the consequence of the masculinisation of wealth. 'The language of money is consistently described in terms of *yours*, *mine* and *ours*. Women are often absent in *yours*, invisible in the *mine*, and too small a part of the *ours*' (Randall, 1996, p. 23). The issue of marriage and divorce is where financial matters always surface.

Many writers have pointed out how pathological attitudes to money often get mixed up with attitudes to sex and food. Thus binge eating, credit card over-spending and sexual promiscuity may all result from the same psychological need either to exercise control, quell discomfort or fill an empty place inside. Buying sprees to feel better, sometimes called *retail therapy*, are seen as a social not a personal pathology. Women typically serve years in prison for writing a bad cheque, for perpetrating credit-card fraud or shop lifting, while men are 'rewarded' with short sentences in resort-like open prisons for orchestrating vast swindles on hundreds and thousands of people.

Feminists admit that there is evidence that society has changed somewhat and many women have a healthier relationship with money. However, powerful social traditions have meant that women remain the victims of a patriarchal society.

While empirical research has not validated feminist theories it has demonstrated significant gender differences in the use of money. Through in-depth interviews with American women and men, Price (1993) found males reported greater confidence, independence of action, risk taking and gambling with respect to money, while females have a greater sense of envy and deprivation. It appears that for men their self-identity, self-esteem and sense of power are inextricably linked with money, while for women it is more simply a means of obtaining things and experiences they can enjoy in the present.

MONEY IN LITERATURE

The sheer number of references to money by dramatists, poets, novelists and wits have merited a long and comprehensive anthology (Jackson, 1995). The editor points out that such a book is not in itself a study in economics 'though a few of the dismal science's more graceful and pungent prose stylists have earned their place beside the poets' (p. vii).

Literature shows well the fantasies, lunacies and dreads which surround ordinary people's experience of money. It has been noted that after love and death few subjects have been more attractive to writers than money.

Many people know of Chaucer's crooks and swindlers and Dickens' Scrooge. Writers satirise avarice, highlight the arrogance of the rich, and may howl outrage, disgust and disdain at those who show love of money. Jackson (1995) believes that the modern novel owes much to the concept of money. Novels often describe the following: spendthrifts, gamblers and philanthropists; embezzlers and blackmailers and swindlers; banks and bankers; merchants and wage slaves; financial manias and young provincial men on the make. The novel gives its characteristic sharp attention to the ways in which the mechanisms of money draw up characters from all levels of society and ease or shove them towards their destinies.

Writers and literature have often been seen as anti-materialists, heroically championing the human values against the cold, pitiless calculations of the market. There is the image of the unworldly poet versus the wicked capitalist. This may be more the vision of idealistic readers than pragmatic writers, whose frequent economic insecurity keeps them sufficiently worldly minded.

Many writers feel and express the inconsistencies and contradictory values about money in their culture. Thus, art alone for its own sake is an indulgence and a trivial thing, but done for money is somehow cheap and 'hackwork'. People like to believe that great writers cannot be bought; that the literary conscience ought to resist the temptations of money.

> Most obviously, money and literature are both conventional systems for representing things beyond themselves, of saying that X is Y. A poem asks us to believe that it represents a nightingale or a raven; a coin asks us to believe that it represents a bushel of wheat or a number of hours of labour. Neither money nor writing would have been possible without the human mind's capacity to grasp that one thing may be a substitute for another dissimilar thing, which is to say that both conventions are a product of out ability to make and grasp metaphors. My love is rose petal; a loaf of bread is a groat.
>
> (Jackson, 1995, p. xiii)

Many writers have reflected on money:

> 'Money talks' because money is a metaphor, a transfer, and a bridge. Like words and language, money is a storehouse of communally achieved work, skill, and experience. Money, however, is also a specialist technology like writing; and as writing intensifies the visual aspect of speech and order, and as the clock visually separates time from space, so money separates work from the other social functions. Even today money is a language for translating the work of the farmer into the work of the barber, doctor, engineer, or plumber. As a vast social metaphor, bridge, or translator, money – like writing – speeds up

exchange and tightens the bonds of interdependence in any community. It gives great spiral extension and control to political organizations, just as writing does, or the calendar. It is action at a distance, both in space and in time. In a highly literate, fragmented society, 'Time is money,' and money is the store of other people's time and effort.'

(McLuhan, 1964)

As ever, writers' and novelists' observations about people's use and abuse of money are considerably more perspicuous, wry and insightful than the writings of social scientists. Like anthropologists and psychologists, writers of fiction dwell on the symbolism of money, its captivating power and the bizarre things individuals do to acquire it.

PUBLIC SENTIMENT, CONSUMER SENTIMENT AND THE POLLS

Most developed countries have regular social survey or opinion polls that attempt to look at general issues like economic optimism or pessimism as well as specific topics like the money spent on certain objects. These are commissioned by governments, newspapers, manufacturers, advertisers and researchers, all of whom want an aggregated picture of how the nation (or specific groups), are spending their money.

For over thirty-five years psychologists have been interested in consumer mood with regard to money (Katona, 1960). Hence, American governments keep a close eye on the Index of Consumer Sentiment, whatever they choose to call it. It may be, from the point of economists, *soft* data, but it is a powerful predictor of consumer spending. In fact, the soft data of mood and sentiment, usually expressed in terms of optimism or pessimism, often explains why governments are not re-elected despite the evidence of economic growth.

A sudden economic shock may have a powerful but delayed effect on the public's perceptions. In periods of gloom people are extremely cautious about investing their disposable cash. In these times the significance of bad economic news is exaggerated and good news discredited or forgotten. Moods of depression may therefore ignore numerous accurate indicators of economic upturn and may, in fact, contribute to their slow development.

Equally, in periods of optimism and public confidence people are brash, even spendthrift, increasing rapidly the circulation of money. Increased spending boosts profits, creates jobs and has a stimulating, self-fulfilling effect on the economy. Indeed this mood may even prevail after economic conditions change.

Economists prefer hard data like the strength of currency, the cost of money, and trade-balance figures to predict the future. Economic psychologists, on the other hand, stress that money-related behaviour results in part from people's attitudes, feelings, beliefs, and even transient moods. Hence the attention to Consumer Sentiment indices. People sometimes spend and save in an attempt to satisfy urges they neither understand nor recognise. Doing this *en masse*, perhaps panicked by stories of large-scale redundancies or political instability, people can patently demonstrate how 'economically irrational' they are. Money may be the servant of society but it can also become its master.

Katona (1975) showed, using large-scale surveys in America, that measures of consumer sentiment, expectations and aspirations provide advance indications of changes in consumers' spending, saving and major changes in their expenditure on durable goals. More importantly, consumers contribute to economic fluctuations far in excess of the impact of changes in their income resulting from variations in the amounts disbursed by the business and government sectors of the economy.

As a result, it is acknowledged that attitudes and expectations are crucial in economic forecasts. Expectations are stable, taking some time to change from optimism to pessimism or vice versa. It has been shown that the consumer sector can exert a decisive influence on economic trends. Further, consumer attitudes and expectations need not follow the trend of incomes, or, indeed, of economic measures. Hence the 'feel-good' factor can last well after all economic indications show economic decline; equally, it may be particularly frustrating for governments to find the 'feel-good' factor does not return even though all monitored indications show strong positive trends.

Katona argued from his impressive data bank that major changes in collective monetary attitudes do not arise without good reason. Further, the origin of the changes may be determined only after the fact. Thus economic information on all objective changes at a given time does not permit the prediction of the resulting changes in attitudes. Also specific factors (news, laws, etc.) that are primarily responsible for changes in attitudes vary from time to time, from group to group. Hence the constellation of objective variables found to be successful in explaining attitude change at any given time, may fail to do so at another.

Consumer sentiment provides a snapshot of the economic mood of a society. This mood is both a consequence of and a cause of economic conditions. It is fickle but not erratic. It can provide governments, businesses and researchers with most useful data to include in their predictive models for the monetary behaviour both of groups and of individuals.

THE SOCIAL PSYCHOLOGY OF MONEY

Social-psychological concepts, methods, and theories have been used to describe monetary behaviour. Certainly, the measurement of attitudes (to money or anything else) is at the heart of the social-psychological enterprise. How attitudes are formed as well as changed and their relationship to (monetary) behaviour are central questions for the social psychologist (see Chapters 2, 3 and 5). How people make sense of their social world can form explanations and attributions for all aspects of monetary behaviour (poverty, wealth, saving, investing, gambling) are also of interest to social psychologists (see Chapter 4). Social-comparison processes, whereby people consciously compare themselves with others, is of considerable interest to social psychologists. Social-comparison processes are ubiquitous: 'keeping up with the Joneses' is a fundamental feature of monetary behaviour for many people.

The role of individual differences and personality traits is clearly important in the study of money attitudes and behaviours. It is noticeable to all lay people that different but clear monetary beliefs and behaviours can be delineated. For the lay person this is almost always done in terms of typologies – the miser, the spendthrift, the show-off, the fashion victim. Personality theorists and social psychologists have been more interested in describing the origins of personality traits and how they relate to monetary behaviour as well as the nature of the processes (cognitive, psychological and social) by which individual differences operate. Personality theorists from very different traditions (psychoanalytic, psychometric) have all taken an interest in personality and money.

Some social-psychological studies on money have been conducted in the laboratory, but by far the most thorough have used interviews, observation and questionnaires. One fairly unusual psychological experiment uses 'miniature economies' where 'token' rather than 'real' money circulates. This may be cigarettes in prisons (or prisoner-of-war camps), schools or mental hospitals. They provide a totally closed mini-society in which various monetary/token behaviours and economic processes can be witnessed. Large-scale surveys on public optimism/pessimism have been particularly useful (see pp. 44–56) as have field observation studies on shopping. The therapist's couch has also provided a lot of material that could be turned into testable hypotheses.

As Lea *et al.* (1987) have indicated in their textbook on economic psychology, there are a vast number of areas of everyday life concerning money, and which require economic and social psychological research. For instance, how monetary rewards (salary) is related to the choice of jobs, satisfaction and productivity at work. What are the major monetary factors in buying intentions, actual buying behaviour, habitual buying and behaviour in shops? Why do people save and whence the morality of thrift in certain cultures? Why do people, seemingly altruistically, give money away? What factors determine charitable giving, and is this behaviour economically rational? There are a host of interesting questions about gambling: what is the difference between normal and excessive gambling; which factors determine who gambles on what and why? Like gambling, which is a moderately taboo topic for research, inquiries into tax avoidance and evasion are very interesting. Does taxation reduce the incentive to work or influence the choice between different kinds of jobs?

Attitudes to and beliefs about money are inevitably closely linked to other economic notions like exchange, property, ownership and work. The latter are concerned with the power base of society. It is no surprise therefore that a person's monetary ideas are closely linked to their politico-economic ideology.

The social psychology of money is primarily about the acquisition of money concepts and attitudes; the imbuing of various forms of money with symbolism and meaning, relating money concepts to other of society's symbols and its habitual use. The rational/utility-maximising approach of economists based on aggregated data is not very helpful at the psychological level. Social psychologists are interested in ordinary individuals' accounts of their own and others monetary beliefs, behaviours and motives. However, theories of monetary motivation need to be integrated with all other motivational issues, which make the undertaking inevitably very large indeed.

The economic and social system influences individuals and vice versa. Ordinary individuals are not simply sovereign causes of economic phenomena based on their attitudes, personality or motives. Nor are they helpless pawns or puppets in the face of over-riding economic forces.

A PSYCHOLOGICAL THEORY OF MONEY

Lea *et al.* (1987) have developed what they call a psychological 'theory' of money. It may be too grand to call it a theory, but they attempt to specify how social and economic psychologists approach the topic. They argue that money represents not only the goods that it can purchase but also the source and how it was obtained. Its meaning is also derived from its form. They believe that money's function of expressing value can be carried out at various levels of measurement.

1　*Nominal*. Here money operates only at the level of equivalence. That is, with a particular kind of money you can buy a particular item of goods or service.
2　*Ordinal*. Here money has different forms, which can be ranked greater or less than each other.
3　*Interval/Ratio*. This means we have a true zero and a ratio scale such that we know and accept the difference between £/$20 and £/$30 is the same as between £/$70 and £/$80. This is the system we have today.

Their theory is that money is deeply symbolic. Behaviour towards and with money can only be understood through an historical and developmental perspective. Principally, money represents an exchange evaluation, but there are many subsidiary meanings, which affect how it is used and can even limit its general applicability.

For large institutions, like banks, the non-economic characteristics of money may be completely irrelevant but they certainly apply to individuals.

What money symbolises differs between individuals and groups but these symbols are limited in number and stable over time. Hence they can be described and categorised. But rather than ask what psychological characteristics money possesses, it is more fruitful to ask how do these characteristics affect behaviour with and towards money. Thus certain coins or notes, either because of their newness, weight or cleanliness may also be spent before others. Similarly, substituting coins for notes may have the effect of stimulating small transactions. It seems a note of a particular denomination (e.g. £10, £5) is needed for a particular amount expressed as a day's average wage. Hence people can, and do, attempt to acquire money because it may satisfy different wants at the same time.

Whether Lea *et al.* (1987) have given us a new theory of money is not clear. But they have drawn attention to some important facts concerning money at the individual psychological level of analyses.

First, there are various types of money in existence in sophisticated societies. A credit card, a bank note, a personal cheque, and a gift voucher can all represent the same amount of money. But how people perceive and use that economical equivalent sum will not be the same. Credit cards are seen as convenient but can be very 'costly' because of the interest rates charged, and their lack of security. On the other hand, their colour and type can be a powerful status symbol. Bank notes are popular and easy to store, but if old and dirty may seem unattractive to use. Notes have the advantage that they are more easily spent and acquired without being traceable (by say, tax authorities); on the other hand, they could be forgeries and hence worth nothing. The personal cheque is possibly safer but less interchangeable than bank notes and practically worthless if in very small denominations because of bank charges associated with processing. Further, they may not be accepted without some specific means of identification. Finally, gift vouchers may be the 'sweetest' kind of money because they are a gift. But they may also be the least useful because they may only be used at certain shops, for certain gifts, and you cannot always ensure you will get change if you under-spend.

The fact that coins and notes take on symbolic value means that they may circulate in the economy at quite different rates for their actual face value. Preferred, attractive, clean, easy to store, safe money is more often hoarded than coins or notes that do not have these characteristics. Next, changes in currency may be met with anything from hostile resistance to immediate adoption, depending on the meaning attached to the symbolism of the coins and notes.

Although it may be possible to draw up an exhaustive list of the major symbolic associates of various types of money, and even document which groups are more likely to favour one symbol over another, a psychological theory of money will only be useful when the symbol is related to behaviour.

Ideally, according to Lea *et al.* (1987), a psychological theory of money has three factors:

1 Factors associated with the *development* of symbolism. Thus for particular individuals in particular cultures, shapes, colours and icons have particular value and importance. Hence national differences in the size, colour and iconography of currency. Note how this changes with major changes in government as in the case of Hong Kong, South Africa, the former Soviet Union and Yugoslavia over the past decade.
2 Factors concerning *symbolism* itself. The range and meaning (positive, negative and neutral) attached to all forms of currency from the traditional (coins, notes and cheques) to more modern forms of currency, including new works of art which are bought not for aesthetic pleasure but as an exclusive source of investment.
3 Factors associated with the *use* of money. Why certain types of money are saved and others spent; why some are considered more safe than others; more personal and more desirable than others. Why money is unacceptable as a gift and why casinos use chips rather than cash. Indeed the meaning of money is more observable in the way it is used.

However, in this book we shall attempt to answer many other questions in addition to those listed here.

Money is not psychologically interchangeable. It is of value and a measure of value. It is a complicated symbol imbued by individuals and communities with particular meanings, which in part dictates how it is used by economic forces. Even the vulgar and naive psychologist and economist recognises issues of multiple causation with feedback loops that contextually shape and describe the individual to the society in which he or she lives. It should be acknowledged that individuals display constant and important monetary behaviours. Individuals act on the economy; the collective behaviour of individuals (sometimes few in number) shape economic affairs. On the other hand, individuals' economic status and situation in society determines not only how much money they have but how they see that money. We shape our economy and it shapes us. The laws and history of a particular economy (i.e. western Europe) do effect in small and big ways the conscious and unconscious behaviour of all the citizens.

One of the most fundamental differences between the major social sciences interested in money (anthropology, economy, psychology and sociology) concerns the fundamental assumption that people believe rationally and logically with respect to their own money. While econometricians and theorists develop highly sophisticated mathematical models of economic behaviour (always aggregated across groups), these nearly always accept the basic axiom of individual rationality. Psychologists, on the other hand, have delighted in showing the manifest number of faulty logical mistakes which ordinary people make in economic reasoning. Sociologists and anthropologists have also demonstrated how social forces (norms, rituals, customs and laws) exist that constantly render the behaviour of both group and individuals a-rational rather than irrational.

The opposite of rational is impulsive, whimsical, unpredictable. Economists accept that there are people of limited knowledge, intelligence and insight. And they know that business people with non-rational motives who make use of non-rational procedure will fail rather than survive. Economic behaviour that reflects human frailty or poor reason is classified as a short-term aberration that has little impact on economic developments in the long run.

The whole rationality issue is a difficult one. Doing unpaid work, giving to charity, and playing the national lottery may all be regarded as irrational. This is often to take a very narrow view of rationality. Clearly, work provides many social benefits while gambling is exciting. What the economist often means by 'rational' is behaving in such a way as to maximise income.

There are various synonyms for rationality like optimising or maximising. But, as Lea *et al.* (1987) note, 'we have seen that, in an analysis of real human choice behaviour, the rationality assumption is at best unproven, generally unhelpful, and sometimes clearly false' (p. 127). Yet they believe it remains reasonable for economists to use rationality assumptions. However, they do point out that economic psychology's preoccupation with the rationality question is futile. Rather than attempt to define whether an individual's behaviour is rational, maximising or optimising we should shift our attention to what is maximised and why. It is rather pointless being obsessed with the rationality question if this leads researchers to ignore the content of that behaviour.

Essentially, the rationality argument can be presented at four different levels:

1 The most strict and least acceptable meaning of economic rationality is that people are almost exclusively materially driven and that with both perfect knowledge and cool logic they choose 'rationally' between material satisfactions. This version has been both theoretically and empirically discredited.
2 The second version is that nearly always people believe rationally with respect to economic situations. Societies and individuals supposedly 'economise'. The trouble with this idea is that although it may be possible to show that in the production and pricing of goods both primitive and modern peoples act rationally they frequently behave quite irrationally in the exchanging of goods within economical gift-giving. In this sense, all individuals and societies are, at once, rational and a-rational.
3 The third position is to treat rationality as simply a provisional set of assumptions upon which to base a theory or model. Rationality is a form of conceptual simplification which can be revised or rejected if unhelpful

or if the data do not fit the theory. Many social scientists would be happy with this level of analysis.

4 The final level of analysis is to treat economic rationality as an 'institutionalized value' (Smelser, 1963). This is more than a psychological or sociological postulate but a standard of behaviour to which individuals and organisations hope to aspire. It is a standard to which people may conform or deviate, and, hence, contains the concept of social control.

As Katona (1975) notes, the real question is not whether the consumer is rational or irrational: consumers' decisions are shaped by attitudes, habits, socio-cultural norms, and group membership. People prefer cognitive short-cuts, rules of thumb, routines – they are rarely capricious and whimsical and, for psychologists, never incomprehensible. Likewise, the behaviour of whole groups follows logical patterns, which may differ greatly from postulated forms of rational behaviour. Few consumers reflect carefully on all the options available to them; they often forget details of past decisions; are not always very clear on how they differ from their reference groups and are rarely up to date on the recent economic data. In short, the consumer behaves psycho-logically. People get multiple benefits from behaviours involving money such as giving and gambling. Thus they may 'pay for' psychological benefits by behaving in a way that does not maximise their income.

Again and again, psychological research has shown that people are not economically rational with their money. The way they do (or do not) save and spend it; the way they deal with their taxation affairs; the way they borrow or give it away; and the way they acquire it at work often defies the axioms of the economists. Most people are not educated sufficiently in monetary and economic affairs to behave 'rationally', though few admit to being illogical or irrational. There are, of course, extreme cases of individuals who, like addicts and neurotics, know their behaviour is self-defeating but seem unable to do anything about it. Most people believe themselves to be sensible about money; they reason about their known choices and follow the examples of others.

Psychological theories of money neither assume monetary rationality nor rejoice in the countless examples of the ir- and a-rationality of ordinary people with respect to their money. They have however, set themselves the task, of trying to understand how ordinary people acquire and demonstrate their everyday monetary attitudes, beliefs and behaviours.

THEMES IN THIS BOOK

Because interest in the psychology of money has been somewhat erratic and because researchers have been interested in quite particular features of how people think about and use money, there are no grand theories of money in psychology as we have in economics. However, there are some very interesting and significant theories that will be covered in this book.

First, there is research on basic attitudes to money; its psychological significance and symbolism. Money has multiple meanings, being both sacred and profane. Further, there are ethical issues about how to acquire and use money, which means money attitudes are linked to other ideologies and religious beliefs. Psychometricians have recently become more interested in devising and validating multi-factorial measures of money attitudes. These questionnaires are a good starting point in research, particularly in order to establish how money attitudes and beliefs are distributed in society at large.

Second, developmental psychologists have become very interested in how children and young people acquire an understanding of the social and economic world. Studies have concentrated particularly on how and when children acquire a knowledge of the meaning, value and origin of money, as well as when they come to understand particular concepts like banking, pricing, profits, possessions, ownership, saving, etc. Most parents are interested in helping their children acquire both a knowledge of and sensible habits with regard to money and attempt to educate them through pocket-money procedures. Various other organisations, like banks, schools and shops have also taken an interest in children's money habits, partly because of their purchasing power.

Third, there has been a growing interest in the way people use money in everyday life: adults spending and saving habits; when and why they gamble; and how they react to taxation. These habits are a reflection of many things: early childhood upbringing, personality, the individuals and the country's particular economic circumstances. Politicians, banks and other institutions are clearly interested in controlling spending and saving, which they do through various mechanisms like taxation, control of interest rates, etc. But these only have limited success because of the sheer number of factors beyond their control. Research on pathological gambling, tax evasion and individual bankruptcy clearly has important applied research, yet there is also an interest in understanding everyday spending and saving from a psychological perspective.

Fourth, one would expect psychologists to be interested in money madness and the rather bizarre and exceptional cases. Psychoanalysts in particular have written extensively about the emotional underpinning of money pathology. They believe that because money represents for different individuals freedom, love, power and security, they react to money in rather pathological ways. Hence one finds the compulsive saver and bargain hunter; the fanatical collector; the money manipulated and empire builder; the love buyer and seller; and those that see money as the only liberator in their lives. Therapists in this area stress the importance of early training, of family experiences and the way societies attitudes encourage or discourage various forms of pathology. There have also been various attempts to measure money pathology.

Fifth, money is used to acquire possessions which are acquired partly to meet real needs, partly to extend life activities, and partly symbolic to enhance self-esteem and identity. Recent research on possessions for individuals have shown how much they are imbued with non-monetary meaning.

Sixth, we shall consider how money operates within families; how it is jointly owned, given to children and controlled by individuals. The family unit represents a mini-economy and various rules are instituted to ensure certain behaviours are adhered to. The sociology of the family throws light on to both historic and current patterns in how families save, spend and distribute money.

Seventh, while economists have primarily been concerned about how people acquire, store and save money, psychologists have become interested in when and why people give money away. Many people make regular, often large, donations to charity. Further, they give a great deal to family and friends at birthdays, Christmas, etc., and when they are in particular need. Some tithe to churches; others expend a great deal of thought on their wills and to whom they plan to leave their money. Again, this behaviour often looks irrational from an economic perspective.

Eighth, there is, of course, a great deal of interest in the whole topic of money 'at work': when and why people go on strike as a function of money; how they like to be paid; and even such topics as the reasons for tipping. Most people acquire nearly all of their money through their work but there are strange anomalies in the amount of money people get paid. The large amounts of profit-related pay given to financiers and the high salaries of chief executives, particularly when compared with such occupations as nurses and teachers, frequently causes concern. Equally interesting and surprising is the poor relationship between pay and job satisfaction.

Last, we shall consider fundamental such questions as, does money lead to happiness? Do the rich benefit society? How do people cope with sudden wealth? And, fundamentally, is the economic model of man correct or useful?

2 Attitudes to money

Money will say more in one moment than the most eloquent lover can in years.

Henry Fielding

Money is the poor man's credit card.

Marshall McLuhan

What's money? It's the only thing that's handier than a credit card.

Anon.

Money isn't everything, but it's a long way ahead of what comes next.

Sir Edmund Stockdale

I would not say millionaires were mean. They simply have a healthy respect for money. I've noticed that people who don't respect money don't have any.

J. Paul Getty

Having money is rather like being a blond. It's more fun but not vital.

Mary Quant

Money differs from an automobile, a mistress or cancer in being equally important to those who have it and those who don't.

John Kenneth Galbraith

To have money is to be virtuous, honest, beautiful and witty. And to be without it is to be ugly and boring and stupid and useless.

Jean Giraudoux

Grocers object to the forgery of cheques, which is a danger to their business, more than they object to the forgery of jam, which puts money in their purses.

Robert Lynd

I don't believe money is no object. Money is the object.
James Gulliver

The chief value of money lies in the fact that one lives in a world in which it is overestimated.
H. L. Mencken

INTRODUCTION

Since the turn of the century, social scientists from various disciplines have speculated on the social and emotional values and meanings attached to money (Wiseman, 1974). The fact that money is emotionally charged and highly symbolic has already been mentioned. The essence of money is that it carries meaning. For instance, the introduction and/or removal of a coin from circulation causes a great public outcry. The use of credit cards as opposed to cash has also altered the way in which people use and perceive money.

Money is easier to spend than earn; and certainly easier to earn than define. Like an umbrella or a tin-opener, it is defined primarily by its use. It is quite simply the medium in which prices are expressed, goods and services paid for, debts discharged, and bank reserves held. But it is also possible to measure attitudes to money and beliefs about it. People hold widely different views about money; these different opinions are a function of their age, social class, wealth, political beliefs and a range of other factors.

In this chapter we will consider attitudes to money, and how to measure them, the meaning of money, and such things as how we perceive our coins and notes.

THE MEANING OF MONEY

All researchers and speculators have remarked how people get caught up in the psychological alchemy that transforms cash into objects, services and fantasies. As we shall see in Chapter 5, money has a way of bringing out the irrational in us. It seems to crawl down to the most remote levels of our personalities and releases avarice, jealousy, resentment and fear. 'People bearing psychological money scars have lost their connection with the original purpose and use of bank notes' (Forman, 1987, p. 2).

The extent to which money is imbued with psychological meaning is clearly apparent from the following quote by Wiseman:

One thinks of kleptomaniacs, or of the women who drain men of their resources, to whom money, which they are always striving to take away, symbolizes a whole series of introjected objects that have been withheld from them; or of depressive characters who from fear of starvation regard money as potential food. There are too those men to whom money signifies their potency, who experience any loss of money as a castration, or who are inclined, when in danger, to sacrifice money in a sort of 'prophylactic self-castration'. There are, in addition, people who – according to their attitudes of the moment towards taking, giving or withholding – accumulate or spend money, or alternate between accumulation and spending, quite impulsively, without regard for the real significance of money, and often to their own detriment every man has, and the pricelessness of objects, and the price on the outlaw's head; there are forty pieces of silver and also the double indemnity on one's own life.

Behind its apparent sameness lie the many meanings of money. Blood-money does not buy the same thing as bride-money and a king's ransom is not the same kind of fortune as a lottery prize. The great exchangeability of money is deceptive; it enables us to buy the appearance of things, their physical form, as in the case of a 'bought woman', while what we thought we had bought eludes us.

Wiseman, 1974, (pp. 13–14)

Snelders *et al.* (1992) argue that money takes many forms and has multiple meanings. In a series of laboratory experiments, one done cross-culturally, they attempted to assess the *prototypicality* of the concept of money. They found that money, whose definition and boundaries cannot be precisely specified, nevertheless is used consistently and efficiently. For both modern and ancient peoples, money has a magic quality about it. For the alchemists whose ultimate blend of magic, religion and science failed, money still held the power of fascination. Most people believe, according to pollsters and clinical psychologists dealing with money problems, that many of their everyday problems will be solved if they had significant amounts of money. The myths, fables and rituals surrounding money have increased with modern society and there is a formidable money priesthood, from accountants and actuaries, to stockholders and friendly/building societies.

THE 'SACRED' OR SPECIAL MEANING OF MONEY

For the economist money is almost profane: it is not treated irreverently or disregarded but it is common-place and not special. For others, however, money is sacred – it is obviously feared, revered and worshipped. Belk and Wallendorf (1990) point out that it is the myth, mystery and ritual associated with the acquisition and use of money that defies its sacredness.

For all religions, certain persons, places, things, times and social groups are collectively defined as sacred. Sacred things are extraordinary, totally unique, set apart from and opposed to the profane world. Sacred objects and people can have powers of good or evil (see Chapter 6 on possessions). 'Gifts, vacation travel, souvenirs, family photographs, pets, collections, heirlooms, homes, art, antiques; and objects associated with famous people

can be regarded as existing in the realm of the sacred by many people'
(Belk & Wallendorf, 1990, p. 39). In essence, they are safeguarded and
considered special. Art and other collections become for many people
sacred personal icons. Equally, heirlooms serve as mystical and fragile
connections to those who are deceased. They can have more than 'sentimental value' and some believe that a neglected or damaged heirloom
could unleash bad luck or evil forces.

Unlike sacred objects, profane objects are interchangeable. They are
valued primarily for their mundane use value. Sacred objects often lack
functional use and cannot, through exchange, be converted into profane
objects. Further, exchange of sacred objects for money violates their sacred
status, because it brings them into inappropriate contact with the profane
realm.

Although money is, by definition, the all-purpose medium of exchange in
Western countries it still can only be used for particular things. Money is
too sterile and ordinary to be used on special occasions. In Western
societies money cannot buy brides, expiation from crimes or (ideally)
political office. As we shall see later in the book, money is thought
unsuitable as a present for various reasons: it may be too precise a measure
of love, no gift-wrapping, etc.

Curiously, the Judaeo-Christian ethic is paradoxical on money. People
with money acquired honestly are seen as superior, even virtuous, and
removing the desire to accumulate money is condemned. So, at one and
the same time, believers are called on to be altruistic, ascetic and selfless,
while simultaneously being hard-working, acquisitional and frankly capitalistic. The sacred and the profane can get easily mixed up (Furnham,
1990).

Belk and Wallendorf (1990) also believed that the sacred meaning of
money is gender and class linked. They argue that women think of money
in terms of the things into which it can be converted, while men think of it
in terms of the power its possession implies. In short, all the money women
deal with is profane (unless used for personal pleasure, in which case it is
evil), while some of the use of money by men is sacred. Similarly, in
working-class homes men tradionally gave over their wages to their wife
for the management of profane household needs with a small allowance
given back for individual personal pleasures, most of which were far from
sacred. Yet in a middle-class house men typically gave, and indeed sometimes still give, their wife an allowance (being a small part of their income)
for collective household expenditure. Again, as we see later, middle-class
couples seem mostly to share their access to money.

Belk and Wallendorf (1990) argue that money (an income) obtained
from work that is not a source of intrinsic delight is ultimately profane,
but an income derived from one's passion is actually sacred. An artist can
do commercial work for profane money and the work of the soul for sacred
money. From ancient Greece to twentieth-century Europe, the business of

making money is tainted. It is the activity of the *nouveau riche* not honourable 'old money'.

Thus, volunteer work is sacred, while the identical job which is paid is profane. The idea of paying somebody to be a mother or home-keeper may be preposterous for some because it renders the sacred duty profane. But the acts of prostitutes transform a sacred act into a formal business exchange. Some crafts people and artists do sell their services but at a 'modest' almost not going-rate, price because their aim is not to accumulate wealth but to make a reasonable income and not become burdened by their work.

> Thus, money obtained from enacting a passion, particularly if it is not a large amount, is sacred, as is money obtained through hard labour by one who will not amass great wealth. Money obtained without labour is regarded as evil and threatens to unleash that power on its owner, even as he or she tries to apply it to sacred uses. Work for profane money may be sacralized to a degree if the worker avoids extremes of greed and acquisitiveness.
>
> (Belk, 1991, p. 55)

Finally, Belk (1991) considers the sacred uses of money. A sacred use – e.g. a gift – can be 'desacralised' if a person is too concerned with price. Sacralising mechanisms usually involve the purchase of gifts and souvenirs, donations to charity, as well as the purchase of a previously sacralised object. The aim is to transform money into objects with special significance or meaning. Money-as-sacrifice and money-as-gift are clearly more sacred than money-as-commodity. Charity giving is a sacred gift only when it involves personal sacrifice and not when there is personal gain through publicity or tax relief. Money used to redeem and restore special objects (e.g. rare works of art, religious objects) also renders it sacred.

Thus to retain all money for personal use is considered antisocial, selfish, miserly and evil. To transform sacred money (a gift) into money (by selling it) is considered especially evil. Many people refuse to turn certain objects into money, preferring to give them away. Money violates the sacredness of objects and commodifies them. Equally, people refuse money when offered by those who have voluntarily helped. The 'good Samaritans' thereby assign their assistance to the area of the gift rather than a profane exchange. Thus a gift of help may be reciprocated by another gift.

The argument is thus: the dominant view of money concentrates on its profane meaning. It is a utilitarian view that sees money transactions as impersonal and devoid of sacred money. But it becomes clear when considering the illogical behaviour of collectors, gift-givers and charity donors that money can and does have sacred meanings, both good and evil. Further, it is these sacred meanings that so powerfully influence our attitudes to money.

MONEY ETHICS

Tang (1992, 1993, 1995) and colleagues (Tang and Gilbert, 1995; Tang *et al.*, 1997) have done a lot of empirical work on what he called the Money Ethic Scale (MES). Tang believes attitudes to money have an *affective* component (good, evil), a *cognitive* component (how it relates to achievement, respect, freedom) and a *behavioural* component. He set out to develop and validate a clear straightforward, multidimensional scale. He started with 50 items tested on 769 subjects, which he reduced to 30 easy statements that had 5 clear factors. The questions and the labels given to the factors are set out in Table 2.1.

The scale had adequate internal reliability. More importantly, various hypotheses were tested and confirmed. Thus the ability to budget money was correlated with age and sex (female). High-income people tended to think that money revealed one's achievement (factor 3) and was less evil, while young people are more likely to see money as evil.

High Protestant Ethic subjects (PEs) reported that they budgeted their money properly and tended to see money as evil and freedom/power. High Leisure Ethic individuals (LEs) were more oriented to see money as good, less as evil, achievement and freedom/power. Also, as predicted, economic and political values were positively associated with achievement respect/ self-esteem and power. Social and religious values were negatively correlated with achievement and power.

Tang (1993) translated and used the scale in Taiwan. He found that Taiwanese students' attitudes towards money were consistent with their inner values, their 'frame of reference', their culture as well as their own personal experience. His results suggested that those who had lower expectations of money tended to report having a happier and less stressful life than those that did not. In other words, anti-materialism was universally related to self-reported happiness.

Tang and Gilbert (1995) found that intrinsic job satisfaction was related to the concept that money is symbolic of freedom and power, while extrinsic job satisfaction was related to the notion that money is not an evil. They found that (mental-health) workers with self-reported low organisational stress tended to believe money was inherently good. Further, those that claimed they budgeted their money carefully tended to be older, of lower income, higher self-esteem and low organisational stress. As before, those who endorse Protestant Work Ethic values tended to think money represented an achievement and is inherently good.

Using a shortened version of the scale, Tang (1995) found many correlates of the total Money Ethic Scale score which indicates people's general positive attitude towards money: it represents success, not evil, and careful budgeting was valued. He found that those who showed a highly positive attitude to money expressed strong economic and political values but not religious values; and they tended to be older, with lower pay satisfaction.

Table 2.1 Factor loadings for the Money Ethic Scale

Item

Factor 1: Good

1	Money is an important factor in the lives of all of us
2	Money is good
17	Money is important
46	I value money very highly
24	Money is valuable
36	Money does not grow on trees
27	Money can buy you luxuries
14	Money is attractive
45	I think that it is very important to save money

Factor 2: Evil

15	Money is the root of all evil
4	Money is evil
21	Money spent is money lost (wasted)
32	Money is shameful
19	Money is useless
37	A penny saved is a penny earned

Factor 3: Achievement

5	Money represents one's achievement
9	Money is the most important thing (goal) in my life
8	Money is a symbol of success
3	Money can buy everything

Factor 4: Respect (self-esteem)

20	Money makes people respect you in the community
31	Money is honourable
25	Money will help you express your competence and abilities
12	Money can bring you many friends

Factor 5: Budget

47	I use my money very carefully
48	I budget my money very well
43	I pay my bills immediately in order to avoid interest or penalties

Factor 6: Freedom (power)

11	Money gives you autonomy and freedom
7	Money in the bank is a sign of security
29	Money can give you the opportunity to be what you want to be
30	Money means power

Source: Tang (1992)
Note: $N = 249$

Thus those who value money seem to have greater dissatisfaction, no doubt because of the perceived inequity between pay reality and expectations. Tang (1995) argued that there are various sources of reward for productivity: job redesign, goal-setting, contingent payment and participation in decision-making. Those who endorse the Money Ethic are usually motivated by extrinsic rewards, and are most interested in, and satisfied by, profit or gain, sharing bonuses and other contingent payment methods of compensation. People who endorse the Money Ethic are clearly materialistic and sensitive to monetary rewards.

More recently, Tang *et al.* (1997) did a cross-cultural analysis of the short MEQ, comparing workers in America, Britain and Taiwan. After controlling for age, sex and educational levels, American workers thought that 'Money is good' and that they 'Budget money very well'. They had the highest scores on the Short Money Ethic Scale (MES), organisation-based self-esteem, and intrinsic job satisfaction. Chinese workers had the highest endorsement of the Protestant work ethic, the highest 'Respect' for money score, yet the lowest intrinsic job satisfaction. British workers felt that 'Money means power' and had the lowest extrinsic job satisfaction.

American workers tended to have higher scores on items with a high 'self-orientation' (factors 'Good' and 'Budget', and the Short MES measure) than their counterparts. Thus, people in an individualistic society (i.e. the USA) tend to score higher on scales or items with a high 'I orientation' or 'the self as the centre of the psychological field' than those in a collectivistic culture.

Chinese workers had the highest endorsement of the Protestant work ethic. Because of their economic success, these workers seem increasingly aware of the importance of the respect that money can offer. Moreover, factors 'Achievement' and 'Respect' were significantly correlated. Workers in Taiwan also have the strongest belief that money means achievement. These findings seemed to support the notion that competitiveness is a powerful stimulant to economic growth. According to Maslow's need-hierarchy theory, when lower-order needs are satisfied, higher-order needs will become more important. Taiwan has enjoyed a long period of peace and economic growth, and is becoming a major player in the world economy. Thus, people in Taiwan may become more interested in money as a sign of achievement and respect than the past. The economic and cultural environment may play an important role in people's money beliefs.

None of these findings is counter-intuitive and Tang has demonstrated empirically what many have observed: that the successful economics of South-east Asia are highly materialistic, stressing hard work and economic rewards.

THE STRUCTURE OF MONEY ATTITUDES

Social psychologists and psychometricians have been particularly interested in measuring attitudes to money. Luft (1957) found that a person's weekly income determines how s/he is perceived by peers. Hypothetically, rich men were seen, in America at the time, as relatively healthy, happy and well adjusted, while the poor person was seen as maladjusted and unhappy. However, subsequent studies in other parts of the world have not replicated this finding. Rim (1982) looked at the relationship between personality and attitudes towards money: stable extraverts seemed more open, comfortable and carefree about their money than unstable introverts. Personality variables seem, however, only weak predictors of money attitudes and behaviour.

Wernimont and Fitzpatrick (1972) used a semantic differential approach (where forty adjective pairs were rated on a seven-point scale) to attempt to understand the meaning that different people attach to money. In their sample of over 500 Americans they used such diverse people as secretaries and engineers, nursing sisters and technical supervisors. Factor analysis revealed a number of interpretable factors, which were labelled *shameful failure* (lack of money is an indication of failure, embarrassment and degradation), *social acceptability, pooh-pooh attitude* (money is not very important, satisfying or attractive), *moral evil, comfortable security, social unacceptability* and *conservative business values*. The respondents' work experiences, sex and socio-economic level appeared to influence their perceptions of money. For instance, employment status showed that employed groups view money much more positively and as desirable, important and useful, whereas the unemployed seemed to take a tense, worrisome, unhappy view of money.

Other researchers have attempted to devise measures of people's attitudes towards money. Rubinstein (1981) devised a money survey for *Psychology Today* to investigate readers' attitudes and feelings about money, to get an idea of its importance in their lives, what associations it evokes and how it affects their closest relationships. Some of these questions were later combined into a 'Midas' scale but no statistics were presented. The free-spenders – classified by questions such as, 'I really enjoy spending money', 'I almost always buy what I want, regardless of cost' – certainly reported being healthier and happier than self-denying 'tight wads'. Those who scored high in penny-pinching had lower self-esteem and expressed much less satisfaction with finances, personal growth, friends and jobs. They also tended to be more pessimistic about their own and the country's future, and many reported classic psychosomatic symptoms like anxiety, headaches and lack of interest in sex. Although over 20,000 responses were received from a moderately well distributed population, the results were only analysed in terms of simple percentages and few individual difference variables were considered.

Rubinstein's (1981) data did reveal some surprising findings. For instance, about half her sample said that neither their parents nor friends knew about their income. Less than one-fifth told their siblings. Thus, they appeared to think about money all the time and talked about it very little, and only to a very few people. Predictably, as income rises so does secrecy and the desire to cover up wealth. From the extensive data bank it was possible to classify people into 'money contented' (very or moderately happy with their financial situation), neutral and 'money discontented' (unhappy or very unhappy with their financial situation). The two differed fundamentally on various other questions (see Table 2.2).

It seemed that the money contented rule their money rather than let it rule them. When they want to buy something that seems too expensive, for example, they are the most likely to save for it or forget it. The money troubled, by contrast, are more likely to charge it to a credit card. Note too how the money troubled appear to have many more psychosomatic illnesses.

Rubinstein also looked at sex differences. Twice as many working wives as husbands felt about their income that 'mine is mine'. Indeed, if the wives earned more than their husbands, over half tended to argue about money. Contrary to popular expectation, the men and women assigned equal importance to work, love, parenthood and finances in their lives. The men, however, were more confident and self-assured about money than the women. They were happier than the women are about their financial situation, felt more control over it, and predicted a higher earning potential for themselves.

There were interesting and predictable emotional differences in how men and women reacted to money (see Table 2.3).

Surveys such as Rubinstein's give a fascinating snapshot of the money attitudes, beliefs and behaviours of a particular population at one point in time. It is a pity, however, that these results were not treated to more thorough and careful statistical analysis. Others, however, have concentrated on developing valid instruments for use in psychological research in the area.

Yamauchi and Templer (1982), on the other hand, attempted to develop a fully psychometrised Money Attitude Scale (MAS). A factor analysis of an original selection of sixty-two items revealed five factors labelled *Power–Prestige*, *Retention Time*, *Distrust*, *Quality* and *Anxiety*. From this a twenty-nine-item scale was selected, which was demonstrated to be reliable. A partial validation – correlations with other established measures such as Machiavellianism, status concern, time competence, obsessionality, paranoia and anxiety – showed that this questionnaire was related to measures of other similar theoretical constructs. Most interestingly, the authors found that money attitudes were essentially independent of a person's income. They argue that the MAS could be used in clinical practice to examine the disparity between the attitudes of couples.

Gresham and Fontenot (1989) looked at sex differences in the use of money using the MAS. They did not confirm the factor structure, finding different but similar factors, labelled *Power–Prestige* (using money to influence and impress), *Distrust–Anxiety* (nervous about spending and not spending money), *Retention–Time* (money behaviours which require planning and preparation for the future) and *Quality* (purchasing of quality products as a predominant behaviour). Clear sex differences were found on all but the retention–time factor. Unexpectedly, despite many views to the

Table 2.2 The money contented and the money troubled

Several survey questions asked people how satisfied they are with their financial situation how much they worry about it, whether money, for them, is associated with fear or anxiety. Their answers were scored, with the top quarter labelled 'Money contented' and the bottom quarter 'Money troubled'

	Money contented (%)	Money troubled (%)
Has inflation substantially altered your way of living in the past year?		
Yes, a great deal	5	40
Yes, somewhat	26	45
No, not very much	46	12
No, not at all	22	2
I think most of my friends have:		
More money than I do	17	59
About as much money as I do	42	32
Less money than I do	41	9
Relative to your present income, how deeply in debt are you?		
Over my head	0	12
Enough to feel uncomfortable	4	44
Not much	37	26
Very little or not at all	59	17
There always seems to be things I want that I can't have		
Strongly agree	7	50
Agree	35	42
Disagree	37	7
Strongly Disagree	20	2
What are your major fears?		
None	24	6
Not having enough money	10	63
Loss of a loved one	43	56
Not getting enough out of life	19	52
Not advancing in career	14	40
Becoming ill	41	51
Which of the following have bothered you in the past year?		
Constant worry and anxiety	7	50
Fatigue	24	49
Loneliness	16	47
Feeling worthless	6	34
Headaches	10	33
Insomnia	10	28
Feeling guilty	6	26
Weight problems	13	25
Lack of interest in sex	12	25
Feelings of despair	4	24

Source: Rubinstein (1981)
Note: Since respondents were asked to circle all that apply, percentages sum to more than 100 per cent

Table 2.3 Emotional differences between men's and women's reactions to money

In the past year, can you recall associating money with any of the following?

	Women (%)	Men (%)
Anxiety	75	67
Depression	57	46
Anger	55	47
Helplessness	50	38
Happiness	49	55
Excitement	44	49
Envy	43	38
Resentment	42	31
Fear	33	25
Guilt	27	22
Panic	27	16
Distrust	23	25
Sadness	22	20
Respect	18	19
Indifference	16	16
Shame	13	9
Love	10	13
Hatred	8	7
Spite	9	8
Reverence	2	5
None	2	5

Source: Rubinstein (1981)
Note: Since respondents were asked to circle all that apply, percentages sum to more than 100 per cent

contrary, females, more than males, seemed to use money as a tool in power struggles. Consistent with the previous literature, the data suggest women are more anxious about money in general than men and also tend to be more interested in the quality of products and services that they buy.

More recently, in a cross-cultural study, Medina *et al.* (1996) looked at Mexican-Americans vs. Anglo-Americans' attitudes to money using the MAS. After a useful review of the literature, they formulated and tested four cross-cultural hypotheses: Compared with Anglo-Americans, Mexican-Americans will have lower Power–Prestige and Retention–Time, but higher Distrust–Anxiety and Quality scores. Only two hypotheses were proven statistically significant, one in the opposite direction to that hypothesised. Mexican-Americans had lower Retention–Time and Quality scores. The authors suggest that the way Mexican-Americans are discussed in the Hispanic consumer-behaviour literature must be called into question. However, it does become clear that different ethnic and national cultures do hold different attitudes towards money and presumably to related behaviours regarding such things as saving, spending and gambling. Attitudes to time and fate (control) are clearly important cultural correlates of attitudes to money.

McClure (1984) gave 159 American shoppers a 22-item questionnaire about money: spending habits, perceived control over finances, importance of money to one's life, preferences about monetary privacy, and conflict resulting from money. He also administered three personality tests. He found that extraverts tended to be more extravagant and less stingy than introverts. People with strong feelings of control over their money reported less general anxiety and tended to be more extroverted. Neurotic introverts considered money more important in their lives and were more private about it compared with stable introverts. Despite clear links to personality, the results showed the attitudes measured in the questionnaire were un-related to demographic differences of gender, education, occupation or religion.

More recently, Furnham (1984) conducted a study which had three aims: (1) to develop a useful, multifaceted instrument to measure money beliefs and behaviours in Britain; (2) to look at the relationship between various demographic and social/work beliefs and people's monetary beliefs and behaviours; and (3) to look at the determination of people's money beliefs and behaviours in the past and the future. Attitude statements used in the study are set out in the list on pp. 50–1. These statements were derived from a number of sources: books on 'money madness' (see Chapter 5); survey research (such as done by Rubinstein, 1981); interviews with people on their attitudes to money and reviews of the extant literature. It was hoped that these attitudes, beliefs and values reflected a comprehensive list of underlying factors that was expected to relate to a person's personality, demographic status and chosen life-style. No attempt was made *a priori* to classify or categorise the items into factors, as this was done statistically.

The results show six clear factors, labelled thus: (1) *Obsession* (items 28, 43, 45, etc.); (2) *Power/Spending* (items 3, 16, etc.); (3) *Retention* (items 7, 9, etc.); (4) *Security/Conservative* (items 14, 55, etc.); (5) *Inadequate* (items 27, 32); (6) *Effort/Ability* (items 51, 53, 54).

Predictably, older, less well-educated people believed their early child-hood to be poorer than that of young, better-educated people, reflecting both the average increased standard of living and the class structure of society. Overall, there were few differences in the subjects' perception of money in the past, but a large number regarding money in the future. Older people were more worried about the future than younger people, possibly because they had greater financial responsibility with families, children and mortgages. Richer people were more concerned about the future than poorer people. Politically Conservative (right-wing) voters believed that the country's economic future was bright, while Labour (left-wing) voters and those with high alienation and conservative social attitudes believed that it would get worse. Although these questions may seem vague they are not trivial because presumably people act on their beliefs about future trends in terms of saving, spending and investing (Rubinstein, 1981).

1 I often buy things that I don't need or want because they are in a sale or reduced in a sale, or reduced in price.

2 I put money ahead of pleasure.

3 I sometimes buy things I don't need or want to impress people because they are the right things to have at the time.

4 Even when I have sufficient money I often feel guilty about spending money on necessities like clothes, etc.

5 Every time I make a purchase I 'know' people are likely to be taking advantage of me.

6 I often spend money, even foolishly, on others but grudgingly on myself.

7 I often say 'I can't afford it' whether I can or not.

8 I know almost to the penny how much I have in my purse, wallet or pocket all the time.

9 I often have difficulty in making decisions about spending money, regardless of the amount.

10 I feel compelled to argue or bargain about the cost of almost everything that I buy.

11 I insist on paying more than my [our, if married] share of restaurant, film, etc., costs in order to make sure that I am not indebted to anyone.

12 If I had the choice I would prefer to be paid by the week rather than by the month.

13 I prefer to use money rather than credit cards.

14 I always know how much money I have in my savings account (bank or building society).

15 If I have some money left over at the end of the month (week) I often feel uncomfortable until it is all spent.

16 I sometimes 'buy' my friendship by being very generous with those I want to like me.

17 I often feel inferior to others who have more money than myself, even when I know that they have done nothing of worth to get it.

18 I often use money as a weapon to control or intimidate those who frustrate me.

19 I sometimes feel superior to those who have less money than myself, regardless of their ability and achievements.

20 I firmly believe that money can solve all of my problems.

21 I often feel anxious and defensive when asked about my personal finances.

22 In making any purchase, for any purpose, my first consideration is cost.

23 I believe that it is rude to enquire about a person's wage/salary.

24 I feel stupid if I pay more for something than a neighbour.

25 I often feel disdain for money and look down on those who have it.

26 I prefer to save money because I'm never sure when things will collapse and I'll need the cash.

27 The amount of money that I have saved is never quite enough.

28 I feel that money is the only thing that I can really count on.

29 I believe that money is the root of all evil.
30 As regards what one buys with money I believe that one only gets what one pays for.
31 I believe that money gives one considerable power.
32 My attitude towards money is very similar to that of my parents.
33 I believe that the amount of money that a person earns is closely related to his/her ability and effort.
34 I always pay bills (telephone, water, electricity, etc.) promptly.
35 I often give large tips to waiters/waitresses that I like.
36 I believe that time not spent in making money is time wasted.
37 I occasionally pay restaurant/shop bills even when I think I have been overcharged because I am afraid the waiter/assistant might be angry with me.
38 I often spend money on myself when I am depressed.
39 When a person owes me money I am afraid to ask for it.
40 I don't like to borrow money from others (except banks) unless I absolutely have to.
41 I prefer not to lend people money.
42 I am better off than most of my friends think.
43 I would do practically anything legal for money if it were enough.
44 I prefer to spend money on things that last rather than on perishables like food, flowers etc.
45 I am proud of my financial victories – pay, riches, investments, etc – and let my friends know about them.
46 I am worse off than most of my friends think.
47 Most of my friends have less money than I do.
48 I believe that it is generally prudent to conceal the details of my finances from friends and relatives.
49 I often argue with my partner (spouse, lover, etc.) about money.
50 I believe that a person's salary is very revealing in assessing their intelligence.
51 I believe that my present income is about what I deserve, given the job I do.
52 Most of my friends have more money than I do.
53 I believe that my present income is far less than I deserve, given the job I do.
54 I believe that I have very little control over my financial situation in terms of my power to change it.
55 Compared to most people that I know, I believe that I think about money much more than they do.
56 I worry about my finances much of the time.
57 I often fantasise about money and what I could do with it.
58 I very rarely give beggars or drunks money when they ask for it.
59 I am proud of my ability to save money.
60 In Britain, money is how we compare each other.

That is, if one believes that future economic trends mean that one might be substantially worse off one might take steps to avoid this.

Hanley and Wilhelm (1992), used the Furnham (1984) measure to investigate the relationship between self-esteem and money attitudes. They found, as predicted, that compulsive spenders have relatively lower self-esteem than 'normal' consumers and that compulsive spenders have beliefs about money which reflect its symbolic ability to enhance self-esteem. They note:

> Descriptively, the findings of this study show that there are significant differences between a sample of compulsive spenders and a sample of 'normal' consumers on five of the six money attitude and belief dimensions under study. Compulsive spenders reported a greater likelihood than 'normal' consumers to be preoccupied with the importance of money as a solution to problems and to use money as a means of comparison. Additionally, compulsive spenders were more likely to report the need to spend money in a manner which was reflective of status and power. In contrast, the compulsive spenders were less likely than 'normal' consumers to take a traditional, more conservative approach to money. Compulsive spenders were more likely to report that they did not have enough money for their needs, especially in comparison to friends. Finally, compulsive spenders reported a greater tendency, than did 'normal' consumers, to feel a sense of conflict over the spending of money.
>
> Hanley and Wilhelm, 1992, (p. 16–17)

Lynn (1991) also used some of the items from Furnham's (1984) scale to look at national differences in attitudes to money over forty-three countries. He argued that various studies have shown that people respond with greater work effort when they are offered financial incentives. It is probable, however, that people differ in the importance they attach to money and therefore in the degree to which they will work harder in order to obtain it, and it may be that there are national differences in the strength of the value attached to money.

There were statistically significant negative associations between the valuation of money and per-capita income among most nations groups. People from more affluent countries attached less value to money. The sex differences show a general trend for males to attach more value to money than females. The male scores are higher than females in forty of the nations, and only in India, Norway and Transkei was this tendency reversed. A possible explanation for this sex difference is that males generally tend to be more competitive. There were also high correlations between the valuation of money and competitiveness across nations.

The results were not dissimilar from related American studies (Rubinstein, 1981; Yamauchi and Templer, 1982). Attitudes towards money are by no means unidimensional: factor-analytic results yielded six clearly interpretable factors that bore many similarities to the factors found in Yamauchi and Templer (1982) such as power, retention and inadequacy, as well as the hypothetical factors derived from psychoanalytic theory (Fenichel, 1947). Whereas some of the factors were clearly linked to clinical traits of anxiety and obsessionality, others were more closely related to power and the way in which one obtains money. Also, some factors more than others proved to be related to demographic and belief variables: obsession with money showed significant differences across sex, education and income, and all the belief variables (alienation, Protestant work ethic, conservatism), whereas the inadequacy factor revealed no significant differences on either set of variables. These differences would not have been predicted by psychoanalytic theory. It should also be noted that feelings of alienation did not discriminate very clearly, so casting doubt on a narrowly clinical approach to money beliefs and attitudes.

These studies do indicate that demographic (sex, age, class), nationality and personality factors are related to monetary beliefs and behaviours. While there are some consistent patterns it is difficult to draw any firm conclusions owing to the paucity of large-population and comparable studies in the area. Females, older people, those from lower socio-demographic groups and those with more evidence of neurosis seem more concerned about money.

Medina *et al.* (1996) have tabulated some of many money questionnaires developed by researchers and the possible factors that influenced them (see Table 2.4). This is a very useful table for the future researcher in the area. It also demonstrates the psychometric interest in money attitudes over the last twenty-five years. What it shows is that there are a number of different questionnaires to choose from if one is interested in research in the area. The choice of questionnaire should probably depend on three things: What one is interested in measuring and the precise dimensions of most concern; the psychometric properties of the questionnaire, specifically reliability and validity; and practical considerations like the length of the questionnaire and its country of origin. What this table does not show, however, is the factor structure of each questionnaire and the overlap. Many have similar dimensions related to such things as obsession with money; concern over retaining it; money as a source of power, etc.

MEASURING ECONOMIC BELIEFS

Money beliefs are embedded in mere general economic beliefs. But there remains a paucity of good instruments by which to assess economic beliefs. Although there exist a number of questionnaires to measure conservatism and authoritarianism, they all attempt to measure *general* social attitudes. Furthermore, these tests have been criticised on numerous grounds including the fact that often all scores go in the same direction and, second, many of the items are vague, ambiguous or culture specific. As a result,

Table 2.4 Empirical studies: methodological characteristics and demographic and personality factors that do and do not influence money attitudes

Empirical studies	Scale used	Sample size	Subjects	Location	Factors that influence money attitudes	Factors that do not influence money attitudes
Wernimont and Fitzpatrick (1972)	Modified Semantic Differential (MSD)	533	College students, engineers, religious sisters, etc.	Large US midwestern city	Work experience socio-economic level and gender	
Yamauchi and Templer (1982)	Money Attitude Scale (MAS)	300	Adults from different professions	Los Angeles and Fresno, CA		Income does not affect money attitudes
Furnham (1984)	Money Beliefs and Behaviour Scale (MBBS)	256	College students	England, Scotland and Wales	Income, gender, age, and education	
Bailey and Gustafson (1986)	Money Beliefs and Behaviour Scale	N/A	College students	US southwestern city	Gender	
Gresham and Fontenot (1989)	Modified Money Attitude Scale	557	College students and their parents	US southwestern city	Gender	
Bailey and Gustafson (1991)	Modified Money Beliefs and Behaviour Scale	472	College students	US southwestern city	Sensitivity and emotional stability	
Hanley and Wihelm (1992)	Money Beliefs and Behaviour Scale	143	N/A	Phoenix, Tucson, Denver and Detroit	Compulsive behaviour	
Tang (1992)	Money Ethic Scale (MES)	769	College students, faculty, managers, etc.	middle Tennessee city	Age, income, work ethic, social, political and religious values	

Tang (1993)	Money Ethic Scale (MES)	68 and 249	College students	Taiwan	
Bailey and Lown (1993)	Money in the Past and Future Scale (MPFS)	654	College students, their relatives and other professionals	Western US States	Age
Bailey et al. (1994)	Money Beliefs and Behaviour Scale	344, 291, and 328	Employed adults related to college students	Arkansas, and Utah, US; Victoria and New South Wales, Australia; Vancouver and British Columbia, Canada	Geographical location

Source: Medina, et al. (1996)
Note: NA = Not Available

investigators have attempted to develop short, accurate and simple measures that are reliable, valid and economical (Wilson and Patterson, 1968).

Furnham (1985a) set about developing a new measure of economic beliefs. The rationale for this test was based on that of Wilson and Patterson's (1968) catch-phrase measure of conservatism which has been shown to be very successful (Wilson, 1973; Eysenck, 1976):

> The solution proposed here then, is to abandon the propositional form of item and merely present a list of brief labels or catch-phrases representing various familiar and controversial issues. It is assumed that in the course of previous conversation and argument concerning these issues, the respondent has already placed himself in relation to the general population, and is able to indicate his 'position' immediately in terms of minimal evaluation response categories. This item format is an improvement in so far as it reduces the influences of cognitive processes, task conflict, grammatical confusion and social desirability.
>
> (Wilson and Patterson, 1968, p. 174)

Although this format may have the disadvantage of being 'caught in time' and in constant need of being updated (Kirton, 1978), as well as revealing a unitary score from a multidimensional inventory (Robertson and Cochrane, 1973), it clearly has many advantages because it is quick and reduces response sets.

A large pool of items was obtained by Furnham from various sources including party-political pamphlets and manifestos, textbooks of modern British politics and questionnaires on political beliefs and outlooks. From a large pool of items fifty were selected to form the basis of the scale. Approximately half of the items represented left-wing and half right-wing politico-economic views, thus controlling the response-category bias. Careful examination of the data reduced this list to the twenty items set out in Table 2.5. Further, as predicted, these items did discriminate those of widely different political beliefs. What the economic beliefs scale measures is politico-economic beliefs. Money and related issues are clearly politically related and this short scale attempts to measure how 'left-' or 'right'-wing people vary with respect to their economic beliefs. The percentage of people who hold left/right-wing economic beliefs changes over time often as a function of socio-political conditions. While the psychometric validity of the scale has been demonstrated it does not, as yet, appear to have been used in money-related research,

EXPERIMENTAL STUDIES OF COINS AND NOTES

On a much more concrete level, attitudes to money have been studied by looking at the public's reaction to their actual currency. One reason for this is the public misunderstanding or misuse of the currency along with hostility to changes in it. Notes and coins, though being overtaken by

Table 2.5 The economic beliefs scale: instructions, items, format and scoring

Economic beliefs
Which of the following do you favour or believe in?
Circle *Yes* or *No*. If absolutely uncertain circle?
There are no right or wrong answers; do not discuss these; just give your first
reaction. Answer all items.

1 Nationalisation	Yes	?	No	12 Informal black			
2 Self-sufficiency	Yes	?	No	economy	Yes	?	No
3 Socialism	Yes	?	No	13 Inheritance tax	Yes	?	No
4 Free enterprise	Yes	?	No	14 Insurance			
5 Trade unions	Yes	?	No	Schemes	Yes	?	No
6 Saving	Yes	?	No	15 Council housing	Yes	?	No
7 Closed shops	Yes	?	No	16 Private schools	Yes	?	No
8 Monetarism	Yes	?	No	17 Picketing	Yes	?	No
9 Communism	Yes	?	No	18 Profit	Yes	?	No
10 Privatisation	Yes	?	No	19 Wealth tax	Yes	?	No
11 Strikes	Yes	?	No	20 Public-spending cuts	Yes	?	No

Source: Furnham (1985a)
Note: Scoring: odd items score Yes = 3, ? = 2, No = 1; even items score Yes = 1, ? = 2,
No = 3. The higher the score the more economically left-wing (socialist) the beliefs

'plastic' and 'electronic' money, are still the physical manifestation of money to most people. Looking at attitudes to national currency certainly gives insight into money attitudes.

One experiment done in 1947 has led to considerable research being done on the psychology of coins from various countries. Bruner and Goodman (1947) argued that values and needs play a very important part in psychophysical perception. They entertained various general hypotheses: the greater the social value of an object, the more it will be susceptible to accentuation, and the greater the individual need for a socially valued object, the more marked will be the operation of behavioural determinants. Rich and poor 10 year-olds were asked to estimate which of an ascending and descending range of circles of light corresponded to a range of coins. Another control group compared the circle of light with cardboard discs of identical size to the coins. They found, as predicted, that coins (socially valued objects) were judged larger in size than grey discs, and that the greater the value of the coin, the greater is the deviation of apparent size from actual size. Second, they found that poor children overestimate the size of coins considerably more than did the rich children. Furthermore, this was true with coins present and from memory.

Because this experiment demonstrated that subjective value and objective needs actually affected perception of physical objects, this study provoked considerable interest and many replications have been done. Studies have been done in different countries (McCurdy, 1956; Dawson, 1975) with different coins (Smith *et al.*, 1975) and with poker chips as well as coins (Lambert *et al.*, 1949) and found that although there have been some differences in the findings, the effects have been generalisable. Tajfel (1977) noted that about twenty experiments have been done on the 'over-estimation effect' and only two have yielded unambiguously negative results. Nearly all the researchers have found that motivational or valuable stimuli had effects on subjects' perceptual judgements of magnitude as well as size, weight, and brightness.

Two other methodologically different studies have looked at the value-size hypothesis. Hitchcock *et al.* (1976) compared eighty-four countries' per-capital income and the average size of the currency to determine whether 'persons in poor countries have greater subjective need than persons in wealthy countries, and whether a country's coinage allows institutional expression of the level of need' (p. 307). They found a correlation of -0.19 ($p < 0.05$) between GNP per capita and the mean size of all coins minted for a country, and a correlation of -0.25 ($p < 0.025$) between GNP (Gross National Product) per capita and the size of least-valued coin. They concluded that this data indicate the potential usefulness of viewing institutional-level data from a psychological perspective. The difference was especially marked when the countries' lowest-level coins were compared. The governments of the poorer countries seemed to be using the principle that although the low-value coins (used more by the poor than the affluent) will buy very little, if they can be given substantial size and weight they will at least be psychologically reassuring.

Furnham (1985a) did an unobtrusive study on the perceived value of small coins. It was assumed that the finder's behaviour (either picking up the coin or not) is an index of the perceived worth of the coin at the time. Specifically, it was hypothesised that the value of the coin would be linearly related to the number of times that it would be picked up. The four smallest coins of the country (England) were dropped in the street and observers recorded how people who saw the coins reacted. In the study of over 200, people 56 people who saw the smallest ($1/2$p) coin ignored it, 44 ignored the 1p coin, 16 the 2p coin, and 10 the 5p coin. It was concluded that because of the fact that money is both a taboo and an emotionally charged topic, unobtrusive measures such as these are particularly useful, particularly in times of high inflation, unemployment or where there were changes in the coinage.

The psychological factors associated with actual coins and notes have received some attention. Bruce *et al.* (1983a) were interested in the introduction of two new coins into British currency which were small relative to their value compared with other coins present in the system. They were made because small coins are cheaper to produce, easier to handle, and brings British coinage into line with the coins of other nations. A number of studies were done on members of the public. In a preliminary series of studies they found that it was not the colour of a coin (gold vs. copper vs.

silver) that made it appear more valuable, but rather its thickness and elaborate edge. Further in Britain, 'seven-sidedness', rather than a purely circular coin, was seen as more valuable. In the main study they found that their adult subjects appeared to follow specific 'rules' about the value-conferring features of coins. These rules refer to the shape, colour, edge and sidedness of the coins.

In a second series of studies Bruce *et al.* (1983b) looked at the extent to which the new British £1 coin might be confused with existing coins. In a series of studies they found that the new coin could easily be confused with a coin one-twentieth of its value and a different colour, but of a similar circumference. Where coins have the same shape and circumference it is most important that the thickness of the more valuable is sufficiently great to make the weight difference between the two coins very easily detectable. They concluded that more ergonomic work is needed before coins are introduced into circulation in order to study problems of confusion to the public.

Both of the Bruce *et al.* (1983a, b) studies were concerned with how people recognised their own currency. However, some work has also been done on how people identify coins they are not familiar with. Furnham and Weissman (1985) showed all the British coins to over sixty Americans (in America) who had never been to Britain, nor previously seen British currency. Only one subject was able to rank order the coins correctly according to worth. Whereas over half of the sample could identify the relative worthlessness of the two smallest coins (1p, ¹/₂p), less than one-third correctly identified the rank of the top five coins. In a second study the authors ask 4–5 and 9–10 year-old children various questions about British coins when showing them all the coins of the realm: for example, 'Which coin can you buy most with?'; 'Point at the 10p piece'. They found that whereas the 9–10 year olds were accurate in their answers (90 per cent or more) in each case 4–5 year olds were often wrong. The 4–5 year olds seemed to be operating on much the same principles as the American adults had done. That is, given the choice, the children (and foreign adults) assumed that size was positively correlated with worth (circumference, not volume) and that silver coins were more valuable than copper- or gold-coloured coins.

Two studies have looked at the effects of inflation on the perception of money, one using coins, the other notes. Subjects are shown paper cuts of circular coins or oblong notes and required to estimate the correct size. Lea (1981) showed that subjects tended to overestimate the sizes of identical coins as a function of inflation. That is, subjects made bigger estimates of coins given their old pre-decimalisation names (2 shillings) than their new name (10 pence). Although there are some alternate hypotheses that may be entertained, the most satisfactory explanation appears to be that because inflation has reduced the actual worth of the same-sized coin, they are perceived as smaller. Furnham (1983) found evidence of the same phenomena when considering notes. Subjects were asked to identify rectangles corresponding in shape to a £1 note withdrawn from circulation in 1979, and a £1 note currently being used. The notes differed slightly in colour, shape and design but were broadly similar. As predicted, subjects tended to overemphasise the size of the old note (10.71cm vs. 9.69cm) and underemphasise the new note (8.24cm vs. 9.05cm).

Together, these studies provide evidence for the value/need money-perception hypothesis and the effects of inflation on the perceived size of actual money. These results could be extrapolated to the abstract, nebulous concept of money rather than just actual coins and notes. Indeed, these results confirm non-experimental observations in the area such as that poorer people overestimate the power of money.

CONCLUSION

Few would disagree with the proposition that everybody has a fairly complex set of attitudes to the abstract concept of money as well as actual currency. Money is clearly symbolic and imbued with moral and emotional meaning. These attitudes clearly play a role in how people use money – whether they are compulsive savers or profligate spenders; whether it includes pain or pleasure; and whether it is sacred or profane. What is abundantly clear from the anthropological, sociological and psychological literature is that money is far from value free and that few people are dispassionate, disinterested, economically rational users of money.

Researchers in the area have attempted through self-report questionnaires to understand the basic structure of money attitudes. Over the past twenty-five years nearly a dozen different instruments have been constructed and psychometrically examined, which purported to investigate the fundamental dimensions underlying money attitudes. While there remains no agreement on the basic number of factors or how they should be described, it is possible to see some overlap. For instance, many of the measures show attitudes about power, prestige and spending, where money is seen as something one can use to influence and impress others. Also most of the measures found evidence of a retention factor which is concerned with saving, investing and carefully planning the use of money.

As well as self-report questionnaires that attempt to measure attitudes to money, there has also been some work on more specific concepts like money ethics or more general concepts like economic beliefs. What these studies show is that money attitudes are inextricably linked with such things as political beliefs and voting intentions.

As well as questionnaire studies, experimental social psychologists have looked at how children and adults react to the national coins and bank notes. Some very consistent findings have been observed such as the link between value and estimation of size of notes. How people use (spend, store), recognise and react to (particularly changes in) their currency is clearly an important issue. What research shows is that it is imbued with powerful feelings, so confirming a central theme in all this work.

3 Young people, socialisation and money

The easiest way for your children to learn about money is for you not to have any.

Katharine Whitehorn

One of the hardest things to teach our children about money matters is that it does.

Anon.

When I was young I used to think that money was the most important thing in life; now that I am old, I know it is.

Oscar Wilde

My father told me that if humanly possible one should never lend people money, as it almost inevitably made them hate you.

Lord Rothschild

Wealth does not corrupt nor does it enoble. But wealth does govern the minds of privileged children, it gives them a particular kind of identity they never lose, whether they grow up to be stockbrokers or communards, and whether they lead healthy or unstable lives.

Robert Coles

Until the age of 12 I sincerely believed that everybody had a house on Fifth Avenue, a villa in Newport and a steam-driven, ocean-going yacht.

Cornelius Vanderbilt, Jr

What I know about money, I learned the hard way – by having had it.

Margaret Halsey

The safe way to double your money is to fold it over once and put it in your pocket.

Frank 'Kin' Hubbard

Always live within your income, even if you have to borrow money to do so.

Josh Billings

Nothing in the world can take the place of persistence. Talent will not; nothing is more common than unsuccessful men with talent. Genius will not; unrewarded genius is almost a proverb. Education will not; the world is full of educated derelicts. Persistence and determination alone are omnipotent.

Ray Kroc

With money in your pocket, you are wise, and you are handsome, and you sing well too.

Jewish proverb

INTRODUCTION

Until recently there has been little research on the economic beliefs and behaviours of young people (Furnham and Lunt, 1996). Still less had been done on *how* knowledge and beliefs are acquired as opposed to the *content* of the knowledge base (Berti and Bombi, 1988; Haste and Torney-Purta, 1992). Furthermore, it has not been until recently that researchers have looked at young people's reasoning about economic issues such as consumption, saving, marketing and work-related knowledge.

Educationalists have been interested in these issues for a very long time. Indeed, there are a stream of papers going back to the turn of the century that concern themselves with children and money (Kohler, 1897; Dismorr, 1902). However, there has been a vigorous research interest in such things as children's knowledge of money and work experience since then (Witryol and Wentworth, 1983; Mortimer and Shanahan, 1994).

A detailed examination of the economic socialisation of children and adolescents is of both academic and applied interest. In Britain in 1996 14–16 year olds had nearly £10.53 per week in disposable cash. This was made up of £4.62 in odd-job earnings, £3.07 in pocket money and the remainder in gifts from friends and relatives. Even the average 5–7 year olds had £2.41 to spend every week (Walls Monitor, 1996). West German 7–15 year olds received DM 7.5 billion (£19 billion) of pocket money and monetary gifts in 1988, and the spending power of 12–21 year olds even amounted to DM 33 billion (£82 billion) annually. Further, in most Western democratic countries teenagers of 18 years are allowed to hold bank accounts, make investments and accrue debts.

Many different aspects of young people's understanding and perception of the economy, their attitudes towards money and possessions, their spending and consumption habits are relevant to the teaching of economic principles in schools as well as to the research of psychologists, educationalists, marketing people and even to economists (Furnham and Stacey, 1991; Lunt and Furnham, 1996).

THE DEVELOPMENT OF ECONOMIC IDEAS IN THE CHILD

What do children know about the economy? How and at what age do they acquire their knowledge? To what extent are there differences of knowledge and beliefs due to gender, age, nationality, socio-economic background and experience with money? Perhaps the most important and programmatic work in this field has been done by two Italian women (Berti and Bombi, 1988), who looked at such issues as the child's construction of work, money, goods, the means of production and ownership from a Piagetian perspective. In a series of very imaginative interview and game-playing studies, they attempted to describe how, and when, children understand economic concepts (like profit) and institutions (like banks).

Lunt (1996) suggests that the history of children's economic socialisation falls into three phases. First, there was a small amount of descriptive work which established that children had a developing understanding of economic life. Second, researchers attempted to map descriptions of children's comprehension of economic matters on to Piaget's theory of the stages of cognitive development producing classic stage-wise theories. Third, an attempt is being made to introduce social factors into the explanation of the development of economic understanding. This 'third wave' show that there has been a burgeoning of research in economic socialisation since the mid-1980s.

Strauss (1952) was among the first to examine the development of money-related concepts. In his 1952 study he interviewed 66 children of both sexes between $4\frac{1}{2}$ and $11\frac{1}{2}$ years and classified the answers into 9 different developmental stages that used the Piagetian idea of the child's advancement by stages rather than by continuum. According to Strauss, the child's concepts of money starts with them believing that they can buy anything with money, to a stage around puberty where they often have a full adult understanding. Six years later, Danziger (1958) asked 41 children between 5 and 8 years questions about money, the rich and the poor, and the 'boss' to examine whether the development of social concepts in the child could be applied to Piaget's theoretical model of cognitive development.

Danziger believed that first hand experience enhances the advancement on to the next level of conception. The children in his study appeared to be at a higher level in their understanding of economic exchange than in production and he attributed this to the fact that they had experience of buying, but none of work.

Sutton (1962) interviewed 85 children between 6 and 13 on money and the accumulation of capital. Irrespective of age, intelligence and socio-economic background the majority of replies were in the beginning stages of conceptualisation, thus emphasising the importance of first hand experience in the development of economic concepts.

Jahoda (1979) conducted a role play study in which 120 working-class Scottish children between 6 and 12 played the role of the shopkeeper and the interviewer that of customer and supplier. Children's responses were grouped according to whether the difference between buying and selling price had been realised. The results suggested that most children did not begin to understand the concept of profit until about the age of 11. The interview that followed showed that the development of the understanding of the concept of profit passed through three stages: in the first stage, children were transforming an ignorance of profit into a conception of profit as observed ritual; in the second stage, buying and selling, understood as separate behavioural systems, were gradually perceived to be connected, although with no price difference between the two activities; in the final stage, an understanding of the difference between what the shopkeeper paid and charged was understood as a profit.

Burris (1983) found general compatibility with the Piagetian view that knowledge develops through a sequence of qualitative cognitive stages from the answers of thirty-two children at each distinct stage (pre-operational, concrete operations and formal operations). More recently Leiser (1983), Schug and Birkey (1985), Sevon and Weckstrom (1989) supported these findings. Schug and Birkey (1985) like Danziger, also stressed that children's economic understanding varies somewhat depending upon their own economic experiences.

Sevon and Weckstrom characterised younger children's perception of the economy as from the viewpoint of *homo sociologicus* (driven by moral and social norms) and the one of older children more as of *homo economicus* (striving for personal hedonic satisfaction). Of the three age groups, 8, 11 and 14, the youngest group when asked about the thinking and acting of economic agents first felt the need to decide whether these agents would become happy or unhappy before thinking about why this was the case (e.g. 'The shoe retailer would be happy about the reduction in shoe prices because "people can save their money" . . . '). The answers of the younger children thus described moral or 'Christian' (concern for other people, other people's approval or disapproval of own behaviour important) rather than *economic* thinking (other people as means, constraints or obstacles to personal satisfaction). Some of the older children, however, saw the economy more as an instrument and the action of the individual as led by the search for opportunity to increase his or her own wealth.

Thus, although there have been a variety of studies which have claimed to support the Piagetian view about the development of economic concepts in the child, these studies have found different numbers of stages. This might be due to several reasons: the age ranges of the subjects were different; the number of subjects in each study were different (sometimes perhaps too small to be representative); variations in the precision in the definition of stage boundaries.

Table 3.1 shows that there is disagreement about the number of stages, points of transition and content of understanding at each stage. The trend among the more recent studies though seems to be that the sub-stages are combined and three broad main phases are defined: (1) no understanding; (2) understanding of some isolated concepts; and (3) linking of isolated concepts to full understanding. By no means do these stages suggest though that the child's understanding of different economic concepts always advance simultaneously. As Danziger (1958) stressed, a child's understanding of, for example, buying and selling may be more advanced than his understanding of work, as he might have had experience of the former but not of the latter.

All stage-wise theories appear to have a number of implicit assumptions. The sequence of development is fixed; there is an ideal end-state towards which the child and adolescent inevitably progress; some behaviours are sufficiently different from previous abilities that we can identify a child or adolescent as being in or out of a stage. By contrast, non-stage theories do not see people progressing inevitably to a single final stage, since environmental forces are given more power to create a diversity of developmental responses. At the one end of the continuum is the view that most of a young person's time is spent in one of several specific stages with short, abrupt transitions between stages.

What is special about economic factors (e.g. property) is that they form the basis of power in society and interpersonal relations, and the concepts/ideology a child develops are therefore of vital concern to educationalists and politicians (Webley, 1983, 1996). The need to relate to the economic structure of the society – an idea more radically expressed by Cummings and Taebel (1978) – and the importance of characterising a child's environment (e.g. exposure to own economic experience) are therefore aspects that might distinguish the development of economic concepts from others. In this sense the understanding of economics, like the understanding of history and politics, is different from that of physics, chemistry and, say, meteorology. Social values and ideology are intricately

Table 3.1 Dates, samples and stages found in studies of the development of economic understanding

Researcher	Year	Subject	Age range	Stages
Strauss	1952	66	4.8–11.6	9
Danziger	1958	41	5–8	4
Sutton	1962	85	grade 1–6	6
Jahoda	1979	120	6–12	3
Burris	1983	96	4/5, 7/7, 10/12	3
Leiser	1983	89	7–17	3

bound up with the latter and not the former and can influence understanding profoundly.

There is increasing criticism of the cognitive stage-wise approach. Dickinson and Emler (1996) argue that the cognitive-developmental approach implicitly treats the public as an undifferentiated mass and ignores social class as a determinant of economic knowledge. They believe that economic transactions take place between people in a variety of social roles. Economy and society are inextricably mixed, and there is no clear and simple domain of economic knowledge separate from the broader social world into which the child is socialised. Different social groups possess different economic knowledge. Knowledge about wealth lags in development and context effects reflect the social distribution of economic knowledge rather than cognitive deficits. They suggest that there are systematic class differences so that working-class children emphasise personal effort as the basis of wage differentials, whereas middle-class children recognise the importance of qualifications. They argue that these differences in attribution bring about a self-serving bias, which acts to justify inequalities and therefore reinforces the *status quo* of socially distributed economic resources.

Similarly, Leiser and Ganin (1996) report a study of the social determinants of choice of allocative system and revealed a complex relation between demographic, social and psychological variables. Increased economic involvement was related to support for free enterprise. Middle-class adolescents supported a version of liberal capitalism, whereas the working classes were most concerned about inequality. Thus the social conditions influence the system of financial allocation within the household, which then creates consumers with particular orientations towards the economy, which in turn reproduces the existing social organisation of the economy.

Clearly, experience of money, through parental socialisation, schooling and everyday experiences, as well as intellectual motivation, determines how quickly children and adolescents come to understand the economic world. The academic question is essentially this: which of these many factors is the most powerful 'educator' and how does it operate?

RESEARCH ON THE DEVELOPMENT OF ECONOMIC THINKING

Although numerous studies of children's understanding of different aspects of the economic world have been carried out, it appears they have concentrated on some topics rather than others (Berti and Bombi, 1988). For example, relatively few studies exist on young people's knowledge of betting, taxes, interest rates, the ups and downs of the economy (boom, recession, depression, recovery, etc.) or inflation. This might be because these concepts are considered too difficult for children to understand, although in a study in former Yugoslavia by Zabukovec and Polic (1990) the children's answers clearly reflected aspects (e.g. inflation) of the then-current economic situation, which shows that the 'difficulty' always depends on the circumstances (exposure to the economic world). There is, however, detailed and replicated research on topics like possession and ownership, wealth and poverty, entrepreneurship, prices, wages, money, buying and selling, profit and the bank. However, the common denominator of all economic interactions in the Western world is obviously money, and therefore its understanding is a prerequisite for all other concepts.

Money

Matthews (1991), a clinician, has recorded the following 'messages' that adults got from their parents. The fact that they can remember them so well, and had such an effect on subsequent behaviour shows the power of early socialisation.

- My mother said only poor people went to heaven.
- My father said only criminals were wealthy.
- My parents warned me not to let anyone know we had money or they would jinx us.
- My parents said I was a popular kid because they were rich enough to have a house with a tennis court. They told me, quite plainly, that if one was without money, one would be without friends.
- My parents told me I had to grow up to be a success, or, being financially unsuccessful themselves, they would end up 'charity cases'.
- My mother always said a smart woman doesn't ever let a man know she's capable of making money.
- My father always said a man should never let a woman know he has money or she'll find a way to take it away from him.
- My parents said there was a 'secret' to making money, but that no one in our family knew what it was. Making lots of money was something of which only 'other people' were capable.
- My parents, who were quite well off, never let me spend a dime without my begging and pleading. They said I must never forget that we could 'wake up poor in the morning'. Sometimes I would lie awake at bedtime, afraid to close my eyes for fear I would wake up hungry and cold.

(Matthews, 1991, pp. 70–1)

As money is the basis of almost all economic actions today, its full understanding is clearly a prerequisite for other, more abstract concepts (e.g. credit or profit). Children's first contact with money happens at a quite early age (watching parents buying or selling things, receiving pocket money etc.) but research has shown that this does not necessarily mean that, although they use money themselves, children fully understand its meaning and significance. For very young children, giving money to a salesperson constitutes a mere ritual. They are not aware of the different values of coins and the purpose of change, let alone the origin of money. Children thus need to understand the nature and role of money before being able to master more abstract concepts.

To investigate children's ideas about the payment for work, Berti and Bombi (1979) interviewed 100 children from 3–8 years (20 from each age level) about where they thought that money came from. These authors too produced a stage-wise theory, but concentrated specifically on money. *Four* categories of response emerged. At *level 1* children had no idea of its origin: the father takes the money from his pocket. At *level 2* children saw the origin as independent from work: somebody/a bank gives it to everybody who asks for it. At *level 3* the subjects named the change given by tradespersons when buying as the origin of money. Only at *level 4* did children name work as the reason. Most of the 4/5 year olds answers were in level 1, whereas most of the 6/7 and 7/8 year olds were in level 4. The idea of payment for work (level 4) thus develops out of various spontaneous and erroneous beliefs in levels 2 and 3, where children as yet have no understanding of the concept of work, which is a prerequisite for understanding the origin of money. Although at that level they did notice occasionally that their parents take part in extra-domestic activities, children did not call them work or even saw a need for them.

Two years later, Berti and Bombi (1981) undertook another investigation (80 subjects between 3–8 years) into the concept of money and its value. Building on the work of Strauss (1952) and others they singled out, six stages: Stage 1: no awareness of payment; Stage 2: obligatory payment – no distinction between different kinds of money, and money can buy anything; Stage 3: distinction between types of money – not all money is equivalent any more; Stage 4: realisation that money can be insufficient; Stage 5: strict correspondence between money and objects – correct amount has to be given; Stage 6: correct use of change. The first four stages clearly are to be found in the pre-operational period whereas in the last two arithmetic operations are successfully applied.

Pollio and Gray (1973) conducted a study with 100 subjects, grouped at the ages of 7, 9, 11, 13 and college students, on 'change-making strategies' and found that it wasn't until the age of 13 that an entire age group was able to give correct change. The younger subjects showed a preference for small-value coins (with which they were more familiar) when making change, whereas the older ones used all coins available. More recent studies have looked at such things as children's actual monetary behaviour. For instance, Abramovitch *et al.* (1991) found 6–10-year-old Canadian children who were given allowances seemed more sophisticated about money than those who did not. This topic will be covered in detail later (see pp. 78–86).

Prices and profit

Buying is one of the earliest economic activities a child can engage in. There are a number of prerequisites before being able to understand buying and selling, and therefore prices and profit: a child has to know about the function and origin of money, change, ownership, payment of wages to employees, shop expenses and shop owner's need for income/private money, which together prove the simple act of buying and selling to be rather complex. Furth (1980) pointed out four stages during the acquisition of this concept: (1) no understanding of payment; (2) understanding of payment of customer but not of the shopkeeper; (3) understanding and relating of both the customers and shopkeeper's payment, but not of the shopkeeper; (4) understanding of all these things.

Jahoda (1979), using a role-play where the child had to buy goods from a supplier and sell to a customer, distinguished between three categories: (1) no understanding of profit – both prices were consistently identical; (2) transitional – mixture of responses; (3) understanding of profit – selling price consistently higher than buying price.

Supporting the idea of gradually integrating sub-systems, Berti, Bombi and de Beni (1986) pointed out that the concepts about shop and factory profit in 8 year olds were not compatible. Despite improving their understanding of shop profit after receiving training, the children were not able to transfer their knowledge to factory's profit, thinking that prices were set arbitrarily. Berti, Bombi and de Beni (1986) showed that, by training, children's understanding of profit could be enhanced. Both critical training sessions, stimulating the child to puzzle out solutions to contradictions between their own forecasts and the actual outcomes and ordinary, tutorial training sessions (information given to children) that consisted in similar games of buying and selling, proved to be effective. However, the results of the post-tests also showed that neither kind of experience was sufficient in itself to lead children to a correct notion of profit, partly due to lack of arithmetical abilities. Nevertheless, Berti *et al.* suggested that although arithmetical abilities are essential, 'making children talk about economic topics they have not yet mastered, far from being an obstacle to learning may contribute to their progress, constituting in itself a kind of training, as Jahoda (1981) also found in different circumstances' (Berti *et al.*, p. 28).

In a study with 11–16 year olds, Furnham and Cleare (1988) also found differences in understanding shop and factory profit. 'Of 11–12 year olds, 7 per cent understood profit in shops, yet 69 per cent mentioned profit as a motive for starting a factory today, and 20 per cent mentioned profit as an explanation for why factories had been started' (p. 475). The understanding of the abstract concept of profit, which depends on the previous under-standing of the basic concept of buying and selling, grows through different phases. Young children (6–8 years) seem to have no grasp of any system and conceive of transactions as 'simply an observed ritual without further purpose' (Furth *et al.*, 1976, p. 365). Older children (8–10 years) realise that the shop-owner previously had to buy (pay for) the goods before he or she can sell them. Nevertheless, they do not always understand that the money for this comes from the customers and that buying prices have to be lower than selling prices. They thus perceive of buying and selling as two unconnected systems. Not until the age of 10/11 are children able to integrate these two systems and understand the difference between buying and selling prices. Of course, these age bands may vary slightly among children (or cultures) as experiential factors play a part in the understanding of economic concepts. Because of the obvious political implications of the ideas of profit and pricing it would be particularly interesting to see not only when (and how) young people come to understand the concepts but also how they reason with them.

Banking

Jahoda (1981) interviewed 32 subjects each of the ages 12, 14 and 16 about banks' profits. He asked whether one gets back more, less or the same as the original sum deposited and whether one has to pay back more, less or the same as the original sum borrowed. From this basis he drew up six categories:

1 No knowledge of interest (get/pay back same amount).
2 Interest on deposits only (get back more; repay same amount as borrowed).
3 Interest on interest and deposits but more on deposit (deposit interest higher than loan interest).
4 Interest same on deposits and loans.
5 Interest higher for loans (no evidence for understanding).
6 Interest more for loans – correctly understood.

Although most of these children had fully understood the concept of shop profit, many did not perceive the bank as a profit-making enterprise (only a quarter of the 14 and 16 year olds understood bank profit). 'They viewed the principles governing a bank as akin to those underlying the transactions between friends: if you borrow something, you return the same, no more and no less - anything else would be "unfair"' (p. 70).

Ng (1983) replicated the same study in Hong Kong and found the same developmental trend. The Chinese children, however, were more precocious, showing a full understanding of the bank's profit at the age of 10. From the same study he discovered two more stages (0 = no idea stage, 2b = interest on loans only – unrelated to profit), in addition to Jahoda's original 6.

A study in New Zealand by the same author (Ng, 1985) confirmed these additional two stages and proved the New Zealand children to 'lag' behind

Hong Kong by about two years. Ng attributes this to Hong Kong's 'high level of economic socialization and customer activity, and the business ethos of the society at large. . . . Their maturity represents, in short, a case of socioeconomic reality shaping (partly at least) socioeconomic understanding'. (pp. 220–1). This comparison demonstrates that developmental trends are not necessarily *always* similar throughout different countries, although they may prove to be so in many cases. A decisive factor seems to be the extent to which children are sheltered from, exposed to or in some cases even take part in economic activity. In Asian and some African countries quite young children are encouraged to help in shops, sometimes being allowed to 'man' them on their own. These commercial experiences inevitably affects their development.

More recently, Takahashi and Hatano (1989) examined Japanese young people aged 8–13 on their understanding of the banking system. Most understood the depository and loan functions but did not grasp the profit-producing mechanism of the bank. Younger children thought of it as a safe-deposit box and none as a stock company. These authors pose the question: why is societal cognition so difficult? They believe the answer is four-fold: first, opportunities for children to take part in political and economic activities is very limited; second, children are not taught about banking in schools; third, humans do not have any 'pre-programmed cognitive apparatus' to understand human organisations; finally, banks themselves do not attempt to educate consumers in what they do. However banks are now, in most countries, very eager to educate young people into the world of banking.

Possession and ownership

The topic of possessions and ownership is clearly related both to politics and economics but has been investigated mainly through the work of psychologists interested in economic understanding. Berti *et al.* (1982) conducted research into children's conceptions about means of production and their owners. They interviewed 120 children of ages 4–13 on three areas to find out children's knowledge about (a) ownership of means of production, (b) ownership of products (industrial and agricultural), and (c) of product use. From the answers they were able to derive five levels:

1 (a) Owner of means of production is the person found in spatial contact with it (bus owned by passengers).
  (b) Industrial and agricultural products not owned by anybody, anybody can make possession of them.
2 (a) Owner is the person who exercises an appropriate use of or direct control over object (factory owned by workers).
  (b) Owner is person closest to or using/constructing object.

3 (a) Owner uses producing means and controls their use by others ('the boss').
  (b) Product ownership explained through ownership of producing means ('boss' must share produce with employees).
4 (a) Differentiation between owner (giving orders) and employers
  (b) Product belongs to 'boss'.
5 (a) Distinction between owner (top of hierarchy) and boss (between owner and worker).
  (b) Products belong to owner of means of production, employees are compensated by salary.

Children's ideas about ownership of means of production develop through the same sequences but at different speeds. The notion of a 'boss-owner' for instance seem to occur at 8–9 years for the factory, 10–11 years for the bus, and 12–13 years for the countryside, perhaps owing to the fact that 85 per cent of the subjects in the study had had no direct experience of country life. Although very few had had direct experience of their father's working environment, they heard him talk a lot about his work and thus acquired their information. In New Zealand, Cram and Ng (1989) examined (172 subjects of 3 different age groups: 5/6. 8/9, 11/12 years) children's understanding of private ownership by noting the attributes the subjects used to endorse ownership. Greater age was associated with an increase in the endorsement of higher-level (i.e. contractual) attributes and in the rejection of lower-level (i.e. physical) attributes, but there was only a tendency in the direction. Already 89 per cent of the youngest group rejected 'liking' as a reason for possessing, which increased to 98 per cent in the middle and oldest groups, whereas the differences on the other two levels were more distinct. This indicates that, surprisingly, 5–6 year olds are mainly aware of the distinction between personal desires and ownership. This does not necessarily contradict earlier work, but makes it necessary to interview children younger than those in this study to find out whether and at what age egocentric ownership attributes are endorsed during earlier stages of development.

For children of all ages the element of control over access to and use of objects seems to be the most important characteristic of possessions. For older children who are more active consumers themselves, possessions often imply power and status and an enhancement of personal freedom and security. This suggests that in societies or groups (like a Kibbutz) where ownership is shared, young people acquire the understanding about possessing in a quite different way.

Concepts relating to means of production seem to develop similarly to those of buying and selling. They also advance through phases of no grasp of any system to unconnected systems (knowledge that the owner of means of production sells products but no understanding of how he gets the money to pay the worker) and to integrated systems (linking workers' payment and sales proceeds), depending on the respective logic-arithmetical ability of the child. Although these concepts seem to follow the same developmental sequence, it cannot be said whether, to what extent, and how the same factors (experimental, maturation, educational) contribute equally to the development of each concept.

Poverty and wealth

In 1975, Zinser *et al.* conducted a study to determine the importance of the affluence of the recipient to pre-school children's sharing behaviour. Most of the children favoured sharing with poor recipients over rich recipients. They were also more generous with low-value items than with high-value items towards both equally and these findings were consistent over all three (4–6) ages. There are two possible explanations for this behaviour: (a) societal values, for example, society already has communicated to these young children that poor people are more deserving as recipients of sharing than rich people, or (b) empathy, for example, perceived need arouses affective reactions in the children that motivate sharing, which in turn reduces affective reactions.

Winocur and Siegal (1982) asked 96 adolescents (of ages 12–13 and 16–18) to allocate rewards between male and female workers in 4 different cases of family constellations, and the results indicated that concern for need decreased with age. Older subjects preferred to distribute rewards on an equal pay for equal work basis whereas younger subjects supported the idea that family needs should be reflected in pay, but there were no sex differences in the perception of economic arrangements. This confirms Sevon and Weckstrom's (1989) suggestions that younger children judge from a *homo sociologicus* and older children from a *homo economicus* point of view.

Leahy (1981) asked 720 children and adolescents of 4 age groups (5–7, 9–11, 13–15, 16–18) and 4 social classes to describe rich and poor people, and to point out the differences and similarities between them. The answers were grouped into different types of person descriptions: (a) peripheral (possessions, appearances, behaviour), (b) central (traits and thoughts), and (c) sociocentric (life-chances and class-consciousness) categories. The use of peripheral characteristics in descriptions decreased considerably with age and thus adolescents emphasised central and sociocentric categories, perceiving rich and poor as different kinds of people who not only differ in observable qualities but also in personality traits. Lower-class subjects tended to refer more to the thoughts and life chances of the poor, taking their perspective, and upper-middle-class subjects tended to describe the traits of the poor, perceiving them as 'others'. On the whole, there was uniformity across class and race in the descriptions and comparisons of the rich and the poor.

To explain these findings two theoretical models are conceivable: (1) a cognitive-developmental model, suggesting that later adolescence is marked by an increased awareness of the nature of complex social systems and (2) a general functionalist model, suggesting that socialisation results in uniformity within different classes and races as to the nature of the social-class system and thus retains stability in social institutions.

Stacey and Singer (1985) had 325 teenagers of $14\frac{1}{2}$ and 17 years from a working-class background complete a questionnaire, probing their perceptions of the attributes and consequences of poverty and wealth following Furnham (1982). Regardless of age and sex, all respondent groups rated familial circumstances as most important and luck as least important in explaining poverty and wealth. With internal and external attributions for poverty and wealth rating moderately important, these findings differ slightly compared with Leahy's (1981) results, as here adolescents clearly thought sociocentric categories to be more important than the other two. A reason for this might be that here all subjects were all from a working-class background and, as Furnham (1982) found out, subjects from a lower socio-economic background tend to attach more importance to societal explanations than subjects from a higher socio-economic background, who tend to offer more individualistic (e.g. lack of thrift and proper money management) explanations for poverty.

Most of the researchers agree that external stimuli (socio-economic environment, personal experience with money, formal teaching, parental practices) have great influence on the child's development of economic thinking and may contribute to early knowledge. For instance, in a study with 87 Polish subjects of ages 8, 11 and 14, Wosinski and Pietras (1990) discovered that the youngest had in some aspects (e.g. the definition of salary, the possibility of getting the same salary for everybody, the possibility of starting a factory) better economic knowledge than the other groups. They attributed this to the fact that these children were born and had been living under conditions of an economic crisis in Poland. They had experienced conditions of shortage, increases in prices, inflation and heard their family and TV programmes discuss these matters. This, too, represents 'a case of socio-economic reality shaping (partly at least) socio-economic understanding' (Ng, 1983, pp. 220–1).

Saving

How and why do children save? Sonuga-Barke and Webley (1993) argue that children's behaviour and understanding of saving, like all economic behaviour, are constructed within the social group and are fulfilled by particular individuals aided by institutional and other social factors and facilities. They believe researchers need a child-centred view of economic activity, examining children as economic agents in their own right, solving typical economic problems such as resource allocation. They argue that the very scant literature on this topic suggests that children save more money as they grow older possibly, quite simply, because they have more money. Certainly, it must be voluntary, though it could be discretionary or contractual.

There have been few studies on children's saving (Dickins and Ferguson, 1957; Ward *et al.,* 1977). Webley and colleagues have done pioneering research in this area (Webley *et al.,* 1991).

Sonuga-Barke and Webley (1993) argue that saving is defined in terms of the quality of a set of actions (going to the counter and depositing money) made in relation to one or other institution (bank or building society), but is also a problem-solving exercise; more specifically, it is an adaptive response to the income-constraint problem. Children have to learn that there are constraints on spending and that money spent cannot be respent until acquired. Thus all purchases are decisions against different types of goods; different goods within the same category; and even between spending and not spending.

In a series of methodologically diverse and highly imaginative experimental studies, Sonuga-Barke and Webley (1993) found that children recognise that saving is an effective form of money management. They realise that putting money in the bank can form both defensive and productive functions. However, neither parents nor banks/building societies seem very interested in teaching children about the functional significance of money. Yet young children valued saving because it seemed socially approved and rewarded. Saving is seen and understood as a legitimate and valuable behaviour, not an economic function. However, as they get older, they appear to understand and challenge these assumptions, but inevitably see the practical advantage in saving.

Cross-cultural, class and gender differences

Various studies in different (mainly Western) countries have been undertaken but few that investigate specifically cross-cultural differences. Furby (1978, 1980a, b) compared American and Israeli (kibbutz and city) children's attitudes towards possessions and found rather more differences between American and Israeli subjects than between kibbutz children and all others.

The most comprehensive and extensive study is a recent cross-cultural project initiated by Leiser *et al.* (1990), the 'Naive Economics Project'. It included samples from 10 countries, Algeria, Australia, Denmark, Finland, France, Israel (town and kibbutz), Norway, Poland, former West Germany and former Yugoslavia, and was administered to 900 children of ages 8, 11 and 14. Topics covered were (a) *understanding*: who decides what, how and why (prices, salary, savings and investment, the mint); (b) *reasoning*: how well do children appreciate the consequences of economic events of national dimensions; (c) *attitudes*: how do they account for the economic fate of individuals. In accordance with previous investigations in various countries, there was an obvious progression with age. However, there were some differences in answers between the participating countries. These could be due to the different political and economical systems and the prosperity of the whole country. The dominance of the government as a visible economic factor was reflected by the frequency with which it appeared in children's answers. The differences in each society's values and attitudes (such as more individualistic attitudes in Western democracies, religion, the work ethic, different moral standards in Christian than in atheist or Muslim countries, etc.) and slight differences in the conditions of the interview are all possible reasons for the disparity in country responses. Furthermore, the size of the sample (ninety subjects from each country) may not have been large enough to provide for representative cross-cultural comparisons. The differences, however, show that the child's understanding of how economic systems work is influenced by various factors in the child's environment, as suggested by the social-learning model.

Class differences were very inconsistently reported by the various researchers in the different countries. Although in some cases there were some indications of class differences, on the whole they were not as significant as the reported age differences. There is a certain difficulty in finding comparable subjects in each country anyway (e.g. 'middle-class' probably had a different meaning in West Germany than in Algeria). Roland-Levy (1990) argues that the comparative economic socialisation literature shows age, gender, social, cultural *and* national differences. She notes: 'It might be promising to ask which underlying variables *can* really explain differences in the way the economy is perceived. If it is not age, it is the way people live their everyday life, what they have already experienced, their relations to other persons, such as peers and family, or to institutional settings in society as well as a reflection of culture and social class traditions' (p. 480).

In a smaller study Burgard *et al.* (1989) replicated a Scottish study by Emler and Dickinson (1985) in former West Germany. They asked 140 children of 8, 10 and 12 years from middle- and working-class backgrounds and 67 parents to estimate the occupational incomes of a doctor, a teacher, a bus driver and a road sweeper, and the cost of some consumer goods. Emler and Dickinson (1985) had found substantial social-class, but no age, differences in their Scottish sample. In West Germany, however, there were significant age but virtually no social-class differences among both parents and children. One explanation might be that socio-economic differences in West German society were less pronounced than in the UK. Furthermore, there was no relationship between parents' and children's income estimates. This, according to the authors, throws considerable doubt on 'Emler and Dickinson's (1985) contention that class-tied social representations outweigh developmental changes' (p. 285).

Similarly, gender differences have been reported through several studies. While some authors have set out quite specifically to measure these phenomena, Kourilsky and Campbell (1984) set up a study '(1) to measure sex differences in children's perceptions of entrepreneurship and occupational sex-stereotyping and (2) to assess differences in children's risk taking, persistence, and economic success' (p. 53). In all, 938 subjects of ages 8–12 took part in an economics education instructional programme over 10 weeks. Before the game, called the 'Mini-Society', entrepreneurship was perceived as a predominately male domain. After Mini-Society there was still a somewhat stereotyped picture of the entrepreneur but the stereotypes had been reduced. This trend was also observable at occupational sex stereotyping. In the Mini-Society, girls were more likely to increase the number of occupations they thought appropriate for women. As to ratings in success (profit made in a mini-business), persistence (sticking to a task until completed) and risk taking (exposure to loss and disadvantages) boys and girls achieved similar results, girls even being slightly in the lead in the first two categories. There are in this study at ages 8–12 thus no sex differences in the major characteristics associated with successful entrepreneurship. The fact that in reality there are few female entrepreneurs must therefore be due to different (e.g. traditional sex socialisation) reasons.

Gender differences most probably may be attributed to children's different upbringing and the role women play in society. If one parent stays at home or works only part-time it is usually the mother. The father is seen as a source of money by young children ('brings it home from work'). Most persons that are thought of as important by the child are men (presidents, 'bosses', headmasters, priests, etc.). Children, therefore, already perceive men and women in different *roles* while growing up. This may again be more or less obvious in different countries. Wosinski and Pietras (1990), for instance, clearly attribute the gender differences they found in their study to traditional sex socialisation, as in Poland economic problems are traditionally left to males rather than females. Other research has demonstrated clearly that women 'control' money, such as in west Africa.

As Kourilsky and Campbell's (1984) study showed, instruction can help change children's perceptions of 'realities' (e.g. gender roles) as well as increase their economic knowledge (see Part III).

ECONOMIC SOCIALISATION: POCKET MONEY

In reviewing the literature on economic socialisation, Stacey concluded that:

> In the first decade of life, the economic socialisation of children does not appear to be strongly influenced by their own social backgrounds, with the exception of the children of the very rich and possibly of the very poor. In the second decade of life, social differences in development appear to be more pronounced.
>
> (1982, p. 172)

One important way in which parents socialise their children in monetary and economic matters is through their pocket money, a weekly or monthly allowance given either unconditionally or for some work. The Americans tend to use the term 'allowance'; the British 'pocket money'. Until recently there has been little academic research in this area and most of the information comes from marketing studies. In Britain, for example, a regular survey of pocket money has been carried out by Bird's Eye Walls. This reveals that the average pocket money in 1989 was £1.40 per week, that it increases with age, that boys get on average slightly more than girls, and that the highest rates of payment are in Scotland, where average payments are almost half as much again as in the south-west of England. Though in some years pocket money has gone up by less than the rate of inflation and in other years by more, overall it was 25 per cent higher in 1989 than it would be if it had simply kept pace with inflation since 1975 (Walls, 1991).

Tables 3.2, 3.3, 3.4 and 3.5 give British data over a seventeen-year period:

Table 3.2 Average weekly pocket money 1975–96

Year ending January	Amount (pence)	% change	Annual inflation rate %
1975	33	–	–
1976	36	+ 9	16.5
1977	45	+25	15.8
1978	62	+38	8.3
1979	78	+26	13.4
1980	99	+27	18.0
1981	113	+14	11.9
1982	95	−16	8.6
1983	122	+29	4.6
1984	105	−14	5.0
1985	109	+ 4	6.1
1986	117	+ 7	3.4
1987	116	− 1	4.1
1988	123	+ 6	4.9
1989	140	+14	7.8
1990	149	+ 6	7.7
1991	169	+13	9.3
1992	182	+14	4.5
1993	187	+ 1	1.7
1994	205	+ 6	3.5
1995	205	+ 1	3.3
1996	240	+30	3.5

Source: Wall's (1991) *Pocket Money Monitor* by Gallup. Inflation data from Retail Price Index (all goods)

Table 3.3 Average handouts (gifts) from friends and relatives 1987–96 (amount in pence)

Year	Total	Boys	Girls	5–7	8–10	11–13	14–16
1987	53	51	55	43	44	54	73
1988	53	54	52	49	55	55	53
1989	72	70	75	57	71	74	95
1990	77	78	77	59	67	63	133
1991	88	96	80	71	70	105	116
1992	91	99	82	61	93	107	106
1993	100	111	91	89	113	99	103
1994	104	101	107	95	104	100	118
1995	115	96	135	134	95	105	125
1996	110	91	135	116	97	93	134

Source: Walls (1991) *Pocket Money Monitor*

Table 3.4 Average weekly earnings from Saturday jobs 1987–96 (amount in pence)

Year	Total	Boys	Girls	11–13	14–16
1987	53	60	46	32	183
1988	43	44	40	49	124
1989	68	68	67	49	276
1990	86	88	83	60	348
1991	118	127	108	61	465
1992	101	104	97	87	372
1993	103	94	112	64	424
1994	113	132	94	52	444
1995	88	95	81	52	338
1996	122	111	134	44	462

Source: Walls (1991) *Pocket Money Monitor*

Table 3.5 Average weekly total income 1987–96 by age and sex (amount in pence)

Year	Total	Boys	Girls	5–7	8–10	11–13	14–16
1987	220	219	220	84	121	228	458
1988	208	213	201	100	154	236	351
1989	271	273	269	124	161	280	605
1990	354	323	385	129	190	353	916
1991	396	411	381	148	235	401	920
1992	386	411	359	127	249	428	851
1993	415	428	403	167	272	404	977
1994	430	452	408	198	263	395	946
1995	418	408	428	214	234	430	890
1996	485	451	526	241	281	432	1053

Source: Walls (1991) *Pocket Money Monitor*

French surveys paint a similar picture but also reveal that parents report giving much lower amounts than children report receiving, essentially because parents focus only on pocket money whereas children count all money they receive (Micromegas, 1993). This gives an idea of when pocket money may be an important socialising agent, since it constitutes 100 per cent of the income of French 4–7 year olds but only 14.5 per cent of the income of 13–14 year olds (half of French 14-year olds work regularly).

The comparative lack of a firm basis of academic research has not inhibited the publication of handbooks and articles that guide parents in the economic socialisation of their children, though ideas about what is appropriate have changed drastically during the last hundred years. At the beginning of the century, parents were encouraged to link pay with children's work, whereas current rhetoric favours a regular allowance that is not tied to work (Zelizer, 1985).

There seemed to have been a flurry of research activity and articles in the 1930s and 1940s on training children in the use of money. Thus, for instance, Prevey (1945) studied 100 American families' practices in training their adolescence about money. They concluded from their results that boys were provided with experiences which are more valuable in training children in the use of money than the girls. This was particularly outstanding in parental encouragement of earning experiences and in discussing family financial status, problems, expenses and goals with children. They found parent practices in training children in the use of money tended to be positively related to later ability to utilise financial resources in early adulthood. Later money habits were clearly related to the parental practice of encouraging earning experiences and the parental practice of discussing family financial problems and expenses with high-school-age children.

Overall, the relationship demonstrated between childhood experiences in the use of money and later ability in money management emphasised the importance of parents' planning as many valuable experiences as possible for children. It appeared important to provide for earning experiences and to help high-school children become acquainted with family finances as a whole.

What evidence is there that such parental practices have the desired effect? Marshall and Magruder's (1960) study appears to be the first that specifically investigated the relationship between the parents' money-education practices and children's knowledge and use of money. Among the many hypotheses examined were: 'Children will have more knowledge of money use if their parents give them an allowance' and 'Children will have more knowledge of the use of money if they save money.' They found, as predicted, that children's knowledge of money is directly related to the extensiveness of their experience of money – whether they are given money to spend; if they are given opportunities to earn and save money;

and their parents' attitudes to and habits of money spending. Thus it seems that socialisation and education would have important consequences on a child's or adolescent's understanding of economic affairs. However, they did not find that children will have more knowledge of money if their parents give them an allowance; nor if children are given opportunities to earn money, will they have more knowledge of money use than children lacking this experience.

In a later study, Marshall (1964) found there was no difference in financial knowledge and responsibility between children given an allowance and those not given an allowance. (Allowance and non-allowance children did not differ in mean scores on any of the ten measures of financial knowledge and responsibility.) Parents who gave their children allowances differed in other practices and in attitudes about money from parents who handled the problem of providing spending money for their children in other ways. Allowance parents differed from non-allowance parents in (a) providing their children with a wider variety of experiences in the use of money, (b) making the purposes of spending money clearer to their children, (c) stating that their children received more spending money, and (d) permitting or encouraging their children to earn money away from home. The two groups of parents did not differ in other money-education practices and attitudes. These early studies did reveal some contradictory findings, no doubt due to the small samples involved.

More recently, Abramovitch *et al.* (1991) have investigated how spending in an experimental store was affected by children's experience of money. Their participants (aged 6, 8 and 10) were given $4 either in the form of a credit card or in cash to spend in an experimental toy store, which offered a variety of items priced from 50 cents to $5. They were allowed to take home any unspent money. Children who received an allowance spent roughly the same amount in the cash and credit-card condition ($2.32 vs. $2.42), but those who did not receive an allowance spent much more with a credit card ($2.82) than when they only had cash ($1.76). After they had finished in the store the children were given a pricing test in which they had to say how much familiar items (e.g. running shoes, television) cost; children who received an allowance scored higher on this test, as did the older children. These results suggest that receiving an allowance may facilitate the development of monetary competence. Since there was no difference in the incomes of the allowance and non-allowance groups, we can exclude the possibility that this is simply the result of their amount of experience with money.

Though the limited evidence does suggest that allowances are effective, it seems as if parents make only limited use of their potential as a vehicle for economic socialisation. Sonuga-Barke and Webley (1993) focused specifically on whether parents used pocket money to teach children about saving. They found that, for most parents, pocket money was seen as money to be spent, not money to be saved. Though there were some half-hearted attempts to foster saving (e.g. by parents offering to match any money saved by the child), this opportunity was rarely taken up.

Probably the most detailed analysis of parent–child money transfer is that of Newson and Newson (1976). They carried out an extensive study of over 700 7 year olds. They found that most of their sample could count on a basic sum of pocket money, sometimes calculated on a complicated incentive system. Some children appear to have been given money which was instituted for the express purpose of allowing the possibility of fining (confiscating); others were given money as a substitute for wages; while some had to 'work' for it. Over 50 per cent of the sample earned money from their parents beyond their regular income but there were no sex or social differences in this practice. This means that it is difficult to determine how much money children get per week, as it varies. They did, however, find social-class differences in children's unearned income and savings. Middle-class children received less (18 vs. 30p) than working-class children, and saved more (90 vs. 48 per cent). That is, 52 per cent of class V (unskilled working-class) children always spent their money within the week, whereas only 10 per cent of class I (professional) or II (semi-professional) children did so. The authors conclude: 'Having cash in hand is equated with enjoying the good life: the relationship between money and enjoyment is specific and direct ... the working-class child already begins to fall into this traditional pattern of life in his use of pocket-money' (p. 244).

Furnham and Thomas (1984a) set out to determine age, sex and class differences in the distribution and use of pocket money. They tested over 400 7–12-year-old British children. They predicted, and found, that older children would receive more money and take part in more 'economic activities' such as saving, borrowing and lending. Class differences were also apparent: working-class children received more money but saved less than middle-class children. Middle-class children also reported more than working-class children that they had to work around the house for their pocket money and tended to let their parents look after the pocket money that they had saved. Overall, however, there were surprisingly few class differences.

Furnham and Thomas (1984b) investigated adults' perceptions of the economic socialisation of children through pocket money. Over 200 British adults completed a questionnaire on their beliefs concerning, for instance, how much and how often children should be given pocket money, as well as such things as whether they should be encouraged to work for it, save it, etc. Females turned out to be more in favour of agreeing with children in advance on the kinds of items pocket money should cover, more in favour of giving older children pocket money monthly, and also more in favour of an annual review of a child's pocket money, than males. Thus all of these differences show females as more willing to treat children as responsible individuals. It is possible that this is due to the tendency for women, both at work and in the home, to have greater contact with children and therefore a better understanding of their capabilities.

As expected, the age differences showed, that, compared with younger adults, older adults were more likely to expect children to spend less on entertainment and more on reading materials. Further, as expected, older adults disagreed less than younger adults that boys should be given a little more pocket money than girls. Younger adults were also more in favour of pocket money's being linked to the performance of household chores. Younger adults tend to view pocket money more as a contractual arrangement between adult and child than older adults. Middle-class adults were more in favour of giving children pocket money and of starting to give pocket money at an earlier age than working-class adults. Over 90 per cent of the middle-class adults believed that by the age of 8 years children should receive pocket money, while just over 70 per cent of working-class adults believed that children of 8 should receive pocket money. All middle-class adults believed that by the age of 10 the pocket money system should be introduced, yet only 84 per cent of working-class adults agreed. Indeed, some working-class respondents did not believe in the system of pocket money at all. A similar class difference was revealed in the question concerning when children should receive their pocket money. Whereas 91 per cent of the middle-class believed children should receive it weekly (and 4 per cent when they need it), only 79 per cent of working-class adults believed children should receive their pocket money weekly (and 16 per cent when they need it). Furthermore, significantly more working-class adults believed that boys should receive more pocket money than girls.

These class-difference findings are in line with previous studies of childhood socialisation (Newson and Newson, 1976) and with figures on class differences in general. That is, working-class adults introduce pocket money later and more erratically than middle-class parents. However, the study of Furnham and Thomas (1984a) revealed far fewer differences, which may be the result of the fact that a greater range of ages were considered in this study.

Miller and Yung (1990) focused on American adolescents' perception of allowance arrangements and reported practices. Contrary to adult conceptions, they found, no evidence that the adolescents understand pocket money to be an educational opportunity promoting self-reliance in financial decision-making and money management. Most adolescents see pocket money as either an entitlement for basic support or earned income. The authors argue that the significance of allowances for adolescents is not the receipt of money *per se* but how the conditions of receipt are evaluated, the extent of work obligations, and monetary constraints on the amount, use and withholding of income. In families, allowances/pocket money are systematically related to all other areas of socialisation. Adolescents' self-concept, plans to delay marriage, egalitarian sex roles, etc., are related to social relationships and hierarchical participation in decision-making and pocket money practices. The authors note: 'Allowances cannot be classified as good or bad for children; rather, it is the way allowance arrangements are managed that instills values and orientations. . . . What we can say is that when their allowance arrangements allow self-direction and egalitarian modes of interaction, they promote development that is likely to encourage further achievement' (p. 157).

All this research on pocket money suggests that, although its role in childhood economic socialisation may be important, it should not be considered in isolation. Parents also provide other resources ('holiday money', 'comics', etc.) and the 'parental package' should be considered as a whole. In particular, we need to consider what use children make of money they obtain from other sources and how the experience of adolescents with money they have earned affects later personal financial management. One also wonders about the extent to which different mental accounts (discussed in Chapter 4) may have their origin in the different sources of income that children have.

Recent studies in different countries have looked closely at pocket money and allowances. In Australia, Feather (1991) examined the relationship between parental reasons and values, and their allocation of pocket money to their children. He found that the amount of pocket money provided was related quite naturally to the child's age, but also with their belief about the need to foster a strong and harmonious family unit. For the older children, parents saw independence training and meeting the child's needs as more important factors, and there was some evidence of the difference between mothers and fathers. The parents' work ethic did not affect the amount they gave yet there was evidence that pocket money is bound up with other parental values and practices.

In Canada, Pliner *et al.* (1996) were concerned with the allowance system of household allocation. They suggest that, although it is the preferred system in many Western households, there is little research on what the underlying learning mechanisms are. They conducted a number of experiments comparing children who received an allowance with those who did not. The children who received an allowance were found to be better able to make use of credit and to price goods. These skills also increase with age and it appears that the allowance system brings forward the acquisition of consumer skills. Pliner *et al.* suggest that the allowance system works because it engenders a relationship of trust and expectation which requires the child to become financially 'literate' and experienced.

In France, Lassarres (1996) found that the best allocation strategy is the giving of allowances paired with discussions of the family budget. The mechanism that makes the allowance system so effective is the possibility it affords for discussions about financial matters within the family. Lassarres suggests that the various reasons for which parents give allowances change as the child develops. The allowance is an attempt to control the increasing demands made by the child. Thus a straightforward pocket money system is often the first thing to be introduced, which then gradually evolves into a full allowance system, which includes a variety of obligations on both parties.

Lunt notes:

> What advice could one extrapolate from the present research to parents and educators concerning possible positive influences on economic socialisation and potential dangers? There is a growing consensus in the literature concerning the advantages of the allowance system which gives early experience of financial arrangement and involves the child in a trusting relationship with parents which subjects them to expectations and obligations.
>
> (1996, p. 8)

Clearly, the setting up of an allowance/pocket money system affords the parents an excellent opportunity to teach their children about money and its functions. The results show strong class differences and suggest it is the discussion of how money is obtained and spent which is as important as the amount given or when the system is introduced.

ECONOMIC EDUCATION

Formal instruction is one means by which young people acquire an understanding of the economic world. Whitehead (1986) investigated the eventual change in students' attitudes to economic issues as a result of exposure to a two-year 'A'-level (twelfth grade) economics course. The 16–18 year-old subjects were divided into a test group of 523 and a control group of 483. The questionnaires did not test economic knowledge but economic attitudes (dis-/agreement on, e.g., 'Private enterprise as the most efficient economic system'; 'Capitalism is immoral because it exploits the worker by failing to give him full value for his/her productive labour'). In absolute terms, considerable correspondence existed between the responses of experimental and control groups with respect to those items where a large majority expressed either conservative or radical attitudes. On the whole, experimental and control group held completely differing views only on three items. For six out of the eighteen items on the scale, though, students who had studied for 'A'-level economics showed a significant shift in their economic attitudes towards capitalism.

In a similar study, O'Brien and Ingels (1987), who developed the economic-values inventory (EVI), an instrument aimed at measuring young people's values and attitudes regarding economic matters, also confirmed their hypothesis that formal education in economics influences students' economic attitudes. The teaching of economics, therefore, not only increases children's understanding of certain economics contexts but also may help them review their values and attitudes, which are mostly influenced by or even taken directly from their parents. Understanding societal independencies better may help learning to question prejudices and therefore contribute to increase maturation.

Economics as a subject is not taught in most countries before university or in some cases secondary school. The majority of adolescents, who drop out of school after nine or ten years of education, therefore never receive economics instruction. As economic knowledge obviously cannot be learned by observation (purchasing something or filling in a cheque might be, but certainly not other fields of economic exchange such as the working of banks or even government borrowing and spending) there obviously is a need for the teaching of economics.

Kourilsky (1977) proved, however, that even kindergarten is not too soon to start educating economically literate citizens. In the 'Kinder-Economy', an education programme, children became acquainted with the concepts of scarcity, decision-making, production, specialisation, consumption, distribution, demand/supply, business, money and barter. Her study examined 96 subjects aged 5–6. Results showed a significant difference between the scores of the subjects in the Kinder-Economy and in the control group, which proved that significant progress was induced by instruction. Out of the 9 topics covered, 4 yielded mastery levels of more than 70 per cent, the total average being 72.5 per cent The mastery level was set at 70 per cent, as a previous testing of 40 elementary-school teachers yielded an average of 68.5 per cent on the same test. This shows that children are in fact able to learn concepts which, developmentally, they are considered to be too young to learn. In other words, a child's success in economic decision-making is more related to education/instruction than simply getting older. She was also interested in what type of school, home and parental/child personality best predicted economic decision-making. Six predictor variables were examined: parent reports, verbal ability, maturation level, general ability, social ability and initiative. The first three proved to be the best predictors of success in economic decision-making; the strongest, parent report, accounting for 62 per cent of the total variance.

Parents' attitudes towards the teaching of economics in kindergarten turned out to be very positive: 96 per cent of the parents were in favour and 91 per cent thought that an economics programme should be continued throughout the rest of the grades. Some even mentioned that they were embarrassed to find out that their children knew more about economics than they did, encouraging them to increase their own knowledge. These findings and the general ignorance of children and adults concerning economic interdependencies and contexts seem to give clear evidence for the importance of economic education as early as possible.

Webley (1983) pointed out that, 'Since we learn about some aspects of the economic world mainly by actually engaging in the behaviour and not, as with the physical world, in two ways – both directly and didactically via the mediation of other – the nature of the construction may be different.'

In the *Journal of Economic Education*, solely dedicated to research into the teaching of economics, Davidson and Kilgore (1971) presented a model for evaluating the effectiveness of economic education in primary grades. A total of 504 second grade pupils in 24 classes from different socio-economic backgrounds were subjects in one control and two different experimental groups. Pupils in the control group were taught their regular social-studies curriculum, the first experimental group was taught with The Child's World of Choices materials, and the teachers in the second experimental group additionally received in-service training. Analysis showed that both experimental groups scored significantly higher results on the post-Primary Test of Economic Understanding (PTEU) than the control group, but neither experimental method proved to be superior to the other. Pupils from lower socio-economic backgrounds (target schools) scored significantly lower on both PTEU pre- and post-tests than pupils from non-target schools. It could thus be concluded that elementary-grade children can be taught basic economic concepts and growth in understanding them can be measured. Specially designed material prompted the pupils' growth in understanding, but an additional full-scale programme in economic education for teachers did not have any significant effects on pupils' advancement.

As to the 'how' of teaching of economics concepts to children Waite (1988) suggested that the child must be the centre of activity, as case studies have shown that the acceleration of children's conceptual understanding can be achieved using a number of different strategies. Since the child's economic awareness is acquired through information channels outside the classroom, case studies seem to be a good way of teaching children about the economy. Ramsett (1972) also suggested that instead of the traditional lecture approach the use of daily-life classroom events, which are either directly or indirectly relevant to economics, as a basis for further discussion and explanation (e.g. if a pupil's family has to move away because his or her mother/father has accepted a new job, the teacher could take this opportunity to discuss employment, incomes, etc.)

More recently, Chizmar and Halinski (1983) described the impact of 'Trade-offs', a special series of television/film programmes designed to teach economics in elementary school, on the performance in the Basic Economic Test (BET). The results indicated that: (1) as the number of weeks of instruction increased, the rate of increase in student scores was significantly greater for students using 'Trade-offs'; (2) there were no sex differences in scores for students using 'Trade-offs', whereas for those being instructed traditionally gender was a statistically significant predictor of student score (girls outperforming boys). Furthermore, the grade-level and teacher training in economics were significant positive determinants of BET performance (see also McKenzie, 1971; Walstad, 1979, Walstad and

Watts, 1985). These findings may indicate that gender differences here could possibly be attributed to the way instruction was given, as boys performed better under 'Trade-offs' than under traditional instruction. Under this premise it would be interesting to examine how sex differences found in other studies possibly could have been caused.

Hansen (1985), acknowledging that the teaching of economics to elementary-school children has proved effective, demanded a firm installation of this subject into the curriculum of the primary grades. He briefly summarised the basic knowledge about children and economic education, which is as follows: what happens in a child's early years – before the end of the primary years – has lasting effects into adulthood; children enter kindergarten possessing an experience-based economic literacy; children can acquire economic concepts and can do so earlier than previously thought; a variety of economic materials and teaching approaches are both available and effective; evaluation procedures are available, and new ones are being established, even though they need continued refinement; economic-education programmes show greater student gains where teachers are well versed in economics.

At present, the apparent opportunity cost of economics (teaching and testing of reading and mathematics, which still have top priority before any other subjects in today's primary schools) are still deemed too high to introduce economics into primary schools. If economics were not considered as a subject to be studied on its own, competing with other subjects in the curriculum, but rather being experienced in connection with already existing subjects such as mathematics (case studies), this problem could be avoided.

COMMERCIAL RESEARCH

Banks, building societies, insurance companies and other financial institutions have taken an interest in children's monetary behaviour presumably because they believe people change their financial institution rarely. Many have produced educational materials aimed at teachers and school children. In Britain, for instance:

1 The *National Westminster Bank* has produced teacher notes, a video and student materials to teach concepts like budgeting, money services and savings, credit and debit for 10–11 year olds.
2 Pearl Assurance have produced glossy materials called *Chance and Change* aimed at 14–16 year olds. It explains the cost of money, risk, etc.

The banks and building societies have been interested in *financial literacy*: the ability to make informed judgements and to take effective decisions regarding the use of money. Young people need to identify what they need to know about financial issues, where to find this out, and how to deal with this information. They need to know about:

- money systems, e.g. barter, coinage, functions of money;
- money services, e.g. a range of financial institutions (banks, insurance companies, building societies), types of account, methods of payment, interest rates on borrowing;
- income, e.g. sources of income (employment, enterprise, investment, tax relief);
- disposal of income, e.g. investment, purchasing, saving, direct and indirect taxation;
- key economic ideas and issues, e.g. supply and demand, 'value for money', 'opportunity and cost', inflation.

Many financial institutions see the advantage in having a financially literate school population and have argued that it needs to be put in the school curriculum. They argue it has specific advantages, such as:

- enabling the development of particular skills and knowledge which will help young people in their everyday lives and in the transition from school to adult life, by developing competencies which enable them to make informed judgements about personal money management;
- fostering the development of transferable process skills, e.g. evaluating options, consequential thinking;
- providing topics which, by being more relevant to pupils' everyday lives, can be a useful starting point from which to build outwards into broader conceptual areas, e.g. economic awareness;
- furnishing a practical vehicle for developing basic skills such as numeracy, problem-solving and planning skills.

Others have completed their own research. Thus, in Britain, the Halifax Building Society, which has a Halifax Quest Club (savings club) of nearly half a million members, regularly publishes data from their surveys. For instance, in 1991, a survey of over 2,000 9–11 year olds found: *pocket money* stood at an average £1.40 per week, an increase of 30p since 1990. This could be due partly to more children claiming to earn all or part of their pocket money. As in 1990, eight out of ten children got regular pocket money. Youngsters in the north continued to receive the highest weekly allowance (£1.80), while children in the south-east and the west said they received substantially less (£1.00 and £1.10, respectively). *Earnings* – 51 per cent of children earned all or part of their pocket money doing jobs around the house (up from 44 per cent a year before), especially in Scotland (59 per cent) and Northern Ireland (57 per cent). Washing-up, tidying up, and making their own beds were the most common jobs. *Saving trends* – almost half of Halifax LittleXtra Club (young savers' club) members saved more of their income than they spent, with an additional 23 per cent claiming to save *all* their money, particularly in the south-east and Greater

London (27 per cent). Only 9 per cent of children spent everything they receive. In that year, children had a broader range of savings goals, including bikes and computers (both 7 per cent). The favourites, however, remained holidays and toys (43 per cent). *Spending habits* – pocket money continued to be spent mainly on sweets, although this trend may be on the decline (42 per cent compared with 48 per cent the previous year). Girls were less likely to buy toys (25 per cent vs. 36 per cent), perhaps showing a tendency to mature earlier than boys.

For these teenagers (13–16 year olds), part-time earnings increased to an average of £12.70 (compared with £9.80 the previous year). Some 62 per cent of 16 year olds earn an average of £18.20 per week, compared with just 11 per cent of 12 year olds earning £5.10 on average. While girls earned an average of 30p more per week than boys, the gap had narrowed substantially since 1990, when girls earned an average of £1.30 more. Most commonly held jobs were paper rounds (31 per cent) and shop work (25 per cent). Other cash earners were baby-sitting (12 per cent), housework/gardening (9 per cent) and waiting/catering jobs (9 per cent). Teenagers in Northern Ireland worked longer hours – 11 against a national survey of 7.5 hours per week.

Just over half of these adolescents saved more of their income than they spent, with a further 9 per cent claiming they saved all of it. Boys appeared to be slightly better than girls at saving all their money (11 per cent against 7 per cent). There seemed to be a difference between the saving habits of teenagers and younger children though.

Fewer 16 year olds were saving for cars than in the previous year (22 per cent from 40 per cent) and more teenagers wanted bikes or motor bikes (7 per cent from 5 per cent the previous year), particularly mountain bikes. Others were saving for computer equipment and software (8 per cent) and music/stereo equipment, clothes and gifts (6 per cent each). Predictably, 5 per cent of 14 year olds were saving for a new pair of trainers (training shoes).

Overall, the most popular ways of spending money were going out, clothes and books/magazines. Younger age groups were more likely to spend money on computer equipment and food and drink, the older ones on going out, clothes, records/CDs, videos and cosmetics. Not surprisingly, more girls spent money on cosmetics (28 per cent compared with 2 per cent of boys), while the reverse applied for computer equipment (29 per cent boys, 3 per cent girls).

EDUCATING CHILDREN AND PARENTS ABOUT MONEY

Because of the perceived importance of children's and adolescents' understanding of the economic world, there are a number of books and articles aimed at both young people and their parents.

Books for children

In a book subtitled 'A Smart Kid's Guide to Savvy Saving and Spending' Wyatt and Hinden (1991) claim to provide a perfect 'hands on introduction to managing money'. Clearly aimed at middle-class, materialistic, American children, the book comes with a (piggy) bank in the shape of a book to facilitate learning. Thus children are encouraged to discuss their allowances (pocket money) with their parents. Suggested questions are provided, such as: How much will I get? What things will I be expected to buy with my allowance? How often will I receive it? Do I have to do any work (chores) for it? What happens if I don't do my chores? Can I do extra chores to earn a bit more? Do I have to save some of my allowance? Can I spend the rest of it as I like?

They are also advised on how to make money. Thus 8–13 year olds are advised to wash cars, rake leaves, shovel snow, mow lawns, walk dogs or deliver newspapers. Children are also encouraged to record their spending; plan a weekly budget; and save money. The authors provide tips for saving as well as shopping. They also consider the consequences of debt, the folly of gambling, and the necessity of taxes.

Rendon and Kranz (1992) aimed their book at teenagers. The approach is part educational, part psychological. Half the book is historical and didactic. It explains such things as the difference between capitalist and socialist economies; the nature of inflation and recession; how the stock market works (what causes high and lows); and the government's role in the economy. But this book is also clearly very psychological. Thus the authors maintain that there are a number of variables which may determine attitudes to money. Rendon and Kranz believe various factors affect young people's attitudes towards money. These include: whether they have more, less or the same amount of money as other people in their community; how closely they live to people who have either a lot less or a lot more money than they do; how much they hear about people who have either a lot less or a lot more money than they do; whether their parents' current money situation is very different from the one they (their parents) grew up with; and how they – and their family – feel their situation compares with the situations of many people they see on television, the movies or in their textbooks.

They argue that these factors shape how people react to both poverty and wealth. Comparative poverty may lead to shame or anger. They note that in every society there are clear, but often isolated, messages about money, such as a person who can't provide for his or her family must be a failure; people who don't dress well are revealing that they have a low opinion of themselves; if you feel bad, buying a present for yourself is one way to feel better.

Rendon and Kranz (1992) suggest that money attitudes are clearly linked to political beliefs. They construct the prototypic beliefs of conservatives, liberals and radicals without clearly siding with any party. Readers are cautioned about popular images of money as depicted in films and on the television. Further, the issue of money among friends is considered, which is clearly of central importance to teenagers. They are invited to consider whether various messages are true such as: if you can't afford the things your friends can afford, you don't belong; you can never talk openly about someone's having more money than someone else; there's something wrong with having less money than other people.

Readers are warned that money is a taboo subject and that society gives many mixed and ambiguous messages about it. Yet they are given clear and helpful advice about finding and getting work from placing and answering advertisements; approaching possible employers; and the nature of the expectations (psychological contract) that both the employer and the employee has. They are told the 'secrets of successful budgeting', the nature of credit cards, and how to save.

The authors point out, accurately, that the major source of money for teenagers is inevitably their parents (guardians). They point out that parental monetary beliefs or behaviours can, and do, have a major impact on teenagers. They begin by getting teenage readers to attempt to appreciate the sort of money pressures parents may be under, such as fear of losing their job; frustration with a dull or unpleasant job, but feeling that no other job that pays well enough is available; anxiety about not having enough money; guilt over not providing a better life for their children; worries about financial security in old age; frustration at not being able to save enough to make a special purchase; anxiety about being in debt, through credit cards, personal loans, or mortgages (loans taken out with a house or a piece of property as security. The underlying message is that a parent's particular monetary beliefs combined with specific pressures can lead them to behaving capriciously, irrationally and frustratingly. Adolescent readers are encouraged to attempt to identify which aspect of their parents' monetary behaviour is particularly frustrating them and then to speak to their parents. However, if they assume their parents are compulsive gamblers, spenders or hoarders, help-line counselling numbers are provided.

Books for parents

There are a number of interesting books on money specifically for parents. Davis and Taylor (1979), both stockbrokers, wrote a book called '*Kids and Cash*' for 'parents who . . . want answers about allowances . . . want their kids to earn and save money . . . believe a job teaches responsibility . . . are interested in preparing their children for the realities of the adult world.' The authors believe parents have two dilemmas: First, how to handle family money matters to include and inform children in a way they feel reasonable and fair; second, how to ensure children acquire the basic money skills and attitudes they need in order to be responsible and productive adults. They believe that all children need a basic understanding of economic reality and that having a job is a critical educational and socialisation experience.

They note various misuses of money that send inappropriate messages to children. Using money (gifts) as a *substitute for love* and 'quality time' is well known, particularly the negative effect of denying the children the opportunity to develop self-reliance. Parents also use *bribery* to prevent or encourage particular behaviours, but its power wanes with use and can cause serious conflict later on. Allowing *third parties*, like relatives, neighbours or teachers, to dictate the money agenda can be very unwise. *Lack of consistency* in applying money rules is clearly unwise, as it causes confusion and makes economic life unduly capricious. *Secrecy* is very common because parents keep their children in a state of total ignorance regarding family finances, which may lead to a very distorted view of reality. Finally, bizarre or neurotic attitudes to money (see Chapter 5) may easily lead a parent to very unwise practices that present a poor model for children.

Davis and Taylor (1979) take a broader Piagetian view with respect to economic cognitive development, though they present no evidence to substantiate this view. They believe all children need to learn quite specific money skills. These include:

- *Spending money*: understanding concepts like scarcity; price differentials the necessity of choices.
- *Budgeting*: planning and keeping to money plans.
- *Saving*: the importance and benefits of postponement of gratification.
- *Borrowing*: the concepts and costs of borrowing.
- *Earning money*: by such things as selling ability, learning to take risks, understanding the competition.

They stress the importance of the allowance/pocket money system: it is the best way to teach children about the value of money and the basis of responsibility. They argue that parents use five systems that do not work, and one that does. The systems that do work are characterised by the following: (1) money is given when needed: irregular, unplanned, capricious; (2) commission system – effectively a pay for work done system; (3) allowances tied to responsibility – money conditional upon chores done; (4) allowances with no strings – paid regularly without responsibilities; (5) allowances with no strings, but supervised spending; (6) allowances with no strings, but responsibilities.

They specify thirteen clear points for the recommended system:

1 The system you will use should be explained to the child at the time it is started.
2 The allowance is initiated at around 6 or 7.

3 The amount should be a reasonable one, and increased as the child grows older when it is expected to cover a wider range of the child's expenses.
4 The parent and child should agree in advance on the kinds of expenses the allowance will cover.
5 The allowance should be paid weekly on the same day each week to younger children, and monthly to kids in their mid-teens.
6 The allowance should always be paid and should not be based upon performance of chores. It should never be withheld as discipline or to influence the child's behavior.
7 Once the amount of the allowance has been established, the child should not be given more money just because he has spent all he had.
8 The child should be allowed to make his own spending decisions.
9 The child should be assigned an agreed-upon chore (or chores), which he will be responsible to do for the benefit of the entire family.
10 No pay is to be expected or received for doing the job.
11 Failure to do the assigned chore must not result in reduction or elimination of the allowance.
12 Parents who are able to pay their kids for doing extra jobs around the house should do so.
13 An annual review should be held yearly on the child's birthday to set the allowance and chores for the coming year.

(Davis and Taylor, 179, p. 50)

Davis and Taylor (1979) believe that children benefit enormously being part of the family budget. Budgeting needs to be carefully explained because ignorance is certainly not bliss. The authors are clearly most interested in helping parents educate their children into the economic world. For instance, concerning the concept of profit they ask and answer such fundamental questions as: What are profits? What difference do they make to a child? How much profit do most businesses make? Where do profits go? There is, of course, no doubt that the authors are free market capitalists. They explain, very much from a monetarist, Adam Smith-type perspective, where jobs come from and the benefits of competition providing the best possible products and services at reasonable cost. They explain in a straightforward way why people pay taxes and why they are so high. They also note why super-taxing the rich is counter-productive.

In simple language, they explain demand-pull and cost-push inflation; how it affects children; and how it could be stopped. They provide parents with clear answers to questions about saving (how much, where, why); even investment (buying stocks and shares). Almost half their book, however, is dedicated to helping children get jobs, for they believe the benefits of part-time work are more important than the money received.

They present six clear arguments for the benefits of work to children. (1) work teaches children the importance of time-keeping; (2) that the world is competitive; (3) that creative innovation can lead to economic success; (4) that all spending decisions are choices; (5) that set-backs are normal; and (6) set-backs can be useful learning experiences rather than disasters.

Further, Davis and Taylor (1978) attempt to rebuff parents' doubts about encouraging their children to work concerning the effect on school-work, what other important activities they may neglect, etc. They believe parents should encourage, give guidance but not too much help in getting jobs, as that is a very positive learning experience. Children should be encouraged to uncover money-making ideas; to create new job opportunities where none existed before; even to start a job club. The authors enthusiastically instruct parents how to encourage their children to start their own business, to advertise their products and services, etc. Finally, the authors recommend that parents take their children into your office to 'shadow' you and help understand what you do and how you earn your money.

In a similar, but more recent, book, Godfrey (1995) sets out to help parents teach their children the value and uses of money. The author, a banker who founded a children's bank, appears on television dealing with 'monetarily dysfunctional families'. She notes:

> What kids don't know about money *can* hurt them. Bad financial habits in childhood can lead to worse problems when you're grown-up . . .
>
> Too much debt can cripple a family – 90 per cent of all divorces are traceable to money issues. It can put you in a hole you'll never get out of – from losing your credit rating (from which you can never completely recover, regardless of what anyone tells you) to losing your home. If you don't know the value of money, you can get swindled easily – it happens all the time. Teaching your kids to have a good grasp on the financial realities is one of the best ways of preparing them to deal with all the unexpected changes life will send their way. Life isn't fair. We all know that, yet it's still a shock every time we're confronted by its unfairness – we need to be solidly grounded so that we're not emotionally devastated. . . . Money is not only a key part of male–female relationships, misunderstandings over it are the chief cause of divorce. Naturally, it's at the heart of every business or employer–employee relationship, and it figures in friendships as well, from transactions as simple as 'Who pays for lunch?' to the sometimes bewildering borrowing and lending that goes on between school-age kids and their friends.
>
> (Godfrey, 1995, p. 17)

In an American survey of 34,000 people, Godfrey (1995) found the results shown in Table 3.6:

The results certainly convinced the author of the necessity of work in this field. The author believes that it is fundamentally important to distinguish

Table 3.6 Attitudes to children and money in America

Question	Yes (%)	No (%)
When I was growing up, I knew how much my father made per year	23	77
I knew how much my family's mortgage/rent payments were.	30	70
I knew what kind of insurance coverage my family had.	23	77
I knew how much it cost to outfit me for grade school.	26	74
I would like my children to understand more about financial realities.	91	9
I would like to understand better how to educate my children about money.	73	27

Source: Godfrey (1995)

between needs (necessities) and wants (luxuries) and therefore between fixed and variable expenses. This distinction leads to negotiable vs. non-negotiable rules of conduct. She considers economic/money education for pre-schoolers, school-age children and teenagers.

For pre-schools, various games are suggested, such as play shopkeepers as well as shopping research games where children 'play in stores'. The educational strategy is clearly seen in the recommendations made for the allowance or pocket money system.

- Pre-school children (3 year olds) should be getting an allowance in the form of pay for work at specific jobs.
- Work for pay means an allowance based on a specific series of chores that are over and above what is naturally expected (i.e. help set/clear the table vs. the brushing of teeth).
- 3 year olds get $3.00 per week, 6 year olds $6. That is, you get $1.00 for every year old you are.

Godfrey (1995) suggests that school-age children should pay tax on his/her allowance. A school-age child should be told that they are a 'Citizen of the Household' and 15 per cent of his or her allowance go in tax. They also need to give 10 per cent to charity. Further, if they save, they should be given interest on that saving. Godfrey strongly recommends family meetings to discuss, openly and honestly, economic affairs. A written agenda should be followed and a log kept. Issues might include product testing the purchases of major items, vacation planning, charity and gift giving. It is also recommended that there is a pool of family money, called the family bank, and the family as a whole should discuss how it is administered and the money spent. Further, the family bank should have an explicitly stated credit policy: hence if a child borrows pocket money ahead of time they have, say, three weeks to pay it back . . . with interest. As children get older their household jobs become harder and they should be taught that they have to be responsible for these jobs. The message to be given is that children, as citizens of the household, should volunteer to do chores and odd jobs.

As children get older and they borrow, lend and trade, they can be taught the importance of verbal contracts, negotiation and the general rule of trading. Also the family and community values on breakages, shoplifting, etc. need to be discussed along with consumer affairs. For instance, it is proposed that pre-adolescents be taught the following simple, but important, consumer concepts: get the best buy for the best price; make sure you know a store's policy; don't forget to keep receipts; shop during sales; know your rights.

In the teenage years, the Citizens of the Household concept can be extended to other concepts, like curfew. Further, they need to be taught good practice about credit cards and budgeting, as well as starting a financial portfolio.

CONCLUSION

The importance of how and when children and adolescents begin to understand money and the working of the economy cannot be underestimated. Lunt has noted:

> The extension of consumer society to include children more and more in economic activity and the relative affluence of young people in contemporary societies have produced children who are actively involved in the economy as they learn about it. Thus the immersion of the child in the economy becomes a potential 'social problem' and a number of issues can be seen to have driven research. . . . The move from a cash to a credit economy, the increase in home ownership and other forms of complex economic activity by ordinary people mean that economic competence is growing in complexity and diversity. The modern consumer is immersed in a complex economy and the demands made upon all of us in terms of economic understanding are constantly developing. Political debate in contemporary western societies is now mainly a question of different approaches to managing the economy, including the consumer economy.
>
> (Lunt, 1996, p. 14)

Research on what young people (children and adolescents) know about and do with money is clearly important not least because of their increasing purchasing power. As children grow older they begin to understand the nature of money and how it is used in society. Their ideas and understanding are affected by motivation and experience. While the former is not easy to influence, the latter is. Various groups are interested in increasing the monetary literacy and sensible behaviour of young people. These include parents who, through pocket money/allowance systems, as well as various discussions and work assignments, attempt to teach their children to acquire, spend and save money wisely.

Schools too play an important role in directly educating and modelling economic behaviour. Banks and other financial institutions, as well as manufacturers, are also interested in young people and their money for obvious reasons. There is both anecdotal and empirical evidence that certain 'unhealthy' money habits are acquired in one's youth and are difficult to change. Hence it is in the interest of many groups that young people be educated consumers and responsible users of money.

Studies have shown how economic understanding is acquired gradually and often goes through recognisable stages. However, personal experience determined by gender, social class, ethical and national culture often powerfully shape how, and when, young people acquire monetary under-standing. Thus whereas in many aspects of cognitive development children from the first (developed, Western) world seem to be more advanced than comparably aged children from the Third (developing) World, the reverse is often true of economic and monetary understanding. This is primarily due to children from the developing world having to be much more involved in day-to-day economic activity. Five year olds may 'man' fruit stalls while their parents are away and soon acquire knowledge of change.

While there is no complete agreement about how to educate children and their parents about money there is an emerging consensus. Indeed, there are an increasing number of self-help books for parents instructing them on some of the details of pocket money or allowance systems that seem to have worked. They are long on rhetoric and short on data, but that is changing, as this important but neglected multidisciplinary research area is attracting more good quality multinational studies.

4 Money and everyday life
Saving, gambling and taxation

If thou lend any money to any of my people that is poor by thee, thou not be to him as a usurer neither shalt thou lay upon him usury.

Exodus 22: 25 (The Revised Standard Version is, ' *If you lend money to any of my people with you who is poor, you shall not be to him a creditor, and you shall not exact interest from him.* ')

Money is a guarantee that we may have what we want in the future. Though we need nothing at the moment it insures the possibility of satisfying a new desire when it arises.

Aristotle

Money, and not morality, is the principle of commercial nations.

Thomas Jefferson

We all know how the size of sums of money appears to vary in a remarkable way according as they are being paid in or paid out.

John Huxley

He is a great simpleton who imagines that the chief power of wealth is to supply wants. In ninety-nine cases out of a hundred it creates more wants than it supplies.

Anon

Money never meant anything to us. It was just sort of how we kept the score.

Nelson Bunker Hunt

Money is the only applause a businessman gets for his performance.

Larry Adler

Making money is easy and slightly boring or at any rate not satisfying.

Jim Slater

We haven't any money, so we've got to think.

Lord Rutherford

To acquire wealth is difficult, to preserve it more difficult, but to spend it wisely most difficult of all.

Edward Parsons Day

INTRODUCTION

Some people spend their money happily and regularly. They may enjoy gambling and be 'retail-therapy' shopaholics. For many they look reckless, self-indulgent, capricious and unwise. On the other hand, many people know the careful (even compulsive) savers who are often regarded as sensible, self-controlled and wise. In this chapter we will look at everyday behaviour associated with money: patterns of saving and spending, who gambles and why, and that sticky problem of tax avoidance and evasion.

Many individuals are happy, regular borrowers of money. They 'clock-up' high amounts on their credit card (at extremely high interest rates) and live entirely for the present. Savers postpone gratification by putting off consumption to some uncertain future date and receive reward (interest) for doing so. Addictive gamblers are often as zealous and difficult to treat as addictive savers. Addictive and compulsive monetary behaviours are not quite the same. Scherhorn (1990) makes the difference clear: 'Addictive behaviour runs out of control because of an overpowering but initially welcome desire: compulsive behaviour, on the other hand, is controlled by unwelcome pressure which the person experiences as alien to himself' (p. 34). We shall also look at attitudes and behaviour associated with paying (as well as evading, avoiding paying) taxes. In this chapter we will not concentrate on the pathological types whose everyday monetary behaviour is clearly abnormal. We will look at that in Chapter 5 (on 'Money and mental illness'). Here we are simply interested in why and how much the average person saves; why, if ever, they get into debt; who gambles and why; and what people think about taxation.

As Price (1993) noted, the psychology of money includes such things as self-concept, monetary beliefs (rich people are mean; hard work leads to wealth) and values (look after the pennies and the pounds will look after themselves). In this sense money has powerful and complex associations, which inevitably have an effect on how people use it (see Chapters 2 and 3).

Sociologists have long recognised the importance of money in society. Marx wrote that 'monies change fidelity into infidelity, love into hate, virtue into vice, vice into virtue, slave into master, master into slave, stupidity into intelligence, and intelligence into stupidity. . . . [Monies] can exchange any quality for any other, even contradictory qualities and objects' (Marx, 1977, pp. 110–11). The sociologist Simmel (1978) also stressed the importance of money in society, which seems for most people the means to any end.

Many adults are self-confessedly ignorant about economics. For some, their embarrassed naivety actually blocks their curiosity. Yet on one level people hold strong views about economic and monetary issues like taxation. People are clearly interested in the allocation of money in families, work and society at large. They are sensitive to, and impressed by, the use of monetary symbols. Lay people know and debate about the differences between the rich and the poor; production costs and prices; and income distribution, taxes, working hours, marketing, etc.

In a Swedish study of everyday thinking about money Bergström (1989) found that complexity in economic understanding increases with age, and seems most affected by one's working life and social role. Women seem to prefer simple, concrete economic arguments and men more abstract arguments. Interestingly, women more than men see themselves as part of the community and yet feel conflict is a natural state of society.

Luna and Quintanilla (1996) have distinguished between personal and social components of attitudes to money. Money is a symbol and artifact of the goods and services exchanged by people and becomes especially relevant in societies where there are high exchange and consumption indices. In the course of socialisation people learn to value money as a social and personal form of expression. Some see money as vitally important and as an index of self-realisation, personal searching and self-esteem, while others do not value it so highly. The extent to which money is valued relates to consumption patterns (compulsive buying vs. shopping) and consumption satisfaction.

It is also probably true that we use money to prize personal worth: that we tend to value ourselves in proportion to the money that others are willing to pay for our efforts. There is evidence from many countries that an offender is less likely to be imprisoned if his/her social status is higher than that of his/her victim, but if so he/she is more likely to be required merely to pay a fine or do community service than go to prison (Black, 1976). It has often been remarked that there is one law for the rich and another for the poor.

If indeed money confers social power it is not difficult to infer worthiness. Money can easily be seen as an index of social adequacy or worthiness (or, indeed, its opposite). Financial status may be both a cause and a consequence of people's position in their organisational, and indeed the wider social, structure. The more powerful are better remunerated; it is also true that financial status may help one acquire more powerful positions through bribery, reputation or intermediary variables like education or the strength and complexity of a personal social network.

Status and power are displayed by such things as dress and the cars one uses. Hence the importance of certain designer or luxury goods whose intrinsic value is not as high or as important as their symbolic or meaning-showing significance. People confer prestige on the ostentatiously economically successful and defer to them. They fantasise that money buys freedom and independence (see Chapter 5).

Certainly, money can have a dramatic effect on emotional states and well-being. An unexpected win or tax demand can have fairly powerful short- to medium-term effects on well-being. Certainly, within organisations, pay influences perceptions of self-worth. Generally, supervisors are paid 30–40 per cent more than employees, and managers 30–40 per cent more than supervisors.

How accurate are people's reports about money in the past? Is their memory accurate or do they sentimentally underestimate or overestimate past prices? Kemp (1991) reported two studies: one done in Germany, the other in New Zealand. He found the Germans were able to estimate fairly accurately general and specific prices of goods for the previous year but tended to overestimate those of fifteen years previously. This study confirms other similar studies in very different countries that shows people underestimate the long-term impact of inflation (Kemp, 1987). In a second study he asked people to date past price changes rather than estimate prices pertaining at past times. Generally, recent price changes were dated too recently and remote ones too remotely. The systematic bias for past prices seems fairly robust. Kemp (1991) has speculated that this means people probably underestimate the future long-term impact of inflation. Further, they may well exaggerate the real returns obtainable from investing in lump-sum insurance schemes, even during periods of low inflation.

The fact that memory for money attitudes and behaviours, as well as economic facts, are not well recalled has, of course, important implications for research, particularly when questioning people about how they saved and spent money in their youth.

There are many aspects of the use of money in everyday life that merit research: help people coping with very serious inflation; why well-off people become shoplifters. But in this chapter we shall concentrate on four major issues: saving, debt, gambling and taxation. Each presents important and interesting theoretical and applied psychological questions, and gives an insight into the meanings people attribute to money.

THE PSYCHOLOGY OF SPENDING/SAVING

There is an extensive consumer psychology literature on shopping, which has not been directly concerned with the psychology of money though it is easy to see how it could be. For instance, in a typical psychographic or life-style analysis, McDonald (1994) found psychometric evidence of quite different types of shoppers. They have been categorised thus:

- *Value* shoppers – interested primarily in obtaining the best combination of price and quality. (Perhaps money obsessionals.)
- *Fashion* shoppers – interested in latest styles, variety and tend to be image oriented and emotional. (Here money may represent power or a self-estem enhancer.)
- *Loyal* shoppers – repeatedly buy from trusted sources and are interested in both quality and image. (Again money is a source of security.)
- *Diverse* shoppers – fickle, capricious and inconsistent. (Money may have powerful conflicting meanings.)
- *Recreational* shoppers – value the fun, enjoyable activity aspects of shopping. (Money may be the primary means to satisfy pleasure drives.)
- *Emotional* shoppers – seem confused, impulsive and less systematic. (Money as a symbol of love.)

There are many psychographic breakdowns like this, some based on specific products and others on a particular type of goods. Sometimes the researchers provide percentages showing what percentage of the population falls into one group or the other, but these are rather unreliable and restricted to the population of a particular country. Nevertheless, they can illustrate the very different ways in which people use money while shopping for the same product. As one might expect, these types use money very differently; though this may also be partly due to mood factors (Babin and Darden, 1996). What is very clear about research on how, why and when people shop is that their behaviour rarely follows the rational model proposed by economists.

Various studies have demonstrated clearly that in judging the quality of goods, people often depend more on the price than the evidence of their senses (smell, taste). Cheap carries connotations of substandard quality. Many believe there is a clear correlation between price and actual quality. Hence manufacturers of 'premium-quality' products have to attempt to explain why they are discounted (Lea *et al.*, 1987).

Equally, there is evidence of a cut-price fallacy when introducing new brands. While cheaper, cut-rate, new brands tend to do well against established brands, once their price is raised to be commercially viable against major competitors, sales diminish dramatically. Customers believe the value of discounted items is low even though they may be of equal or superior quality to other goods. Despite the evidence, most people retain the forlorn hope that price differences accurately reflect quality differentials (Lea *et al.*, 1987).

Fank (1994) set out to develop a (German-language) questionnaire to measure risk taking, housekeeping, handling money and assets. He developed two questionnaires, each with more than 600 items, which were factor analysed to reveal 60 primary factors. These latter were then converted into questionnaire items and given to 225 German males. Factor analysis reduced the 60 items to 13 factors which were then factor analysed again. In the end there were 3 clear factors, labelled: *luxury* (optimistic preference for luxury goods, believing money solves problems); *investment/speculation* (concerned with investments, speculation, while accepting losses calmly); and *saving/working hard* (stressing saving and strict financial control).

Fank believed that risk behaviour is the underlying theme of much money handling. He was impressed by the great range of scores in his sample indicating those with extreme risk aversion as well as its opposite. How attitudes to, and beliefs about, money relate to everyday shopping and spending remain somewhat unresearched.

Why do people save? There has been some limited work in psychology (rather than economics) on saving behaviour. Katona (1975) noted that in American surveys done over a number of years there was a consistent pattern in the reasons people gave for saving. Most commonly, people mentioned emergencies (illness, unemployment), because they felt the future to be uncertain and hence reserve funds were necessary. A second major concern was retirement (old age), expressed by comparatively young people (in their 30s). The other reasons were children's needs (primarily education) and the buying of a house (and, to a lesser extent, durable goods). Katona noted:

> First of all, references to saving for the purpose of later consumption or improving one's standard of living at a later date are infrequent. . . . Secondly, hardly any consumers mentioned saving for the purposes of earning additional income in the form of interest or dividends, or in order to bequeath money to heirs. . . . On the whole, surveys revealed that the accumulation of savings constitutes a highly valued goal. Savings are associated with important values and are seen as a goal for

Table 4.1 Assumptions about changes in personal saving in good and bad times

Factor	During a recession	During an upswing
1 Instalment buying (i.e. purchasing in easy instalments)	Net saving grows because not reduced by extensive credit incurrence	Net saving declines, because reduced by extensive credit incurrence
2 Unusual cash expenditures (non-ordinary payments of cash)	Net saving grows because not reduced by extensive withdrawals from bank accounts	Net saving declines because reduced by extensive withdrawals from bank accounts
3 Frequency and size of income increases	Net saving declines because income increases less frequent and less substantial	Net saving grows because income increases frequent and substantial
4 Strength of saving motives	Net saving grows because people strongly motivated to save	Net saving declines because people less strongly motivated to save

Source: Adapted from Katona (1975)

which it is worthwhile to strive. Not saving is regretted and sometimes considered morally wrong. The high value attached to thrift has puritan undertones that persist among many people despite the much-lamented 'thing-mindedness' of our age.

(1975, pp. 234–5)

Katona suggested that the demographic characteristics of savers depend to some extent on the definition of saving. Discretionary (vs. contractual) saving is mainly done by middle-aged people with high incomes. However, it is noted that saving is a function of periods of prosperity and recession, and the interest rates being offered. According to British data (*Central Statistical Office*, 1996, p. 116) the 'savings ratio' (that is, of household savings to income), is now 3.3 per cent but was negative in the late 1980s. However, if one includes pension and mortgage 'contractual' payments the rate goes over 10 per cent. Gianotten and van Raaij (1982) examined consumer credit and saving as a function of income and confidence. They found that the expectation of being able to save remains stable over time, while the utility of saving shows a cyclical pattern. The young and wealthy respondents in this Dutch survey have more positive expectations to be able to save but the wealthy have a low motivation (and may prefer bonds, shares and real estate to a savings account). Generally, the more optimistic one is about the general economic situation, the more one expects to save, but the utility of saving is unrelated to general economic expectations. The Katona model, wherein saving is determined by income and saving expectation/ motivation, applies only to savings institutions.

Both economists and psychologists have speculated on this issue, though they do not necessarily have similar definitions. Unlike lay people, economists see instalment paying as saving as well as residual amounts left in bank accounts and not spent. In countries with high home ownership (like Britain) one of the most common ways of saving is through a mortgage. For home owners, nearly always their home is their most valuable possession and that which they hope to leave to their children. Saving, via mortgage payments, is thus very regular and contractual and may easily take up to a third of a person's post-tax income. Hence, when property prices suddenly fall and the mortgage is higher than the value of the property ('negative equity'), people experience considerable anger and distress. Savings then can be done contractually through insurance, pension or mortgage schemes as well as on an *ad hoc* or occasional basis. Sonuga-Barke and Webley (1993) believe there are essentially two types of theories of saving, which can be distinguished in terms of the importance they place on the economic functions of saving. First, there are a number of theories based on individualistic notions of rational action; these assert that saving is motivated by specifically economic concerns – people save for future consumption or they save for interest. Second, there are those theories that are based on the idea that saving is a socially acceptable goal in itself or the response to a drive developed during early childhood. These latter theories argue that saving is not motivated by specifically economic concerns. One set of theorists see the economic function as paramount, others do not.

Katona (1975) distinguished between voluntary and involuntary saving, which can also be extended to borrowing. Involuntary saving occurs when there is no intention or decision to save. Households which pay their gas bills through a regular payment scheme may well discover at the end of the year, when they get a rebate, that they have been saving involuntarily. Conversely, if they get a bill from the gas company, they have been borrowing involuntarily. Voluntary saving and borrowing are, of course, the opposite, but may take some unusual forms. Cordes *et al.* (1990) point out that overpayment of federal income tax is found in three-quarters of all individual tax returns in the United States and that the average overpayment is $1,000 (£650). People use the tax system to engage in forced saving, so that they will get a refund later. Katona has made a further distinction between two other forms of saving: contractual saving such as pension plans, which are fixed, regular obligations that require no new decisions but are not always regarded by the individual as saving *per se*; and discretionary savings, which are deposits of income in various places and seen as a means of accumulating reserve funds.

Theories of saving

Keynes (1936) listed eight main motives or objectives that people have for saving money, though he provided no data in support of his categories. The eight motives were:

1 Precaution: to build up a reserve against unforeseen contingencies.
2 Foresight: to provide for an anticipated future relation between the income and needs of the individual or his or her family different from that which exists in the present (old age, education).
3 Calculation: to enjoy interest and appreciation – because larger real consumption in the future is preferable to a present smaller consumption.
4 Improvement: to enjoy a gradually increasing expenditure, since most people look forward to a gradually improving standard of living.
5 Independence: to enjoy a sense of independence and power to do things, though without a clear idea of definite intention of specific action.
6 Enterprise: to secure a capital mass to carry out speculative or business enterprise.
7 Pride: to bequeath a fortune to others.
8 Avarice: to satisfy pure miserliness.

In a passage that has become famous, Keynes (1936) noted:

These considerations will lead, as a rule, to a greater proportion of income being saved as real income rises. . . . We take it as a fundamental psychological rule of any modern community that when its real income is increased it will not increase its consumption by an absolute equal amount, so that a greater amount must be saved.

(Keynes, 1936, p. 96)

Keynes' ideas have been challenged by economists as well as sociologists. For instance, Duesenberry (1949) proposed a sociological theory that separated the propensity to save from the absolute level of income, relating it more directly to social factors such as the relative position of the person in the income distribution of his or her social group. Therefore, over a period of rising income the savings ratio should remain approximately constant. Hence, a person with a high income will be able to satisfy all the social and cultural requirements put upon him or her and will have a residue for saving, while the low-income consumer will never have enough to save, as all the money is consumed by meeting cultural demands. Duesenberry explicitly based his theory on the idea that consumption expenditures are strongly influenced by *comparisons* with other persons' consumption and that the utility index is a function of the relative, rather than absolute, consumption expenditures. Thus, expectations do change over time with changes to income, but at a given time expectations out-weigh actual income changes in effects on consumer behaviour, and the level of expressed satisfaction is strongly dependent on relative economic condition. It is not surprising, then, that the raising of the incomes of all does not increase the happiness of all – what is true for the individual is not true for the society as a whole (Easterlin, 1973) (see also Chapter 11).

Duesenberry's ideas can be understood in the context of the reference-group concept (Hyman, 1942), which states that people act in a social frame of reference yielded by the groups of which they are a part. The concept has been applied to problems as various as mental illness and consumer behaviour, and always aims to systematise the determinants and consequences of the processes of evaluation and self-appraisal in which the individual takes the values of norms of salient groups as a frame of reference. Thus, feelings of poverty or wealth depend not so much on a person's absolute income and savings but on feelings of *relative* deprivation compared with one's chosen reference group. Furthermore, a person's habits of, and beliefs about, saving money will be partly determined by the norms and standing of that person's reference group. Thus, from this perspective, a person's habits and beliefs about saving money will be dependent not so much on absolute income or wealth, but on the saving norms of the reference group. If the reference group tends to save a fairly large proportion of income in order to maintain a secure source of income in the future, an individual might do likewise. Similarly, if the reference group tends to save little, preferring to spend money on goods and services that bring immediate pleasure, the individual will probably do likewise.

The most influential economic theories assume that the prime motive for saving today is so that one can consume tomorrow; in other words, people are making choices between spending now and spending later. Most theoretical effort has been concentrated on the issue of how individuals deal with variations in income across their lifespan. The best known of these theories is the life-cycle hypothesis, developed by Modigliani and Brumberg (1954). Thaler provides a succinct summary:

> The essence of the life-cycle theory is this: in any year compute the present value of your wealth, including current income, net assets, and future income; figure out the level of annuity you could purchase with that money; then consume the amount you would receive if in fact owned such an annuity.
>
> (Thaler, 1990, pp. 193–4)

For most people, this is of course a very difficult calculation. It seems, therefore, unlikely that very many behave in this way. This suggests that people are rationally determining how much they can consume over the remainder of their life so as to maximise utility and that in any given year the difference between this level of consumption and income will be the amount saved (or the amount borrowed). Young people will borrow to pay for consumption, the middle-aged save for retirement, and the old spend those savings (this is the so-called 'hump'-shaped saving profile). Many older people plan to leave their money to their children. Some have argued that this is the manifestation of a deep sociobiological need. Hence there are many voices raised in the community when the government suggests that old people should sell their houses to pay for long-term care. Equally, middle-class people are often very concerned with job insecurity and worry about unwanted early retirement.

More recently, Friedman (1957) proposed a permanent income-saving theory that is purely economic and rational. It is assumed that savings are provisions for the future, not a residual phenomenon. The 'actual' consumer saves to even out his or her income over their lifespan to ensure a permanent income, though the time considerations may be longer for some categories and shorter for others. Of course, aggregated data can be provided to support or refute these theories, yet it cannot be shown by economic or statistical analysis whether the motives that people have for saving are indeed those proposed by economists.

Though these theories are elegant, they do not really correspond with the data: consumption (and therefore savings) seems to be very sensitive to income. The young and the old consume less (save more) than they should according to the life-cycle hypothesis and the middle-aged save too little. A further problem is that those in retirement often add to their savings because of greatly decreased household expenses and because of the departure of children and well-planned pensions. Many older people worry about inter-generational capital transfer either to their children or grandchildren. People are not inheriting money until much later than in former times.

The traditional life-cycle model assumes that people work out an optimum consumption plan and then stick to it. It is very easy to refute the theory, by showing that on questioning a sample of adults from the population few, if any, say that they have worked out a savings plan based on Friedman's model. People are far less rational and logical than economists believe! Also, savings do not necessarily go up with interest rates or down with inflation (Lea *et al.*, 1987). There is also a large body of evidence that shows that people have great difficulty in delaying gratification and if offered a choice between a small reward now or a larger one later they are likely to take the small immediate reward.

Shefrin and Thaler (1988) have, however, made a spirited defence of the behavioural life-cycle hypothesis. They divide people into two categories, far-sighted planner and myopic doer, both of whom operate rationally but with different preference functions. The planner is concerned with maximising lifetime utility, while the doer wants immediate gratification. So the planner invents self-imposed rules and makes use of external rules (such as commitments to save regularly through a pension plan) to control the doer's behaviour.

Shefrin and Thaler (1988) also propose that people have a number of mental accounts at their disposal which operate fairly independently of each other. In a simple stylised version, these accounts are hierarchically organised according to the source of income: current disposable income, assets and future income. Individuals are predisposed to spend money from these different accounts (the psychological equivalent of the jam jar on the mantlepiece) differently; they will spend most of their current income and almost none of their future income, with the propensity to spend assets falling somewhere between these two. Notice that this means that people may borrow while they have savings; they may borrow to buy a car knowing that the bank will ensure that they repay the loan while keeping their savings intact because of a fear that they, unassisted, would be unable to build them up again.

The final feature of the Shefrin and Thaler (1988) model is the idea of framing, which essentially asserts that income will be spent differently, depending on how it is perceived by the recipient. This very closely resembles the idea of mental accounts; however, it is not clear what it adds to the overall theory.

The behaviourial life-cycle hypothesis is quite striking. It does a good job of accounting for some of the saving data (although few of its predictions have so far been directly tested) but, more interestingly, it is explicitly (if extremely simplistically) psychological. The two-self model may seem very naive, but it is one step on a road to the fusion of economic and psychological models. Despite the modifications to the initial life-cycle model, this approach is still firmly based on the idea of individual rational action: both the doer and the planner 'act' rationally according to their preferences.

Household and everyday saving

Furnham (1985c) set out to establish the determinants of people's attitudes towards, and habits of, saving money in Britain. Although people save through a variety of means (such as shares, investments, property specula-tion) the focus of his paper was the saving of *money*. Attitudes towards savings are assumed to be deeply rooted and connected with upbringing and life-style (Lewis *et al.*, 1995). The study had a number of aims: (1) to determine the structure of beliefs about saving and whether, as Keynes (1936) and Katona (1975) imply, nearly everyone has positive attitudes and beliefs towards saving; (2) to investigate the demographic and psycholo-gical determinants of these beliefs and habits in order to determine whether income or some other set of variables are the most powerful determinants of saving habits and values; (3) to determine the range of people's motives for saving, which is partly revealed in how they save (bank, building society, property, art), in order to compare the ideas of Keynes, Duesen-berry, Friedman and Katona.

First, it was demonstrated that attitudes towards saving are by no means unidimensional and involve such things as beliefs about the benefits vs. the pointlessness of saving, how one should save, whether saving secures wealth, and the self-denial implicit in saving. Katona's (1975) early work seems to imply that saving money was universally considered a positive goal, possibly linked to the Protestant work ethic. Furnham's (1985c) study demonstrated that both these assumptions do not necessarily hold in Britain, as some people appear to believe the saving of money to be pointless, and that overall Protestant work ethic beliefs are not strongly related to saving habits and beliefs. The reason for this difference may be in a number of areas: the then depressed economic climate in Britain vs. the comparatively well-off early 1960s in America; the different political and welfare arrangements in the two countries, sampling differences, and so on. Suffice to say, there do not appear to be universally positive beliefs about the benefits of traditional forms of saving money, even when inflation is comparatively low.

Furnham found age was directly and linearly related to saving (older people are more positive about saving), education was curvilinear with the most and least educated being negative about saving as such, but not investment (no doubt for quite different reasons). Income did not discri-minate between saving beliefs much, except that as income increased, beliefs about the pointlessness of saving decreased. Whereas alienation was positively correlated with beliefs about the pointlessness of saving, the opposite was true of conservative beliefs – the more conservative one is in social attitudes, the more important one sees saving to be. There were practically no differences (age being the only exception) in how *regularly* or what *percentage* of their income people saved. Income revealed *no* significant differences, so invalidating the speculations of Keynes (1936) but not that of Friedman (1957) or Duesenberry (1949). These results did not suggest that higher-income people save less than lower-income people but rather that the percentage of money saved is the same, hence casting doubt on the discretionary concept. It is possible that people will forgo certain goods in order to save a constant percentage of their income. Yet other reviews have concluded that saving does increase with wealth and income which is to be expected.

Lunt and Livingstone (1991a) used a wide range of economic, demographic, and psychological variables to attempt to distinguish between savers and non-savers, as well as to predict recurrent saving and total saving. They argue, from the social-anthropological perspective, that saving is regulated by social and moral context, and accrues specific social meanings. It seemed to them that saving relates to individuals' life events, coping strategies and social networks. They gave a 20-page questionnaire to nearly 250 British adults to discriminate savers, non-savers and non-savers with savings. They also used regression analyses to attempt to predict both recurrent and total savings. They found savers tended to have higher incomes and more education than non-savers. Savers tended to be more optimistic; (compared with non-savers). They also

- thought they managed their finances better than their parents;
- felt better off than their parents at a similar age;
- expected to be better off in a year's time;
- thought that the economy, as a whole, was doing well;
- were less fatalistic in their beliefs; felt more in control of their finances;
- believed lack of discipline to be a cause of others' money problems;
- were less likely to spend whenever they felt like it.

Non-savers tended to give up control over finances, thinking themselves the victims of external events, but seemed to chastise themselves when things go wrong. Non-savers tended not to tell friends or relatives of their financial position, keeping their finances private. Savers, through talking to friends and relatives, got social support for their approach to finances and information about ways of coping with finances. Non-savers seemed to feel themselves as victims of external circumstances, coped by blaming themselves and getting upset, and did not avail themselves of social support. Savers tended to shop in a few favourite shops compared with non-savers, who tended to shop around. Non-savers thought that credit makes life complicated and is both useful and problematic, while savers tended not to endorse these attitudes. This fits with the flexible strategies of the non-saver and the simplifying strategies of the saver. Overall, the saver believed in personal control over finances, in budgeting, in keeping things simple, whereas the non-saver tended to make life more complicated and felt less under control.

Impressively, Lunt and Livingstone (1991b) found that they could account for 65 per cent of the variance in predicting actual recurrent saving. Economic variables predicted most, which was also the case for explaining total savings. The total amounts people had saved were not predictable by psychological variables but were instead explained by income and demographic variables. However, the amounts of money people commit to regular savings were predicted by a variety of psychological reasons, including valuing enjoyment, shopping behaviour and social networks.

Livingstone and Lunt (1993) were interested in the relationship between saving and borrowing. Habitual or regular savers were found to have different psychological motivations from borrowers, seeing debt either as a failure or as a normal part of everyday life. People who saved and had savings, while simultaneously having debts, felt more optimistic and in control of their lives than those who had debts but no savings. Thus, debt seemed to be related to moral issues and savings to optimism.

Dahlbäck (1991) argued that saved money is often used as a protection against economic risks and therefore an individual's risk preference probably affects their savings. The argument was that risk taking is a fairly stable trait, which is presumably related to total net accumulated capital, debts, liquid assets and total value of capital. The propensity to take risks was measured by a sixteen-item questionnaire. As predicted, the author found that cautious, risk-averse subjects tend to have a lower burden of debt and more money in the bank than risk-taking subjects, but there was no relationship between risk, total net capital and the ability to manage sudden, extra expenditures.

Psychological studies on saving are in their infancy. Much more research needs to be done on where and why people save, and what determines their patterns of saving. More importantly perhaps, rational economic theories for how and why people save need to be put to the test, not only through examining aggregate econometric data but also by large-scale representative surveys and small-scale studies of particular groups.

DEBT

Debt is the involuntary inability to make payments which the payee expects to be paid immediately, as opposed to credit use, which can be characterised as agreed postponement of payment. Usually, debt can be divided into mortgage debt (currently standing at 2.3 times income) and consumer debt, which varies with the economic cycle. There remains some debate as to whether debt is a sign of wealth or poverty: certainly, prosperous households often have high levels of debt, but do so out of necessity rather than choice, as do low-income households.

Lea *et al.* (1995) listed eight factors associated with debt:

1 Attitudes to/social support for debt: as society has moved from abhorrence of debt to acceptance of credit, so modern consumer society accepts (even encourages) debt.
2 Economic socialisation: families that model acceptance of debt perpetuate it.
3 Social comparison: if people compare themselves with a richer inappropriate reference group, they may easily get into debt 'keeping up with the Joneses'.
4 Money-management styles: poor ability to manage money reflects both disorganised life-style and problematic finances.
5 Consumer behaviour: inappropriate purchasing patterns (believing luxuries are necessities) soon causes debt.
6 Time horizons: the less realistic a person's time horizon, the easier it is for he or she to run into debt.
7 Attitudes to debt: clearly, if one is neither worried nor embarrassed by debt, it is easier to fall into it.
8 Fatalism: the more people have an external locus of control the more they are likely to fall into debt.

This list should best be seen as a series of hypotheses that merit testing. There is a paucity of research in this area but what does exist provides some evidence that each of the above factors plays a role.

In a study to try to examine the main determinants of debt Lea *et al.* (1995) divided their large sample into non-debtors, mild and serious debtors. They found, as predicted, that non-debtors have more money-management facilities (e.g. bank accounts) than debtors, and rated their abilities at money management more highly. Debtors had shorter time horizons than non-debtors. There was some evidence that other factors also discriminate between the groups – use of credit card and other aspects of consumer behaviour – but not strongly.

In a related study of student debt, Davies and Lea (1995) found students (low-income, high-debt group) tolerant in their attitudes to debt. They gave a 14-item questionnaire to 140 British post-graduates and found age, religion, some kinds of expenditure and fatalism linked to attitudes to debt. Higher levels of debt and greater tolerance of debt were found in students who had been at university longer. They believe the results are understandable within life-cycle theory and a behavioural theory of attitude change. That is, student attitudes are a function of the temporary phase they find themselves in the life-cycle, which will change as their circumstances change.

Lunt and Livingstone (1991a, b) were interested in how personal debt is discussed, analysed and explained in the mass media and everyday conversations. In two studies they found that lay people seem to believe that commercial pressures, through advertising, influence normative pressures and the motivation to buy, and affect both the credit system (credit-card availability) and lack of self-control (careless budgeting). Lay people appear to see a powerful force at work, starting with marketing and advertising pressures, through the explosion of credit facilities and social-comparison processes ending with a stressed individual with careless budgeting, in debt with no savings. The study of who, why and when people get into (and out of) debt remains largely ignored, despite its obvious importance.

GAMBLING

Why do people gamble? Walker (1995) listed eleven questions that the gambling research literature needs to address, such as: 'What is the real prevalence of problem gambling?'; 'What are the typical personality traits of gamblers: neurotic or stable, intelligent or dim, moral or immoral?'; 'What demographic characteristics are associated with gambling: sex, age, socio-economic class, religion?'; 'What role does gambling fulfil in society: distraction for the working class or re-enactment of the real-life drama of pre-historic hunting groups?', etc.

For some, the answer as to why people gamble is straightforward: to win easy money and have a thrill, of course! But psychoanalysts have speculated that, paradoxically, some people gamble to lose (Bergler, 1958), though this is, for most people, highly improbable. There are, however, case histories of gambling addicts which show that this is often true. According to Ferenczi (1926), a member of Freud's group, the feeling of absolute certainty which is familiar to anyone who has ever speculated on the stock market or gambled at a casino is a lingering form of 'infantile omnipotence'. Ferenczi maintained that infants do not look upon themselves as weak and helpless but rather as all-powerful omnipotent beings, whose needs are met by obedient adults who have no voice in the matter. Infants are able to maintain this wholly unrealistic self-concept because they lack the means to find out how weak, dependent and helpless they really are. With time, they encounter reality; disillusioning experiences teach them the facts of life.

Maturity means learning not only what you can do but also what you cannot do. Most of us have lost the feeling of omnipotence by the time we go to kindergarten, but it re-emerges from time to time in later years, especially when we want something very much and are convinced that we can have it – no matter what.

The speculator, for example, knows a few things that may affect the price of his desired option or commodity, but he/she does not know everything. Most important, he/she does not know how significant his bits of information are, relative to all other relevant information. Hence he/she does not know what the odds are for success. Not knowing the odds permits him/her to place an exaggerated value on what he knows. He/she wants very much to play and so calls upon the magic of his never-quite-forgotten infantile omnipotence to rationalise the plunge. This feeling of infinite power is characteristically strongest after he/she has had a string of losses. The weaker his/her financial position, therefore, the more convinced he/she is that he is *certain* to win this time.

As Wiseman (1974) said: 'This is exactly the gambler's passion; whipping himself up into a state of hallucinatory *knowing*, whereby we can actually see the numbers that will come up. One is bound to see in such ill-judged ventures – that so patently go against the laws of probability, and yet are attended by the certitude of success – the workings of the losing drive' (p. 47).

Observational studies show the addicted gambler in a state of tension and suspense, which s/he hides behind a mask of calm stoicism – the well-known 'poker face'. The gambler is unable to relax because s/he is continually reading racing tip sheets, arranging card or dice games, making bets, or raising funds to gamble or pay off debts. Just as the alcoholic hides bottles of liquor in secret places to get through some future 'dry period', the addicted gambler maintains a reserve fund – the 'betting money' – which s/he will not use for other purposes even though personal or family needs may be desperate.

Obviously, not all gamblers are addicts. Millions of people have a 'regular flutter' on horse-races, lotteries, bingo games and slot machines in pubs. It is seen as stimulating fun but some still argue that encouraging people in the belief they can achieve more than their fair share of what society has to offer is not healthy.

Despite a fairly considerable effort devoted to attempting to measure the real expenditure on gambling on a national basis, figures are unreliable and probably grossly underestimate the actual amount gambled in any one year. Various commissions have attempted a fairly objective assessment of the economic significance of gambling, monitoring how much is waged. The introduction of a national lottery which has regular large prizes has radically changed gambling habits. Hence it is now more difficult than ever to attempt to determine accurately how much discretionary income the average household gambles per month but recent figures seem to suggest it is around £2.12 per week (*Central Statistical Office*, 1996).

Attempts to understand how and why people gamble have been limited and partisan. First, gambling is a highly emotive topic with moral overtones and opinions are expressed that do not accord with facts. Second, the sociological, psychological, psychiatric, psychoanalytic and experimental work on gambling is not consistent. Third, three assumptions are often made by both theorists and researchers, which are both erroneous and obfuscatory:

1 By reason of their behaviour alone, gamblers may be distinguished from non-gamblers. This ignores both the quantitative and the degree-of-

participation aspects, which tends to lead researchers to look for one or two motivations common to all members of either group.

2 People who gamble can be regarded as engaging in the same basic activity. This ignores the fact that different types of gambling offer different experiences and rewards; involve more or less luck vs. skill; and are available to different groups in the community.

3 Explanations for the initial decision to gamble will be closely related to those used to explain persistent gambling. This assumption erroneously assumes that the motives which explain the continuance of gambling also account for its initiation.

Although compulsive gambling has been fairly extensively studied from a number of perspectives, very little work has been done on 'normal', non-compulsive gamblers. Most of the existing literature attempts to explain what motivates people to gamble, though there are some psychological studies on people's perceived probabilities of winning and losing at gambling. The reasons gamblers (and non-gamblers) give for their behaviours are usually discounted because of dissimulation and attributional errors, as well as the fact that few appear to have real insight into their behaviour.

Psychoanalytic theories

Psychoanalysts have long been interested in gambling (Bergler, 1958). Freud (1928) examined the case of the writer Dostoyevsky, who was a pathological gambler, and linked pathological gambling to other compulsive neurotic traits, especially the Oedipus complex. Later research has shown Freud's insights could be generalised to other gamblers. Central to psychoanalytic thought is the idea that the compulsive gambler is driven by an overwhelming desire to lose – to savour victimhood and injustice, and to revel in remorse and self-pity. For Bergler (1958), six features characterise the 'pathological' gambler: (1) the gambler *habitually* takes every chance to gamble; (2) the gambler's game precludes *all* other interests; (3) the gambler is full of optimism and apparently never learns from defeat and loss; (4) the gambler never stops when winning; (5) despite initial caution, the gambler eventually risks too much; (6) tension and thrill is experienced during the game.

Psychoanalytic accounts of gambling attempt to specify the psychological function of gambling for the individual. The basis for gambling occurs in childhood and typically involves defective relations between the parents and the child. The gambling may be the means by which the child recreates the love of the mother; the means by which the child is punished by the father for seeking the love of the mother; or the means by which the child is testing reality. The problem for all psychoanalytic accounts is one of generating testable hypotheses and then providing evidence for their validity.

Further, for many people, the hypotheses in the first place are either fantastical or patently wrong.

Personality-based predisposition

Others have argued that the compulsive gambler is psychophysically predisposed to self-arousal. Lozkowski (1977) exposed subjects previously classified on their preferences for stimulus levels to high and low-risk gambling situations. Subjects who preferred high environmental stimulus levels consistently preferred gambling with high risk, and vice versa. This is clearly linked to the extensive psychological literature on extroversion and sensation seeking.

Goffman (1961) also supported the hypothesis that gambling is a surrogate for the risk taking which has been removed from everyday life. He also believed that occupation was related to gambling: both those with very high- and very low-risk jobs would indulge in high-risk gambling while those in middle-risk jobs would take part in low-risk gambling.

Evaluations of probabilities and pay-offs

A third approach has considered gambling from a mathematical or cognitive viewpoint (Strickland *et al.*, 1966). This has primarily been concerned with how and why individuals choose *between* gambles not with why they gamble at all. Furthermore, it assumes that individuals both know and understand all the relevant information (probabilities, pay-offs) required in making a logical decision. Yet it attempts to provide a systematic treatment of the cognitive variables involved. These studies have demonstrated that gamblers are by no means logical or rational in their gambling in an objective sense. For example, if roulette players were rational they would play in such a way to maximise their gains or to minimise their losses, but this does not happen (Edwards, 1953). They would, for instance, bet on even chances (red or black; odd or even numbers) rather than placing amounts on single numbers with a 36 to 1 chance of winning. Simple expectation theories based on the idea that people bet to maximise expected gain do, however, hold up in some situations. More complex models have been proposed which provide reasonable explanations in terms of economic motivation for some forms of gambling (e.g. lotteries) but cannot account for other types of gambling or individual variation. Cohen (1972) has noted that most experimental studies on gambling rest on two assumptions: the worth of a bet to a gambler is the product of the utility of each outcome and its corresponding probability summed over all outcomes; and that the gambler chooses that gamble which yields the maximum sum of products of utility and probability. Yet these ideas have been criticised, primarily because they neglect so many obvious salient psychological variables such as the belief in luck and skill, the subjective nature of risk taking, etc.

More intelligent people tend to prefer gambling games where the element of choice is minimised (e.g. some card games), while less intelligent people tend to prefer games of chance where the outcome is beyond their control (e.g. lotteries). Schoemaker (1979) examined the role of statistical knowledge in gambling decisions which is central to this approach to gambling. He found that statistically untrained subjects tended to simplify judging gambles by focusing more on certain risk dimensions than others. The price of strategy is to reduce consistency and confidence in the resulting decision. Gilovitch (1983) examined biased evaluations and persistence in gambling. As predicted, subjects spent more time explaining their losses than their wins – they described their losses but bolstered their wins. There is a growing and very interesting literature on judgemental heuristics and illusion of control, all of which stress the problem of conceiving of the rationality of gambling behaviour in economic terms.

Sociological theories

There are numerous sociological theories of gambling. Devereux (1968) developed a structural-functionalist theory which saw gambling as the perfect scapegoat for the contradictions of capitalism. Capitalism seeks to encourage economic self-interest of a 'rational' kind; competition with a visible correlation between effort and reward; institutional mechanisms of banking and credit, which service both producers and consumers; and the Protestant work ethic, which stresses rationality and avoidance of reliance on risk and luck. Gambling survives and flourishes because it meets personal and social needs frustrated in capitalist societies, or acts as a protest against budgetary constraints, rationality and ethics, while providing thrill, aggression behind a playful facade, and artificial and short-time problem-solving of issues differentiated from real life. Or, more simply, gambling occurs because it is the only way some people believe they might be able to better their condition. More importantly, gambling is counter-religious because it stresses ultimate ignorance and helplessness over luck which has to be constantly tested. This, according to sociologists, accounts for the many contradictory and ambivalent attitudes to gambling in the West, where it is tolerated in practice and yet often illegal in principle, this ambivalence being strongest in the middle class where Protestant work-ethic values are at their strongest. Downes *et al.* (1976) have suggested that gambling is deeply rooted in working-class culture with its limited deferment of gratification and strong beliefs in luck, fate and destiny. Of course, many working-class people also have a more urgent need for money, having less disposable cash and being more frequently in debt. Evidence for this is found in various surveys, which found that lower socio-economic class people predominated in the major forms of gambling. Social class inevitably plays a very large part in all sorts of gambling decisions – where to 'play', how much to spend, etc.

Downes *et al.* (1976) tested various theories of gambling. As independent variables they included thirty-eight measures including socio-economic characteristics (age, education), beliefs, leisure activities, political beliefs, etc. Large samples in three areas of Britain were used to test various theories:

1 *Anomie.* The more people experience anomie the more they gamble (propensity to gamble is inversely related to socio-economic level)
2 *Alienation.* The more people experience alienation the more they gamble as an expression of self-assertion.
3 *Working-class culture.* The working class gamble more than the middle class because they believe more in luck, fate and destiny.
4 *Decision-making.* People who have no scope for decision-making in their work gamble more than those who have opportunities to make decisions.
5 *Risk taking.* Those whose jobs are more hazardous (action-oriented) and those whose are least action-oriented gamble most.

Some evidence was found to support 2 and 3 but many of these sociological theories are highly speculative and difficult to test. What they have in common, however, is the assertion that a major factor associated with the propensity to gamble is socio-economic circumstance rather than personality profile.

Though the authors appreciate the limitations of their study for assessing the overall merits of these sociological theories, they do believe their results to be a useful ground for better theory testing. No support was found for anomie theory, working-class culture ideas or risk taking, yet there was equivocal support for other theories, like risk taking. They did, however, find a strong intergenerational pattern of gambling, which exists irrespective of class, suggesting 'that broad class-based theories of gambling are ill founded, and that the factors making for variations in involvement and gambling, whatever they are, are permeated throughout the social structure rather than localised in one sector' (Downes *et al.*, 1976, p. 77).

Like Cornish (1978), Downes *et al.* (1976) explored social variations in gambling activity as well as describing the distribution of gambling for their entire sample. They conclude making statements in support of the structuralist-functionalist and decision-making viewpoint. They stress that all macro and micro-sociological theories of gambling implicitly or explicitly rely on a functional analysis, and that one needs to make sense of gambling in sociological terms. Yet they do acknowledge that these theories cannot provide an adequate explanation for the variability in different forms of gambling in small-scale contexts. Furthermore, many myths surround the increase and decline in gambling, which need to be examined empirically and historically. Finally, they consider the social policy implications of gambling.

> Social objectives – the goal of minimizing criminal entrepreneurship – clashes with fiscal ends – the goal of drawing in some revenue for the state from gambling profits: the larger the revenue drawn from gambling, the greater the inducement to make illegal books. The overall trend, however, is towards gambling as a key component in large-scale, interlocking 'leisure' industries.
>
> (Downes *et al.*, 1976, p. 212)

Other approaches

It should be pointed out that there are other approaches to gambling which have been mentioned. *Structuralists* or *situationalists* attempt to describe and identify key environmental features which stimulate, maintain or suppress the incidence of gambling. Factors which have been considered include:

1 The frequency of opportunities to gamble, such as the regularity of lotteries, the number of betting shops, fruit machines, etc., and the number of horse/dog-race meetings.
2 The pay-out interval, which refers both to how long people have to wait before they know of the result of the bet and how long they have to wait for their winnings.
3 The range of odds and stakes available, which may be quite variable.
4 The degree of personal participation and the exercise of skill as gamblers feel more active when present at the gambling event and when they are able to select the odds of the bet.
5 Probability of winning an individual bet and pay-out ratio.

Many more cognitive or mathematical models of gambling leave out the obvious point that for many gambling is a social occasion. Bingo, horse-racing and gambling, for example, are primarily social occasions and for some the idea of winning money is almost secondary to the benefits of being with other people.

Another approach is based on classic learning theory and the principles of operant conditioning, which stresses schedules of reinforcement. Gambling usually provides intermittent schedules of reinforcement (variable ratios) which, though not the best schedule for establishing a particular response pattern, is probably the most addictive – that is, maintaining the response pattern over long periods of time. There is a very low reinforcement schedule for the national lottery, yet it remains enormously popular, no doubt off-set by the size of the prizes. Indeed, organisers prefer few, bigger prizes, which seem better for generating interest in the lottery itself. Experimental studies have looked at resistance to extinction as a function of the duration of previous reinforcement with mixed results. But there are very wide differences in behavioural terms between different forms of gambling such as event frequency, expected values, etc. Thus it may be that the reinforcers differ from person to person, and from one type of game to another. Precisely what is reinforcing (feedback, exercise of skill, excitement, etc.) is extremely important.

Clearly, as Cornish (1978) stresses, both personal (psychoanalytic), individual difference (trait) and situational (sociological learning theory) factors are important in understanding the development of all forms of gambling behaviour. Personal factors are important as they attempt to isolate which demographic and psychological differences (cognitive, belief and personality) account for the fairly large behavioural variance noted in all forms of gambling. Situational characteristics are relevant, as they limit the range, frequency, type and amount of reinforcement available as well as the social and economic consequences of gambling. An eclectic approach does not, however, necessarily mean an uncritical acceptance of all aspects of all approaches. What needs to be done is to attempt to delineate which theory best accounts for either (or both) the initiation *or* the maintenance of which type of gambling with which particular group of people.

Walker (1995) has listed nine factors which may interact to predispose a person to gambling, all of which have been confirmed in the research in this area:

1 *Culture*: which may prescribe or proscribe various forms of gambling.
2 *Reference groups*: groups with which an individual identifies and on which he or she may model various types of gambling behaviour.
3 *Social learning*: the way in which novice gamblers learn the techniques and consequences of gambling.
4 *Personality*: individual difference factors which relate to the particular consequences of gambling.
5 *Crisis and stress*: the extent to which gambling is used as a coping mechanism.
6 *Leisure time*: the degree to which gambling makes up an important aspect of leisure time activities.
7 *Social rewards*: the social contact and environment within which gambling takes place.
8 *Physiological-arousal needs*: the extent to which gambling functions as a stimulant drug that people use to regulate arousal.
9 *Cognitions*: beliefs and understanding associated with the gambling experience.

Many of the very different gambling theories and approaches given above, even the most disparate, share similar problems. Some do not make clear, testable, falsifiable hypotheses which may be used to test their usefulness (see Downes *et al.*, 1976). Second, many are very similar and may be seen as complementary rather than contradictory, so that the same evidence may be used to support (or refute) more than one approach at the same time. Third, many studies have simply not provided supporting evidence. Furthermore, it is never difficult to cite a range of examples that contradict any one theory. This is particularly true of psychodynamic approaches. Fourth, because these are mostly general theories (with the exception of psychoanalytic approaches) it is not always easy to make specific predictions about individuals' gambling behaviour. Next, there appears to be some vagueness about motives that account for people's beginning to gamble and those that continue to do it. Because individual differences are ignored it is not clear why some people from much the same background are heavy, others moderate, and still others infrequent gamblers. Finally, and perhaps most importantly, many theories have been derived from, and hence are applicable to, specific (and very different) types of gamblers or types of gambling. Hence studies of compulsive roulette players may not provide useful insights into football-pools gamblers. General accounts can offer broad explanations for the prevalence and social distribution of gambling, in terms of social structures and socio-economically determined expressive needs, which can complement or compete with simpler accounts in terms of economic motivation. But they are neither suited nor intended to provide more detailed information about the relationship between particular motives and particular types of gambling. Where they occasionally appear to provide such information it is either because they are particular accounts masquerading as general ones, or general accounts which offer so many possible motives for gambling as to be consistent with virtually any explanation for any form.

TAXATION

It has been argued that taxes are what we pay for a civilised society. They are the subscription we pay for a stable, supported social environment. Tax is a social contract between individuals who tacitly agree to pay for particular social benefits. The levying of taxes is the way governments become self-supporting and are able to provide the facilities that people expect of them. There are many different types of tax: both direct (or income) and indirect (on specific goods or sales). For some people (particularly in the USA), they have to pay income, state, city and sales tax. Taxes are levied on all sorts of things and can have profound influence on behaviour. The window tax, levied by the British authorities in the eighteenth century to finance war, has consequences which can still be seen today with many beautiful Georgian buildings having bricked-in windows. According to British data the average income tax is 17 per cent of income, and indirect taxes (e.g. VAT [Value Added Tax], GST [Goods Sales Tax]) are another 21 per cent (*Central Statistical Office*, 1987).

Ultimately, any government ability to finance its expenses through taxation depends on the extent to which the public feels identified with the particular programme being funded and trust those who are carrying out the specified politics. Inevitably, if people disapprove of the policies, feel the taxes are too high (and unfair), dislike the parties in power or learn or believe taxation is corrupt and/or capricious, taxpayers become disaffected and thence dishonest.

Taxes have always been and will continue to be unpopular. Hence governments try to find ways to tax indirectly or less obviously to raise the revenue they require. Some exploit the mood or prevalent ideology of their voters. Hence, 'sin' taxes on tobacco, alcohol and gambling can be reasonably popular and even good for the health of the nation.

Painless, widely accepted, trouble-free and easy-to-collect taxes do not exist. However, there is some consensus around the concept of progressive or graduated taxation. Most countries avoid flat-rate, fixed percentage of income taxation, though there are exceptions. Much depends on the political mood of the time, which has swung from 'sting-the-rich' envy to a dramatic reduction in the top rate of income tax in most countries. However, there remains popular support for the severe punishment of the tax evaders and the acceptance of strong investigative policies on the part of tax officials.

All legislators attempt to find the exact point of setting taxes high enough to pay for the services people want and expect but not so high that they will be deeply unpopular, resisted or evaded. However, it becomes difficult to know what this particular point or zone is: it changes with various economic conditions. Various governments have attempted solutions to this problem. Thus Swedes recognised the need to give the creativity and drive of the entrepreneur full rein, in order to promote economic development and production, and thus increased the tax base. The initiative of individuals who wish to launch businesses is encouraged by tax rates that are set as low as possible during the developmental stage. Then, when businesses are well under way, their taxes are reset at levels that will compensate the state for its earlier leniency, but not so high that economic motivation is inhibited or destroyed. The Swedish state also encourages business leaders to volunteer to aid in planning public works, training public employees, and becoming involved in a wide range of activities and operations. This collaborative, participatory approach is quite different from what occurs in other countries, where the relationship between taxpayers and their government is often grimly adversarial.

Tax avoidance is legal; tax evasion is not. The former idea is to look for legal loopholes or maximise exemption claims. All governments attempt to encourage particular behaviours (i.e. saving, house-buying, family, charity-giving) by offering tax deductions. Tax evasion is cheating and appears to be fairly widespread. It is more common where people believe 'everyone cheats' and the underground, black economy is enormous. Further, if people believe their tax rate is unjustified and taxes unfair, they may 'fiddle' their tax returns (Lindgren, 1991). The tax evaders often rationalise their cheating by pointing out government waste, incompetence or inequity. They even assume the role of victim of the corrupt government rather than that of criminals. Others cleverly point to the fact that governments themselves attempt tax avoidance when paying international loans, etc., and politicians themselves have a rather dodgy history of honesty. Governments that attempt to finance their expenses by borrowing or printing money seem to be avoiding taxation. For people to be honest taxpayers, it seems they need to feel that their government is worthy of support and that its members are ultimately interested in their welfare.

What determines fiscal preferences or attitudes to taxation? In the United Kingdom voting preference is probably the single most important factor associated with fiscal preferences (Edgell and Duke, 1982, 1991; Lewis, 1982). Liberal Democrat and Labour voters (who have some things in common with Democratic voters in the United States) are more likely to favour increased expenditure on health and welfare provisions than Conservative Party voters (with ideological overlaps with the Republicans), who instead are more enthusiastic about increased expenditure on the police and armed forces. Conservative Party supporters are generally happier with lower taxes, which to an extent fits with their general lack of enthusiasm for state-control provisions. And although the fiscal connections between tax and state spending are rarely salient in the mind of 'ordinary' people, if the 'fiscal connection' (that is, the 'tax price' of government expenditure) is specifically mentioned in survey questions, enthusiasm for increased spending on health and education wanes. Even under these conditions it is still the case that Labour supporters are generally prepared to pay more in income taxes to see. What underpins these differences in fiscal preferences? Swift *et al.* (1992) pointed out that what divides Conservative from Labour supporters is not different conceptions of what justice requires (for instance, there was a consensus among their respondents that an unequal distribution of income was fair as long as there are equal opportunities) but different perceptions of how far these requirements are actually met in Britain today.

Inevitably, the role the state should take in the provision and distribution of welfare is a political and moral question. A central concept of 'welfarism' is that state bureaucracies, acting as 'benevolent dictators', distribute goods on the behalf of consumer/voters equitably, fairly and in accordance with strict guidelines. If people do not approve of the taxation and public-expenditure policies of government, of how much or how little they spend on health, education, police and the armed forces, they must register their disapproval by not voting for them at the next election. If politicians want to be re-elected it is in their best interests to take account of the wishes and preferences of consumer/voters especially as elections approach. One of the reasons fiscal referenda have been introduced in some states of America has been precisely because, some have argued, governments have not been responsive enough and have been more interested in feathering their own nests, resulting in an increase in administration and a concomitant decrease in efficiency. Advocates wishing to see a reduction in the size of the public sector have not always had their way as a result of fiscal referenda, however; as voters become more aware of and interested in the fiscal connection between taxes and spending they sometimes become keener on expenditure programmes rather than becoming more 'fiscally conservative'.

Tax evasion is a moral, economic and legal issue. In most Western democracies people comply with legal requirements. Even when taxes are seen as legitimate and government expenditure desirable, taxes are unpopular. How prevalent is tax avoidance (legal) vs. evasion (illegal)? Various different methods have been used to try to calculate this very difficult to measure behaviour. It seems that between 2 and 10 per cent of GDP (Gross Domestic Product) is lost (Cowell, 1990). We know very little about how (how much and how often) people actually or attempt to evade tax. Even guarantees of anonymity by disinterested researchers are unlikely to yield honest answers by a representative sample of the population. There is also the curious possibility in some countries of 'tax evasion by legal means'. That is, governments institute special and specific schemes (TESSAs [Tax Exempt Savings Scheme Accounts], PEPs [Personal Equity Plans]) that are tax exempt in an attempt to get individuals to save more, plan for retirement, etc. Equally, many big organisations have accountants carefully looking for legal ways to avoid paying tax.

Why do some individuals and, apparently, many small and large businessmen and businesswomen evade taxes? The simplest answer (and one that lies at the heart of economic models) is that people are greedy, that they are motivated by economic gain. The classic economic model (Allingham and Sandmo, 1972) assumes that the decision to evade tax is influenced by the benefits of evasion (which will be determined by factors such as the tax rate) and the costs (the probability of detection and the penalties of fraud). This suggests that if detection is likely and penalties are severe few people will evade taxes. The empirical evidence for this very plausible proposition is conspicuously absent. However, there are also more sociological models of tax evasion. One model that has been particularly important is that of Vogel (1974), who presented a theoretical framework which specified three objective factors (the individual's exchange relationship with the government; social orientation; opportunities for evasion) which have both direct and indirect effects on tax attitudes and evasion. There is strong evidence that these factors are important and in survey investigations opportunity has often been identified as the most important explanatory factor. But it is Vogel's typology of taxpayers that is particularly interesting. This is based on Kelman's (1965) distinction between internalism, identification and compliance. Compliance is behaving as an authority requires without changing one's beliefs. A *compliant* taxpayer is thus one who pays taxes because s/he fears the consequences if s/he does not, and not one who believes that it is morally right to pay taxes. *Identification* involves a change of beliefs to be akin to an admired person; so if a friend evades taxes and you respect him/her you may evade taxes yourself. *Internalisation* involves a genuine change of beliefs such that belief and behaviour are in line. By combining these distinctions with two kinds of taxpayers' behaviour (compliant and deviant), Vogel derived a six-fold classification of responses to the tax system. Conformist internalisers will pay their taxes in full because they believe that it is morally right to do so: deviant internalisers will evade taxes for the same reason (a good example would be some poll-tax protestors in the United Kingdom). Conformist and deviant identifiers pay taxes (or not) because of the behaviour of their reference group. Conformist compliers pay taxes because they fear the consequences if they do not; deviant compliers evade taxes because they believe that the likelihood of being caught is low.

A second conceptual framework is that of Smith and Kinsey (1987), who argue that people do not make a single decision to evade tax. In each decision they weigh up material consequences, normative expectations, socio-legal attitudes and expressive factors. Attitudes towards government spending and attitudes towards the tax system as a whole are considered to be the most significant. As many individuals do not recognise the connection between taxation and government spending, attitudes towards the latter are seen as having indirect effects on attitudes towards the system, which themselves have indirect effects on material consequences. Expressive factors are rather different: these are simply the subjective costs and benefits involved in paying taxes, such as the irritation caused by incomprehensible tax forms.

A third approach sees tax evasion as a social dilemma. Weigel *et al.* (1987) claim tax-evasion behaviour is a function of social and psychological conditions. A social dilemma involves a potential conflict between what is best for an individual and what is best for the group. The prototypic and famous example is an open common where an individual benefits if s/he alone grazes more animals but where everyone will suffer (as the quality and amount of grass is reduced) if most or all people do this. Similarly, an individual may benefit if s/he evades taxes but the whole system will break down if too many people do this.

CONCLUSION

The scattered but fascinating research on money in everyday life gives a rather different picture depending whether it is done by anthropologists, economists, psychologists or sociologists. Whereas some stress individual differences (personality traits, childhood experiences) others focus more clearly on the social context of monetary behaviour. Thus some see the motive for gambling, compulsive spending and not saving in the need for stimulation or low self-esteem for individuals. Others stress the importance of commercial pressures, the growth of credit cards, casinos and social-comparison processes. Sometimes a concept can bridge the social sciences: thus *risk aversion* is a concept used both by economists and psychologists to explain saving behaviour.

Elegant, rational utility-maximising models are explanations of economists and are challenged by the individual-differences and developmental approaches of psychologists. But it soon becomes obvious to the disinterested observer that psychological, sociological and economic factors *together* best explain everyday monetary behaviour. Thus, while total amount of disposable income is probably the best predictor of saving, it can be better predicted by taking into account certain personality factors like risk aversion. A multi-factor, multidisciplinary approach seems most obviously the best way to proceed. Yet as Lewis *et al.* (1995) have noted, while economists incorporate psychologists ideas into their models, they are not truly integrative. The social scientists interested in this area soon retreat to their favourite ideas and methods, only occasionally acknowledging the importance of other ideas.

But disciplines are moving closer together. Economic psychologists and psychological economists have written about consumer sentiment, the 'feel-good' factor, and economic optimism and pessimism. Furnham (1997) has recently devised a way to measure this quite simply.

The willingness, as opposed to the ability, to save, borrow, spend and buy is to a large extent a function of consumer confidence and sentiment – the evaluation and expectation people have of the economic circumstances of their household and of the national economy as a whole. What is particularly interesting about consumer sentiment, be it essentially optimistic or pessimistic, is that it supposedly precedes a noticeable movement in the economy. Thus changes in favour of optimism occur before a noticeable pick up in the economy. Equally, the gloom of pessimism of the average consumer seems to occur before the economy takes a downward dive.

One final point needs to be made in this chapter, which is the point the book opened with, and it concerns the research neglect of everyday life behaviours with respect to money. This chapter has concentrated on four everyday topics but various others have not been considered. For instance, we know little about how people do their personal budgeting or their particular and peculiar shopping habits. Reports of carefree non-savers and self-denying obsessional savers usually only describe unusual and extreme cases, and give little insight into the behaviours of 'normal' people with respect to such activities. However, they do appear to be changing and there is a noticeable increase in interest in all aspects of everyday money usage by researchers from various different research disciplines and traditions.

5 Money madness
Money and mental health

Nothing in the world is worse than money. Money lays waste cities; it sets men to roaming from home; it seduces and corrupts honest men and turns virtue to business; it teaches villainy and impiety.

Sophocles

I have no money and therefore resolve to rail at all who have.
William Congreve

There are two fools in this world. One is the millionaire who thinks that by hoarding money he can somehow accumulate real power, and the other is the penniless reformer who thinks that if only he can take the money from one class and give it to another, all the world's ills will be cured.

Henry Ford

An optimist is always broke.
Frank McKinney Hubbard

A moderate addiction to money may not always be hurtful; but when taken in excess it is nearly always bad for the health.

Clarence Day

If a man runs after money, he's money-mad; if he keeps it he's a capitalist; if he spends it, he's a playboy; if he doesn't try to get it, he lacks ambition; if he gets it without working for it, he's a parasite and if he accumulates it after a lifetime of hard work, people call him a fool who never got anything out of life.

Vic Oliver

Some people who make a lot of money are afraid of spending it; they use it as a security blanket. I've always felt that this is not a rehearsal. Real wealth is your health and freedom and money helps you see as much of this blue and beautiful planet as you can.

Mickie Most

INTRODUCTION

Many philosophers and playwrights have written about the irrational, immoral and downright bizarre things that people do with, and for, money. Newspapers, magazines and television programmes frequently focus on compulsive savers and hoarders (who live in poverty but die with literally millions in the bank) or impulsive spenders (who utterly recklessly 'get rid of' fortunes often obtained unexpectedly): the former of whom are compelled to save money with the same urgency and vengeance that the latter seem driven to get rid of it. Robbery, forgery, embezzlement, kidnapping, smuggling and product-faking are all often quite simply money motivated.

There are celebrated cases of money pathology. In America, the billionaire Howard Hughes became, over time, more reclusive and paranoid. In Britain, Viv Nicholson was famous for her 'spend, spend, spend' philosophy which saw her win and lose a money fortune in a few years. While it is possible to observe the extreme parsimony, obstinacy and orderliness with which some people approach money, it is equally possible to observe the hustlers, wheeler-dealers, thrusting acquisitors and carefree spendthrifts. Wiseman (1974) pointed out that there is no obvious biological drive to amass wealth and get rich, yet the 'purposeless drive' appears to be one of the most powerful known to man. Money is both intoxicating and inflaming, and the fairy tale dream of acquiring great riches appears to have affected all cultures for all time.

Journalists, like clinicians, are fascinated by fairly regularly occurring cases where otherwise normal people behave completely irrationally with respect to money. Typical cases are people who spend money they know they do not have; or scrimp and save, leading chronically deprived lifestyles when they do not have to. Incredible arguments and acrimony over money can strain and break friendships, marriages and cause very long-lasting family feuds. As we shall see, money represents different things to different people: power, love, freedom and security, and money madness is associated with each. Hence misers see money as a primary source of security, as does the bargain hunter. Tycoons enjoy the power of money and compulsive gamblers the excitement their money brings. We will look at the various neurotic types associated with money later in the chapter.

Money is frequently discussed – the tax rates, cost of living, price of property – but remains a taboo topic. Celebrities and ordinary mortals seem happier to talk about their sex lives and mental illnesses long before their monetary status, salary or frequent financial transactions. Secrets about money matters are surprising in our society but not in all cultures. In the openly materialistic cultures of South-east Asia, enquiries into others' and open discussion of one's own financial affairs seem quite acceptable. It is often denied, overlooked or ignored in courtship, argued about constantly during marriage, and the focus of many divorce proceedings. Contested wills between different claimants can turn mild-mannered, reasonable human beings into irrational bigots.

There are all sorts of reasons why money remains a taboo subject. Various theories have been put forward to explain this:

- Rich people, who dictate etiquette, eschew discussing their money lest the poor figure out how to get it for themselves. Or because friends and relatives might want it or become envious of it.
- It is superstitious to talk of money: it means it could be taken away.
- Boasting about money could encourage envious others to inform tax authorities.
- If money is associated with food, avoiding discussing it reduces hunger, need, greed and vulnerability.
- If money is associated with filth in the eyes of the people, shunning discussing it can be a way of fending off feelings of shame.
- On some levels we know our attitudes to money reveal a lot about us which we would rather keep private.

This chapter is about money pathology: the hypocrisies, inconsistencies, lies and paradoxes that surround money. To an outsider, the industrialised Westerner is inconsistent about money. Many stress that you only get what you pay for, but spend hours trying to seek genuine bargains. Monetary greed is thought of as sinful and repulsive but it remains clear that wealth commands respect. Money is self-evidently a measure of personal worth in the United States, for example, where it is a better indication of social class. Those that seek it often endure significant intimidation and humiliation by those who have it. Money hypocrisy is widespread – money is publicly disavowed, privately sought after; simultaneously it is the most important quality in the world but spoken of as having little value.

What is not really known is how common psychological monetary problems are in society. There have been no good population samples of monetary pathology, and thus, no quantitative evidence of their rarity or commonness. Because extreme cases are so memorable and interesting it is possible their occurrence is overestimated. On the other hand, because research on this taboo topic and the 'hidden problem' is so scarce, it could well be that the actual frequency of serious money neurosis in society is, in fact, underestimated.

It is apparent from Table 5.1 that the majority (often the vast majority) claimed not to be victims of money insanity, claiming 'yes' to those items. A quarter of the items showed that 30 per cent or more of the respondents did say 'yes', however. This does suggest a skewed distribution, which is not surprising given the fact that this was a 'normal' population and also that the likelihood of faking was good.

This chapter is particularly about the pathological meaning and use of money. It is, curiously, an area of research with a plethora of interesting

Table 5.1 The results of the 'money-sanity' subscale

Question	(%) Yes	(%) No
1 Do you find yourself worrying about the spending, using or giving money all the time?	29.3	70.7
2 Are you inhibited about talking to others about money, particularly about income?	28.4	71.6
3 Do you buy things you don't really need because they are great bargains?	19.2	80.8
4 Do you lie awake at night trying to figure out a way to spend less money and save more, even though you are already saving money?	14.0	86.0
5 Do you hold on to, or hoard your money?	22.2	77.8
6 Do you regularly exceed the spending limit on your credit card?	12.0	88.0
7 Does gambling make you feel a burst of excitement?	15.1	84.9
8 Would you walk blocks out of your way to save a bus fare you could easily afford?	13.9	86.1
9 Are you constantly puzzled about where your money goes or why there is none left at the end of the month?	42.7	57.3
10 Do you use money to control or manipulate others?	3.7	96.3
11 Do you refuse to take money seriously?	14.0	86.0
12 Do you resent having to pay the full price for any item when you shop?	26.3	73.7
13 Do you often gamble and spend large sums on your bets?	3.7	96.3
14 Do you spend a large proportion of your free time shopping?	18.9	81.1
15 When you ask for money, are you flooded with guilt or anxiety?	34.5	65.5
16 Are you increasingly anxious about whether you can pay your bills each month?	33.5	66.5
17 Do you spend money on others but have problems spending it on yourself?	35.2	64.8
18 Do you buy things when you feel anxious, bored, upset, depressed or angry?	33.7	66.3
19 Are you reluctant to learn about practical money matters?	16.5	83.5
20 Do you think about your finances all the time?	31.3	68.7

Source: Furnham (1996a, b)

and unusual case studies and a paucity of theory. There are few, if any, money-specific theories developed to explain pathologies associated with money. There may be a number of reasons for this. First, money madness may be extremely interesting but fairly unusual and hence not worthy of scientific interest. More likely, however, is the fact that pathology associated with money means that money is simply the focus of the pathology. It could equally be associated with time or dirt. That is, just as it has been suggested that the same pathology may underline seemingly separate pathologies such as early disorders, kleptomania and sexual promiscuity, so money pathology may almost be accidental in the sense that money becomes the focus of the issue.

Anthropologists, social psychologists, sociologists and theologians have all suggested possible explanations for money pathology.

- *Early Learned Experience*: growing up in poverty, economic recession or clear economic comparative difficulty has been suggested as a motive for some individuals to be driven to secure, in both senses of the word, large sums of money.
- *Intergroup Rivalry*: the concept of *pity* by the rich for the poor; and the *envy* and *hatred* of the poor for the *rich* provide plenty of opportunity for intergroup conflict. Threats to security, status, reputation and ego can act as powerful forces as well as a psychological threat to attempt to control money.
- *Ethics and Religion*: feeling guilty about money and being personally responsible for the poor is at the heart of many religions. The self-denial, self-depreciation and guilt associated with certain puritan sects has often been invoked for the strange behaviour of individuals taught that too much money acquired 'too easily' or displayed too ostentatiously is sinful.

However, there exists no well-formulated articulate theory of individual differences with respect to money. That is, with the exception of psychoanalysis.

THE PSYCHOANALYSIS OF MONEY

In an essay entitled 'Character and anal eroticism' Freud (1908) argued that character traits originate in the warding off of certain primitive biological impulses. In this essay in his collected papers he first drew attention to the possible relationship of adult attitudes to money as a product of eroticism. In fact, he later wrote 'Happiness is the deferred fulfilment of a pre-historic wish. That is why wealth brings so little happiness; money is not an infantile wish.' Many psychoanalytic thinkers, like Fenichel (1947) and Ferenczi (1926), have developed these notions. The latter described the ontogenic stages through which the original pleasure in dirt and excreta develops into a love of money. Freud (1908) identified three main traits associated with people who had fixated at the anal stage: orderliness, parsimony and obstinacy, with the associated qualities of cleanliness, conscientiousness, trustworthiness, defiance and revengefulness.

O'Neill *et al.* (1992) found evidence that the anal personality, characterised by obstinacy, orderliness and parsimony, enjoyed toilet humour more than non-anal types so providing modest evidence for the theory. According to the theory, all children experience pleasure in the elimination of faeces. At an early age (around 2 years) parents in the West toilet-train their children, some showing enthusiasm and praise (positive reinforcement) for defecation, others threatening and punishing a child when it refuses to do so (negative reinforcement). Potty- or toilet-training occurs at the same stage that the child is striving to achieve autonomy and a sense of worth. Often toilet-training becomes a source of conflict between parents and children over whether the child is in control of its sphincter or whether the parental rewards and coercion compel submission to their will. Furthermore, the child is fascinated by and fantasises over its faeces, which are, after all, a creation of its own body. The child's confusion is made all the worse by the ambivalent reactions of parents who, on the one hand, treat the faeces as gifts and highly valued, and then behave as if they are dirty, untouchable and in need of immediate disposal. Yet the children who revel in praise over their successful deposits, come to regard them as gifts to their beloved parents, to whom they feel indebted, and may grow up to use gifts and money freely. Conversely, those who refuse to empty their bowels except when they must, later have 'financial constipation'.

Thus the theory states quite explicitly that if the child is traumatised by the experience of toilet-training, it tends to retain ways of coping and behaving during this phase. The way in which a *miser* hoards money is seen as symbolic of the child's refusal to eliminate faeces in the face of parental demands. The *spendthrift*, on the other hand, recalls the approval and affection that resulted from submission to parental authority to defecate. Thus some people equate elimination/spending with receiving affection and hence feel more inclined to spend when feeling insecure, unloved or in need of affection. Attitudes to money are then bimodal; they are either extremely positive or extremely negative.

Evidence for the psychoanalytic position comes from the usual sources: patients' free associations and dreams. Freudians have also attempted to find evidence for their theory in idioms, myths, folklore and legends. There is also quite a lot of evidence from language, particularly from idiomatic expressions. Money is often called 'filthy lucre', and the wealthy are often called 'stinking rich'. Gambling for money is also associated with dirt and toilet-training: a poker player puts money in a 'pot'; dice players shoot 'craps'; card players play 'dirty-Girty'; a gambler who loses everything is 'cleaned-out' (see Chapter 4).

Psychoanalytic ideas have inspired a good deal of empirical work (Beloff, 1957; Grygier, 1961; Kline, 1967). Although there are a number of measures that have been constructed to measure dynamic features, Kline (1971) developed his own test of the anal character. This scale includes the following questions.

1 Do you keep careful accounts of the money you spend? (Yes/No)
2 When eating out, do you wonder what the kitchens are like? (Yes/No)
3 Do you insist on paying back even small trivial debts? (Yes/No)
4 Do you like to think out your own methods rather than use
   other people's? (Yes/No)
5 Do you find more pleasure in doing things than in planning
   them? (Yes/No)
6 Do you think there should be strong laws against spending? (Yes/No)
7 There is nothing more infuriating than people who do not
   keep appointments? (Yes/No)
8 Do you feel you want to stop people and do the job
   yourself? (Yes/No)
9 Most people do not have high enough standards in what
   they do? (Yes/No)
10 Do you make up your mind quickly rather than turn things
   over for a long time? (Yes/No)
11 Do you think envy is at the root of most egalitarian ideals? (Yes/No)
12 Do you like to see something solid and substantial for your
   money? (Yes/No)
13 Do you easily change your mind once you have made a
   decision? (Yes/No)
14 Do you disagree with corporal punishment? (Yes/No)
15 Do you regard smoking as a dirty habit? (Yes/No)

This scale has been used in Ghana as well as Britain and has attracted a good deal of research. For instance, (Howarth (1980, 1982) found the anal scale quite separate from measures of neuroticism or psychoticism. However, O'Neill (1984) found anality related to various Type A characteristics like time consciousness and obstinacy, which suggests they may be difficult to treat.

Empirical research into the anal character has been reviewed by Hill (1976) and Kline (1972). Both reviewers were critical of the methodology of studies done in this area, but came to the conclusion that there is evidence for the existence of the anal character as described by psychoanalytic thinkers. For instance, Stone and Gottheil (1975) tested the Freudian idea that proctological and ulcer patients would have oral personality structures, and those with obsessive compulsive disorders would be clearly anal. While there was some evidence of the latter, it was only a weak association and the link on oral traits was not significant. No doubt the quality of the psychometric evidence could be criticised and psychoanalysts may be tempted to point out that psychometricians like Kline have not understood the concept of the anal character, combined too many anal traits together or that through lack of insight or dishonesty anal characters have responded dishonestly to simple questionnaires. In short, it seems that there is fairly good evidence for an anal trait, but less good proof of its link to money-related issues.

THE EMOTIONAL UNDERPINNING OF MONEY PATHOLOGY

Freudians and their fellow-travellers have suggested that many money-linked attitudes disguise other powerful emotions. Many Freudians rejoice in the paradox whereby some outward, visible behaviour disguises or masks the opposite motive or desire. Thus pity towards the poor may in fact disguise hatred, racial prejudice and feelings of threat. Threat of physical violence or political clout with attempts legally or illegally to remove the wealth and concomitant status, reputation or ego of the well-to-do is a powerful motive. The poor are a psychological and economic threat to the latter because they may be prepared to work for very low wages, but can easily be stigmatised and victimised as dirty, dishonest and worthy of their fate.

One emotion frequently associated with money is *guilt*. This has been associated with puritan values of asceticism, denial and anhedonia (Furnham, 1990). Puritanism preaches the sinfulness of self-indulgence, waste and ostentatious consumption. Values such as conscientiousness, punctuality, thrift and sobriety make people with these beliefs or this socialisation guilty not about the acquisition but more about the spending of money. It is not antagonistic to the concept of money or receiving equitable rewards for hard work, but puritanism opposes money gained too easily (i.e. by gambling, inheritance) or dishonestly or sinfully, and particularly money being frivolously spent.

Guilt about money, indeed anything, can cause a sense of discomfort, dishonesty, unhappiness, even self-loathing. This guilt may be consciously felt and steps made to reduce it. Goldberg and Lewis (1978) believe that money guilt may result in psychosomatic complaints, transferred to feelings of depression. Psychoanalysts have documented cases of the fear of affluence in those schooled in the Puritan ethic. The basis of this fear is apparently loss of *control*. Money controls the individual; it dictates how and where one lives; it can prescribe and proscribe who are friends and associates; and can limit as much as liberate one's social activities. The Puritan ethic focuses on limits and the conservation of such things as time, money, resources, even emotions. If money were in super abundance there would seem little, certainly less, reason to exercise any control over it. In this sense one could lose the need for control. Maintaining control – over physical factors and emotions – provides a person with an illusory sense of security.

Psychoanalysts believe that one reason for those who suddenly become rich being unable to deal with their wealth is that they lack the self-discipline and, of course, actual experience to handle it. 'Where controls have not been internalized and realistic self-discipline has not evolved, the individual is dependent upon external controls to provide a sense of security' (Goldberg and Lewis, 1978, p. 75). Large amounts of money seem to imply, for many individuals, that one can use it irrespective of the consequences, and this uncontrolled behaviour creates anxiety. Paradoxically, if the money dries up or disappears, order and security are restored to life. Further, if people have made sudden and dramatic changes to one's life, getting rid of the money and all it bought may mean a return to normality.

As well as guilt money can represent *security*. Studies of the self-made, very rich in America have shown a much greater than chance incidence of these rich people's experiencing early parental death, divorce or other major deprivation (Cox and Cooper, 1990). Psychoanalysts believe that these people, in adulthood, set out to amass so much money that they would never be stranded again. Having had to assume adult responsibilities at an early age, they may have felt the need to prove to themselves and to others their lack of need for dependence on the parents. The desire to amass wealth therefore may be nothing more than a quest for emotional, rather than physical, security.

Money greed for psychoanalysts may relate more to orality than anality (Goldberg and Lewis, 1978). They point here to terms like 'bread' and 'dough' referring to money. The money-hungry person who seeks and devours money with little regard for social etiquette reacts to money as a starving person does to food. This behaviour, it is said, derives from a deprived infancy.

As we shall see, psychoanalytic writers have tried hard to categorise people in terms of the underlying dynamics of their money pathology. For psychoanalysts and other clinicians from diverse backgrounds, money has psychological meanings: the most common and powerful of which are *security*, *power*, *love* and *freedom* (Goldberg and Lewis, 1978).

Security

Emotional security is represented by financial security and the relationship is believed to be linear – more money, more security. Money is an emotional life-jacket, a security blanket, a method of staving off anxiety. Evidence for this is, as always, clinical reports and archival research in the biographies of wealthy people. Yet turning to money for security can alienate people because significant others are seen as a less powerful source of security. Building an emotional wall around themselves can lead to fear and paranoia about being hurt, rejected or deprived by others. A fear of financial loss becomes paramount because the security collector supposedly depends more and more on money for ego-satisfaction: money bolsters feelings of safety and self-esteem.

Goldberg and Lewis (1978) specify several 'money-types' that all, consciously or not, see money as a symbol of security. They provide typical 'case-history' data for the existence of these various types, though they offer little quantitative rather than qualitative research findings.

A   *The Compulsive Saver.* For them saving is its own reward. They tax themselves and no amount of money saved is sufficient to provide enough security. Some even become vulnerable to physical illness because they may deny themselves sufficient heat, lighting or healthy food.

B   *The Self-denier.* Self-deniers tend to be savers but enjoy the self-sacrificial nature of self-imposed poverty. They may spend money on others, however, though not much, to emphasise their martyrdom. Psychoanalysts point out that their behaviour is often a disguise for envy, hostility and resentment towards those who are better off.

C   *The Compulsive Bargain Hunter.* Money is fanatically retained until the situation is 'ideal' and then joyfully given over. The thrill is in out-smarting others – both those selling and those paying the full price. The feeling of triumph often has to validate the irrationality of the purchase, which may not really be wanted. But they get short-changed because they focus on price not quality.

D   *The Fanatical Collector.* Obsessed collectors accumulate all sorts of things, some without much intrinsic value. They turn to material possessions rather than humans as potential sources of affection and security. They acquire more and more but are reticent to let any go. Collectors can give their life a sense of purpose and avoid feelings of loneliness and isolation. Objects are undemanding and well-known collections can bring a sense of superiority and power.

Power

Because money can buy goods, services and loyalty it can be used to acquire importance, domination and control. Money can be used to buy out or compromise enemies and clear the path for oneself. Money and the power it brings can be seen as a search to regress to infantile fantasies of omnipotence. Three money-types who are essentially power-grabbers are, according to the psychoanalytic-oriented Goldberg and Lewis (1978):

A   *The Manipulator.* These people use money to exploit others' vanity and greed. Manipulating others makes this type feel less helpless and frustrated, and they feel no qualms about taking advantage of others. Many lead exciting lives but their relationships present problems as they fail or fade due to insult, repeated indignities or neglect. Their greatest long-time loss is integrity.

B   *The Empire Builder.* They have (or appear to have) an overriding sense of independence and self-reliance. Repressing or denying their own dependency needs, they may try to make others dependent on them.

Many inevitably become isolated and alienated, particularly in their declining years.

C *The Godfather*. They have more money to bribe and control so as to feel dominant. They often hide an anger and a great over-sensitivity to being humiliated – hence the importance of public respect. But because they buy loyalty and devotion they tend to attract the weak and insecure. They destroy initiative and independence in others and are left surrounded by second-rate sycophants.

As Goldberg and Lewis (1978) note, power-grabbers felt rage, rather than fear as a child, and express anger as an adult. Security collectors withdraw with fear, power-grabbers attack. Victims of power-grabbers feel ineffectual and insecure, and get a pay-off by attaching themselves to someone they see as strong and capable. They may therefore follow 'winners', particularly if they have enough money.

Love

For some, money is given as a substitute for emotion and affection. Money is used to buy affection, loyalty and self-worth. Further, because of the reciprocity principle inherent in gift giving, many assume that reciprocated gifts are a token of love and caring.

A *The Love Buyer*. Many attempt to buy love and respect: those who visit prostitutes; those who ostentatiously give to charity; those who spoil their children. They feel unloved not unlovable and avoid feelings of rejection and worthlessness by pleasing others with their generosity. However, they may have difficulty reciprocating love, or their generosity may disguise true feelings of hostility towards those they depend on.

B *The Love Seller*. They promise affection, devotion and endearment for inflating others' ego. They can feign all sorts of responses and are quite naturally particularly attracted to love buyers. Some have argued that forms of psychotherapy are a love buyer–seller business transaction open to the laws of supply and demand. The buyers purchase friendships sold happily by the therapist. Love sellers gravitate to the caring professions.

C *The Love Stealer*. The kleptomaniac is not an indiscriminate thief but one who seeks out objects of symbolic value to them. They are hungry for love but don't feel they deserve it. They attempt to take the risk out of loving, and being generous are very much liked, but tend only to have very superficial relationships.

Overall, then, it seems that whereas parents provide money for their children *because* they love them, parents of potential love dealers give money *instead* of love. Because they have never learnt to give or accept love freely they feel compelled to buy, sell or steal it. The buying, selling, trading and stealing of love is for Freudians a defence against true emotional commitment, which must be the only cure.

FREEDOM

This is the more acceptable, and hence more frequently, admitted meaning attached to money. It buys time to pursue one's whims and interests, and frees one from the daily routine and restrictions of a paid job. Goldberg and Lewis (1978) find there are two sorts of autonomy worshippers.

A *The Freedom Buyers.* For them, money buys escape from orders, commands, even suggestions that appear to restrict autonomy and limit independence. They want independence not love: in fact, they repress and hence have a strong fear of dependency urges. They fantasise that it may be possible to have a relationship with another 'free spirit' in which both can experience freedom and togetherness simultaneously. They are frequently seen as undependable and irresponsible, and can make those in any sort of relationship frustrated, hurt and angry.

B *The Freedom Fighters.* They reject money and materialism as the cause of the enslavement of many. Frequently political radicals, drop-outs or technocrats, they are often passive-aggressive and attempt to resolve internal conflicts and confused values. Camaraderie and companionship are the main rewards for joining the anti-money forces. Again, idealism is seen as a defence against feeling. There may be a large cost if the person gets involved with cults.

An underlying theme is that dependency on other people and on the world early in life was perceived as a threatening rather than a rewarding experience. This typology is based on clinical observations and interpreted through the terminology of a particular theory. For some, this may lead to interesting hypotheses that require further proof either by experiment or, at least, evidence from a much wider, normal population.

Goldberg and Lewis (1978) argue that psychotherapists see money madness as of secondary importance. They also note that the different money-types, not unnaturally, seek out therapists that fulfil their particular needs. Thus, those concerned with authority will seek out a less conventional therapist, while the security collector will be attracted to the least expensive therapist in the local market. Because (nearly) all therapists charge money for their services (though there is not necessarily any relationship between cost and quality of treatment), entering psychotherapy means spending money on oneself. Yet money remains a relatively taboo subject between therapist and client. Clearly, all therapists need to understand the shared meaning attached to payment and non-payment for services throughout the course of therapy. Also, paying shows commitment.

Finally, Goldberg and Lewis (1978) try to specify which psychological factors often lead to serious money problems. They mention ten:

(1) *gambler's fallacy*: throwing good money after bad;
(2) *greed*: the ally of manipulator and con artist;
(3) *fear*: inhibits reasonable risk taking;
(4) *envy*: it distracts one, may limit opportunity and wastes psychic energy;
(5) *anger*: can destroy business relationships and negotiations;
(6) *self-concept*: believing they do not have the ability to become rich;
(7) *contentment*: simply being happy with one's lot;
(8) *honesty*: not being prepared to sacrifice certain principles for gain;
(9) *compassion*: emotional softness, tenderness and caring that may lead to poor economic decisions;
(10) *sentiment*: attachment to traditions, possessions that make people not value being rich to sufficiently want to achieve it.

For these clinicians, particularly in materialistic societies, people who have emotional problems may incorporate money into their faulty behaviour pattern. Where money is a measure of worth it can attract powerful emotions and associated behaviours.

Psychotherapists believe that money beliefs and behaviours are not isolated psychic phenomena but integral to the person as a whole. People who withhold money may have tendencies to withhold praise, affection or information from others. People who are anxious about their financial state may have something to learn about a fear of dependency or envy. Therapists attempt to help people understand their money madness. Money can become the focus of fantasies, fears and wishes, and is closely related to denials, distortions, impulses and defence against impulses. Money can thus be associated with

> armour, ardour, admiration, freedom, power and authority, excitement and elation, insulation survival and security, sexual potency, victory and reward. Thus, money may be perceived as a weapon or shield, a sedative or a stimulant, a talisman or an aphrodisiac, a satisfying morsel of food or a warm fuzzy blanket . . . so having money in our pockets, to save or to spend, may provide us with feelings of fullness, warmth, pride, sexual attractiveness, invulnerability, perhaps even immortality. Similarly, experiencing a dearth of money may bring on feelings of emptiness, abandonment, diminishment, vulnerability, inferiority, impotency, anxiety, anger and envy.
>
> (Matthews, 1991, p. 24)

For all psychoanalytically inclined clinicians the money personality is part pleasure-seeking, frustration-avoiding *id*, part reasonable and rational *ego*, part overseeing, moral, *superego*. This accounts for the oft-reported but curious paradox of seeing people lethargic and depressed after a major win and elated, even virtuous, after financial depletion.

Rather than typologies of money madness, Matthews (1991) sees a continuum from mild eccentricities with subtle symptoms through moderate money neurosis to full-blown money madness. Again her data is obtained from treating patients and running workshops, with all the limitations that that implies. Further, she believes that money attitudes and behaviours are influenced by the emotional dynamics of early childhood; interaction with families, friends, teachers and neighbours; by cultural and religious traditions, and more; by modern technology and by the messages in the mass media.

For Matthews (1991) money has many functions – which she calls corrections and conceptions. These include: money can be used to express mistrust and suspicion; can be used to foster alliances between family members and to exclude other members; can instigate manipulation; can cause projection of emotion and blame; frequently can be invoked as an instrument of control; can be used to foster unnatural dependencies; be used to assuage parental guilt; be offered in lieu of heartfelt apology; can be used to express boundary problems which occur when family members cannot quite tell where they end and someone else begins.

Matthews (1991) has observed that many money disorders are learned from 'family disorders'. The message families send about money are, however, simultaneously overt and covert, and often paradoxical, inconsistent and confusing. Parents can, and do, express their feelings towards their children through money: reinforcing good habits, success at school.

In most cultures women have had much less opportunity than men to handle significant sums of money. Pocket money and allowances are negotiated with the father by boys, though girls may be encouraged to charm their fathers into opening their wallets. Hence some girls come to believe that financial wheeling and dealing is a masculine activity and shun all money matters for fear that it renders them somehow less feminine. On the other hand, if boys equate money with masculinity they feel very inadequate in the company of others with money, or, overspend that which they have as a means of making a statement about their 'male assets'.

Psychoanalysts point out that some children respond to parental messages by doing the precise opposite. One can find this with money: financially over-cautious parents spawn profligate and imprudent children. Other children attempt to outdo or exaggerate the financial behaviours of their parents. Some people appear completely indifferent to money and unworldly. A common theme running through their money attitudes is that they do not deserve it. Inevitably, those who believe they do not deserve a fair financial return for their labours will not receive it.

Yet, as well as early and later childhood experiences, inevitably cultural values and habits prescribe and proscribe money-related behaviour. Thus societal values dictate what is rich and what is poor; how money should be made; on what one's disposable income should be spent; who are monetary heroes and anti-heroes. Schools formally and informally socialise children into financial attitudes and habits. Equally, the media tends to reinforce culturally acceptable money values and habits, which naturally appear a little bizarre to culture travellers. All societies also have their messages about money sacrificing; donations and gifts to others.

Matthews (1991) believes there is a host of reasons why people run so easily into debt. People may buy too many things that boost their capacity for self-esteem or to try and fulfil a fantasy they have about themselves. Some may overdebt out of an unconscious desire to impoverish themselves, or to get rid of their money because on some level they find it loathsome. Alternatively, they may overdebt because they feel unfulfilled and frustrated in some significant aspect of their lives and because spending temporarily takes their mind off their sense of emptiness and unhappy circumstances. People may overdebt because compulsive behaviour of one sort or another runs in their family or as a reaction against a family of origin where thriftiness was excessively prized. People may overdebt to try to keep up with their peers, or because they are unable to resist media messages which instruct them to 'shop till we drop'.

Matthews (1991) also speculates about the 'pack-thinking' (conformity of views) of investors who play stock markets and whose greed and belief in eccentric experts can lead to spectacular monetary successes and failures. Economic shamans, the stars and superstitions all appear to play a major role in a highly capricious and unpredictable world. Many behave quite irrationally to allay feelings of uncertainty and insecurity about financial matters.

The literature on the emotional underpinning of money problems is certainly fascinating. Written by therapists and mainly from a psychoanalytic background it also has severe limitations. There is clearly overlap between various different systems or descriptions and there is no agreement on typologies or processes. More important, there is little corroborative empirical evidence for many of the points made. While it is possible that many of these concepts and processes are correctly described, we need disinterested, empirical evidence demonstrating the validity of these writings. We do not need to know how widespread these pathologies are in the general population. Indeed, it is striking from the (scant) sociological and epidemiological research on money how common money pathology is, not the reverse. There is also no evidence on the incidence of these pathologies in the population as a whole, nor whether therapy (of any sort) cures these problems. Long on speculation and short on evidence, this area of research warrants good empirical studies to examine these ideas.

MEASURING MONEY PATHOLOGY

Forman (1987) believes of all the neuroses, money neurosis is most widespread. Like all neurotic processes it involves unresolved conflict associated with fear and anxiety that may relate directly to maladaptive, self-defeating, irrational behaviour. Money cannot buy love and affection, personal states of mind like inner peace, self-esteem or contentment, or particular social attributes like power, status or security. Forman believes too many people have a simple equation like money equals love or self-worth, or freedom, power or security. To help people identify their neurosis, he developed a money-sanity scale, which Furnham (1996b) has attempted to evaluate.

In his book, Forman (1987) describes five classic neurotic types:

1 The *miser*, who hoards money. They tend not to admit being niggardly, have a terrible fear of losing funds, and tend to be distrustful, yet have trouble enjoying the benefits of money.
2 The *spendthrift*, who tends to be compulsive and uncontrolled in his/her spending and does so particularly when depressed, feeling worthless and rejected. Spending is an instant but short-lived gratification that frequently leads to guilt.
3 The *tycoon*, who is totally absorbed with money-making, which is seen as the best way to gain power status and approval. They argue that the more money they have, the better control they have over their worlds, and the happier they are likely to be.
4 The *bargain hunter*, who compulsively hunts for bargains even if they are not wanted because getting things for less makes people feel superior. They feel angry and depressed if they have to pay the asking price or cannot bring the price down significantly.
5 The *gambler* feels exhilarated and optimistic taking chances. They tend to find it difficult to stop even when losing because of the sense of power they achieve when winning.

Forman considers in some detail some of the more fascinating neuroses associated with everyday financial and economic affairs like saving, paying insurance and taxes, making a will, using credit cards. He does not speculate directly on the relationship between those various money complexes appearing to suggest that are all related to the same basic pathology. He developed a forced-choice (ipsative) questionnaire and a way for people to self-diagnose. The idea is that if one agrees with the majority of items in any one section one may have that pathology.

Furnham (1996b) has done some empirical evaluation of the Forman (1987) scale and typology. He argued that most psychological research in this area appears to have concentrated on a limited number of these 'money complexes' and hence this multidimensional questionnaire has the advantage of examining different manifestations of the same disorder. It is possible that the five money-types outlined by Forman (1987) are related to other established psychological variables. Thus one may expect *spendthrift* to be positively correlated, but all other scales to be negatively correlated, with the Protestant work ethic (Furnham, 1990). It is also likely that *miser* and *tycoon* are positively correlated with neuroticism. However, it is probable that individual scores on these five money-attitudes subscales are most closely correlated with socio-political beliefs and attitudes to work, both of which are partly about the generation and distribution of wealth (Furnham, 1984, 1990). He gave the questionnaire to over 300 British adults selected by a market-research company. The first question concerned the relationship between the types (see Table 5.2).

Table 5.2 also shows modest positive correlations between the subscales. While these indicate some overlap between the different money 'pathologies' it appears to be slight. However, the correlation between the five scales and the overall pathology scale do appear to indicate that it taps into a general attitude: when the five money-pathology scores were totalled (to include 50 items) the alpha rose to an acceptable 0.75. Thus it seems the money pathologies are sufficiently unique but related to the general-pathology questionnaire.

The second question was how internally consistent the various types were. Because of the low alphas an initial exploratory factor analysis of the latent structure of the fifty items was performed. The results indicated that items from the *gambling* and *spendthrift* scales load most clearly on the first two factors respectively. Items from the *miser* and *bargainer* scale load together on the third factor, suggesting some considerable overlap between the two subscales (and concepts). Three of the ten *tycoon* items load on to the fifth factor, but two *tycoon* items also load on the first factor. These results confirm the results from the internal reliability and correlational analysis, notably that gambler and spendthrift subscales are most internally coherent and unrelated to each other.

Table 5.2 Means, alphas and correlations between the scales

Scales	X*	SD	Alpha	M	S	T	B	G	T
Miser (M)	20.12	3.94	.43						
Spendthrift (S)	20.46	4.47	.65	−.01					
Tycoon (T)	18.40	3.82	.56	.17	−.04				
Bargainer (B)	19.90	4.12	.56	.20	.24	.22			
Gambler (G)	25.21	3.41	.70	.10	.16	.29	.22		
Total Pathology (T)	103.58	11.79	.75	.51	.55	.60	.69	.55	
Money Sanity (MS)	35.73	2.91	.65	.24	.23	.32	.47	.19	.48

Source: Furnham (1996b)

Notes: Correlations of >.14 are $p<.001$
   * For Forman, scores of 23 or over indicate clear health scores or 7 points or less extreme pathology

Table 5.3 Correlations between the money-sanity scales and other self-report measures

	Money sanity[a]	Miser	Spendthrift	Tycoon	Bargainer	Gambler	Total pathology
Job involvement	−.05	−.01	.17**	−.17**	.02	.09	.00
Work ethic	−.19***	−.13*	.12*	−.28***	−.18**	−.04	−.21**
Organisational belief	−.10*	−.04	.06	−.01	.00	.04	.03
Marxist-related belief	−.29***	−.02	−.02	−.06	−.15**	−.06	−.12*
Humanistic belief	−.11	.22***	−.02	.03	.02	−.02	.03
Leisure ethic	−.05	.08	−.23***	.12*	−.03	−.06	−.02

Source: Furnham (1996b)
Notes: *** $p < .001$; ** $p < .01$; * $p < .05$ (Low scores indicate high 'pathology') [a] Money sanity is the total score on the 20-item scale

Table 5.3 shows correlations between various attitudinal measures and the six money-related scales. Various patterns emerged: while three-quarters of the correlations with the money-sanity scale were significant, none was significant with the gambler subscale. The work ethic and beliefs in economic alienation seemed the most consistent correlates of the money-related beliefs.

Money sanity was correlated negatively with all but one of the five work beliefs, i.e. the *leisure* ethic (indicating that those with greater money complexes were more against the work ethic), as well as the *humanistic* belief scale (the idea that personal development in a job is more important than output), *Marxist*-oriented belief scale (the idea that most work represents worker exploitation) and the *organisational* belief scale (the idea that working in a group is important). Money sanity was negatively correlated with four economic values: trust in business, economic alienation, believing in government welfarism or the economic *status quo*; however, it was positively correlated with three scales, suggesting the government should not be involved in price setting, anti-union attitudes and the belief that workers are fairly treated. Money sanity was also correlated with the economic comparison measure indicating that money sanity was associated with negative comparison of others. In other words, money sanity seemed to be associated with optimistic and liberal economic 'views'.

The correlations with the various money-related scales showed a consistent pattern with the exception of the spendthrift scale which tended to show the opposite trend. This may be expected, since to some extent a miser and a spendthrift could be thought of as opposites.

This study set out to investigate attitudinal and demographic correlates of money-related beliefs or behaviours, a much-neglected topic in psychology. The measures listed in this study showed themselves to have face validity but weak internal reliability. While this may be due to certain artifacts (social desirability, the length of scale, the forced-choice format), it does suggest further work needs to be done on devising psychometrically valid measures of ordinary money-related behaviour. The same problem has dogged other measures of money attitudes (Wernimont and Fitzpatrick, 1972; Goldberg and Lewis, 1978; Furnham, 1984). However, the totalled money-pathology scale (see Table 5.1) had quite acceptable internal reliability, partly as a function of its length.

The subscale of money pathology seemed to indicate that while being a miser or spendthrift seemed unrelated to the other subscales, they were moderately positively correlated and all systematically related to the simple twenty-item sanity scale (where a low score indicated 'insanity'). Indeed, it was this scale that was most clearly and strongly related to the various attitudinal scores. However, the totalled money-pathology scale (including all five specific money pathology subscales, which totalled fifty items) was also correlated with many of the work- and economic-related beliefs and values scales. Thus, despite the attempts of clinical, organisational and social psychologists to taxonomise different money-related attitudes, the psychometric properties of many of their devised questionnaires remain weak.

It was the regressional analysis, however, that demonstrated that the more people endorse the work ethic the more they are indeed 'obsessed' by money. In fact, the second chapter of Weber's monograph is almost exclusively concerned with the amassing, but not the spending, of money.

These results are similar to those of Furnham (1984), who also found political beliefs (in that case, voting patterns), the Protestant work ethic and sex to be statistical correlates of money attitudes. He found, using canonical correlations, that females who endorsed the work ethic tended to be more obsessed with money. Similarly, Lynn (1991) found Protestant work ethic beliefs and attitudes to saving money were closely related. He also found consistent sex differences in attitudes to money (Lynn, 1994). Tang's (1992, 1993) research on money ethics also established the link between attitudes to money and the work-ethic beliefs.

Furnham (1990), in his review of the work ethic noted that both a historical view of the writing on the Protestant work ethic and what limited empirical work that there has been, suggests that Protestant work ethic beliefs are associated with security, collecting, miserliness and saving, but also to autonomy and power. At the heart of Protestant work ethic is an obsession with money as a sign of success (and grace) and hence a powerful psychological indicator of Protestant work ethic beliefs. It seems all writers in this field have emphasised the money beliefs and behaviours are established fairly early in childhood and maintained in adult life. If this is indeed the case, and Protestant work ethic beliefs are closely associated with money, this provides an interesting and important insight into the early socialisation practices of Protestant work ethic parents, who, no doubt, inculcate the belief in their children. However, a problem in interpretation may arise here because either too much or too little specific parental behaviour may be associated with obsessions with money. The Protestant work ethic values and practices, like training in postponement of gratification and stress on autonomy and the necessary contingency of all behaviour, are more likely to relate to late monetary beliefs and behaviours.

The second factor most consistently related to money pathology was political beliefs. People who labelled themselves as right-wing (either somewhat, or very radical) tended to have more pathology. Note that this variable predicted money pathology independent of the work or leisure ethic. Furnham (1984) also showed political beliefs related to attitudes towards money.

Money pathology seems closely linked to moral and political issues. Writers in the area from Freud to the present-day have noted that money is about freedom, power, security and autonomy, which are socio-political concepts. It may, then, be inappropriate to treat money pathology as another form of mental illness, but rather as what the Victorians called 'moral madness'. Attitude to, and habits of collecting and disposing of money, which are acquired in early childhood, may be closely linked to morality and ideology rather than to neurosis.

This study showed that, although it clearly taps into certain specific money-related attitudes, Forman's (1987) questionnaire requires further modification based on psychometric evaluations such as provided in this study. Specifically, the miser, tycoon and bargain-hunter subscales require further work to ensure higher internal reliability.

THERAPY FOR MONEY DISORDERS

Forman (1987) considered a range of therapies that he believes may be successfully used to help those with money neurosis, though of course the therapies may be applied to many other psychological problems. First, he notes how *cognitive behaviour therapy* may address negative attitudes. Self-defeating thoughts are characterised by self-blame, guilt, unresolved anger and low self-esteem. They are riddled with distortions, including *overgeneralisations* (in which a single negative event is seen as a never-ending pattern of defeat), *arbitrary conclusions* (in which one thought does not follow from another), and *black-or-white thinking* (in which everything is all or nothing).

The first step is developing a contract for how the patient will behave – the rewards and penalties for compliance and non-compliance with objectives. Next is to uncover automatic, money-related thoughts and attitudes. The third step is to recognise the harmful effects of these thoughts, and then to replace them by healthy thoughts on the subject. The final step is to change behaviour in line with the new healthy thoughts.

Another recommended therapy is *de-stressing or systematic relaxation*, which is an attempt at stress inoculation. The idea, somewhat tenuous, is that money neurosis is exacerbated by stress. Next, psychoanalysis is recommended, which also has set steps.

Assertiveness training is also recommended to help some people turn down unreasonable money requests which does not let them or the requester feel uncomfortable. Various other therapies are considered, including 'thought-stopping therapy' and role playing. Alas this eclectic approach to therapy has little or no evidence to support it, nor a full explanation of the processes at work.

Yet therapists have written about money in analysis: how they 'charge' their patients. Unlike sex and death, money does seem to remain a taboo subject, Haynes and Wiener (1996) have pointed out that the analyst's complexes and practices about money can clash badly with those of the client, causing particular problems. Sending of fees, presentation of bills, charging for cancellation, and increases of fees can present problems. But higher fees do not necessarily mean better work. Yet payment is received for work in progress which cannot guarantee results. Therapists' fees confirm their self-esteem, professional status and belief in efficacy. Thus when this is challenged by patients, the therapists have to confront their own attitudes to money and then negotiate that meaning with the patient. Again it is asserted that self-knowledge and insight is the best cure.

MONEY MADNESS

Fluctuations in the economy – particularly observable in inflation, unemployment and interest rates – can be a source of great stress. Suicides following the Wall Street crash as well as psychological depression during the great (economic) depression lead demographers, economists and sociologists to see if there were any noticeable changes in the nationally recorded statistics between economic variables and data like mental-health hospitalisation and suicide.

Dooley and Catalano (1977) noted that the well-known fact that people of lower socio-economic status are more frequently diagnosed as mentally ill than middle- or upper-class people has led to various interpretations. One hypothesis is that changes in economic security have most negative impact on the poor, who are thenceforth more psychologically vulnerable. Further, economic fluctuation can reduce social cohesion, increase alienation and suicide. Thus Pierce (1967), who followed data in the years 1919 to 1940, found a clear strong positive relationship between sudden changes in American common stock prices and suicide. Similarly, Brenner (1973) looked at admissions to New York State mental hospitals from 1914 to 1967, and found a clear relationship between them and the manufacturing employment index. Counter-intuitively, Brenner found good economic times were associated with increases in mental hospitalisation for some groups. Clearly, the unemployment impairs mental health argument is far too simple.

The lag between economic change and mental disorders can be very useful for planning purposes. Dooley and Catalano (1977) argue that if they can disentangle and understand the relationship between economic change and behavioural outcome, this research is of the utmost importance. In one study they found mental-health workers receptive to the ideas but not well informed about them.

However, from a research point of view, they wisely suggest that both economic changes and behavioural outcomes should be measured retrospectively. Also less severe factors than suicide and institutionalisation need to be considered. Further, of particular interest for the psychological level of analysis, individual coping strategies should be focused on to see how they affect both the consequences of economic change and remedial interventions. All sorts of outcome variable could be considered: life events, psychological symptoms, changes in coping strategies, and demand for mental-health services.

CONCLUSION

The research on money pathology is nearly all psychoanalytically oriented and case study based. Different writers have come up with rather different typologies of madness, though there is clearly overlap between them. Many of the descriptions are of 'serious cases' whose money pathology influences their whole lives. Inevitably, ordinary people may experience some of these 'problems' to a lesser extent. Most individuals know people who are self-denying, mean and miserly, as well as those whose carefree and excessive spending habits mean they are frequently in debt. Most money-pathology syndromes are naturally related to other disorders.

What this limited but fascinating literature does show is that money comes to symbolise something that can meet psychological requirements for security, safety, love and power. While money can, in part, satisfy some of these needs externally it cannot, however, buy those psychological characteristics it is sought to achieve. Because many people assume this lack of success is caused by not having sufficient money, many redouble their efforts to achieve this. Hence the miser, the spendthrift, and the gambler get worse over time. Moreover, they become ambivalent about money and may begin to distinguish between good and bad money.

Attempts to distinguish and describe pathological money types have all the problems associated with typologies. For example, there is overlap and movement from one category to another. The typologies only describe the predominant characteristics, and often there are contradictory signs. The categories are open ended and fluid, and while some have a clearly stated aetiology others do not.

Two other major criticisms could be made about the 'clinical' literature. The first is the evidence on which it is based. Much seems to be based on the case notes and observations of a few – mostly American, psychoanalytically trained – clinical psychologists. As such, we do not know how widespread these problems are in the population as a whole. Nor do we have any corroborative evidence based on other observers or methods, other than the 'therapy session'.

Second, these theories all trace money problems and issues to childhood problems and perhaps later difficulties with satisfying particular needs. But they neglect other psychological, sociological and economic factors. Thus, the trait of impulsivity, physiologically based, influences, in part, how money is spent. Family size, parental socio-economic status, and sibling examples are all sociological variables which inevitably influence money beliefs and values. Further, politico-economic variables can and do have an influence on individual money behaviour: for example, whether one's society is basically communist or socialist; the distribution of wealth in the society.

The attitudes to and behaviour of the *nouveau riche* attests to sociological forces at work on individuals. All societies develop an etiquette about money such as how and when to tip, what presents are acceptable, and when invitations should be reciprocated. Societies as a whole endorse, prescribe and proscribe money-related behaviour, which in some instances becomes pathological. Indeed, the society as a whole may dictate what is, or is not, pathological money madness, mere eccentricity or complete normality.

6 Possessions

Wealth consists not in having great possessions, but in having few wants.

Epicurus

In our culture we make heroes of the men who sit on top of a heap of money, and we pay attention not only to what they say in their field of competence, but to their wisdom on every other question in the world.

Max Lerner

Money is not an aphrodisiac; the desire it may kindle in the female eye is more for the cash than the carrier.

Marya Mannes

A man's treatment of money is the most decisive test of his character – how he makes it and how he spends it.

James Moffatt

When you want something from a person, think first of what you can give him in return. Let him think that it's he who is coming off best. But all the time make sure it is you in the end.

Sir Ernest Oppenheimer

I get so tired listening to one million dollars here, one million dollars there. It's so petty.

Imelda Marcos

Keep looking tanned, live in an elegant building (even if you're in the cellar), be seen in smart restaurants (even if you nurse one drink), and if you borrow, borrow big.

Aristotle Onassis

MONEY AND POSSESSIONS

A great deal of expenditure is on possessions – this is obviously one of the main things which we need money for. Yet it turns out that some of our most valued possessions have little monetary value. There are many kinds of personal possessions – houses, land, cars, animals, clothes, furniture, domestic and leisure equipment, collections (such as books and pictures), photographs, computers and other information technology. Some possessions are 'necessities', including what is biologically necessary to survive, and also what is needed to take part in everyday life such as telephones and washing machines. There are various kinds of less necessary items, such as cars and TV sets, which add to life and make more things possible or easier. Finally, there are more symbolic objects, such as jewellery, antique furniture and works of art, which, as we shall see later, are valued because they express the self, or enhance social status, though for a few they may be seen as investments. Many of these possessions are greatly valued by their owners, but this value may lie more in the history and associations of the object than in its monetary value, as is found in studies of what people in old-people's homes are most attached to.

Some possessions are regarded by their owners as 'necessities', others as 'luxuries'. Economists define necessities as objects which are bought in the same quantity regardless of changes in prices or incomes, while luxuries are bought only when they can be afforded (Douglas and Isherwood, 1979). What the rest of the population regard as necessities depends on the culture – TV sets are now so regarded, though they are scarcely necessary for survival. The things needed for biological survival and basic needs are certainly necessities, but so are many items in the 'uses' category. Lunt and Livingstone (1992) found that most of their sample thought that telephones, cars and washing machines were classed as necessities, and single individuals thought that stereo systems were necessities, while CD players, video recorders and microwaves were regarded as luxuries by the great majority. The line between necessities and luxuries keeps changing, as different items are needed to participate in, and be a normal member of, society. Townsend (1979) argued that poverty is relative, that individuals or families can be said to be in a state of poverty 'when they lack the resources to obtain the types of diet, participate in the activities and have the living conditions and amenities which are customary, or at least widely encouraged and approved, in the societies to which they belong'. Buying things is one of the main reasons that people want money: in Britain 42 per cent of our expenditure is on buying cars, clothes and other non-consumables.

People believe, furthermore, that these purchases will make them happy; but this is far from true. Objects are commonly valued in monetary terms; however, we shall see that some of the most-valued objects are things like photographs and souvenirs, which have little or no monetary value.

The most expensive item that most British families own is their house; 67 per cent of families own one, more than for other European countries, the average cost is £65,720 (in 1996 prices), and paying for them costs about 16 per cent of regular expenditure. Sixty-nine per cent of British families own a car, 24 per cent more than one, they spend 5 per cent of the family expenditure on buying them, and a lot more on running costs. Household goods, such as refrigerators, washing machines and the like, take up another 8 per cent, while leisure equipment such as videos take up a further 5 per cent. There is constant change here as new gadgets are invented and marketed, as shown in Table 6.1. A breakdown of expenditure on different goods and services is shown in Table 6.1.

Various studies have asked people what they would like to own. Lunt and Livingstone (1992) asked a sample of 219 respondents in the Oxford area 'Is there something between £50 and £200 that you really want to have?', and also between £200 and £1,000. The results are shown in Table 6.2a, b.

Several studies have asked people what they valued or treasured most. The objects mentioned vary greatly with the age and sex of the respondent (see Table 6.3, p. 166). Similar studies have been done by Csikszentmihalyi and Rochberg-Halton (1981) and in Britain by Dittmar (1992). A curious feature of these studies is that what might seem important possessions in terms of monetary value are rarely mentioned, for example, houses, clothes and kitchen equipment. On the other hand, sentimental objects, which cannot be replaced, have little or no monetary value.

We shall see in Chapter 12 that money has a small but positive effect on happiness, and this is mainly for people at the lower end of the income scale. Possessions also have a small positive effect, but different items give satisfaction at different ages (Oropesa, 1995). But in surveys which have applied controls for income, possessions have been found to have no effect on happiness (Veenhoven, 1994). The only exception is that owning a car has a positive effect. Yet some individuals, who have been labelled as 'materialists', believe that more possessions will make them happier, more successful and lead to self-fulfilment (Richins and Dawson, 1992). McCracken (1988) argued that buying expensive items is not greed but a quest for an ideal and happier time in the present or in the future; that they form a bridge to an ideal way of life. Part of the explanation of these beliefs

Table 6.1 Average family expenditure per week in 1994–5

Item of expenditure	£
Clothing and footwear	17.13
Household goods	22.66
Leisure goods	13.89
Housing (mostly mortgage payments)	46.42
Personal goods and services, assume 50% goods	5.40
Cars	14.47
Total	119.97
Total expenditure	283.58

Source: Central Statistical Office (1995)

Table 6.2a Is there something between £50 and £200 that you really want to have?[a]

Object	%
Clothes	19
White goods (microwave, tumble drier, etc.)	8
Camera/camera equipment	6
Home improvements	6
Colour TV	6
Holiday	6
Furniture	6
Electronic goods (cassette, walkman, etc.)	6
Video recorder	4
Hobbies	4
Garden plants/equipment	4
Compact-disc player	3
Typewriter	3
Shoes	2
Guitar	2
Bicycle	2
Carpet	2
Hi-fi equipment	2
Furnishings	2

Source: Lunt and Livingstone (1992)
Note: [a] Goods listed by the 43 per cent of respondents who answered 'yes'

Table 6.2b Is there something between £200 and £1,000 that you really want to have?[a]

Object	%
Holiday (mainly abroad, $\frac{1}{3}$ specified places)	22
Car (often replacement car or second car)	14
Home improvements (new kitchen, shower, porch, etc.)	10
Hi-fi equipment	8
Video recorder	5
Word-processor/computer	4
Carpet	4
Furniture	4
Kitchen, white goods	4
Bicycle	4
Compact-disc player	4
Music equipment (piano, organ, amp, etc.)	3
Cooker	3
Boat	3
Dishwasher	2
Television	2
Three-piece suite	2

Source: Lunt and Livingstone (1992)
Note: [a] Goods listed by the 52 per cent of respondents who answered 'yes'

in the benefits which objects might convey is probably exposure to advertisements, which make extravagant claims for the benefits that the product will bring. And expensive items may bring problems – insurance costs, danger or robbery, for example. Income is positively related to happiness at the lower end of the income scale, for both individuals and countries, because for poor people money means more food and other necessities of life, and this adds greatly to satisfaction, while for rich people it means objects which are less immediately useful, like jewellery and works of art. Indeed, there is no limit to what can be desired and bought, but for the very rich these new things may not add very much to life.

There are class differences in number and type of possessions, and even greater differences between countries in what people possess. Individual Americans own more than most Europeans do, and those in Third World countries a lot less. In many traditional cultures there is very little personal property, and most of it is owned communally. There is least property in nomadic tribes, who have no permanent homes and have to carry everything with them.

Compared with earlier historical periods and with poorer countries, Britain and other industrialised countries are experiencing in the 1990s a high level of 'economic activity', with periods of 'economic boom', that is, many people spend a lot of money on possessions, and they are encouraged to do so by department stores, easy credit, massive advertising and fashion magazines. Some of this desire for things leads to cultural growth, as when people were persuaded that they needed to buy cars, telephones and other items which turned out to be very useful, and which became widespread. Other objects made life much easier, such as central heating, washing machines and microwaves. Some new possessions added to leisure, as with TV sets and CD players. Other items are bought simply to enhance social status, such as buying a larger house or car. And a lot of purchases are for none of these reasons, they are to keep up with 'fashion'. This applies most obviously to clothes, but also to cars, interior decoration, and to some extent all possessions. So people are encouraged to buy new ones, just to keep up to date, because otherwise their self-image will suffer. However, fashion victims with their false wants may be good for the economy.

Why we need possessions

Biological needs

There may be a biological basis for possessions, at least for some of them. This is supported by the fact that animals have possessions too. The most important kinds of 'possession' for animals are: (a) territory; (b) sleeping places or nests; (c) hoarded food; (d) females and children, which may be treated as property; (e) attractive objects for decoration or adornment (Beaglehole 1931; Ellis, 1985).

Is this possessive behaviour in animals due to an 'acquisitive instinct'? This idea has generally been abandoned, in favour of the view that territory and other possessions are directly instrumental to the provision of food and water, shelter, and family life. Nevertheless, these unlearnt patterns of animal behaviour must be regarded as 'instinctive'.

According to sociobiologists, these unlearnt patterns of animal behaviour can be found, in weaker form, in humans, as has been found for non-verbal communication, for example, and sexual behaviour, and possibly in altruism. Is there a similar instinctive basis to human possessions? The alternative view is that any such residual innate patterns are overlaid in humans by the much stronger effects of culture and socialisation. We shall see that human children, at an early age, manage to possess things, such as toys, and will fight over them. They also, again at an early age, make collections, of attractive but usually useless objects, though this varies with the culture. However, territory, sleeping places and food supply are central to the existence of humans as well as animals.

The universality of human possessions

Anthropological evidence from more traditional societies has shown that in all of them there is ownership of clothes, weapons and decoration, as was found in a survey of 300 such societies by Hobhouse *et al.* (1915). In more developed societies there is ownership of land or territory, houses, animals, tools and symbolic objects.

- *Territory or land.* The simplest tribes, the hunters and gatherers, control hunting rights over land; in more settled agricultural tribes there is control over grazing of animals and land for cultivation. In the simplest societies the tribe or clan own land communally; in more advanced, agricultural, societies land is owned by individuals or families, and in the most developed tribes it is owned by chiefs or nobles, as in the later feudal system. Sometimes land is very plentiful, as in New Guinea, where the Mailu feel no need to actually possess it. (Hobhouse *et al.,* 1915)
- *Houses.* In the simplest societies, which are nomadic, there is only temporary accommodation, and this is usually communally owned. It is with the development of settled agricultural societies that individual families have their own huts, and have more possessions generally (Rudmin, 1990).
- *Animals.* Goats, sheep, cattle, pigs and other beasts play an essential role in agricultural communities. Animals are not only a source of food and power, but also status symbols, displaying the owner's wealth, and even a form of money, as when wives are bought with a number of animals.

- *Wives.* These are bought from their families, and are enjoyed, controlled and used by their husbands; they are essentially a form of property, and usually have little rights of their own. Children are also regarded as property; they are set to work, and when they grow up can be sold.
- *Tools and weapons.* These are individually owned; as we said weapons are among the most universal forms of possession. Canoes are usually individually owned, with the exception of war canoes, which are communal property (Beaglehole, 1931).
- *Clothes.* These might be thought to be the most universal kind of property, but the peoples of the lower Sudan, like the Nuer and Dinka, wear almost nothing. In addition, personal decoration is universal, and includes symbolic objects, such as the shrunken heads of enemies who have been vanquished.
- *Symbolic and immaterial possessions.* In addition to items of personal adornment, there may be other possessions whose significance is entirely symbolic. These include amulets, fetishes, talismans and totems, as well as religious icons (Belk, 1991). The decorated shells and other deeply valued but otherwise useless objects circulated in the Trobriand Islands in the Kula are one example. The gifts, mainly useless, donated at feasts in the Potlatch of the Kwatkiutl Indians, serve only to raise the status of the giver. Some possessions are non-material, such as having ceremonial rights, or knowing magical rites or procedures.

The ways in which possessions are acquired in primitive society are fairly obvious. One way is simply to appropriate them: when an individual or family has had the object for some time it is regarded as theirs. More than that, in the case of clothes, and sometimes weapons, they are regarded as part of the person who wears or uses them. Second, objects may be acquired by putting in the labour necessary to make them. Third, they can be inherited.

At later stages of development, the culture changes, largely as a result of additions to the material culture, so that work is done more efficiently, for example, better clothes and houses are made, or more powerful weapons invented. The main driving force over a long historical period was the need for food, drink, shelter and security, as with animals – though different human groups have worked out different ways of satisfying these needs. But, as with animals, there is a clear biological basis for acquiring possessions.

Possessions which are used to enhance life

Even in the primitive world there are a lot of additional possessions which do not meet obvious biological needs, but which are used to enhance life, to make more things possible. These are much more numerous in the modern world. We suggest that there are four main categories of these:

1 Cars, bicycles and other transport, help us get to work, but also to take part in leisure activities, and to see friends and kin, and to find mates, a biological motive. Anything that adds to mobility must be socially useful.

2 Domestic equipment, such as ovens, refrigerators, washing machines, dishwashers, central heating, vacuum cleaners, which make domestic life easier, and save a lot of time. At a previous historical period, when there was a lot of home working, the tools needed were important possessions. This is to some extent happening again with home working via computers and other electronic links.

3 Leisure equipment such as musical instruments, sports equipment, books, radios, TV sets, video recorders and CD players, which make possible a greater range of leisure activities.

4 Communication and information equipment, such as telephones, computers and fax machines, which increase social contacts and add to information available. Books can be counted here too.

Symbolic objects can be said to add to life, through their aesthetic merits or power to arouse emotions.

A prominent theory about possessions is Furby's (1978) proposal that to possess something is to be able to control access to it, and thus to enhance control over the environment and other people. This is derived from studies with children, which will be described later, and has been generalised to adults. Beggan (1991) found in laboratory experiments that subjects strong in internal control, who had received a manipulation in which they experienced less control, compensated by saying that their possessions gave them more control. External controllers, on the other hand, compensated by choosing different possessions, things which were judged to give more control. However, many of the items chosen in this study, as in others, do not seem to provide much control, for example, jewellery, pets and stuffed animals.

Possessions as symbols

In his review of the possessions of the 'simpler peoples' Hobhouse *et al.* (1915) found that one of the universal kinds was decoration worn on the self, such as beads. These are of no immediate biological use or instrumental purpose, but since such decorations are universal they are probably important in some way. As well as beads, houses and clothes and other possessions, all carry additional messages about the owner, from their design, size, cost, etc. Evans-Pritchard (1940) described the Nuer spear as a symbol of the self:

> A man's fighting spear (mut) is constantly in his hand, forming almost part of him . . . and he is never tired of sharpening or polishing it, for a Nuer is very proud of his spear . . . in a sense it is animate, for it is an

extension and external symbol . . . which stands for the strength, vitality and virtue of the person. It is a projection of the self.
(cited by Csikszentmihalyi and Rochberg-Halton, 1981).

Prentice (1987) studied the dimensions by which students classify possessions. The first factor was Self-expressive vs. Instrumental. Their other dimensions were Recreational vs. Practical, Cultured vs. Everyday, and Prestigious vs. Common. Possessions are status symbols. There is widespread agreement on the prestige of different makes of car, shops for clothes, and suburbs (Felson, 1978). Cars will all take us places, but they also send messages about their owner. Status may be enhanced by driving the latest model, or large and expensive cars. In modern society there are changing fashions, for clothes but also for other possessions. Veblen (1899) proposed that it is the rich who start fashions, and others follow, so that there is a 'trickle down' of fashions, and status symbols keep changing. As soon as lower-status groups have adopted a fashion the rich start a new one to distinguish themselves from their social inferiors.

Social status is not the only message symbolised by possessions; another is group membership. For example, football fans, punks and other youth groups proclaim their solidarity with the group by wearing the 'uniform' of that group. Such symbols express solidarity with other members of the group, and emphasise shared identity. Other symbols express uniqueness, deviation from the norms of groups, showing that someone is a *scientific* doctor, a *high-church* clergy person, a *left-wing* politician, etc. It is hardly necessary to send signals announcing whether an individual is male or female, but it is common to signal aspects of sexual orientation, for example, being gay, promiscuous. For women at work it may be important to signal their degree of masculinity or femininity by their clothes, and whether they get a job may depend on this. This whole process depends on there being shared meanings for objects; however, these shared meanings are not mainly created by special groups like the rich, but more by the media, such as advertising (Dittmar, 1992), and also the norms of different groups, for example, among clergy, 'the higher the blacker'.

These symbols of status, femininity and the rest do affect the impressions formed by others, as many studies have found. Non-verbal signals can have more impact than verbal ones, since simply telling others how rich, famous or feminine you are is likely to be greeted with mirth and disbelief, while material symbols appear to be genuine. There are several motives for this 'self-presentation': for immediate goals such as getting a job, or other professional purposes, to enhance self-esteem, and to help in the construction of the self – if others accept the identity signalled, then you can believe it yourself. All this really works; for example, it has been found that if newsreaders do not wear the 'right' clothes viewers believe and remember the news less (Harp *et al.,* 1985). If a shabbily dressed person stops people in the street to ask for minor help, he is less likely to be helped.

However, the identity offered has to be believable, and it may be necessary to negotiate an image acceptable to both sender and receiver, that is, to both the owner and the observer of possessions. One of the present authors (MA) knew someone who displayed coats of arms and other items suggesting that he belonged to the French royal family, but no one believed this, partly because there isn't one now, and he had to abandon these symbols (Argyle, 1994).

Possessions as symbols can also affect the owner directly. Wicklund and Gollwitzer (1982) argued that possessions can help with symbolic self-completion, so that perceived inadequacies are compensated for by impressive equipment, clothes, briefcases, etc. There is not very strong evidence that such compensation actually works. Indeed, thick briefcases may be seen as a sign of low social status. However, Turkle (1984) reports an interview with a young man who had failed an engineering course, but on acquiring a programmable calculator became confident and optimistic, seeing himself as capable of learning mathematical skills. We describe later the importance to old people going into nursing homes of keeping treasured possessions, which help to sustain their self-image. It is often reported that people who have been burgled have a feeling of violation of the self through loss or contamination of their possessions.

Possessions can also communicate information about the personality of their owner, and here self-presentation is less relevant; the owner is simply being his or her self, and not trying to show that they have a certain kind of personality. Dittmar (1992) found that aspects of personality such as forcefulness and warmth were communicated via the stereotypes of rich and poor. Later we shall describe studies in which clothes were found to communicate personality qualities more directly. The home has been described as an 'identity shell', an 'illustrated history of the self, as well as an expression of current social standing, interests, religious and political beliefs, personal tastes and qualities' (Dittmar, 1992).

HISTORY AND CULTURE

Material possessions have played a central part in human history and the growth of civilisation. Steam engines, spinning wheels and many other aspects of 'the means of production' have totally changed the world of work, and greatly enhanced what can be produced by it; they have also changed the relations between people, creating differences between owners, workers, technicians and others. New kinds of possessions have changed leisure as well as work, with the availability of cars, TV, cinema and the rest (Argyle, 1996).

Another historical change has been the development of new attitudes to possessions, and a 'consumer society', in which status-seeking individuals can buy objects which will enhance their social status. Historians report some degree of conspicuous consumption in the ancient world, among members of the court, but it is in the period between the late 1500s and the late 1700s that it became an important cultural phenomenon, not only throughout Europe but also in China and Japan. Several reasons have been advanced to explain this phenomenon – the influence of the royal courts, the emergence of the new rich in big cities, and cultural diffusion (Burke, 1993). In all these countries there was conspicuous consumption among the nobility, with extravagant clothes, food, furnishing and art.

For a long time, however, this was confined to the nobility and wealthiest of the commercial class, not to the middle class as a whole; this came later (Weatherill, 1993). Indeed, there have been 'sumptuary laws' which prohibited the new rich from wearing silk clothes, and in Japan they were forbidden to have houses with more than two storeys. In Europe there was an ideological restraint from the Protestant work ethic which disapproved of personal extravagance. Nevertheless, conspicuous consumption did spread to other social classes.

> The extravagant life-style of a ruling elite which seemed to live in a blaze of conspicuous consumption, and also the more modest but cumulatively more influential rise in middle class standards of living, made the inequalities of a highly commercial, cash-based economy glaringly plain.
>
> (Langford, 1984, p. 381)

The driving force behind this cultural change was partly the commercial acumen and effective marketing by people like Josiah Wedgwood, who invoked, and perhaps discovered, the Veblen principle to persuade people to buy more to enhance their social status (McCracken, 1987). However, these ideas have been criticised, and it has been argued that much acquisition of domestic equipment has little to do with status striving and more to do with making domestic life easier (Weatherill, 1993). It is the desire for social status together with the usefulness of new objects which have driven social change and continues to sustain the economy.

Figure 6.1 shows the recent rapid growth in ownership of microwaves and video recorders, the saturation of TV, washing machines, telephones and deep freezers, and the more recent growth in computers. It was some time before the working classes became caught up in consumerism, though this slowly grew between 1830 and 1950 in Britain. The present condition of mass consumption dates from the middle of the twentieth century; it was accelerated by TV advertising, which has often been aimed at working-class consumers, who are the people who watch most TV (Agnew, 1993).

Advertising has played a central role in the growth and sustaining of consumer demand. Adverts often appeal to real needs: how a car will go faster, use less petrol, be safer, etc. They also appeal to more nebulous, symbolic needs, and this happens with petrol, for example, where all brands come out of the same hole in the ground, cannot easily be distinguished from one another, and can only be sold by offering an image.

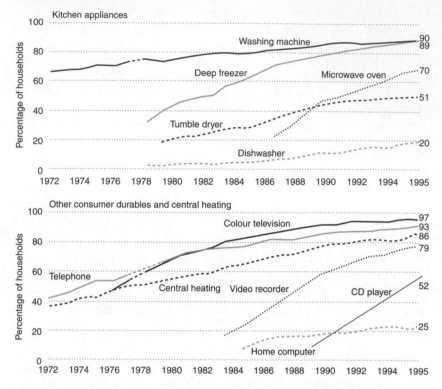

Figure 6.1 Percentage of households with consumer durables in Britain, 1972–94
Source: OPCS (1996)

Consumer goods have been described as 'symbols for sale' (Dittmar, 1992), and this applies both to useful objects like cars and to objects which are mainly symbolic. Early adverts concentrated on the Veblen principle and offered social status. They can offer the promise of romantic success, by the use of hair preparations and cosmetics, for example. When buying a certain brand of petrol you are buying an image of being a 'get-away person'.

The drive to possess material objects has been described as 'material-ism', and has been the object of much social criticism from Karl Marx onwards. Scitovsky (1992), for example, believes that we have become 'spoiled', and have acquired the habit of endless acquisition of goods in the insatiable quest for social status. Another criticism came from members of the 1960s 'counter-culture', who rejected the comforts of middle-class life in favour of a simpler way of living.

Richins and Dawson (1992), cited by Dittmar (1992), devised a scale for measuring materialism in individuals, with questions about the importance attached to acquiring possessions, such as whether people believe posses-sions are necessary for happiness, and whether people judge their own success by the number and quality of their possessions. Individuals who scored high on this scale were found to be less happy, and they were more often disappointed or anxious after buying things. Belk (1984) devised a different materialism scale, with items about envy, possessiveness and non-generosity. Again the materialists had lower life satisfaction.

The reason for the failure of materialism to bring happiness may be that people are really seeking non-material goals as personal fulfilment, the meaning of life, success, happiness or wisdom, and are disappointed when material things fail to provide them (Dittmar, 1992). In three studies of young people Kasser and Ryan (1993) found that those who rated financial success as a more important goal than family, community feeling, affiliation or self-acceptance were lower in self-actualisation, vitality and self-acceptance, and higher in anxiety and depression.

Csikszentmihalyi and Rochberg-Halton (1981) are critical of what they call 'terminal materialism', where consumption becomes an end in itself, the endless pursuit of more and more things in the hope that they will add to happiness or social status. They accept, however, another kind of materialism, 'instrumental materialism', which 'involves the cultivation of objects as the essential *means* for discovering and furthering goals' (p. 231). One can see how acquiring a musical instrument, a computer or a boat, for example, could open the way to the extension of life. This view is an example of the growth of a more positive attitude to consumerism, which is less puritanical than earlier ones, and in favour of certain kinds of self-indulgence (Agnew, 1993). Increased wealth affects the happiness of the poor, but has little effect on that of the rich, indeed very little for those in the top half of incomes. The reason for this is that the things which rich people buy often do very little to enhance life, for example, jewellery and antiques; all they can do is play a small role in the quest for a better life.

Group differences in possessions

Gender differences

The effects of gender and age on what are regarded as treasured possessions are shown in the Kamptner study (1991) (see Table 6.3). Women valued jewellery, photographs and silverware, and teenage girls clothes, whereas men valued cars, and teenage boys sports equipment. In another study, Csikszentmihalyi and Rochberg-Halton (1981) interviewed a varied group of 315 Americans in Evanston, Illinois, 30 per cent of them black, and asked them to list the 'objects which are special for you'. The respondents produced 1,694 such objects. The men often mentioned TV, stereos, musical instruments, sports equipment, vehicles and trophies; while women mentioned photographs, pictures, plants, plates, glass and textiles more often, they never mentioned vehicles. The authors conclude that men value objects for their instrumental uses, while women value objects for their

Table 6.3 Most frequently named treasured possessions: relative percentage by subject grouping

	Total group		Males		Females	
Middle	Stuffed animals	26	Sports equipment	28	Stuffed animals	31
childhood	Sports equipment	16	Stuffed animals	22	Dolls	15
(*n* = 112)	Childhood toys	10	Childhood toys	20	Music	12
	Dolls	8	Small appliances	13	Jewellery	12
	Small appliances	8	Pillows/blankets	4	Books	10
Adolescence	Music	13	Music	17	Jewellery	16
(*n* = 249)	Motor vehicles	11	Sports equipment	17	Stuffed animals	11
	Jewellery	10	Motor vehicles	11	Music	10
	Sports equipment	10	Small appliances	9	Clothing	9
	Small appliances	8	Clothing	6	Motor vehicles	6
					Small appliances	6
Early	Motor vehicles	21	Motor vehicles	33	Jewellery	22
adulthood	Jewellery	17	Music	10	Photographs	16
(*n* = 72)	Photographs	13	Photographs	10	Motor vehicles	13
	Memorabilia	8	Jewellery	10	Pillows/blankets	9
	Stuffed animals	5	Memorabilia	7	Stuffed animals	7
	Pillows/blankets	5	Artwork	7		
	Music	5				
Middle	Photographs	13	Photographs	18	Dish/silverware	18
adulthood	Jewellery	13	Jewellery	15	Jewellery	12
(*n* = 72)	Dish/silverware	11	Books	9	Artwork	10
	Artwork	10	Sports equipment	6	Photographs	10
	Books	7	Motor vehicles	6	Memorabilia	8
			Small appliances	6	Furniture	8
Late	Photographs	17	Small appliances	26	Jewellery	25
adulthood	Jewellery	16	Photographs	17	Dish/silverware	19
(*n* = 72)	Small appliances	14	Motor vehicles	11	Photographs	17
	Dish/silverware	11	Artwork	11	Religious items	6
	Artwork	7	Sports equipment	9	Furniture	6

Source: Kamptner (1991)
Note: Numbers are in percentages (*n* = 577)

links with family and friends, and for the memories and associations they evoke. This was confirmed by the reasons the subjects gave for choosing the objects they did.

In a small-scale interview study Livingstone (1992) found that men and women had different attitudes to domestic equipment. Women saw these objects in terms of their impact on family life, the microwave for heating the husband's supper, another TV to stop the children from quarrelling, the telephone as a life line. Men, on the other hand, saw these objects in terms of their functions and inherent properties, not of their effect on family life. To put this together, it seems that men value objects in a more instrumental way, while women value objects partly for their sentimental value, reminding them of other people, and partly for their impact on family life.

Class differences

Much has been said about the importance of possessions as status symbols, so it would be expected that people of higher status would have more or different possessions, and that their status could be identified from these possessions. Does this happen? There are extensive class differences in the ownership of most kinds of possessions, but not in all; Table 6.4 shows some of them, from the Central Statistical Office (1995) study.

Dittmar (1992) made a vigorous attempt to examine class differences, and used business commuters and the unemployed, as well as students. She did not find very great differences in the types of objects valued, though the business people valued antique grandfather clocks and sofas rather than the basic beds and cookers valued by the unemployed, and the business people also valued sentimental objects and decorative knick-knacks more. There were clearer differences in the reasons given for valuing their possessions. The business people valued things as symbols of personal history, for sentimental reasons, and for leisure, while the unemployed valued their possessions for their immediate usefulness and their financial value.

Do people use possessions as indicators of others' social class? If people are asked 'Which two of these [from a given list] would you say are the most important in being able to tell which class a person is?', as many give 'way of life' as the main criterion as give occupation or income (Reid, 1989). In another study 'the way they spend their money', 'the way they dress', and 'the car they own' were thought more important than occupation or income (Reid, 1989). Clearly, possessions are widely regarded as indicators of social class. Attempts have been made to use possessions as measures of social class for survey purposes, by checklists for what is in the living room. A recent American example included the

Table 6.4 Class differences in ownership of domestic equipment

	Highest 10%	Lowest 10%
Central heating	97.2	74.3
Washing machine	99.0	63.8
Telephone	99.7	69.6
Video recorder	93.0	36.1
Second dwelling	8.8	0.6
Tumble drier	74.3	18.7
Microwave	85.5	36.2
Dishwasher	55.0	2.0
CD player	73.6	15.2

Source: Central Statistical Office (1995)

items 'motorcycle in living room' (−10), and 'original oil painting by recognised international artist' (+6) (Fussell, 1984).

Dittmar (1992) showed adolescents videos of a young man or a young woman seen either in a wealthy home or in a fairly impoverished one. Subjects were asked to rate the characteristics of the target persons. Both working-class and middle-class students who judged the videos thought that the persons seen in the rich home were more intelligent, educated and successful, and a little more forceful, while when seen in the impoverished home they were thought to be warmer, friendlier and more self-expressive. The same individuals were judged to have the characteristics commonly believed to be found in members of higher and lower classes (Argyle, 1994).

Age differences

Children develop a very clear idea about which things are 'mine' from about age 2 onwards, and have frequent quarrels with other children such as their siblings over toys, porridge bowls and the like. At age 3 children have a very clear idea of ownership and will defend and be unwilling to share toys which have been said to be theirs (Eisenberg *et al.*, 1981). They feel that an object is owned if it has been 'earned' and the rights of the owner are respected (Staub and Noerenberg, 1981). Child psychologists have seen this as part of the development of the idea of self, defining its boundaries, rather than as 'selfishness'. Furby (1978) carried out interviews with 270 children and concluded that children have a drive to control the environment. They discover which things they are able to control, and regard these as parts of the self, as 'possessions'. They find they are able to control access to these objects, that is, they can control other people.

Furnham and Jones (1987) studied a total of 102 children, aged from 7–8, 9–10, 12–13 and 16–17, and found that possessions have a number of links with other people. They found that most children thought they could control who used their possessions, especially older children, while a quarter of younger ones thought their parents controlled them. Most children owned some objects jointly with other members of the family, and the younger ones preferred these objects. About half of the children said that they were prepared to lend their possessions; the younger ones to people they liked, the older ones depending on the needs of the other. Younger children preferred objects given by parents, but older ones preferred the objects they had acquired themselves.

At age 10–11 children's most treasured possessions are teddy bears and the like, toys, sports equipment and, for girls, dolls. By adolescence, age 14–18, in California, the treasured objects are music, motor vehicles, sports equipment and, for girls, jewellery (Kamptner, 1991). For British students the five most valued objects most often included music equipment, photos and mementoes, diaries, musical instruments, clothes and books (Dittmar, 1992).

At the other end of life, among the elderly, Kamptner (1991) found that the most-treasured possessions were photographs; for men, small appliances and cars, and for women, jewellery and silverware. The reasons given were most often links with family and friends, enjoyment and memories. Csikszentmihalyi and Rochberg-Halton (1981) also found that for their oldest group the most-cherished objects were most often photographs, but also furniture, books and art. These objects were said to be important because of the memories they evoked, together with links with the past, definition of self, and links with family and kin.

When old people go into a nursing home, they are distressed at the loss of their personal possessions. Those who have possessions with them adapt better to nursing homes, especially if these provide historical continuity, and links with other people (Wapner *et al.*, 1990). Many writers have stressed the benefits of allowing old people and mental patients to have some of their possessions with them, since it maintains their self-image (Dittmar, 1992). When people emigrate, able to take few possessions, or go into an old-people's home, they take with them a few objects of importance to them. These are things which remind them of their past life and their relations with others. Diaries of the Mormon pioneers for example found that they took with them possessions of these kinds, including objects with sacred meanings (Belk, 1991).

Dittmar (1992) criticises Furby's theory that possessions are mainly about control, since it overlooks the use of possessions as symbols. While children's favourite things seem to be mainly for use rather than symbolism, for example, toys and sports equipment, for old people the most important items are symbolic ones like souvenirs. However, having clothes, shoes and other equipment which are in fashion is very important even to children, and causes parents great expense, so Dittmar's criticism is probably correct.

Some of the main kinds of possessions

Land and houses

Animals have territories containing sources of food, water and shelter, and nests or other shelter for sleeping, eating, mating and rearing young. Humans in traditional societies also have land and huts or other dwellings for the same purposes. The land is used for herds of animals or for food production. With the growth of cities, only a minority now live in the country and own land; about 4 per cent of the population of Britain work on the land, and most of them do not own it. We shall look at the problem of inheritance of land in Chapter 8 – the problem is that it is not possible to keep dividing it up between a number of children without making the farm too small to support a family. Some food is still grown in urban gardens, and allotments, but more as a leisure activity for most gardeners, and most gardens have more lawn and flowers than vegetables.

However, nearly all people live in houses or apartments, and 67 per cent of families in Britain own the property they live in; 25 per cent own it outright, 41 per cent have a mortgage, and 34 per cent live in rented property. The percentage of families in Britain who own their homes is less than in Ireland (80 per cent) and more than in Germany (38 per cent). More professional-class families (86 per cent) own their homes, 75 per cent with a mortgage. (Central Statistical Office, 1995). The average price paid for houses, new and old, in England in 1994 was £65,720. The average family income was £15,570 after benefits and taxes, so house values are 4.2 times average annual earnings (*Social Trends*, 1996). The average amount spent per week on housing was £46.72 plus another £6.60 on repairs (19 per cent of income). Rex and Moore (1967) invented the concept of 'housing classes', of which there were six, from outright ownership of the whole house, to tenancy of rooms in a lodging house. They believed that everyone wanted to move up this hierarchy and to move out to the suburbs. However, it is now known that there is a sizeable minority who prefer living in the inner city, and another sizeable minority who prefer the independence of renting (Couper and Brindley, 1975).

Homes are designed, in each historical period, to meet the needs of those who will live in them. So the big houses in north Oxford, which were built between 1860 and 1890, had large reception rooms, a study near the front door, a second servants' staircase, and several small bedrooms for servants on the top floor (Hinchcliffe, 1992). No such houses are being built in Oxford or anywhere else today.

Houses are the main possession in most families; they meet many needs: do they also serve symbolic needs? Most visitors only see the front room, hall and dining room; Goffman (1956) called this the 'front region', where the family put on a performance for visitors, this being prepared in the kitchen and other 'back regions', where visitors are not allowed. There is some support for this view. Canter (1977) found that people thought of their houses as divided up in this way, and found that people put their best pictures and other valuable objects in the front room where they can be seen. There are some variations on this theme, for example in the Middle West of the USA it is common to receive visitors in the kitchen. It is possible to assess a family's social class from the contents of their living rooms, and it is likely that everyone realises this.

Csikszentmihalyi and Rochberg-Halton (1981) asked their subjects about their attitudes to their homes: 36 per cent gave an emotionally positive response, 9 per cent negative, and 55 per cent neutral. Women were most positive, boys the most negative. The older generation, still living in the same homes, valued the continuity of memories. Many individuals had an 'inner sanctum' where they felt most at home. For children this was their bedroom; for their parents it was more often the living room or kitchen; for fathers it was often their study; for mothers the kitchen.

Cars

There has always been a need for transport, and for many years this was provided by animals, mainly horses, ridden or pulling carts and carriages. The next development was the bicycle, and in the East, as well as in Oxford and Cambridge, and in Holland, this is still a major means of locomotion, and to a lesser extent of carrying things (both authors cycle, quite happily, to work). Since about 1900 the car has become all important in industrialised countries, to the extent that it is now creating social problems of pollution and overcrowded roads. The rapid growth of the car was stimulated by Ford in the USA and Morris in Britain, marketing very cheap vehicles, aimed at large sections of the population. However, Chrysler then competed with Ford in producing a more impressive vehicle, beginning the use of cars as status symbols (Stokvis, 1993). Thus cars gradually became bigger and more powerful, and impressive and attractive objects apart from their usefulness for transport.

In all, 69 per cent of British families now own a car, and 24 per cent have more than one car. Twenty-four per cent of first cars are bought with credit, more than any other object apart from houses, and most people regard cars as a necessity rather than a luxury (Lunt and Livingstone, 1991a,b). Cars are the next most valuable item most of us have, after the house; they cost between £7,000 and £18,000 new and a lot less second hand, but still a good fraction of the average annual family income. A new Ford Escort would take 1,846 hours of averagely paid work to earn, about 11 months, but cars are on average 7 years old and worth a lot less than when new. People spend on average £21.60 per week on running costs and another £14.50 on buying cars, about 12 per cent of total family income (*Social Trends*, 1996).

Cars are obviously extremely useful, for getting to work; 68.3 per cent of British workers drive to work, with an average distance of $7\frac{1}{2}$ miles. They also drive to church, sporting facilities or other leisure, and to see families and friends. Dittmar (1992) found that men in particular valued their cars primarily for their practical use. In an interesting statistical study of numbers of friends, Willmott (1987), found that having a car added on average 2.36 friends, and having another car added the same again.

People can do other things in cars apart from driving about; Kinsey *et al.* (1953) found that 38 per cent of American women, even in that more restrained period of social history, had had sexual intercourse in a car. Of course, American cars are larger than British ones. It is widely accepted that cars can act as status symbols, and this is confirmed by interviews with the owners of Rolls Royces and Cadillacs. 'My Cadillac has become to me a thing I deserve. . . . I've had comments: "You're Rich", from customers.

They may even resent it – I don't care. It shows you make so much more money' (Csikszentmihalyi and Rochberg-Halton, 1981).

Dittmar (1992) found that her businessmen greatly valued their Porsches, BMWs and Lamborghinis. Indeed, cars form a status hierarchy of their own, depending on cost, make, size, age, etc.; indeed, they are marketed with a range of income brackets in mind.

An American study using the Adjective Check List found clearly different images of several makes. Drivers of Chevrolets were seen as 'poor, low-class, ordinary, plain, simple, practical, common, average, cheap, thin, small, and friendly'. Drivers of Buicks (the second author once had one, and was very fond of it) were seen as 'middle-class, brave, masculine, strong, modern and pleasant' (Wells *et al.*, 1957).

However, cars convey other messages as well as status. Marsh and Collett (1986) carried out interviews about the perceptions of the drivers of different cars, and found that there are several dimensions in car stereo-types: (1) young, trendy, sporty and aggressive, vs. middle-aged, conservative and family people, for example, Golfs vs. Volvos; (2) professional, successful, status-conscious men vs. warm, ordinary, friendly and hard-up people, for example, Rover 2000s vs. Citroen 2CVs; (3) young, ambitious, professional females, who drive Metros and 2CVs. These authors found stereotypes for a wide range of cars.

Some of these car images have been created by advertising. Four-wheel drives have been marketed with images of tough masculinity and rugged terrains, convertibles with images of youthful freedom and sexuality. Interviews of subjects under hypnosis have obtained evidence of people entertaining unconscious fantasies about their cars. The most common themes to emerge were about power, success and sex, all escapes in fantasy in the imagination of car owners (Black, 1966).

Clothes

Unlike animals, humans need clothes, for warmth and protection from the weather, but also to cover the private parts, and for personal adornment. As Table 6.1 shows, we spend on average 6 per cent of the family budget on clothes and shoes. Beggan (1991) asked American students to list their five favourite possessions, and found that clothes came third in popularity. Kamptner (1991) asked 577 subjects to their list 5 most-treasured possessions, and found that clothes were mentioned most by adolescent girls.

Clothes are the possessions which change meaning the most rapidly, because of constant changes of fashion. New fashions try to out-do those of the year before, until a limit is reached and the changes are reversed. This has happened to the length of women's skirts, which have been found to have 20–25-year cycles with a longer 100-year cycle (Richardson and Kroeber, 1940). This gives lots of scope for the Veblen (1899) trickle-down theory, and such theories are based mainly on clothes.

Clothes vary with and signal social class, though less than they used to in the days of top hats and cloth caps and clogs. Richer people go to more expensive shops and buy clothes of better materials and workmanship, and they are usually cleaner, newer and better cared for. The symbolism is straightforward: wearing gold tells its own story, and so does wearing clothes like high-heeled shoes, which are obviously unsuitable for work (Veblen, 1899).

Clothes can communicate a lot more than social class. Burroughs *et al.* (1991) found that their subjects thought that clothes were more represen- tative of an individual's personality than other information such as their room or records; when clothes were shown there was good agreement between self- and other-ratings in a number of areas such as formal/ informal, optimistic/pessimistic, and hard/soft. Gibbins (1969) studied 15–16-year-old girls in the north of England, who were asked to judge the characteristics of girls who would wear various clothes; they were agreed that some outfits meant that the wearer was snobbish, or fun-loving, rebellious, shy, would drink, etc. But what are the features of clothes which carry this information? There is a high level of agreement in the studies cited that, for example, girls with short skirts, bright dresses and a lot of make-up are sophisticated and immoral (Hamid, 1968). In recent years ambitious people have been advised to 'dress for success', with smart suits for men and dark costumes for women. And there is some evidence that this works, in studies in which personnel managers are asked to rate people wearing different clothes for jobs (Forsythe *et al.,* 1985).

Physical attractiveness is very important for women, not only for rela- tionships but also for jobs and salaries. It depends partly on the shape of face and body, and on hair and grooming, but it also depends on clothes, being smart, glamorous and in the latest fashion. Finally, clothes also show very clearly the groups to which individuals belong. There are other groups in addition to social-class groups. There are rebellious youth groups like skinheads, punks and the rest. There are the uniforms of the police, post- men, doctors and nurses, lawyers and judges. Members of religious groups, political groups and occupational groups can also often be identified from their appearance.

Veblen's theory was extended by Simmel (1957), who pointed out that while the followers imitate, the upper-status group differentiate themselves from their followers: it is they who adopt new styles. Does it work for clothes, as Veblen claimed it did? In an early American survey, Hurlock (1929) found that 40 per cent of women and 20 per cent of men said that they would follow a fashion to appear equal to those of higher social status, and about half said that they changed their styles when their social inferiors adopted them. It looks as if the theory worked in America in 1929. How- ever, the fashion scene has changed since then. The clothing industry now produces new styles at all price levels at once, so there is less fashion lag. The trickle is more horizontal than vertical (Kaiser, 1990). Some fashions have even trickled upwards from the styles of punks and other rebellious youth. Nevertheless, there is still constant change in fashion, and to be out of fashion is to invite scorn and rejection and to be perceived as of lower status. But this can be explained by an older and simpler model of social behaviour–conformity pressures, and the rejection of deviants. If there are leaders of fashion they are less likely to be the upper classes, since most people would not like to be like them anyway, but rather pop singers, TV personalities and other opinion leaders:

> When blue denim work shirts are selling at New York's Bloomingdales and when rock star Mick Jagger is voted one of the world's best-dressed men, there is obviously something wrong with the theory that sees fashion styles established at the top and trickling down.
>
> (Blumberg, 1974, p. 494)

Who, then, starts the new styles? There is some evidence that leaders of clothes fashion are young, well-educated, and of high social status, venturesome and non-conformist in other ways (Millenson, 1985). The second author carried out a study on one of the former Oxford women's colleges, and located three leaders of fashion: one was very rich, one had a mother who was a model in Paris, and the other had a mother who owned a dress shop. But Campbell (1992) thought that there may be more than one kind of innovator: some of them are 'romantic bohemians' who want to shock, while others belong to groups of car, computer or other enthusiasts, who value minor technical improvements. The followers, he thinks, are daydreaming pleasure seekers, looking for new experiences, and for something else in life.

House contents

Animals do not have any furniture or equipment in their dwellings, and traditional peoples have very little. The growth of industrial civilisation has seen a tremendous growth in the things inside houses. Many of these things are useful, labour saving devices, which make life easier, and have enabled even those who can afford them to do without servants. Others are for leisure. We saw in Table 6.2 above that about 8 per cent of average family budgets are spent on household goods and another 5 per cent on leisure goods. Many of these items are of fairly recent invention, and Figure 6.1 shows the recent rapid growth since 1972 in the ownership of microwaves and video recorders. There are extensive class differences in the ownership of most of these objects, but not in all, as Table 6.4 shows.

Surveys of treasured objects find most of them inside the house. The most expensive items are washing machines, freezers and other equipment, though they do not appear much in lists of treasured objects. They are, however, important, since they make life easier and save a lot of time. They do more than save time, since they affect the whole pattern of family life.

Livingstone's interviews (1992) showed how women valued telephones, second TV sets and microwaves because of the difference they made to life in the family. However, some of her subjects thought that the time saved by washing machines and microwaves was the most important. Furniture scores quite high as treasured items, and this too is closely connected with patterns of family interaction, round the dining room table, for example.

Leisure equipment is valued more than domestic equipment, for example, TV, sports equipment and musical instruments, as are pictures and other collections. We have already seen how leisure equipment is valued, since it extends what can be done. New items are being devised and sold all the time. What's next? Computers and more complex kinds of information technology, multi-media sources of information and entertainment, and the Internet, which seem to be used mainly for entertainment at present.

Pictures and photos are valued as records of personal history, the house acting as an 'identity shell'. There are many items, which may be of no monetary value, but which are important to their owners, such as gifts, souvenirs, heirlooms, antiques, dolls and other items with special meanings or associations (Belk, 1991).

Art and sculpture, though this is less common, are often very expensive, so they can act as symbols of wealth, indeed, they are one of the things that rich people, who have everything else, spend their money on. And art requires expertise, so it symbolises taste.

What about collections? The most active collectors are children; Newson and Newson (1976) found that the great majority of 4 and 7 year olds had collections – of stamps, birds' eggs, etc.; later in life some resume collecting more seriously, mainly men. Formanek (1991) tried to find out the motivation for collecting; the most common reasons given were (1) self-esteem or extension of the self; (2) relating to other collectors; (3) preserving history, making links with the past; and (4) as an addiction or a source of excitement.

Collecting can be regarded as a form of serious leisure, a hobby; once the interest has developed it becomes a source of continuing enjoyment, of relations with other collectors, and of intense joy when new items are found (Olmsted, 1991; Argyle, 1996). This fits some collectors known to the second author, for example, collectors of pewter and old weighing machines. Books are different: most academics and writers in a sense collect books, since these are tools of their trade, and records of past activities. They may also act as a form of self-presentation, displaying the enormous erudition of the owner.

CONCLUSIONS

A large part of domestic budgets is spent on possessions. Some are essential to life, others extend what can be done in life. Some of these are very useful – cars, telephones and washing machines, for example. Others are mainly symbolic, like jewellery and antique furniture. However, the useful ones are often also symbolic, and are usually more expensive than they need be because of the desire to keep up with the Joneses, and have the latest model. New cars and clothes give pleasure and satisfaction to their owners, though this can lead to endless expenditure and a 'materialistic' attitude to consumption. And some of the most-valued possessions are photographs and other souvenirs, reminders of the past or of other people, which have no monetary value at all. There is little relation, if any, between the cost of possessions and their value to their owners.

Belk (1991) suggested that goods are not mere commodities, but have a 'more numinous character', when owners: are unwilling to sell for the market value; are willing to buy regardless of price; will not exchange the good for another; refuse to discard the good when no longer used; are depressed when the good is lost or damaged; and are elated when the good is in perfect condition, or when it is thought of as a person.

7 Money and the family

Whoever said money does not buy happiness didn't know where to shop.

Anon.

Money frees you from doing things you dislike. Since I dislike doing nearly everything, money is handy.

Groucho Marx

Money has no ears, but it hears.

Japanese proverb

If American men are obsessed with money, American women are obsessed with weight. The men talk of gain, the women talk of loss, and I do not know which is more boring.

Marya Mannes

When I had money everyone called me brother.

Polish proverb

The rich man and his daughter are soon parted.

Frank Hubbard

I'd seen how hard times could affect a family and I knew that with money you could get up into the clouds and stay there. I hope I never have to come down to earth.

Sir Nigel Broackes

People who have made money always want to look like people who have inherited money.

Mario Bualte

If you want to know what God thinks of money, look at the people he gives it to.

Anon.

THE ECONOMICS OF THE FAMILY

The exchange of money and goods inside the family is quite different from outside it. When money comes in from outside it becomes, in different degrees, the common property of all the members. The relations between family members and kin are different from those in the market economy outside; there are special bonds between them, and they last for life. It is unusual for family members to pay one another; when money is transferred, as with pocket money, this is not in return for work done, but for the needs of the recipient. Property and income are shared, on an informal basis and without bargaining. The family is often a production unit, where there is farming or a family business, and above all it is a consumption unit, where money is spent on food, shelter and all the other needs of the family.

In simple societies there is no money, and commodities are exchanged by barter. The family is universal, consisting of at least one adult of each sex and their children. In tribes of hunters and gatherers there are usually nuclear families, but where there is animal husbandry and agriculture extended families are much more common (Nimkoff and Middleton, 1960). It has been suggested that the invention of the plough in Europe made possible the accumulation of capital and led to the rise of the family, as separate from the clan, which did not happen in the African hoe culture (Casey, 1989). In Britain, in the thirteenth century, peasants farmed strips of land under the feudal system. They could buy and sell land, but as part of a community with obligations based on status, age and family (Homans, 1961). So brothers would look after one another as parts of 'stem' families; indeed, they were needed to deal with sudden needs for help incurred by farm animals. The independence of a household depended on how much land they had. If this was under 2 acres they needed to work for others as well or engage in commerce. If they had between 2 and 10 acres they co-operated with kin but were not independent.

In Britain and the rest of Europe until the Industrial Revolution the family was an important production unit, either in farming or in cottage industry, where the whole family worked as a co-operative. There was a lot of self-provisioning of households. In the sixteenth and seventeenth centuries in Britain many families were large; 39 per cent of people lived in families of 8 or more, and a quarter of families had servants, who were treated as part of the family, mainly children from other families who left home at 10 or later and were servants till they married. A few families had 30–40 members, run by senior servants, like Malvolio and Maria in *Twelfth Night*, with miscellaneous relatives, like Sir Andrew Aguecheek (Laslett, 1983). Women played an active part in all kinds of work until about 1800, when there was a shift of ideas, partly due to the early Protestants, and it was thought that work was for men to do, and that women should play a more subservient role in the home (Pahl, 1984).

Since the Industrial Revolution the most common form of the family has been the nuclear family, of husband, wife and children. There is some evidence that it preceded the Industrial Revolution and some evidence that it followed it. In any case the nuclear family has the great advantage for the industrialised world that labour is more mobile.

At the end of the nineteenth century there was a lot of unemployment, though many women went out to work in the factories, and some working-class men did the domestic work at home (Pahl, 1984). Anderson (1980) found that in the 1850s in Preston families and their kin provided and received a lot of mutual help in times of hardship. Some husbands came home exhausted from work, gave the wife some money to pay for all the costs of the family, and drank the rest. Kin became important, this time to give wives support, and female kin acted as a kind of female trade union.

In the twentieth century the situation of the family changed radically in several ways. During the early years, and especially between the wars, few women went out to work, but after the Second World War many did, some earned more than their husbands, and there was a move towards what has been called the 'symmetrical family' (Young and Willmott, 1973), though, as we shall see shortly, this has not gone very far. There was less need for kin, and the nuclear family became fully independent and more home-centred, especially for working-class families. Men did more housework than before, and women's work in the home was eased by domestic equipment. Better methods of dividing up the family finances were devised than those common in the previous century. Since the Second World War there has been a decline in full-time employment, with a high rate of unemployment in all industrial countries. There has also been a rise in self-employment, and in the 'informal economy', where no money changes hands.

THE SHARING OF DOMESTIC WORK

At all periods of history a lot of work has been done in the home, and unlike work outside this is not paid for. The question is who does it, and how are they rewarded? The short answer, of course, is that women do most of it, and they are not paid for it, though they are provided for by their husbands or other male members of the household. With a small sample of forty-seven British women, Oakley (1974) found that some of them liked housework, but others did not, and found it boring and repetitive. Much work in textile mills and offices which is done by women is also boring and repetitive, and an American national sample survey by Robinson (1977) found that 25 per cent obtained 'great satisfaction' from housework, 23 per cent from cooking, and 17 per cent from shopping; watching TV scored only 17 per cent. Many men regard cooking as a form of leisure. So there is some reason to doubt Oakley's views of housework. However, it must be admitted that being a housewife is a job which is not greatly esteemed, it may be felt that any fool can do it, and it can lead to social isolation. On the other hand, it is possible to do it well, and well-kept houses, well-cooked meals and well-behaved children can be a source of pride, and the conditions of work are much better than those down the mine or in many other places of work.

There is no doubt that women do most of it – even when they also have full-time jobs. Time budget studies have found that housewives, that is, wives without jobs, do 67.5 hours housework a week, wives with full-time jobs do 45.6 hours and men with full-time jobs do 26.2 hours. So if both are working full-time the wives do 63.5 per cent of the housework, and if the wife is not employed she does 72 per cent (Henley Centre for Forecasting, 1985).

Horrell (1994) reports a smaller-scale but detailed study of 110 house-holds, using diaries, of the time spent on housework and other activities when the wife was working, full-time, part-time or not at all. Some of the results are given in Table 7.1.

It can be seen from Table 7.1 that wives did less housework when working full-time, while husbands did a little more, 1.5 hours, but still only 23 per cent of it. The fully employed wives found the extra time by doing much less child-care, and had less leisure. They also slept less and spent a little less time shopping. The total amount of time spent by the two together was a lot less for housework, especially for meal preparation, and also for eating meals and for child-care.

Even when both partners have exactly the same kind of job women still do most of the work. Elston (1980), cited by Reid and Stratta (1989), studied 400 couples where both were doctors; the wives still did 85 per cent of the shopping, 81 per cent of the cooking, 80 per cent of looking after sick children, and 51 per cent of the cleaning (hired helps did the rest). If women were paid for this work it has been estimated from the level of skill and the hours worked that £370 per week, £19,000 p. a., would have been a proper rate in 1987 (Legal and General, 1987). It may be argued that women are paid by being supported and consume a share of their husband's income. But they are not paid for what they do, there is no rate of pay, no wage bargaining, and the wives of rich men do less work for more of such 'pay'. It has also been calculated that wives, by not working outside the

Table 7.1 Time spent on housework and other activities when wife working full-time, part-time or not at all

	Wife's time (hours)		
	Non-employed	*Part-time*	*Full-time*
Total housework	23.7	21.5	12.7
Child-care	18.5	6.7	1.4
Leisure	40.9	34.8	35.3
	Husbands time (hours)		
Total housework	2.4	3.4	3.9
Child-care	5.4	3.6	0.9
Leisure	34.5	37.4	38.2

Source: Horrell (1994)

home, forgo about £202,500, in 1990 prices, some 46 per cent of their potential life-time earnings (Joshi, 1992).

In all cultures, from the most primitive onwards, there is considerable division of labour between husbands and wives, the men doing the heavy outdoor work, the women looking after children, cooking and other housework (Blood, 1972). In the Israeli kibbutz the original plan was to have no such division of labour, but soon the women returned to the home to look after the children and ended up doing much as before, partly because of their need to care for the children, partly because of the physically demanding farm work done on the kibbutzim in the early days (Blood, 1972). The current division of jobs in Britain is shown in Table 7.2. It can be seen from Table 7.2 that the only job done mainly by men is repairs of equipment. It could be added that they look after the car too, and do outside work in the garden. In a similar American study Blood and Wolfe (1960) found that husbands looked after repairs (70 per cent), lawn mowing (66 per cent), and path clearing, i.e of snow (61 per cent).

Why do women do all this domestic work, more or less unpaid? There are several possibilities. (a) Pahl (1984) argues that it is following an economic strategy where men use their greater earning power outside the home and women use their free time to do the housework. This assumes that women have little or no earning power, which is not the case, though on average women still receive lower wages than men. (b) 'Resource theory' suggests that men do heavy outside jobs because they are stronger, repairs because they have the mechanical skills, and women do the rest because they have the resource of time (Blood and Wolfe, 1960). But we have seen that even when husband and wife have exactly the same amount

Table 7.2 Household division of labour by marital status in Britain, 1984

Task	Actual allocation of tasks (%)		
	Mainly man	Mainly woman	Shared equally
Household tasks			
Washing and ironing	1	88	9
Preparation of evening meal	5	77	16
Household cleaning	3	72	23
Household shopping	6	54	39
Evening dishes	18	37	41
Organisation of household money and bills	32	38	28
Repairs of household equipment	83	6	8
Childrearing			
Looks after the children when they are sick	1	63	35
Teaches the children discipline	10	12	77

Source: *Social Trends* (1984, p. 36)

of time available, the wife still does most of the work in the home. (c) Exchange theory in sociology argues that there is a satisfactory exchange of husband's economic support and wife's work in the home, leading to an affectionate relation between them (Scanzoni, 1979). This overlooks the fact that the wife has very little choice in this matter, and may dislike housework (Heath, 1976).

(d) There may be a widespread cultural assumption, passed on through socialisation, that housework is women's work, that their identity is to be found in the home, and that this is not real work, not economically productive and not paid (Oakley, 1974). Housework is not regarded as real work because its products are only for internal consumption, not for the market, it does not need to be paid, since it is done as part of a relationship. This was not so in the days of cottage industry before the Industrial Revolution, and it is not true of farm families and small businesses today (Delphy and Leonard, 1992). There appears to be a deeply ingrained set of beliefs, a kind of ideology, to the effect that men go out to work and women do the housework.

(e) Another possibility is that the links between women and child-care, and women and food-provision, have an innate biological basis; perhaps there is a similar link between men and the provision of shelter. This would explain why the division of labour is so pervasive throughout all known cultures.

Since women are often such useful and unpaid domestic workers, it is not surprising that in many cultures they have to be paid for. 'Bride price' is paid by the husband or his family to the wife's family to compensate them for their loss, and may consist of a considerable amount in money or cattle. This practice is still common in Turkmenistan, though it is slowly becoming less widespread. Berdyev and Il'yasov (1990) carried out a large survey of students, and found that 45 per cent of them thought that *kalym* (bride price) is incompatible with love. Bride price is much more common in those societies where the couple live in the village of the husband's family; it is perhaps partly to compensate the bride, who has to leave her own family and village (Murdoch, 1949). Since the husband's family will usually have to pay, this gives them considerable power over the choice of whom he marries.

THE CONTROL OF INCOME AND EXPENDITURE

Husbands and wives may divide their income in a number of different ways. Vogler and Pahl (1994) report a survey of 1,235 couples from the Social Change and Economic Life Initiative (SCELI), and distinguish several methods, whose frequencies are shown in Table 7.3.

- *Female whole wage.* Here the wife manages all of the family income, or nearly all of it, or gives her husband some pocket money. This is found

Table 7.3 Household allocative systems showing different forms of pooling

	%	N
Female whole wage	27	343
Female-managed pool	15	205
Joint pool	20	250
Male-managed pool	15	191
Male whole wage	10	118
Housekeeping allowance	13	153

Source: Vogler and Pahl (1994)

among the poorest families, including the unemployed and retired, where it is necessary to keep very close control of the budget. It is also found in areas where many women are employed. The wife may be responsible, since she receives social-security benefits and is no longer dependent on her husband.

- *Housekeeping allowance.* Here the husband controls how much money is passed on to his wife; this may exclude the bills which he pays. The wife may not know how much her husband earns. This method is most common among skilled workers in heavy and traditional industry, like mining and fishing, where there is a lot of male solidarity and little women's work, and during the period of child-rearing. The wife has no control over the money she receives; there is an incentive for men to earn more, for example, through overtime.
- *Pooling systems.* Here both partners have access to the joint income. This is found in richer families, where there is less need for tight control of the budget, in the newly married, and in later life when the wife is working. Three varieties of pooling are distinguished in Table 7.4, managed by the male, by the female, and jointly.
- *Male whole wage.* This is like the female equivalent.
- *Independent management.* Another method has been reported, though not in this study, and is quite rare, where each partner keeps his or her income separately and pays some of the bills. This is found among some cohabiting and homosexual couples, and may represent a lower level of commitment (Reid and Stratta, 1989; Morris, 1990; Pahl, 1995).

Vogler and Pahl (1994) used 1,211 of the couples from the SCELI Survey to compare the effects of these different systems. There was greatest equality of power to control finances with the joint pool, and the two female-managed methods, greater male power with housekeeping allowance and male whole wage. There was a similar pattern for access to personal spending money. And while wives usually felt more financially deprived, this was strongest with the two female-managed systems.

These authors also examined the conditions under which these different systems were adopted. The most important factor was 'socialisation', i.e.

the method used by parents, though there had been some historical changes. Next came husbands' education, the most educated using the joint pool, the least educated the female whole wage. Third was husbands' sexist attitudes to women's working and the division of housework: non-sexist husbands used the joint pool. Fourth was women's job status – full-time employment went with use of the joint pool method. This study also found some historical changes, when subjects were compared with their own parents. Has there been a shift towards greater equality? The very unequal house-keeping allowance is much less used now, and there has been a large increase in pooling, but only a small increase in joint pool, and increases in the unequal forms of pooling. There has been an increase in the female-managed systems, both of them associated with female deprivation.

Many women feel that they have little control, and if they leave their husbands find that they are worse off but feel better off, since they have control (Graham, 1987). Disagreement over money is one of the most common sources of marital conflict (Argyle and Henderson, 1985); it has been argued that it should play a more important part in marital therapy (Poduska and Allred, 1990). The allowance system leads to most marital dissatisfaction, the pooling system to the least. The process of division of income may be unclear to wives, especially those who do not know their husband's incomes. As a result they may not benefit from wage increases, and are vulnerable to inflationary increases in the cost of food. Usually wives pay for food and other regular household expenses, while husbands pay larger and less regular bills. The balance of power varies with different areas of expenditure. Edgell (1980) found that, for middle-class British couples, husbands made or thought they made decisions about moving, finance and cars, which were thought to be very important, wives about food and other domestic spending, and children's clothes, which were not thought to be important. Some other important areas were decided jointly – about the house and children's education.

Pahl (1989) studied a small but representative sample of 102 couples in Kent. She found that wives who were responsible for the spending had most responsibility for spending on their own clothes, food, children's clothes, school expenses, papers and books, charities and Christmas. Husbands paid most for meals out and trips, repairs and decorating, drinks in the pub, car or motorbike, their own clothes, fuel, telephone, insurance and consumer goods.

Although money all looks the same, it can be seen to be 'earmarked' for certain purposes. In particular, people may feel that they have greater access to what they have earned themselves. In the study by Pahl (1989), there was quite a strong feeling that the wife's earnings were hers to spend (see Table 7.4)

While the husband's income was seen as belonging to the family, the wife's income was seen by many husbands as well as wives as being hers to spend as she liked. Burgoyne (1990) interviewed a number of middle-class

Table 7.4 'How do you feel about what you earn: do you feel it is your income or do you regard it as your husband's/wife's as well?'

	Husband's income		Wife's income	
Income belongs to:	Husband's answer (%)	Wife's answer (%)	Wife's answer (%)	Husband's answer (%)
The earner	7	24	35	52
The couple/family	93	76	65	48
Total number	99	100	100	100

Source: Pahl (1989)

English couples. She found that in most cases money was controlled by the husband, who earned more, and that the wives felt inhibited from spending from the joint account if they hadn't earned it; they also felt a need to have some money they could call their own.

Blood and Wolfe (1960) surveyed 900 families in Detroit, USA, and found that overall power to make decisions depended partly on the incomes of the partners, but also on their education, job status, and membership of churches and other organisations. White husbands had more domestic power than black ones. They interpreted these results in terms of the 'resources' provided by each partner – though it is not at all clear why going to church or being white count as resources in this context. This version of exchange theory, where the person providing the least rewards is in a weaker position, since they have more to lose. Support for this theory came from a study by Crosbie-Burnett and Giles-Sims (1991) of stepfather families. Marital power was increased by prior ownership of the home, having been happy while single, and relative age.

However, the 'money leads to power' theory has been criticised on the grounds that power really depends on the alternatives available. In fact, exchange theory in social psychology says that people will stay in a relationship if the balance of rewards over costs is better than in the alternatives available (allowing for the costs of transfer) (Thibaut and Kelley, 1959). Applying this thinking to marriage, Heer (1963) observed that rich husbands are in a strong position, since wives would not get such a rewarding situation elsewhere, nor would wives with small children, while wives of poor husbands might well do better.

Sometimes husband and wife work together in a family business. If it is a farm the wife might do part of the work, such as milking the cows. It has been suggested that the home functions as a kind of family business (Willmott and Young, 1960). There have been many recent sales of British council houses; this has produced many more home owners, some of them from occupational groups with the skills to repair them; this has led to a great increase of DIY (do-it-yourself) sales and activity. The family home is usually jointly owned, it may show a large profit over a period, and it represents the major part of the family's possessions. It is also the focus of family life and leisure.

THE ECONOMICS OF CHILDREN

Throughout the developing world – and in Britain until the last century – children have been regarded as a major economic asset. Children were regarded as their parents' property to use as they wanted. From an early age, sometimes as young as 3 or 4, they were set to work in the fields as agricultural labourers; this became less necessary in many countries with the advent of mechanisation in agriculture. Or they may have been set to work in the home, engaged in the family cottage industry. The children would inherit family land or business and it was expected that they would look after their parents in old age. In England before the Industrial Revolution, if children were not needed for farm or domestic work, and the family could not support them, they were often sent as servants to richer households, from the age of 10 onwards, where they would stay until marriage; many households had servants at this time, and these servants, many still children, lived together with the children of the family (Laslett, 1983). In the nineteenth century in Britain there were many domestic servants, most of them daughters of rural labourers (Scott and Tilly, 1975). Many children were sent to work in factories, and as recently as 1870–1900 some children in Britain were doing this at the age of 11–15; when this was prevented by a series of changes in the laws governing child labour and education, people had smaller families. Those who cannot have children today and have difficulty in adopting may pay large sums of money to buy them from poorer families, usually in poorer countries. An important change of the 1980s and 1990s has been the increase in single-parent families, consisting of mothers and their children, where the mothers have either never married or have separated from their partners. In the USA 50 per cent of black-American families now are like this.

Children are valued for other than economic reasons. The pleasure and emotional satisfaction, the companionship, which they give is one of the major sources of marital satisfaction for most couples; children also give stimulation and fun, a purpose in life, a feeling of being adult and mature, and of achievement (Hoffman and Manis, 1982) (Table 7.5). They are also a status symbol and evidence of virility. The number of children that families have depends on a number of factors. Those of higher occupational class have a little fewer, educated wives want fewer, because the wives have careers, and because of the expense of the education thought desirable (Argyle, 1994). In the USA there was the famous 'baby boom' during the increased prosperity following the end of the Second World War.

Children also incur costs, economic and otherwise. The mother usually

Table 7.5 The value of children (percentage of sample)

	Women		Men	
	Parents	Non-parents	Parents	Non-parents
Advantages of children				
Primary group ties and affection	66	64	60	52
Stimulation and fun	61	41	55	35
Expansion of the self	36	34	32	32
Adult status and social identity	23	14	20	7
Achievement, competence and creativity	11	14	9	21
Morality	7	6	6	2
Economic utility	5	8	8	10
Help expected from sons/daughters				
Give part of their salary when they begin working	28/28	18/18		
Contribute money in family emergencies	72/72	65/63		
Support you financially when you grow old	11/10	9/9		
Help around the house	86/92	88/91		

Source: Hoffman and Menis (1982)

has to stop work for some years, children have to be fed and clothed, and given pocket money; as adolescents they cost more than adults in these respects; they have to be educated; daughters' weddings have to be paid for; and children need help in setting up house when they marry. The cost of education can be considerable, as it is in the case with British private schools and American universities. Education is the main route to good jobs and social mobility, and parents want their children to do as well as themselves or preferably better. The wife may go out to work to pay for such education. These are all very sizeable costs, which take up a large proportion of the domestic budget, and for poor families can be hard to meet, and for all families the result is that other things cannot be afforded. Blood and Wolfe (1960) found that financial costs were said to be the greatest costs incurred by children, followed by their illness and difficulties with child-rearing. Small children are very hard work for mothers, who may become exhausted, isolated and depressed during the years of infancy; a few years later there is often conflict with adolescents, which can be severe enough to wreck the marriage. The conflict with adolescents is partly over money; Conger *et al.* (1994) studied 451 families in Iowa, USA, and found that when families were in economic difficulties there was more financial conflict with adolescents, leading to hostility towards them and to antisocial and aggressive behaviour by them.

The age at which children leave home varies with the culture. In black-British families they leave in adolescence. In middle-class white families they leave when they go to college or equivalent. In working-class white families they stay at home longer, until their early 20s and can afford to marry; many aged 20–4 are still at home, most of them working (Leonard, 1980). Children's earnings make up 28 per cent of household income on average. When they go to work first they follow the 'whole-wage' system and hand over all of their earnings to mother, not being used to such large sums, and she gives them pocket money. This is more common for children with lower incomes and in the north of England. A little later on they follow the 'board' system and pay a regular amount to their mother for their board and keep, though mothers are generous here and charge much less than the commercial rate (Morris, 1990). In the USA it is more usual to charge nothing at all. In a British study mothers admitted that there was an implicit bargain here, in which spoiling led to keeping children close (Leonard, 1980). As with husbands and wives, earning more gives children more power in the household, in this case to be independent, to defy parents, to have priority over siblings in choosing the TV channel, though they may also help to support unemployed siblings (Blood and Wolfe, 1960).

Children usually receive pocket money, and this was discussed in Chapter 3. Children are expected to help with the housework, especially during the ages 11–15, and especially older daughters. They are not usually paid for this, except when there is a need for extra effort, such as when mother is out at work, in which case they may get extra pocket money. In fact, their mothers still do most of the housework. If children are asked to do too much housework there is a danger that they may leave home sooner (Morris, 1990). A lot of children do part-time jobs, such as paper rounds or Saturday jobs, and the proceeds from this are spent on their own recreation.

Parents are in a sense very generous to their children, who consume a large part of the domestic budget; quite poor families charge very little board from children who are at work, and a lot is spent on their education, weddings and setting up house. We saw earlier that parents give their children seven times as much in presents as vice versa, and we shall see later that most of their inheritance goes to the children. There is almost no negotiating or bargaining about this, and money inside the family does not change hands in the same way as outside it. It is as if the money were jointly owned, or were owned by some members more than others; and it is owned for a time before being passed to others.

The most basic use of money for children is to feed and clothe them, the basic concern is for their physical well-being and survival. There may be a sociobiological factor here, that is, parents are motivated to perpetuate their genes. It is not known whether parents spend any more money on biological compared with adopted children; common experience suggests not. What has been found, however, is that there is much less child abuse or neglect of biological children compared with stepchildren (Daly and Wilson, 1988). Alternatively, it may be because of the attachment, the bonding between parents and children, which is due more to the closeness between them in the early years, when some kind of conditioning or other emotional learning may take place. This could explain why parents enjoy their children so much – their presence arouses positive emotions.

MONEY AND THE EXTENDED FAMILY

We have discussed economic relations within the nuclear family; we now turn to economic links with other kin – children who have left home and their parents, adult siblings, and others. In earlier historical periods we have seen that larger groups of kin lived together and formed economic units, for example, farming together. Now those who live apart are financially independent, but there are still economic links.

A basic kind of exchange is with buildings; roofs may be mended by builders, but this can also be done by the occupants, or by their relatives and friends. In many traditional societies it is common for groups of kin to give help in building houses, which requires the co-operation of a group (Mead, 1937). In our own society, too, roof repairs would not be paid for, though there might be reciprocation with other services. This is part of the 'informal economy' (Pahl, 1984). Help of this kind can best be provided by those who have the skills and the equipment to do it, and skilled manual workers are most likely to have these. Although there has been a long-term decline in work done in and around the home, there are signs that this has now been reversed, as shown by the great increase in the sales of DIY, tools, wood, and of home decorating, garden and car-maintenance equipment. A women might be paid for ironing, if she were a paid domestic worker. However, she might be doing it for her husband, mother or sister, in which case she would not be paid, or for a sick relative or neighbour, or for a dramatic society production, which are all different parts of the informal economy, where no money is exchanged (Pahl, 1984).

People give and receive a lot of help from adult kin; Hill *et al.* (1970) found this in a study of a three-generation family in Minneapolis, WA (see Table 7.6). The direction of such economic help depends on who is better off; while it is more common for money to flow from parents to children, this may be reversed when the parents are retired or the children do particularly well. This goes further in Africa, where the news of economic prosperity circulates rapidly, and many kin expect a share in it. The large family network in Africa has often been seen as a kind of alternative to the welfare state – 'African families are universal providers of limitless generosity'. However, it doesn't always work: Seeley *et al.* (1993) found in Uganda that in a sample of AIDS patients the relatives provided rather limited help, because of lack of food and money and responsibility for other family members, some of them old or ill. In Britain working-class

Table 7.6 Help given and received from kin (USA)

		Parents	Married children	Grandparents
Economic	given	41	34	26
	received	17	49	34
Household management	given	47	33	21
	received	23	25	52
Childcare	given	50	34	16
	received	23	78	0
Illness	given	21	47	32
	received	21	18	61

Source: Hill *et al.* (1970)
Note: Percentages have been rounded up, so may sum to over 100%

Table 7.7 Help by friends and relations (by percentage)

		Middle-class	White collar	Working-class
Advice on a personal matter:	friends	64	67	39
	relatives	34	33	58
Source of financial loan:	friends	26	23	9
	relatives	74	73	86
Main source of help in child's illness:	friends	39	45	19
	relatives	56	55	77

Source: Willmott (1987)

people seek help from kin as opposed to friends, when in serious need, but this is less the case for the middle-class, as found by Willmott (1987) in a survey in London (see Table 7.7).

There is a flow of money from older to younger kin, and from richer to poorer, in the form of presents, as we saw earlier, inheritance, as we saw earlier, and financial help for particular needs, such as buying a car or paying school fees. There is also a lot of help for the elderly, both financial and by caring. In Britain one adult in seven was providing unpaid care in 1985, and, costed at £7 per hour this is equivalent to the entire cost of the National Health Service (Offer, in press). There is also a lot of domestic help, for example, in cases of illness of other family members.

Kin are also very interested in the occupations of their young members, because this will affect the prosperity and the social status of the family as a whole. Kin will give advice and help with jobs, and in some cultures what we regard as 'nepotism' is common, that is, giving jobs to kin rather than other applicants. In our society employing young people in family businesses is similar, though there is another reason for this, that kin can be trusted as partners, because of the unbreakable bond. The reason for making friends or partners into 'blood brothers', by a ceremony of mixing blood, in some cultures is to create a bond with similar strength to kinship; it is believed that if the other lets the partner down the latter's blood in them will kill them (Argyle and Henderson, 1985).

In China elderly parents traditionally lived with and were cared for by their children. However, since the Cultural Revolution, the old have lost their power and the next generation is less willing to look after them. This is because during this Revolution the old were supported by the community, there is no longer inheritance of land, and there are heavy expenses for bride price, weddings and housing (Yang and Chandler, 1992). In Taiwan most couples start by living with the husband's parents; many move out later, but many still visit every day, and give substantial financial help (Freedman *et al.*, 1978). However, all this altruism does have benefits for the giver. We showed earlier that there is a sense in which it is more blessed to give than to receive, and it has been found that two-directional social support provides psychological benefits for the main giver (Maton, 1987). This is consistent with the theory of 'communal relationships' which are closer than exchange relationships, and where those involved are more concerned with the needs of the other than with their own rewards (Clark, 1986).

In Britain young couples rarely live with the husband's parents; and mothers in law are found to give presents to the son's wife rather than do things for them, as mothers do (Fischer, 1983). In some pre-literate societies there is the practice of mother-in-law avoidance, in some cases forbidding looking at her. Cousins in modern society are a voluntary form of kinship, but only some are kept up with. Often they are encountered at the grandparents' home, so the relation depends on their being alive. Cousins are closest if their mothers are sisters, since these female bonds are stronger. Adams (1968) found that cousins were more likely to stay close if they had been childhood companions. Grandparents stay in closer contact than cousins, since the two parent–child bonds are strong, and they often form direct links with grandchildren, which can be quite close, since they have no disciplinary responsibility. Again links in the female line tend to be stronger, but the relation of grandparent has to be earned and is not automatic.

GIFTS IN THE FAMILY

The acquisition and distribution of family money can be a fraught topic. We shall start by looking at the psychology of gifts. Gifts are a form of charity, except that they are given to known individuals, family and friends, or others in close relationships. Further, gifts are often reciprocated: we get something in return. Charity is given in response to a state of need or distress on the part of recipients, but gifts may not be related to any actual need of the recipient. There is a set of beliefs about gifts, that they are voluntary and spontaneous acts of affection, quite different from a payment or bribe, and do not seek any return (Carrier, 1995). However, there are quite specific rules, for example, *who* should be given Christmas or birthday presents, *what* items are suitable as presents, and *how* they should be reciprocated. Large sums of money are often involved, and the exchange of gifts and other aspects of finance in the family can be regarded as an alternative to the market economy (Offer, in press).

Gifts may consist of money, or of gift vouchers such as book tokens, and most gifts have their monetary value, except for home-made ones. However, gifts more often do not consist of money, and money is thought to be unsuitable for many gift-giving occasions. Gifts may be practical, such as household objects or clothes, in which case they have to be transformed into gifts by being wrapped and presented. Or they may be useless and redundant, like cards and flowers, in which case the gift consists mainly of the message it conveys. Gifts send a message, by their size, and what they symbolise. Gifts of money also convey a message, mainly by their size.

Gifts are of interest to psychologists, since they are a form of altruism which has so far been little studied. Does their explanation lie in the psychology of interpersonal attraction, or in sociobiology, or in the functions of social systems of rules and ritual? Gifts have been of great interest to anthropologists; some of the most complex rituals which they have discovered have been systems of gift-giving; this raises the question of whether similar processes are operating in our own society, for example, the competitive, status-seeking ritual of the potlatch, and the elaborate circulation of gifts in the Kula.

TEN QUESTIONS ABOUT GIFT-GIVING

1 How much is given?

Gifts account for a proportion of household expenditure. Davis (1972) analysed British consumer data and concluded that on average 4.3 per cent of budgets was spent on presents, not including charity, which, we shall see later, comes to another 1 per cent. Davis believes this is probably an underestimate, since it does not include gifts which are made or grown in the domestic economy. American surveys have found much the same, for example, Garner and Wagner (1991) surveyed 4,139 households and found that 3.7 per cent was spent on gifts and about three-quarters of this is spent on Christmas presents, the rest on birthdays and occasional weddings. The proportion spent on presents is much higher than this in some other cultures.

2 Who gives most?

Four factors appear to be important here:

- *Income.* Richer individuals give more, on average, in proportion to their incomes, but the proportion also rises with income, especially over the middle ranges of income, suggesting that gifts are to some extent a luxury, for those who can afford them (Garner and Wagner, 1991).

- *Education.* Independently of income, more-educated individuals give more, possibly because they have larger social networks.
- *Gender.* Women give a lot more presents than men, though men tend to give more expensive ones. Caplow (1982) found that 84 per cent of Christmas presents were given by women, alone or in combination with men, when they would do the choosing, and only 16 per cent were given by men alone. Women are often in charge of Christmas arrangements, buying joint presents, arranging swaps instead of presents, and, of course, producing the Christmas dinner. Women give a lot of presents to other women friends, for example, at wedding showers in North America.
- *Age.* More presents are given by the middle aged, those whose children have left home, who have the money and time to do it.

3 Who are the recipients?

Most gifts are given to close family – mostly to a spouse if there is one, followed by children, siblings and other kin, and then friends. Caplow (1982) studied a large sample of Christmas presents in Middletown, USA, and found the following proportions: Children receive seven times as much from parents as they give parents, and similar ratios affect other relations with a generation gap. Presents may also be given to teachers, doctors, to service workers and to work subordinates, in these cases much smaller ones than those given to kin.

	Token (under $5)	Modest ($5–25)	Substantial (Over $25)
Immediate family	19	56	26
Secondary kin	28	59	13
Tertiary kin	49	56	3
Non-kin	69	25	6

Figure 7.1 Christmas presents and kin (USA)
Source: Caplow (1982)

4 Are there cultural differences?

More traditional peoples, in societies of hunters and gatherers, do not give presents. In some cultures, which do not have money, gifts play an important part in life and there are elaborate rules and rituals connected with them, such as the potlatch of the Kwakiutl and the Kula of the Trobriand Islands. In the Kula two kinds of shell circulate, in opposite directions, round the islands. They are never used, consumed or exchanged for commodities, but their exchange is believed to keep the peace for other trading. The shells each have an original owner, who in a sense continues to own them; they are 'inalienable' (Mauss, 1954).

In more developed, but still Third World, cultures, there are extended families, with the result that more presents are given to kin than in modern societies. This is found in Mexico, and in the Hausa tribe, where 10.6 per cent of income is spent on presents, to a wide range of relatives. The latter may be an overestimate, since the percentage is based on external income and here this does not include food and other things made or grown at home, so the income is higher and the percentage of it spent on presents is less (Davis, 1972). Migrants from Pakistan, Egypt, Turkey, Portugal and former Yugoslavia, when working in Britain, Germany or other more prosperous countries send remittances over a long period to their families. The Chinese, on the other hand, give more to friends, reflecting the collectivist nature of Chinese society. Japan is a special case, in that many presents are given, about twenty-six per month, and they should come from a special gift shop so that their value can be judged and an equivalent gift returned. It is said that this leads to some circulation of unopened gifts, which may go bad, and hence are not opened in the presence of the donor (Morsbach, 1977). Sometimes presents circulate in Britain too.

Every culture has its own rules and rituals about gifts. Cheal (1988) describes the gift culture in Winnipeg, Canada, where it is normal, for example, to give money as a gift to pay for weddings, and where Christmas presents have to be displayed round the Christmas tree and opened at the time of Christmas dinner, while on the day before a wedding the bride's female friends hold a wedding shower and give her household objects. These arrangements are different in Britain and Germany. The force of these rules is such that giving presents is not as voluntary or spontaneous as the ideology of gift-giving assumes – it is more or less compulsory to give presents at Christmas and weddings. There is a pretence that gifts are spontaneous, and also that there is no expectation of return: they are signals of affection, not moves in a game.

5 Gifts for different occasions?

The value of gifts varies a lot between occasions. Table 7.8 shows the average amount spent on presents in Cheal's (1988) Winnipeg study. It can

Table 7.8 Financial value of gifts by occasion

Occasion	Value of gifts*	
	Mean ($)	Standard deviation ($)
Anniversary	85.70	266.90
Birth	23.10	23.30
Birthday	27.00	40.20
Pre-wedding	44.10	114.90
Christmas	21.40	38.30
Easter	9.00	7.00
Father's Day	21.00	16.00
Mother's Day	34.20	100.20
Reunion	11.90	9.90
Valentine's Day	8.60	7.20
Visit	22.10	28.10
Wedding	117.10	394.40
Sympathy	14.80	10.80
Farewell	18.30	36.00
Party	29.00	69.90
Other	49.10	112.70

Source: Cheal (1988)
Note: * Home-made gifts excluded (interviewees made 3.5 per cent of the gifts they gave on all special occasions in 1982)

be seen that wedding presents were by far the most expensive, followed by anniversary and pre-wedding presents. Birthday and Christmas presents were much cheaper, and much more numerous. In this and other studies it was found that wedding presents were either practical, such as household goods, or of money. Easter and Saint Valentine's presents on the other hand were more likely to consist of flowers or chocolates – they were 'expressive' rather than 'instrumental'. Birthday and Christmas presents could be either practical or expressive, or both; often they were toys, or clothes.

There are conventions about what should be given on silver, diamond and other wedding anniversaries, popular with the jewellery trade, and promoted by advertising, but usually not followed. For presents given within institutions, there are presents which are obviously suitable; for example, in an academic setting books are usual. Many others would be unsuitable, as we will show later.

6 Who reciprocates gifts and why?

Reciprocity of gifts has been regarded as a cultural universal (Gouldner, 1960); it has been said that there is a moral duty to reciprocate gifts (Mauss, 1954). There is evidence for short-term reciprocity, and this principle can be used to elicit donations. Laboratory experiments also find short-term reciprocity. Cheal (1988) found that 53 per cent of gifts were reciprocated in the course of a year. In British and American studies it was found that this operates between equals, such as siblings and friends, and happens particularly at Christmas. However, this depends on anticipating what others will give, since Christmas presents are given simultaneously. An alternative explanation of this apparent reciprocity is that those concerned know the rules about who should give presents to whom, and the scale which is appropriate. There is often reciprocity of birthday presents, but weddings take place more rarely. There is reciprocity about neighbours' doing jobs or lending things; they do not want to be paid but would prefer to be reciprocated by a 'gift' of their neighbours' time, skill and effort, for example, in baking cakes, repairing cars, etc. (Webley *et al.*, 1983). According to some theories in social psychology, if a person can't reciprocate he or she feels indebted, in the power of the other, even inferior; it is reported that gifts and favours are sometimes avoided, since they may produce such consequences. The unemployed may fail to go to the pub because they can't afford their round, with the result that they become socially isolated. Politicians or others in public office have to avoid receiving gifts, since they would feel under pressure to grant favours or be accused of bribery.

There are other relationships where there is definitely not reciprocity. We have seen that parents give children seven times as many presents as they receive from children. Similar differences apply to grandparents, uncles and aunts, and anyone who has a nurturant family relationship. Research on relationships has distinguished between 'exchange' relationships, where people expect help or other favours to be reciprocated, and 'communal' ones where they do not look for or count such rewards, but instead are concerned with the needs of the other (Clark and Reis, 1988). Relationships with children and other loved ones would be counted as communal ones, and exchange would not be expected, unless we count looking after aged parents many years later. And 70 per cent of old people in the world depend entirely on their families for support though there is much less support of old people by their children in advanced societies (Offer, in press). Women are more involved than men in communal and nurturant relationships, and there may be a more general gender difference here.

There is no reciprocity with regard to presents to teachers, doctors, service workers, or employees, unless these presents are seen themselves as reciprocation for past favours. These would all be seen as exchange relationships.

7 What is the meaning of gifts?

Giving a present at all conveys a message – of concern or affection for the recipient. Not giving a present is a sign of rejection. Accepting a present is also a sign of affection, or at least of accepting the relationship. The degree of this concern or affection is shown by the cost of the present, and also by the trouble taken in choosing, acquiring or wrapping it. A gift can act as a long-term reminder of the donor, in the cases of photographs or jewellery, for example. Gifts can strengthen a bond in another way, for example, in giving away valued heirlooms, or other objects with a special history.

There are many ways in which gifts can convey the wrong meaning. Davis (1992) cites the case of Lord Ashburton, a Scottish nobleman who started Baring's Bank, inviting Thomas Carlyle and his wife for Christmas. Thomas was given a jig-saw puzzle for a present, very suitable as this was a new invention, but Mrs Carlyle was given a black silk dress, which was totally unacceptable, since this would be a normal present for a cook. Giving clothes for a fatter, shorter or older person is equally offensive, as would be giving deodorants, or ointment for spots.

Gifts can convey another kind of message, when they suggest a new interest or activity, such as a tennis racket, roller skates, telescope, computer or a book on a new interest. This is a common type of present for children. But children much dislike being given presents suitable for a younger child.

8 Is money suitable as a present?

It is often felt than money is unsuitable as a gift. Webley and Wilson (1989) asked students to rate the acceptability of a variety of gifts for different others. Money was regarded as the least acceptable in all cases, and especially when the other was of higher status. It is found to be unsuitable as part of an exchange between neighbours, for food borrowed, or jobs done (Webley and Lea, 1993). In a study with Dutch business students 41 per cent thought that money was not acceptable as a present, and they liked the present and the donor more when there was a real present, and effort had been made, for example, by wrapping it. Money was seen as impersonal and the donor as lazy. Money was acceptable if it had been asked for, if the recipient was in great need of money or was saving up for something, or if the donor had a reputation for giving bad presents (Pieters and Robben, 1992). There is no evidence that children object to being given money.

Only 9 per cent of Middletown Christmas presents and 7 per cent of Winnipeg ones consisted of money. On the other hand it was common in Winnipeg to give money for weddings, partly to pay for the wedding, and this has also been found in Greece. A number of reasons are given for why money is felt to be unsuitable – it means that the donor didn't bother to choose; it is a weak symbol of the relationship; it has little symbolic meaning; it is too exact for a measure of love, and so on. This last explanation must be wrong, since gift vouchers, like book tokens, which are just as exact, are nearly as acceptable as ordinary presents (Webley and Wilson, 1989). It would be absurd if A and B both gave each other money, though they may give each other presents of the same value – this shows that the extra, non-economic meaning is important.

If gifts are primarily signals for affection or regard, since these are things which are not for sale, money is an unsatisfactory way of sending the message.

9 Do gifts strengthen relationships?

A common kind of explanation of social systems in sociology from Durkheim onwards is that they have the function of integrating society, of strengthening relationships. The Kula in the Trobriand Islands, for example, is believed by anthropologists to sustain peaceful relations between the islands, so that commodity exchanges can be made. Cheal (1988) went further and suggested that presents strengthen weak relationships, and that the three main gift-exchanging relationships particularly need this support – between spouses, parents and children, and between other kin. However, there is no evidence that these are particularly weak relationships. It could be argued that kin relations last a lot longer than friendships, for example, so that it is rather friendships which need strengthening. There is a lot of tension at work between colleagues and with work superiors, so that it is these who should be given presents. Inside the family there is most tension with in-laws, so that on this theory they need the most presents. However, presents may be used to strengthen particular relationships.

An alternative explanation of why the three relationships mentioned have the most presents is in terms of sociobiology, which would predict that gifts would go to those sharing the most genes – children and siblings, followed by other kin, while spouses would also get them because they are instrumental in producing and rearing children. Children receive much more than their parents, since they still need nurturance. However, Caplow (1982) found that sons- and daughters-in-law received as many presents as sons and daughters, and that wives gave as much to their husband's relatives as to their own, despite the lack of shared genes. An explanation might be to say that rules of fairness have been added to avoid conflicts within the family.

Another explanation of the distribution of presents is that we give presents to those we like best, for example, spouses. Such liking may be based on genetic links, on early shared family experience producing attachment, or on rewarding experiences in later life. Receiving a present is interpreted as a sign of affection, and sometimes surely it is. However, friends, whom we usually like very much, receive small or token presents or none. Close kin receive presents regardless of how far away they live, so that those who would be seen rarely and provide few rewards, still get their presents (Caplow, 1984), all of which supports the sociobiological explanation. On the other hand, we have seen that present-giving is governed by strict rules, which to a large extent over-ride real feelings, and also modify the effects of shared genes. So strict are these rules that present-giving inside the family is far from voluntary – presents have to appear as spontaneous expressions of love, but they may not be.

10 Is there conspicuous consumption in present-giving?

The potlatch of the Kwakiutl Indians on Vancouver Island has continued to fascinate anthropologists. The giving away and destruction of property, in the course of complex rituals in the potlatch, is done to seek social status, in a highly competitive way. As Heath (1976) points out, this is fairly irrelevant to our society since status is based on occupation and achievements rather than giving things away. Heath found that those who gave bigger presents than they received did not feel superior, but embarrassed or annoyed. On the other hand, there is an element of the potlatch about weddings, which are extremely expensive, perhaps competitive, and very wasteful, since the couple could make better use of the money to set up house.

THE GIFT ECONOMY

The gift economy has a number of interesting and distinctive features, which make it quite different from the market economy, and also quite different from giving money away to charity.

Most people, in all but the very simplest cultures, give presents, costing them typically 4–5 per cent of their budgets. More presents are given by women than men, and most presents are given to close kin, together with smaller ones to friends. In Western culture, most presents are given at Christmas, birthdays and weddings. There is much reciprocity between equals, but none between parents and children or others in close and nurturant relationships. Gifts are governed by a complex system of rules, which are generally followed; however, there is no evidence that this system has the function of strengthening weak relationships; the rules of the gift economy can better be interpreted in terms of genetic closeness. On the other hand, gifts do function as non-verbal signals, for affection, and carry many other meanings as well.

Anthropological models do not fit the gift economy in modern societies, though expensive weddings have some similarity to a potlatch. The modern gift economy does not seem to have any equivalent of the Kula, where the shells are 'inalienable' possessions of the giver; where there is money and property, gifts soon become separated from their donors, even though they may act as reminders of them.

For economics, the gift economy is different from the market economy in that money is normally not used for gifts, and is often thought unsuitable, partly because of its poor symbolic power; in addition, there is no reciprocity in some relationships. Where there is reciprocity, there is some pretence that no return is expected, and certainly no bargaining. For psychology, the gift economy is a case of a rule system, whose functions are not yet clear, but which is probably based on sociobiology, while the gifts themselves function in a very similar way to other non-verbal signals.

INHERITANCE

The largest 'gifts' are given in wills, and mainly to close members of the family. When families own land, or businesses, this is an important part of this social process. Most people who own farms have inherited them, and, as we see later, most of the very rich in Britain have inherited a lot of money. Nowadays the main kind of property that most people inherit is houses; in traditional society they also inherited ritual offices, and some in our own society inherit titles and seats in the House of Lords.

During feudalism, those with land usually passed it on to their eldest son, 'primogeniture'. In feudal times women did not inherit, and much the same is true of many farming families today – because sons will put in more years of devoted labour on the farm than either daughters or possible sons-in-law. When land or farms are inherited, the oldest son is often given the greater part, since subdividing the property would produce plots too small to support a family. In Ireland, about a third of farming families still do this, especially those with farms of intermediate size; this can be seen as an exchange, where the eldest son works for many years at a low rate of pay, knowing that he will eventually inherit. This will be the result of negotiation and understanding over a long period. There is further exchange in that the elderly parents, no longer able to work effectively, are looked after by these sons, very few living alone (Kennedy, 1991). The other sons may have worked for years on the farm too, more or less unpaid, and will end up poorer and of lower status than the eldest son. However, in France, and to a lesser extent in England, there was a kind of joint inheritance, making a 'stem' family; although one son took over the father's land, the sons continued to live near each other, with a strong sense of solidarity and mutual obligation. In France, the Civil Code of 1804 required equal inheritance between children. Since this would make farms uneconomically small, in practice one son ran the farm and money was spent educating the rest for other careers. Another motive behind the Civil Code was to prevent the aristocracy emerging again (Casey, 1989). In America, in the early 1800s, primogeniture was practised in some of the southern states, but not in the north, with the result that estates became too small and children had to move west (Matthaei, 1982).

Most people today do not own land in Britain, but many own houses, and this is the main property to be passed on. Munro (1988) found in Glasgow that overall 56 per cent of families owned the house they lived in; after a parent's death it was passed on to the spouse and then to the children, but that 72 per cent of the 'children' were already owner-occupiers. Since people are now living longer this inheritance of houses is coming later in life, when the recipients are middle-aged or even older.

Inheritance is mainly within the family, first to a surviving spouse, then to children; very little is left to grandchildren, or to others outside the family. Wives leave less to husbands than vice versa: Judge and Hardy (1992) found that in California 42.4 per cent of wives left their property to their husbands and 69.8 per cent of husbands left it to their wives; probably wives feel that men have greater earning power. Young wives, and those with children from another marriage, are left less. Children are usually treated equally now, and there is a lot of conflict between them if they are not.

Different kinds of property are passed on to males and females. While male descendants are given land and businesses, women may get money and valuables. Widows are likely to get building-society funds as well as houses (Delphy and Leonard, 1992). A study of inheritance in France found that families passed on not only family businesses, but all the goodwill and social relationships which went with them. This made it possible to pass on the family's social status to their children (Bertaux and Bertaux-Wiame, 1988).

Some of these findings suggest a sociobiological interpretation, that is, individuals pass on their property to those who share most genes, who will be their children or sibs. But it is found that adopted children are treated the same as biological ones for inheritance purposes (Judge and Hardy, 1992) (they can't inherit titles in aristocratic families). These systems of inheritance are partly due to the need to solve social problems, such as keeping farms big enough to support a family, and preventing the reappearance of the French aristocracy. There are also some empirical regularities about the emergence of different systems; for example, 'patri-lineal' inheritance, that is, through the male line, is more common under certain conditions, such as sons and their families living near the sons' fathers (Murdoch, 1949), while a market economy and access to jobs and property leads to the decline of these single-sex descent groups in primitive societies (Blood, 1995).

There are two other major kinds of transfer of property within families. In primitive societies there is a 'bride price' paid to the wife's family when she marries, and in the Middle Ages 'dowries' were paid to the bride by her family (Casey, 1989). Another important kind of transfer is to the wife if there is divorce. These transfers will be discussed later. The family is believed by sociologists to have several functions – sexual, reproductive, economic and educational. It may have lost some of these functions, but it is still important as a unit of consumption, though less so as a unit of production, and it is important as a source of social support and socialisation of the young (Fletcher, 1966).

CONCLUSION

How far does the family operate like a rational market economy? It did so more in earlier times, for example, when women and children were expected to work in the fields or in the family workshop. It is less like that today. Members do not pay each other, or negotiate bargains. When money or other possessions enter the family they are to a large extent jointly owned, though some have more control over them than others.

This may be because kinship relations are communal not exchange relations, and members give others what they need rather than what they have earned (Clark and Reis, 1988). Pocket money works like this, as does helping kin in times of hardship or other crisis. It is women who operate most clearly in this way; they look after children, and keep the kinship network intact.

Any rational economic system here is upset by ideologies, which create social systems, for example, the belief that women should do the housework and men should earn money from outside. Money may be earmarked, some of it can only be spent by the wife because she earned it, or must be spent on food. It may be felt necessary to live close to kin, or to look after grandparents.

There are biological factors here, in the bonding between marital partners and in the attachment to and care of children. The latter are the recipients of large gifts, unearned pocket money, free board and lodging, and eventually inheritance.

There are some exchanges, however. The main earners in the family have more power to do what they want and to influence decisions; this applies to children as well as to spouses. Those who earn more do less housework too. Elderly parents often do what they can in return for any help, such as baby-sitting. This goes against doctrines that exchanges are made with the same kind of rewards (Foa *et al.*, 1993). There are some exchanges of similar goods. If one member of the family performs some service such as mending the roof, this is likely to be returned in kind, but not in money.

8 Money at work

O money, money, how blindly thou hast been worshipped, and how stupidly abused! Thou art health and liberty, and strength; and he that has thee may rattle his pockets at the foul fiend.

Charles Lamb

Nothing links man to man like the frequent passage from hand to hand of cash.

Walter Richard Sickert

Where money talks, there are few interruptions.

Herbert V. Prochnow

Money is good for bribing yourself through the inconveniences of life.

Gottfried Reinhardt

Each dollar is a soldier that does your bidding.

Vincent Astor

It happens a little unluckily that the persons who have had the most infinite contempt of money are the same that have the strongest appetite for the pleasures it procures.

William Shenstone

Money is a good servant but a bad master.

H. G. Bohn

When a fellow says, 'It ain't the money, but the principle of the thing', it's the money.

Elbert Hubbard

Money is certainly too dangerous an instrument to leave to the fortuitous expediency of politicians.

Prof. Friedrich Hayek

Making money doesn't oblige people to forfeit their honour or their conscience.

Baron Guy de Rothschild

INTRODUCTION

It comes as a surprise to many people to be told, or find out for themselves, that most psychology textbooks that deal with work (occupational, organisational, industrial psychology) are unlikely to refer to money at all. It is rare for the term 'money' to be in the appendix of any psychology book. Money, *per se*, is usually seen as one of many rewards for work done, and in itself not particularly important. But to the lay person, particularly the supervisor, who finds it difficult to motivate his/her staff to work harder, it is a crucial and powerful motivational tool: the ultimate carrot.

Furnham (1996a) has commented on the power of money as a motivator. Psychologists cite support for their relative disregard of norms from surveys in which workers were asked which factors were most important in making a job good or bad; 'pay' commonly came sixth or seventh after such factors as 'security', 'co-workers', 'interesting work', 'welfare arrangements'. This has been confirmed in more recent surveys, which have found that pensions and other benefits are valued more than salary alone. Money is important, but not that important relative to other factors. However, these results may be misleading, since people may not have accurate insight into their motivations, or may want to give socially desirable answers. Furthermore, not all these surveys are done on representative populations and it may be that because of their other benefits and sheer size of salary, senior managers underestimate the motivational power of money for poorer people with fewer perks.

The basic psychology of incentives is that behaviour can be influenced if it is linked to some desired reward. Speed of work is an example. There is little doubt that people work harder when paid by results than when paid by the time they put in.

Other studies have shown the effects of an incentive plan for reducing absenteeism, which fell immediately as soon as the plan was introduced, and rose again when it was discontinued. There is also evidence that money can act as an incentive for people to stay with their organisation: 'golden handcuffs' as they have been called.

If, indeed, money *is* a powerful motivator or satisfier at work, why has research consistently shown that there is no relationship between wealth and happiness? In fact, this will be taken up in Chapter 11.

REWARD SYSTEMS

Every job has an inducement/incentive and, one hopes, an agreement between inputs (amount of work) and outputs (e.g. pay). This wage–work bargain is in fact both a legal and a psychological contract which is often very poorly defined (Behrend, 1988).

Organisations determine pay by various methods, including historical precedents, wage surveys, and job evaluations (using points). They have to bench-mark themselves against the competition so as to meet or exceed the market rate (Miner, 1993). Certainly, it is believed that monetary rewards are better at improving performance than such things as goal-setting (management by objectives) or job-enrichment strategies.

Nearly everyone is paid – in money – for work. But organisations differ widely in how money is related to performance. The question of central interest to the organisational psychologist is the power of money as a motivator, which works in several ways:

1 *Piece work.* Here workers are paid according to how much they produce. It can only be judged when workers are doing fairly repetitive work where the units of work can be counted.
2 *Group piece work.* Here the work of a whole group is used as the basis for pay, which is divided between them.
3 *Monthly productivity bonus.* Here there is a guaranteed weekly wage, plus a bonus based on the output of the whole department.
4 *Measured day work.* This is similar except that the bonus depends on meeting some agreed rate or standard of work.
5 *Merit ratings.* For managers, clerical workers and others it is not possible to measure the units of work done. Instead their bonus or increments are based on merit ratings made by other managers.
6 *Monthly productivity bonus.* Managers receive a bonus based on the productivity of their departments.
7 *Profit-sharing and co-partnership.* There is a guaranteed weekly wage, and an annual or twice-yearly bonus for all, based on the firm's profits.
8 *Other kinds of bonus.* There can be a bonus for suggestions which are made and used, and there can be competitions for making the most sales, finding the most new customers, not being absent, etc.
9 *Use of other benefits.* Employees can be offered other rewards, such as medical insurance or care of dependents.

The money – whether in cash or deposited electronically in a bank account – that employees receive in exchange for working in an organisation is tied up with many other fringe benefits (insurance, sick leave, holiday, pensions), and they are difficult to separate. If money/pay itself satisfies a variety of important and fundamental needs of employees, it should be/is a good motivator to the extent that good job performance is necessary to obtain it. If employees' needs are complex and not clearly related to income, or if the quality or quantity of work performance are not directly related to reward, it serves as a much weaker motivator.

A topic of considerable interest is the whole issue of *performance-related pay*: the idea of linking pay with performance. Piece work and related methods are used most for skilled manual work. There have been many studies of rates of work when there is payment by results. For example, a British study of six factories where payment by results had been introduced but no other changes found an increase in output of 60 per cent and of earnings of 20 per cent (Davison *et al.,* 1958). A meta-analysis of 330 American intervention programmes found that introducing financial incentives had the greatest effect, of up to 2.12 times the standard deviation (Guzzo *et al.,* 1985, see Table 8.1).

However, these findings may be exaggerations, since when an incentive scheme is introduced there are usually other changes as well, such as improved methods of working or of delivery of supplies. When incentives are based on the performance of groups, as in the American Scanlon plan, this has the effect of improving co-operation, but the effect of such wage incentives is less in larger groups (Marriott, 1968). Where it is difficult or undesirable to measure an individual's contributions, it is possible to have group wage-incentive plans. While between one-fifth and a quarter of industries have wage-incentive plans, many studies suggest they increase productivity by anything from a third to a half more than before/without the plan.

Wage incentives can also reduce absenteeism, when a bonus is given for regular attendance. These schemes work better if there is participation over their introduction (Steers and Rhodes, 1984), and simply increasing the rate of pay can have dramatic effects in reducing labour turnover, in one case from 370 per cent to 16 per cent (Scott *et al.,* 1960). Use can be made of non-pay incentives, such as more free time or recognition, but financial incentives have the most effect (Guzzo *et al.,* 1985).

Problems with these plans arise where particular workers have differential opportunities to produce a higher level – that is, some workers may be unfairly disadvantaged under such a system. Further wage incentives that reward individual productivity can, and often do, decrease co-operation among workers. Rewarding team productivity is an obvious solution but, of necessity, as the size of the team increases, so does the clear relationship

Table 8.1 The average effect on output of various organisational interventions expressed as standard deviation units as found in a meta-analysis

Intervention	Standard deviation units
Financial compensation	2.12
Training	.85
Decision-making strategies	.7
Socio-technical changes	.66
Goal-setting	.65
Work redesign	.52
Supervisory methods	.51
Management by objectives	.45
Appraisal and feedback	.41
Work rescheduling	.3

Source: Guzzo *et al.* 1985

between any individual's productivity and his/her pay increases. As Johns (1991) notes, without wage-incentive schemes the productivity in any organisation tends to be 'normally distributed' in a bell-shaped curve, but the introduction of a system sometimes leads to a restriction of production when workers come to an informal agreement about the norms of production. That is, there is often a restriction of range. This may be because workers fear increased productivity will lead to lay-offs, and/or that rate of payment will be reduced to cut labour costs. Obviously, the restriction of range is in part a function of the history and climate of trust in any organisation.

With the current emphasis on teamworking (Furnham, 1996a) group-level incentive plans have been popular. Profit-sharing is a good example. It is assumed that the synergistic benefits of greater co-operation (one hopes, leading to greater productivity) can offset the theoretical benefits of paying for individual performance. Gain-sharing plans is a system where bonuses are based on the measurable cost reductions (in labour, materials, supplies) that are under the control of the workforce. These plans involve all members of the work unit, even support staff and managers.

Trade unions the world over oppose individual incentive plans, arguing that it promotes unhealthy competition, increases accidents and fatigue, and disadvantages older or less well workers. Some even oppose group-incentive schemes because they argue that they ultimately lead to a reduction in the quality of working life.

For managerial jobs and support staff merit-pay plans can be based on appraisals done by the managers, supervisors, peers, subordinates and customers (Furnham and Stringfield, 1994). Wage incentives are often applied to sales, and over 85 per cent of firms use it for some of their staff. It is even used for professors. Managers may have a bonus based on the performance of their section. But, for many employees, productivity is more difficult to measure, so incentives are based on appraisals and merit ratings. The great advantage of these schemes is that they are very flexible and many aspects of work performance can be rewarded, including stress tolerance, delegation, initiative, oral expression or anything else. As Johns (1991) notes, overall, the evidence suggests that managers like these systems and that there is a clear, measurable reward between performance and (monetary) reward. Yet problems with introducing fair systems and ensuring that raters of performance are both fair and differentiating means many organisations severely curtail the amount of merit pay. Hence seniority and job level account for much more variance in performance pay than actual job performance.

The major problems with performance-related pay systems are, first, the fact that ratings of performance tend to drift to the centre. Feeling unable to deal with conflict or anxiety between people in a team, managers over-rate under-performers and under-rate better performers, so undermining the fundamental principles of the system. Next, as has been pointed out, merit increases are too small to be effective. Paradoxically, in difficult economic times, when higher motivation and effort are required, the size of merit pay awards tends to be slashed.

The secrecy that surrounds merit pay means many employees have no way of comparing their salary with others so seeing the benefits (or not) of an equitably administered system. If working well, an open system that shows the amount of merit pay separate from other increases (i.e. cost-of-living) is most effective. This is partly due to the fact that many managers overestimate the pay of their peers and subordinates, and underestimate the pay of their superiors. These tendencies reduce satisfaction with pay and the perceived link between performance and rewards.

The aims of such systems are straightforward: good performers should be pleased with, satisfied by, and motivated to continue to work hard because they see the connection between job performance and (merit-pay) reward. Equally, poor performers should be motivated to 'try harder' to achieve some reward.

There are different types of PRP (Performance-related pay) systems, depending on who is included (to what levels); how performance will be measured (objective counts, subjective ratings or a combination) and which incentives will be used (money, shares, etc.). For some organisations the experiment with PRP has not been a success. Sold as a panacea for multiple ills it has sometimes backfired to leave a previously dissatisfied staff even more embittered and alienated. There are various reasons for the failure of PRP systems.

First, there is frequently a poorly perceived connection between pay and performance. Many employees have inflated ideas about their performance levels which translate into unrealistic expectations about rewards. When thwarted, employees complain, and it is they who want the system thrown out. Often the percentage of performance-based pay is too low, relative to base pay. That is, if a cautious organisation starts off with too little money in the pot, it may be impossible to discriminate between good and poor performance, so threatening the credibility of the whole system.

The most common problem lies in the fact that, for many jobs, the lack of objective, relevant, countable results requires heavy, often exclusive use of performance ratings. These are very susceptible to systematic bias – leniency, halo, etc. – which render them neither reliable nor valid.

Another major cause of failure is resistance from managers and unions. The former, on whom the system depends, may resist these changes because they are forced to be explicit, to confront poor performance, and tangibly to reward the behaviourally more successful. Unions always resist equity- rather than equality-based systems because the latter render the notion of collective bargaining redundant.

Further, many PRP plans have failed because the performance measure(s) which are rewarded were not related to the aggregated performance objectives of the organisation as a whole, that is, to those aspects of the performance which were most important to the organisation. Also, the organisation must ensure that workers are capable of improving their performance. If higher pay is to drive higher performance, workers must believe in (and be capable of) performance improvements. But PRP plans can work very well indeed, providing various steps are taken. First, a bonus system should be used in which merit (PRP) pay is not tied to a percentage of base salary but is an allocation from the corporate coffers. Next, the band should be made wide while keeping the amount involved the same: say 0–20 per cent for lower-paid employees and 0–40 per cent for higher levels. Performance appraisal must be taken seriously by making management raters accountable for their appraisals; they need training, including how to rate behaviour (accurately and fairly) at work.

Information systems and job designs must be compatible with the performance-measurement system. More importantly, if the organisation takes teamwork seriously, group and section performance must be included in the evaluation. It is possible and preferable to base part of an individual's merit pay on team evaluation. Finally, special awards to recognise major individual accomplishments need to be considered separately from an annual merit allocation.

In short, Miner (1993) has argued that five conditions need to be met to ensure that any sort of incentive plan works.

1 The employee must value the extra money they will make under the plan.
2 The employee must not lose important values (health, job security, and the like) as a result of high performance.
3 The employee must be able to control their own performance so that they have a chance to strive further.
4 The employee must clearly understand how the plan works.
5 It must be possible to measure performance accurately (using indexes of performance, cost effectiveness, or ratings).

Similarly, Lawler (1981) has provided an excellent summary of the consequences of merit-pay systems (see Table 8.2).

For many workers, job security is regarded as more important than level of wages, and this is particularly true of unskilled, lower-paid workers, and those with a family history of unskilled work. Having a secure job is not only important for the family, it is also a status symbol. Worry about job insecurity has increased in the 1990s as the result of many jobs being taken over by computers. This is a major problem with the contemporary work scene; the big companies in Japan have succeeded in offering job security to their staff, but the losses are then taken by the subsidiary firms. And wage incentives affect whether or not people will work at all; in the past this was a choice between work and a life of leisure for some, today it is choice between work and social security.

However, there are definite limitations to the effects of money on work.

Table 8.2 Effectiveness of merit-pay and bonus-incentive systems in achieving various desired effects

Type of compensation plan	Performance measure used	Desired effects			
		Tying pay to performance	Minimising negative side effects	Encouraging co-operation	Gaining acceptance
Merit-pay Systems					
For individuals	Productivity	Good	Very good	Very poor	Good
	Cost-effectiveness	Fair	Very good	Very poor	Good
	Ratings by superiors	Fair	Very good	Very poor	Fair
For groups	Productivity	Fair	Very good	Poor	Good
	Cost-effectiveness	Fair	Very good	Poor	Good
	Ratings by superiors	Poor	Very good	Poor	Fair
For organisation as a whole	Productivity	Poor	Very good	Fair	Good
	Cost-effectiveness	Poor	Very good	Poor	Good
Bonus Systems					
For individuals	Productivity	Very good	Fair	Very poor	Poor
	Cost-effectiveness	Good	Good	Very poor	Poor
	Ratings by superiors	Good	Good	Very poor	Poor
For groups	Productivity	Good	Very good	Fair	Fair
	Cost-effectiveness	Fair	Very good	Fair	Fair
	Ratings by superiors	Fair	Very good	Fair	Fair
For organisation as a whole	Productivity	Fair	Very good	Fair	Good
	Cost-effectiveness	Fair	Very good	Fair	Fair
	Profit	Poor	Very good	Fair	Fair

Source: adapted from Lawler (1981, p. 94)

Some people are less interested in earning more money; it depends on how much their friends and neighbours earn, how large their family is, whether they are trying to buy a house or a car. On the other hand, they may raise their level of financial aspiration, and want a bigger house or car, or they may find new things to buy, or they may regard money as an index of success.

A FAIR DAY'S WAGE: EQUITY AND RELATIVE DEPRIVATION

There is substantial evidence that, beyond a reasonable level, the absolute amount of pay is not as important as the comparative amount. In any society salary is an index of status and prestige, and there is an obvious disparity in this relationship. Pay is a form of social approval. Low pay indicates low skills and less important work to most people. Strikes for more money are as much about desire for respect as they are about salaries (Lindgren, 1991). As in divorce courts, money becomes a symbolic compensation for hurt feelings. Equally, pay differentials are imbued with many psychological and economic factors (Anikeeff, 1957).

There are anomalies that may be in part explained by the concept of psychic income or, more prosaically, intrinsic motivation. Thus the clergy, artists, novelists, social workers and academics receive poor pay but it is generally accepted that low pay with high psychic income exceeds the value of high pay with low/no psychic income. Hence, often the over-supply of applicants for poorly paid but intrinsically satisfying jobs like acting. Of course, jobs that are rich in both intrinsic and extrinsic rewards are the most satisfying.

Equity theory, borrowed by psychologists from economics, views motivation from the perspective of the social comparisons that people make among themselves. It proposes that employees are motivated to maintain fair, or 'equitable', relationships among themselves and to change those relationships that are unfair, or 'inequitable'. Equity theory is concerned with people's motivation to escape the negative feelings that result from being treated unfairly in their jobs once they have engaged in the process of *social comparison.*

Equity theory suggests that people make social comparisons between themselves and others with respect to two variables – *outcomes* (benefits, rewards) and *inputs* (effort, ability). Outcomes refer to the things that workers believe they and others get out of their jobs, including pay, fringe benefits or prestige. Inputs refer to the contributions that employees believe they and others make to their jobs, including the amount of time worked, the amount of effort expended, the number of units produced, or the qualifications brought to the job. Equity theory is concerned with outcomes and inputs as they are *perceived* by the people involved, *not* necessarily as they actually are, although that in itself is often very difficult to measure.

Not surprisingly, therefore, workers may disagree about what constitutes equity and inequity on the job. Equity is therefore a subjective, not an objective, experience, which makes it more susceptible to being influenced by personal factors.

Equity theory states that people compare their outcomes and inputs to those of others in the form of a ratio. Specifically, they compare the ratio of their own outcomes/inputs to the ratio of other people's outcomes/inputs, which can result in any of three states: *overpayment*, *underpayment* or *equitable payment*.

- Overpayment inequity occurs when an individual's outcome/input ratio is *greater than* the corresponding ratio of another person with whom that individual compares himself/herself. People whom are overpaid are supposed to feel *guilty*. There are few people in this position.
- Underpayment inequity occurs when an individual's outcome/input ration is *less than* the corresponding ratio of another person with whom that individual compares himself/herself. People who are underpaid are supposed to feel *angry*. Many people feel under-benefited.
- Equitable payment occurs when an individual's outcome/input ratio is *equal* to the corresponding ratio of another person with whom that individual compares himself/herself. People who are equitably paid are supposed to feel *satisfied*.

According to equity theory, people are motivated to escape the negative emotional states of anger and guilt. Equity theory admits two major ways of resolving inequitable states. *Behavioural* reactions to equity represent things that people can do to change their existing inputs and outcomes such as working more or less hard (to increase or decrease inputs), or stealing time and goods (to increase outputs). In addition to behavioural reactions to underpayment inequity, there are also some likely *psychological* reactions. Given that many people feel uncomfortable stealing from their employers (to increase outputs), or would be unwilling to restrict their productivity or to ask for a salary increase (to increase inputs), they may resort to resolving the inequity by changing the way that they think about their situation. Because equity theory deals with perceptions of fairness or unfairness, it is reasonable to expect that inequitable states may be redressed effectively by merely *thinking* about their circumstances differently. For example, an underpaid person may attempt to *rationalise* the fact that another's inputs are really higher than his/her own, thereby convincing himself/herself that the other's higher outcomes are justified.

There are a number of different reactions to inequity. People can respond to overpayment (i.e. being over-benefited) and underpayment (i.e. being under-benefited) inequities in behavioural and/or psychological ways, which help change the perceived *inequities* into a state of perceived *equity*. Table 8.3 shows the two 'classic' reactions to inequity.

Table 8.3 Reactions to inequity

	Type of reaction	
Type of inequity	*Behavioural*	*Psychological*
Overpayment inequity (guilt): 1 < 0	Increase your inputs (work harder), or lower your outcomes (work through a paid vacation, take no salary)	Convince yourself that your outcomes are deserved based on your inputs (rationalise that you work harder, better, smarter than equivalent others, and so you deserve more pay)
Underpayment inequity (anger): 1 > 0	Lower your inputs (reduce effort), or raise your outcomes (get pay increase, steal time by absenteeism)	Convince yourself that others' inputs are really higher than your own (rationalise that the comparison worker is really more qualified or a better worker and so deserves higher outcomes)

How people will react to inequity depends on how they are paid. If they are paid by the time they are there they can reduce the rate of work, but if they are on piece work they may reduce the quality of work. Similarly, a salaried employee who feels overpaid may raise his/her inputs by working harder, or for longer hours or more productively. Similarly, employees who lower their own outcomes by not taking advantage of company-provided fringe benefits may be seen as redressing an overpayment inequity. Overpaid persons (few though they are!) may readily convince themselves psychologically that they are really worth their higher outcomes by virtue of their superior inputs. People who receive substantial pay raises may not feel distressed about it at all because they rationalise that the increase is warranted on the basis of their superior inputs, and therefore it does not constitute an inequity.

Research has generally supported the theory's claim that people will respond to overpayment and underpayment inequities in the ways just described. For instance, Pritchard *et al.* (1972) hired male clerical workers to work part-time over a two-week period and manipulated the equity or inequity of the payment that the employees received. *Overpaid* employees were told that their pay was higher than that of others doing the same work. *Underpaid* employees were told that their pay was lower than that of others doing the same work. *Equitably paid* employees were told that their pay was equal to that of others who were doing the same work. People who were overpaid were more productive than those who were equitably paid; and people who were underpaid were less productive than those who were equitably paid. Moreover, both overpaid and underpaid employees reported being more dissatisfied with their jobs than those who were equitably paid.

However, these experiments are all in the short term, and it is doubtful how far the effects would persist over time, partly because the workers who are overpaid come to see themselves as worth more and those who are underpaid as worth less (Kanfer, 1990). Nevertheless, real-life perceptions of inequity do affect behaviour. Summers and Hendrix (1991) found in a study of 365 managers that received pay inequity did not affect job performance but did affect labour turnover. And in an American study by Berkowitz *et al.* (1987) it was found that the strongest predictor of pay satisfaction was current inequity ($-.49$). Equity theory says that people seek fair distribution of rewards in relation to 'inputs', which can include amount of work done, ability, etc., and will be discontented and leave the situation if this cannot be achieved, or they may try to increase equity in other ways such as by more absenteeism or stealing from their employers. What is seen as equitable depends to a large extent on comparisons. Brown (1978) found that industrial workers would choose a lower salary, if it meant that they would receive more than a rival group.

An ingenious method of tackling the effects of inequity was devised by Clark and Oswald (1993). They calculated the 'comparison incomes' of 10,000 British workers, that is, the average incomes of those with the same jobs, education, age, etc. They found that while income had little effect on job satisfaction, comparison income had a clear effect – the lower it was the higher was job satisfaction ($-.25$ to $-.30$). In other words, with income held constant the less people expect, the greater their job satisfaction. An American study with 4,567 employees found the same, and it was also found that pay satisfaction was greater if there were procedures for ensuring fair incomes (Leicht and Shepelak, 1994).

Women are paid less than men, and have often been found to be contented with lower earnings, because they compared their pay with that of other women, and felt entitled to less than men (Jackson, 1989). However, when women do exactly the same work as men they start to compare their wages with those of men, and are no longer contented with lower wages (Loscocco and Spitze, 1991). Phelan (1994) studied a sample of managers and professionals and found that women were as satisfied as men, although they had lower pay. Several explanations were tested, and it was found that pay was not a predictor of satisfaction at all, after the intrinsic rewards and the importance of jobs had been taken into account.

As one might expect, equity theory has its problems: how to deal with the concept of negative inputs; the point at which equity becomes inequity; the belief that people prefer and value equity over equality. Nevertheless, the theory has stimulated an enormous literature, which partially addresses itself to the issue of motivation and money's role in it.

INTRINSIC AND EXTRINSIC MOTIVATION

Some jobs and some tasks are intrinsically satisfying. That is, by their very nature they are interesting and pleasant to do. They can be enjoyable for a wide variety of reasons and much depends on the preference, predilections and propensities of individuals.

Intrinsic satisfaction implies that merely doing the job is, in itself, its own reward. Therefore, for such activities no reward and no management should be required. But the naive manager might unwillingly destroy this ideal state of affairs.

Take the case of the academic writer scribbling at home on a research report. The local children had for three days played extremely noisily in a small park near his study and, like all noise of this sort, it was highly stressful because it was simultaneously loud, uncontrollable and unpredictable. What should be done? (1) Ask them (politely) to quieten down or go away? (2) Call the police or the parents if you know them? (3) Threaten them with force if they do not comply? (4) All of the above in that order?

The wise don did none of the above. Unworldly maybe, but, as someone whose job depended on intrinsic motivation, the academic applied another principle. He went to the children on the fourth morning and said, somewhat insincerely, that he had very much enjoyed their being there for the sound of their laughter, and the thrill of their games. In fact, he was so delighted with them that he was prepared to pay them to continue. He promised to pay them each £1 a day if they carried on as before.

The youngsters were naturally surprised but delighted. For two days the don, seemingly grateful, dispensed the cash. But on the third day he explained that because of a 'cash flow' problem he could only give them 50p each. The next day he claimed to be 'cash light' and only handed out 10p. True to prediction the children would have none of this, complained and refused to continue. They all left in a huff promising never to return to play in the park. Totally successful in his endeavour, the don retired to his study, luxuriating in the silence.

This anecdote illustrates a problem for the manager. If a person is happy doing a task, for whatever reason, but is also 'managed' through explicit rewards (usually money), the individual will tend to focus on these rewards, which then inevitably have to be escalated to maintain satisfaction. This is therefore a paradox: reward an intrinsically motivated person by extrinsic rewards and he/she is likely to become less motivated because the nature of the motivation changes. Unless a manager can keep up the increasing demands on the extrinsic motivator (i.e. constant salary increases) the person usually begins to show less enthusiasm for the job.

The use of reinforcers – i.e. paying people – is counter-productive when the task is intrinsically interesting. That is, intrinsic motivation decreases with extrinsic rewards. Deci and Ryan (1985) demonstrated, however, that reinforcement of progressively improved performance produced no loss (nor gain) of intrinsic interest. Eisenberger has argued that all jobs and tasks have a mix of intrinsically and extrinsically interesting features and levels of difficulty:

Even if a student finds that an academic subject is generally interesting, the acquisition of a good understanding of the subject matter requires the study of some topics found to be dull and repetitive and other topics that, although interesting, are discouragingly difficult to master. An increased secondary reward value of high effort may encourage selection of, and persistence on, difficult academic tasks. Reinforced high effort on dull, repetitive tasks can even be used to increase subsequent effort in intrinsically interesting tasks. For example, pre-adolescent children who had been rewarded for accuracy on a monotonous pronunciation task produced more accurate subsequent drawings and stories than did students who had been rewarded for simply completing the pronunciation task. These findings attest to the heuristic value of the secondary reward theory of generalized industriousness.

(1992, p. 263)

Some activities are rewarding because they satisfy curiosity, some because they produce an increased level of arousal. Deci (1980) proposed that intrinsic motivation is increased by the activity's giving a sense of mastery and competence, through the use of skills, and also by a sense of control and self-determination by exercising autonomy to choose how the work is done; both these factors have been found to increase motivation. In addition to the enjoyment of competence, leisure research shows that people often enjoy the sheer activity, for example, of dancing, music or swimming, though they enjoy these things more if they are good at them (Argyle, 1996). Hackman and Oldham (1980) proposed five job characteristics which should motivate work performance. These are skill variety, task variety, task significance, autonomy and knowledge of results. They also proposed that the effect of these job characteristics would be greater for individuals with more 'growth need strength', that is, for those who enjoy interesting and demanding work. This theory predicts job satisfaction successfully, but the findings on motivation have been more mixed.

Experiments with children showed that if they were given external rewards for doing things which they wanted to do anyway, intrinsic motivation decreased. However, later research with adult workers has found that pay or other extrinsic rewards can increase intrinsic motivation, for example, if the external rewards also give evidence of individual competence (Kanfer, 1990).

The Protestant work ethic (PWE), which we discussed in Chapter 5, is another source of intrinsic motivation. Those strong in the PWE enjoy work for its own sake, and in a number of experiments they have been found to work harder at laboratory tasks, and to improve their performance more after negative feedback; in work settings their absenteeism is lower and they are more committed to the organisation (Furnham, 1984). Workaholics can be seen as an extreme case of the PWE; they work very long hours, have almost no leisure, no holidays, and enjoy their work very much (Machlowitz, 1980). It is not only workaholics who enjoy their work for non-economic reasons. Those who have retired say that they miss the work and they miss their workmates (Parker, 1982).

Achievement motivation is important at work. The main application has been to managers, but also to scientists and other academics. A number of studies have found that individuals scoring high in n.Ach. (Need for Achievement) get promoted more, publish more papers, etc. It is most relevant to the promotion and success of entrepreneurs, managers in small firms, and those in sales (McClelland, 1987). It is managers and others with careers for whom promotion or other aspects of success seem very important. Managers are found to be preoccupied with success, and are very dissatisfied when they don't get it. Herzberg *et al.* (1959) found that experiences of recognition and achievement were the greatest sources of positive satisfaction for managers. A related approach to achievement at work is Csikszentmihalyi's concept of 'flow', a deep state of satisfaction which is obtained when there is a strong challenge which can be met with sufficient skills; he found that flow is experienced more at work than at leisure (Csikszentmihalyi and Csikszentmihalyi, 1988).

Organisational commitment is another source of work motivation, and is a major source of low labour turnover and absenteeism. It is greater for those who are satisfied with their pay (Cohen and Gattiker, 1994), and for those who have a financial interest in the firm, or who have 'investments' such as retirement and pension plans. However, there are also non-financial causes of commitment to the organisation, such as having spent a long time with the organisation, participation in decisions, and having had responsibility (Argyle, 1987).

ECONOMIC MOTIVATION TO WORK

There are those who work without pay. Voluntary work (e.g. that done for the old and the ill) makes it clear that money is not the only reason for working. There are also people who do not need to work, but still do so. Of those who win lotteries, 17 per cent stay in full time work afterwards (Smith and Razzell, 1975). Many people in good jobs now work longer hours than in the past, while average hours of work have declined. For some it is because they enjoy their work, as in the cases of scientists and other academics, but this is not the only reason. There are also a lot of people in full-time work who are already so rich that they do not need any more money, so presumably are working for some other reason.

Money-like incentives have been used with success in 'token' economies. Lately, the method has been used at work to discourage smoking or make people use safety equipment. Many experiments have found that token economies are successful in influencing behaviour; the only exceptions have been with stopping drug use, and in one study 9–11-year-old boys were more affected by the immediate reward of breakfast. It has been found that there are also effects on non-target behaviour, especially social interaction and well-being. There has been less success with bringing about permanent changes in behaviour however (Lea *et al.,* 1987).

Money plays an important part in occupational choice – most people prefer a job with a larger salary, but money is not the only factor. Many studies have been made of 'work values', that is what people seek and enjoy at work. In an early study Rosenberg (1957) found that students scoring high on extrinsic-reward orientation chose sales, hotel management, estate agency and finance. These were the ones who particularly valued money. On the other hand, students high on his people-oriented scale were more likely to choose social work, medicine, teaching or social science, while students scoring high on his self-expression scale were more likely to choose journalism, art or architecture. Mortimer and Lorence (1989) found three dimensions of work values: (1) challenge and autonomy, (2) dealing with people, and (3) high pay. They also found that over time experience of jobs reinforced these values. Individuals high in achievement motivation, at least in the USA, also want to make money, and are prepared to take risks, for example, as entrepreneurs and small businessmen, in order to do so (McClelland, 1987).

Later studies have factor analysed work values and produced tests for them like the Minnesota Importance Questionnaire (MIQ). The work-value factors assessed in these questionnaires are typically achievement, money, working with people, creativity, independence, prestige and interest. Follow-up studies have found that if people do jobs which match their work values they have greater job satisfaction ($r = .30$ to $.50$), but it has not yet been shown that values predict occupational choice (Davis, 1992).

Another approach is via 'job interests', such as in science, social welfare, aesthetic expression, clerical, business, outdoor work, physical drive, adventure versus security, and aesthetic appreciation. These too have been measured by tests like the Strong Vocational Interest Blank. Note that money does not appear among these interest factors. When jobs match interest scores, the prediction of occupational choice and how long individuals stay is better than for work values, but the prediction of job satisfaction is weaker (Davis, 1992).

The upshot of this work on job values and job interests is that money comes out as one job value among about seven value factors, and job values predict job satisfaction, but are less good at predicting occupational choice; this is better done from job interests, and money does not emerge as one of these.

Those who seek less highly paid jobs do so because these fit their values or their personality. For some this is definitely a matter of 'vocation', as with clergy, monks, some teachers, and some nurses. There may be no great sacrifice here, they are maximising satisfaction by choosing work they enjoy doing. If a person takes a job which is too demanding or too stressful, for example, he or she will become distressed, and may have to give it up. They may have to 'downsize' and find they enjoy a less well paid and less demanding job more. The second author knows a number of individuals who are much happier in their new, lower-powered job.

Women often seek different things in their work from men: they want to work with people and be helpful to others, and are concerned with self-expression and creativity; men often want jobs that pay well, are secure and have prestige, and are quite happy to work with things. As a result many women become secretaries, nurses, teachers, social workers, hairdressers and shop assistants, and most of these are less well paid than many men's jobs. We have seen that women expect to be paid less than men.

There are also class differences in what people seek from work. Working-class youths tend to seek money, while middle-class ones tend to seek challenge, autonomy, career prospects or service to others, and are prepared to start at a lower salary, and usually delay starting paid work. The value of autonomy, self-direction and challenge is derived from parents, who themselves have jobs with these properties (Kohn and Schooler, 1983). Parents also affect the occupational choices of their children more directly, as many children go into the same or similar occupations as their parents. Schools are also important, and in any given community there is a range of the occupations which are normally entered (Argyle, 1989).

CONCLUSION

Financial incentives are successful in making people work harder, when they are paid by results, and also affect job satisfaction, and money also affects absenteeism and labour turnover, but is a minor factor in occupational choice. The absolute effects of pay are less than comparisons with the wages of others, and there is discontent and strikes when employees feel that they are unfairly rewarded, greater job satisfaction when they are paid more than they expect. There are several kinds of intrinsic motivation to work, apart from money, and voluntary workers and others work unpaid. The effects of wage incentives depends on how much individual workers need money, which partly depend on comparisons with other people's life-styles.

9 Giving away money

*Thy money perish with thee, because thou hast thought that
the gift of God may be purchased with money.*

Acts VIII, 20, c. 75

*Money is of a prolific generating nature. Money can beget
money, and its offspring can beget more.*

Benjamin Franklin

Money is always there, but the pockets change.

Gertrude Stein

*Gentility is what is left over from rich ancestors after the
money has gone.*

John Ciardi

INTRODUCTION

This is one of the most interesting topics in the psychology of money. The
fact that people do give money away requires explanation, for both
economists and psychologists. For economists it presents a challenge to
the doctrine of the 'rational' economic man who seeks his own self-interest
and is 'insatiably greedy' (Lea *et al.*, 1987). It presents problems for
psychology too: theories of altruism which work for giving to family and
friends, such as reciprocity and empathy, which were dealt with in Chapter
7, do not work for giving to charity or to strangers. On the other hand,
charitable giving provides a more realistic setting for the psychological
study of altruism than the laboratory experiments involving unlikely
scenarios with electric shocks, often used to investigate this phenomenon.
And we shall see that there is extensive evidence from charity surveys as
well as field experiments about giving money away. In a final section we
will discuss the closely related phenomenon of tipping.

   From the earliest times, giving to the poor has been an important part of
life. In primitive societies, and in much of the Third World today, this is
seen as a responsibility of the family, and it is common to call on quite
distant relatives, such as second cousins, for help; the family is the basis of

social welfare. There was also an obligation to look after other members of the tribe. Gifts, often large ones in tribes which had a potlatch, were given, not for charity, but for social competition, to keep the peace, and to ward off evil (Mauss, 1954). However, the amounts given would vary greatly, and depend on the local cultural norms.

By the time of the ancient civilisations of Egypt, Greece and Rome, moral and religious ideas had become important, ideas of justice, self-denial and sacrifice, and rewards in heaven (Nightingale, 1973). The early Jews believed that those who could afford it should give a fifth of their income to the poor. Christians believed that the poor were blessed, tithing was often practised and was seen as the route to heavenly salvation. Indeed, all religions have attached great importance to charity: 'If thou wilt be perfect, go and sell that thou hast, and give to the poor, and thou shalt have treasure in heaven' (St Matthew's Gospel chap. 19). In the Middle Ages the monks were a major source of social welfare, by looking after the poor, and a lot of charity was channelled through the church. Meanwhile, quite a lot was done for the lower orders by their superiors on feudal estates.

With the growth of cities the problem of the poor became too much for these medieval arrangements, and there was gradual evolution of secular arrangements throughout Europe, such as the poor laws in Elizabethan times. But the poor rate was small, and really only worked in emergencies, so there was still need for charity, religious and secular. Charity in the seventeenth and eighteenth centuries was partly motivated by fear of trouble from the poor, by fear of a falling population, and to show the social status of the rich and keep the poor in their place.

During the early Industrial Revolution there was some ambivalence of attitudes to the poor, on the part of those hard-working individuals inspired by the Protestant work ethic, who believed that poverty was due to idleness. In the nineteenth century in Britain the country gentry enjoyed looking after the poor in their villages, though the Lady Bountiful image had begun to have a bad name. The middle classes enjoyed the poor less, but were active in setting up voluntary agencies, while the wives were active in voluntary work. Early socialists were against charity, since it delayed more fundamental reforms, which were indeed soon to come.

The welfare state emerged in the twentieth century, first in Britain, Australia and Scandinavia, and this removed much of the immediate need to give to the poor – those who had incomes already 'gave' a substantial amount of them in income tax, a lot more than the 10 per cent of tithing for most. But there are many who are still in need in one way or another, and many charities have grown up to meet these needs. They help those for whom the welfare state has failed, like the homeless, and the poor in other parts of the world, as well as many medical and other causes (Ross, 1968; Nightingale, 1973).

A further development has been in 'corporate giving' by firms and other organisations. It is not known how much this comes to, but a survey of 159 large firms in Britain in 1992–3 found that they gave a total of £149 million, and a survey of small firms suggests that they gave between £0.5 billion and £1 billion (Lee, 1989; Charities Aid Foundation, 1993). This is comparable with, though a little less than, the total from individual giving. Corporate giving involves administrative activities by managers, who may also become involved in the administration of charities themselves. In the USA, in particular, this can play an important part in the careers of businessmen (Ross, 1968). In addition, there may be regular contributions by employees by means of payroll deductions.

Fortunately, for our immediate purposes, there is extensive social survey material on individual charitable giving on which we can draw. There are also many experiments in social psychology about the conditions under which people can be persuaded to give away money. There are several competing kinds of explanation for why people do it. Economists have argued that there are economic advantages in giving money away. Sociologists have argued that it is all based on reciprocity between individuals in social relationships. Social psychologists have found that altruism is motivated by empathy, and also by various kinds of social motivation; giving money away puts donors in a good mood, so this is one sense in which it is better to give than to receive.

HOW MUCH MONEY IS GIVEN?

There have been two regular surveys of giving in Britain. The *Family Expenditure Survey* (FES) is done by the Government Social Survey, and interviews about 13,000 adults every year; they are also asked to keep a two-week diary of giving. There is extensive demographic data on the characteristics of the subjects. The *International Giving Survey* (Charities Aid Foundation, 1994) is carried out by the Charities Aid Foundation. It uses a smaller sample, of 1,020, and it is a quota sample, but it asks more detailed questions, 8 questions about each of 17 forms of giving over the past month. It includes forms of giving not covered by the FES, such as buying at charity gift shops, and as a result it finds that more people report some giving, and that the overall level of giving is a little higher (Lee *et al.*, 1995). There are data about American giving from a different source – income-tax returns, to the IRS (the Inland Revenue Service) and we shall make use of these later.

There is a very uneven distribution of giving, as Figure 9.1 shows, using IGS (International Giving Survey) data. According to the IGS surveys, in 1993, 81 per cent of British adults gave something to charity; according to the FES the figure was 73 per cent. The average given in 1993 was about £10 per month in both surveys, but with such a skewed distribution the median is a more informative figure; it was only £2.50 per month, i.e. half the population gave more and half gave less than this. The top 1 per cent of givers donated over £100 per month, which is one reason why the mean is

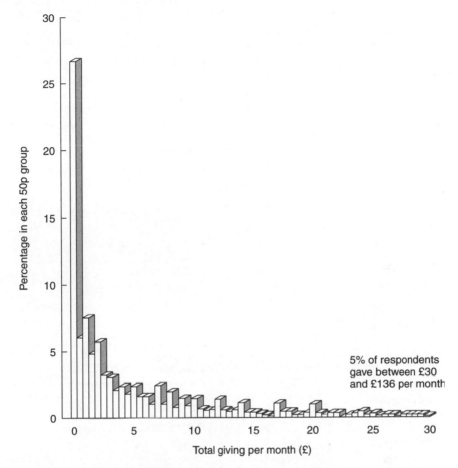

Figure 9.1 Distribution of total individual giving per month (all respondents)
Source: Charities Aid Foundation, (1991)

so much larger than the median; without them the mean comes down to £7.35 per month. These figures may be overestimates, since 42 per cent of them are due to purchases at charity shops, raffles, etc., which give some clear gain or hope for gain to the donor. This is shown in Figure 9.2 which gives the percentages of respondents who gave by each method, and Table 9.1 which shows how much they gave.

While these individual contributions may seem rather small, the total amounts given are of course very large, over £5 billion a year in Britain to the main charities (Charities Aid Foundation, 1994), large enough to make a number of important contributions. They give an average 1.4% of income; most people give a lot more than this to members of their families, about 4 per cent as we saw in Chapter 7, and have to give a lot via income tax, an average of 17 per cent of income being paid in income tax in Britain.

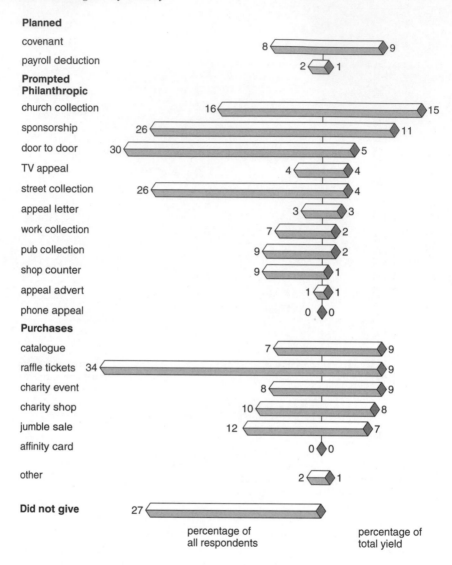

Planned

covenant

payroll deduction

Prompted Philanthropic

church collection

sponsorship

door to door

TV appeal

street collection

appeal letter

work collection

pub collection

shop counter

appeal advert

phone appeal

Purchases

catalogue

raffle tickets

charity event

charity shop

jumble sale

affinity card

other

Did not give

percentage of
all respondents

percentage of
total yield

Figure 9.2 Ways of giving in the past month and the proportion of total yield (based on those who said how much money they gave)
Source: Petipher and Halfpenny (1991)

WHO RECEIVES CHARITY?

A great deal of charity goes to registered charities, and the donations in Britain to the top 500 are shown in Figure 9.3.

The largest amount went to health and medicine, about £525 million per annum. Of this, the largest shares went to cancer research, the physically disabled and the blind. The second-largest group of charities were for

Table 9.1 Typical (median) donation per annum by each method (donors who specified the amount they gave)

Method of donating	Median annual donation [a]	Median donation on each occasion of donating [b]
Tax-efficient	£60	
covenant	£77	
payroll deduction	£24	
Gift Aid	£300	
Non-tax-efficient	£55	
(1) Philanthropic	£24	
appeal letter		£5
television appeal		£5
buy goods for charitable organisation		£4.50
appeal advertisement		£4.15
sponsor someone in an event		£1
church collection		£1
collection at work		£1
door-to-door collection		£1
pub collection		70p
street collection		50p
shop-counter collection		25p
(2) Purchases	£60	
subscription/membership fees		£6.75
buy through a catalogue		£5
attend a charity event		£4.50
buy in a jumble sale		£3
buy in a charity shop		£2.50
buy raffle tickets		£1
All methods	£60	

Source: Charities Aid Foundation (1994)
Notes: [a] rounded to the nearest £1
[b] rounded to the nearest 5p
[c] the medians for telephone appeal, affinity card and other methods are omitted because fewer than eight people gave in these ways

various categories of people in need, such as children, the aged and the homeless; this is the closest to traditional giving to the poor. The third group were for overseas charities, mostly concerned with famine relief and refugees in the Third World. The remaining groups of charities received much less money: these were animals, the environment, missionary work, the arts and so on.

This does not include giving to old schools and colleges, which is a major source of their funds in the USA. Nor does it include giving to individuals such as beggars.

There are a number of individual difference factors in giving.

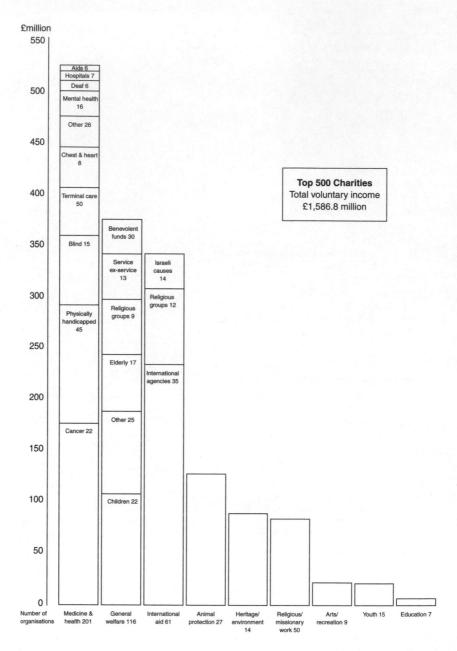

Figure 9.3 Voluntary income of the major sectors
Source: Charities Aid Foundation (1993)

Income

It would be expected that those who have more money would be able to give more of it away. In previous periods of history it was part of the role of the rich to give to the poor; 'charity' balls and dinners were a very public way of doing this. Lords of the manor, or their wives, looked after the poor in their village to some extent.

There is still a relation between giving and wealth. The amount given is more for the rich, though the correlation between income and donations is only about $r = \cdot 13$. The proportion of the rich who give something is also a little greater. What about the percentage of income that is given away? The most accurate British data comes from the FES, and in 1992 this showed a rise from 1.02 per cent of income for those earning about £80 per week, to 1.75 per cent for those earning about £475 per week, though the curve was fairly flat over the middle incomes, 1.4 per cent being the average. Of those earning over £275 per week in Britain 11 per cent gave nothing, and 74 per cent gave over £30 per month. Of those earning under £80 per week, 42 per cent gave nothing, and 23 per cent gave over £30 per month. There is a similar relation with social class, but the relationship is much weaker – it is income not class which affects giving most. There is a similar relation with education, but this is weaker still (Halfpenny and Lowe, 1994).

American charity surveys show a rather different pattern. They show a U-shaped curve of percentage donations in relation to income, where the rich and the poor both give a higher percentage than those in between. This is shown in Figure 9.4.

At all levels there is great variability in how much is given, but particularly at the top end. Table 9.2 shows that for US millionaires the most generous 25 per cent give an average of $132,000 per annum, while the least generous 25 per cent give only $6,821, a ratio of 22: 1. For the poorest group the equivalent ratio works out at 3: 1. Put another way, 5 per cent of the richest group give 80 per cent of the donations in this group, and the top 10 per cent give 86 per cent (Auten and Rudney, 1990).

What is the explanation of the U-shaped curve for American giving? There is no agreed explanation as yet, but, as we shall see shortly, it is mainly due to donations to churches, and especially by the most generous givers, at both ends. Jencks (1987) suggests that the larger donations of the rich are due to 'giving away your surplus': rich people mix with many who are poorer than themselves, and spend at a similar rate; what is left over is given to hospitals and universities, whose donations mainly come from the rich.

Since the rich give more, indeed a larger proportion of their incomes, charitable giving is regarded by economists as a 'luxury', that is, something unnecessary that you buy when you can afford it (e.g. Garner and Wagner, 1991). But it seems misleading to group charitable giving with the buying of jewellery and expensive clothes. Economically, they may be similar but psychologically they are not.

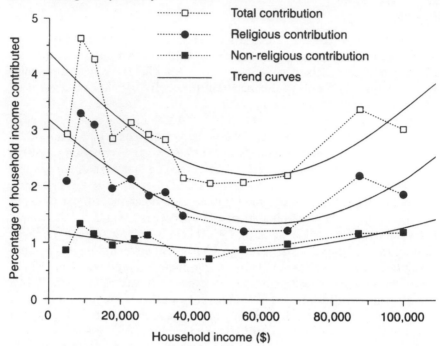

Figure 9.4 Percentage of household income contributed by contributing household for total, religious and non-religious contributions
Note: In this figure, the upper curve is the trend for the total contribution as a percentage of income for households who reported non-zero contributions. The middle and lower curves are the trends for the percentage of income contributed to religious and to non-religious organisations, respectively, by these same households.
Source: Schverish and Havens, 1995

Age and sex

There is a curvilinear relation of giving with age: most is given away by those between 30 and 65; the FES shows that the 50–65 age group give most. The old give less and the young give much less. It is understandable that the young and the old should give less. The retired and unemployed are also less likely to give, but most of the sick and disabled still make donations.

Sex differences in giving are small, but women give a little more, 9 per cent more in American data (Jencks, 1987): in Britain, 25 per cent of women give nothing (33 per cent for men), and 43 per cent give over £30 per month (39 per cent for men). This is perhaps surprising, since men earn more than women. The comparison with voluntary work is interesting: women do considerably more voluntary work than men (Pearce, 1993).

Family size

In American surveys it is found that married couples give 20–40 per cent more than single people with the same income. Couples with children at

Table 9.2 Giving over a five-year period, 1971–5

| | | | | Distribution of giving | |
Economic income class	No. of taxpayers	Average giving ($)	Median giving ($)	Lowest quartile ($)	Highest quartile ($)
$4,000–$10,000	1,313,848	403	245	164	572
$10,000–$20,000	8,158,249	389	266	147	426
$20,000–$50,000	4,543,156	639	467	246	753
$50,000–$100,000	491,697	1,881	973	592	1,981
$100,000–$200,000	114,689	4,920	2,409	760	4,969
$200,000–$500,000	22,128	12,161	3,324	711	12,352
$500,000–$1,000,000	3,649	34,256	6,682	2,211	39,678
$1,000,000 and over	1,032	124,351	43,808	6,821	132,487
Total	14,648,448	562	321	172	572

Source: Auten and Rudney (1990)

home give away 50 per cent more than those without. In both cases those with more dependents to look after are prepared to give more, though they have less income per capita (Jencks, 1987). The British CAF (Charities Aid Foundation) surveys found similar differences, though these were not so great.

Importance of religion

This is one of the strongest predictors in both British and American surveys. In 1993, those in Britain who said that religion was 'very important' to them gave £23.75 per month, while those for whom it was not very important gave on average £7.94. In American surveys, weekly attenders report giving away 3.8 per cent of their income, occasional attenders 1.5 per cent, and non-attenders 0.8 per cent (Myers, 1992). As Figure 9.2 shows, church contributions make up more than half of these donations, and it is these which have a U-shaped distribution. The authors of this study also found that the U-shaped pattern was partly due to the minority of high contributors. They separated those who gave more than two standard deviations above the mean for their income group, who constituted about 5 per cent of the sample, and found that they gave 10.42 per cent of income to churches and another 4.18 per cent to other causes; they were, in religious language, 'tithing'. The explanation of the lower end of the American U-shaped curve may be that many poor Americans belong to Pentecostal or similar churches, who command great loyalty, and have a large influence over the behaviour of their members, including the donations which they make to the church. Another American study found that members of evangelical churches were more likely to give to charities, to believe that such contributions are 'absolutely essential' or 'very important', and to be active in voluntary work (Clydesdale, 1990).

In Britain, people give much less to churches, and there is no U-shaped curve. It has been pointed out that 'donations' to churches are in any case not all charity, since some of it is like the fees to any other club, to provide the facilities needed by members; it has been estimated that perhaps 70 per cent of church contributions are like this (Schverish and Havens, 1995).

Personality

There is evidence that individuals show some degree of consistency in their helpfulness and generosity. Altruistic behaviour is found to be related to personality factors such as empathy, but little is known yet about personality in relation to charitable giving (Batson, 1991).

National differences

The level of giving in the USA is much higher than in Britain. Table 9.3 shows the levels of giving in North American and several European countries. One reason that North American levels of giving are so high is that churches there expect high levels of contributions, some of this being passed on to charities, though, as we have seen, most of it is probably to meet church expenses, such as clergy salaries. A second reason is that charitable contributions are tax deductible in the USA. Jencks (1987) concludes from many studies that making donations tax deductible adds about 25 per cent to the amount given away, though other economists disagree. Covenanting is popular in Britain and has the effect of giving more to the charity, but it is probably not perceived to be of any advantage to the donor.

Britain is different from the other four countries in Table 9.3 in the low level of giving, and the fact that this is largely made up of many small contributions; money is raised by charity events, charity shops, door-to-door and street collections. It is given mainly for medicine and social welfare, and more is given than in other countries for international causes and animals. And in Britain blood is all given free, while in the USA and many other countries you have to pay for it. In the USA and Canada money is collected mainly through churches and for churches; in the USA little is given for social welfare or medicine. France has an odd distribution in that 73 per cent give nothing but a minority give a lot. It is given in response to radio and TV appeals and to letters, and through churches, and it is given most for medicine. In Spain, the greatest source is lottery tickets, and the main beneficiaries are social welfare and the church (Charities Aid Foundation, 1994).

It might be expected that charitable contributions would be greater in those countries which do not have welfare for the poor. In Third World countries there is a lot of real poverty, and most people do give alms to beggars, though exactly how much is not known. In pre-literate societies a

Table 9.3 Total donations per person in the month prior to interview (all respondents)

Total amount given per month	Britain (%)	Canada (%)	France (%)	Spain (%)	USA (%)
Nothing	35	38	73	29	45
Unspecified amount	4	7	6	3	6
1p–£1	19	2	2	8	4
£1+–£5	22	15	5	25	11
£5+–£10	9	10	4	14	8
£10+	11	28	10	21	26
Average donation per person per month	£7.20	£21.80	£5.40	£6.90	£17.10
Typical donation per donor per month	£2.00	£10.50	£10.10	£7.00	£12.00

Source: Charities Aid Foundation, (1994)

lot is given to the poor, and to strangers, as well as to kin; it is regarded as a normal part of life to give to the poor, partly for religious reasons, partly because people have a strong sense of collective identity, of being part of a community. D'Hondt and Vandewiele (1984) surveyed 840 16–20 year olds in a Senegal school. Most of them said that they gave alms to beggars, partly for religious reasons (giving alms is strongly prescribed for Muslims), or for humane concerns, to appease their consciences, or to ward off evil spirits. There are several kinds of beggars in Senegal – some devout religious groups, the very poor, for example, through being handicapped, special groups like mothers of twins and those recently circumcised, and the bone idle. Some of these schoolchildren thought that being a beggar was a kind of job.

In China, and other parts of Asia, it has been found that people behave in a collectivist way, as opposed to the individualism of the West. In collectivist cultures there is a greater emphasis on sharing material resources. In a series of studies, Hui and Triandis (1986) have found that Chinese give, or say they would give, more to others, including complete strangers.

WHEN IS MONEY GIVEN AWAY?

We have just seen that money is raised in different ways in different parts of the world. The CAF surveys have found out in some detail how successful different methods of fund-raising are in Britain.

Table 9.4 shows the proportions of individuals who said that they would be likely to give in response to an approach by each method. The greatest likelihood was for sponsorship, a score of 1.16 being just above 'quite likely'. Several of the other methods had a very low estimated probability of success; a telephone appeal scoring −1.46, close to 'very unlikely'. The main point of interest to social psychologists is the finding that many of these forms of collection involve social contacts or social events of some kind. Some of them are from other individuals who are already known, as in the case of raffles and sponsorship. Table 9.1 shows the median amount given on each occasion by each method. Many of these donations are quite small, £1 a time or less. Table 9.5 shows that 10 per cent is collected by covenant or payroll deduction, 42 per cent by collections of various kinds, and 44 per cent by raffles and other charitable sales.

However, we should remember that the most effective methods of fund-raising are different in other countries. In the USA and Canada most money is raised through the church; in Spain by lotteries; and in France through TV and radio appeals and letters. In Britain, the National Lottery is becoming a major source of charity, and charities in other countries might do well if they used sponsorship and the other methods which work well in Britain.

Table 9.4 Likelihood of donating by each method of non-tax-efficient donating (all respondents)

Method of donating	Mean score
Philanthropic	
quite likely	
Sponsor someone in an event	1.16
door-to-door collection	0.66
street collection	0.54
neither likely nor unlikely	
church collection	0.22
collection at work	0.19
buy for a charitable organisation	−0.06
shop-counter collection	−0.06
television appeal	−0.08
pub collection	−0.23
unlikely	
appeal advertisement	−0.61
appeal letter	−1.05
telephone appeal	−1.46
Purchases	
quite likely	
buy raffle tickets	0.72
neither likely nor unlikely	
attend a charity event	0.42
buy in a jumble sale	0.40
buy in a charity shop	0.25
buy through a catalogue	0.04
unlikely	
subscription/membership fees	−0.62
affinity card	−1.09

Source: Halfpenny and Lowe (1994)
Note: mean score calculated by scoring:

'very likely to give'	= 2
'quite likely'	= 1
'neither likely nor unlikely'	= 0
'unlikely'	= −1
'very unlikely'	= −2

The relation between asker and donor

The person who is asking or 'soliciting' is usually a voluntary worker; the money will go to the cause, some of it to individual recipients. Only in the case of beggars is the asker also the recipient.

Research has demonstrated there are clear factors associated with giving money away.

The attractiveness and other features of the asker

There is extensive research on the effect of different sources of influence, but mainly on attitude change, and there is not very much on the effects on

Table 9.5 Total value of donations per annum by each method of donating (donors who specified the amount they gave)

Method of donating	Total donation (£) by all donors [a]	% of total donation
Tax-efficient	15,700	13
covenant	11,100	9
payroll deduction	800	1
Gift Aid	3,800	3
Non-tax-efficient	105,900	87
(1) Philanthropic	51,100	42
church collection	9,400	8
door-to-door collection	7,800	6
sponsor someone in an event	7,600	6
buy goods for charitable organisation	4,800	4
street collection	4,400	4
appeal advertisement	4,300	4
television appeal	4,100	3
appeal letter	2,900	2
pub collection	2,600	2
collection at work	1,900	2
shop-counter collection	1,100	1
telephone appeal	200	b
(2) Purchases	53,800	44
buy in a charity shop	12,800	11
buy through a catalogue	12,400	10
buy raffle tickets	8,400	7
subscription/membership fees	6,900	6
buy in a jumble sale	6,600	5
attend a charity event	6,300	5
affinity card	500	b
(3) Other	900	1
Total	121,500	100

Source: Charities Aid Foundation (1991)
Notes: [a] rounded to the nearest £100
[b] between 0 and 0.5%

giving money away. Physical attractiveness has been shown to have financial consequences. For example, attractive individuals, of both genders, have been found to be paid more for the same job, 18.5 per cent more for men and 26.4 per cent more for women (Quinn *et al.*, 1968), and in other studies attractive defendants have been fined less in experimental trials. Many studies have shown that attractive individuals have more influence when delivering a persuasive message, and it seems very likely that they could persuade others to give money successfully. Cialdini (1984) reports how he was visited by a 'stunning young woman', who pretended to start a social-survey interview, and then succeeded in persuading him, against his will, to buy an expensive club subscription.

Similarity has been found to be important for social influence. Emswiller *et al.* (1971) found that stopping students and asking for a dime to make a telephone call was more likely to be successful if the asker was dressed in the same way as the student, i.e. hippy or straight.

Expertise, authority and trustworthiness are also important in social influence, but have not been studied much in connection with giving money. Kraut (1973) compared door-to-door charity fund-raising by collectors who explained that they had been involved in working for handicapped children for two years, while other collectors said they had been given the job by the office. The average donation was 54c for the involved collectors versus 34c for the others. Other research has shown the effects of prestigious clothes, uniforms, etc. on persuasion but this has not been studied here for collecting money.

Non-verbal communication

Touch has been found to be a powerful additional source of social influence. If the asker touches the target, the latter is more likely to give 10 cents for the telephone, return 10 cents left in a telephone box, as well as a number of other kinds of help (Argyle, 1988). If waitresses touch diners they get bigger tips; if touched on the hand the tip was 16.7 per cent (Crusco and Wetzel, 1984).

Gaze functions in a similar way to touch. Bull and Gibson-Robinson (1981) studied a door-to-door collection. If the collector looked the potential donor in the eye while asking for money twice as much was given as when the collector looked at the collecting tin. In a related study on the effect of facial disfigurement, the effect of gaze was less evident; and a 'facially disfigured' collector received less money, but this only applied in a working-class area, not the middle-class one (Bull and Stevens, 1981).

Other aspects of non-verbal communication have been found to affect social influence – facial expression, tone of voice, spatial proximity and gestures are all important, but these have not yet been studied in connection with giving money (Argyle, 1988).

Reciprocity

This is a powerful source of social influence. 'There is an obligation to repay' (Mauss, 1954). We saw earlier that reciprocity is an important principle in gifts within the family and between friends. Regan (1971) ran an experiment in which an experimental confederate bought some subjects a bottle of Coca-Cola, then worth 10 cents, during the experiment; at the end of the experiment the confederate asked subjects if they would buy a 25 cent raffle ticket. Twice as many of those who had received a bottle of coke bought raffle tickets – which cost two and a half times as much. This principle is sometimes used in fund-raising. Members of Hare

Krishna and some other religious groups approach people at airports and give them a flower or a small religious book, refusing payment and saying that it is a gift. They then ask for a donation to funds. Often the 'gifts' are thrown away by their recipients, and are gathered up by the sect members to be given again. Many find it easier to deal with this situation by avoiding the sect members or refusing a gift rather than simply failing to reciprocate (Cialdini, 1984).

Relations with recipients

The recipients of money may be individuals, as with beggars, or they may be large groups of unknown others, who are poor, ill, old, etc. They may be the future members of schools or colleges. They might really be the donors themselves, when they contribute, for example, to medical charities for diseases which they have or think they might suffer from later. They may be whales or other animals. Charities also raise money for environmental or political causes, where there are no direct recipients at all.

Research on helping behaviour finds that empathy is an important process. Empathy is 'an understanding of and compassion for another's distress' (Sabini, 1995); it is seeing another's position or point of view and imagining how they are feeling. It is not the same as distress, it is imagining another's distress. Batson (1991) has shown that when empathy is aroused subjects will volunteer to take electric shocks in the place of another; empathy was aroused by saying how the victim came from the same town or college. However, empathy has not so far been shown to be effective in producing monetary gifts. For example, Warren and Walker (1991) tried to manipulate empathy by asking some of the 2,648 people approached in Perth, Australia, to 'imagine how they would feel in the situation', but this did not increase donations. However, it seems likely that very little empathy would be aroused in this way, where there are no actual individuals to empathise with. Being confronted by a beggar could arouse empathy, except that beggars are usually so different from most potential donors that little empathy would occur. Emler and Rushton (1974) found that with 7–13 year olds generosity was unaffected by empathy.

The arousal of pity may be a little different. The sight of a handicapped child from another culture, for example, would not be expected to produce empathy, since the child is in a totally unfamiliar situation and culture. However, this might evoke another kind of concern in the form of pity. Fund-raisers have attempted to arouse this by showing a photograph of a typical recipient. Thornton *et al.* (1991) did this, and it was successful in raising twice as much money when the photograph was part of a passive counter display in a shop, but it did not work as part of door-to-door collection. Isen and Noonberg (1979) found that fewer contributed in a door-to-door collection when a photograph of a handicapped child was shown; this was thought to be due to distraction. However, more gave when the child was shown smiling. Radley and Kennedy (1992) showed twelve photographs of different kinds of needy recipients. Manual workers responded by pity to some of these, especially cases of children in need, or individuals with cancer and the elderly; business people and professionals were not affected by pity in this way. In a study in north Wales, Eayrs and Ellis (1990) found that some posters for the mentally handicapped elicited feelings of sympathy, pity and guilt, especially one of two mentally handicapped children looking appealing and pathetic; respondents said they would give more in response to these posters, but that they would be less likely to think of the recipients as capable, valuable and having the same rights as others.

Research on helping behaviour finds that more help is forthcoming when the other's distress was externally caused, and not their own fault, through being drunk, for example. Benson and Catt (1978) found that more was given to a charity when the external causation of the victims' plight was emphasised.

A long tradition of intergroup research has found that people give preferential treatment to members of the in-group, for example in allocating sums of money. This has been found in laboratory studies and also with groups of workers (Brown, 1978). This affects voluntary workers, for example retired people providing meals for even older ones. This principle works against many charities, where the recipients are likely to belong to very different groups from the donors. However, large donations are given to old schools and colleges, and some charities target in-group members when raising money for distressed gentlefolk, out-of-work musicians, etc. American Jews give a median amount of $175 per year to Jewish charities and $75 to non-Jewish; those who gave larger amounts gave much more to Jewish charities. This does not include synagogue dues of $500–1,000 p. a. (Rimor and Tobin, 1990). Black-American churches give a lot to charities and organisations outside their church, and these are mainly to black organisations (Carson, 1990).

Research on helping behaviour finds that more help is given to others who are liked, attractive or similar to the helper. Again, this principle works against most money-donating situations, when the recipient is either quite unknown, or is distinctly dissimilar, and often unattractive. Yet these may be the people who most need help, a point often brought up in religious discussion of this topic.

Relations with other donors

Modelling and conformity

All social behaviour is affected by these processes. The difference between them is that a model may be followed who is outside the group, and conformity is partly due to fear of disapproval by other group members.

Catt and Benson (1977) found that more was given in a door-to-door collection if people were told that over three-quarters of their neighbours had contributed than when told that under a quarter had (62c. vs. 41c.); more was given in the three-quarters condition if they were told that this proportion of neighbours had given over $1 than when told they had given less than $1 (74c. vs. 51c). This was described as an experiment on modelling, but they mentioned that contributors would receive a window sticker, so that their neighbours would know, and so was also a case of conformity. In a similar study Reingen (1982) showed longer or shorter lists of others who were said to have contributed. With a list of 12 who were said to have given over $5, 65 per cent contributed versus 40 per cent without this information, and the average donation was 4.2 times as great. Both length of list and alleged size of donation made a difference. This looks more like modelling than conformity; however, conformity is not only due to fear of disapproval, but also to taking norms as a source of information, in this case that there is a need to be met. Modelling is clearer in the case of children learning to be generous. Grusec *et al.* (1978) found that children were influenced to be generous by watching an adult model, later behaving generously when the model was absent. In this and earlier studies it was found that a nurturant, that is rewarding, model was more influential, while the behaviour of a model had more effect than what he or she said should be done; practice had more effect than preaching.

Diffusion of responsibility

This is a familiar cause of not helping – when there are others present who could do it instead, and the more there are the less likely an individual is to help. Wiesenthal *et al.* (1983) found that when solitary individuals were approached they gave more than when approached in groups, in pubs (which introduces another factor), and that when 1,346 students were approached in classrooms of different sizes, the larger the class the smaller the donations.

The effect of different ways of asking for it

Large versus small requests

This kind of information in very useful for those engaged in fund-raising for charities. Weyant and Smith (1987) studied two door-to-door appeals for the American Cancer Society. In one of them 6,000 people were approached; when the options offered were fairly small ones ($5, $10 and $25), 35 per cent gave something, but when larger alternatives were suggested only 14 per cent paid up, and the average amount given was slightly less, $12 as compared with $12.14. Cialdini and Schroeder (1976) took this a step further and added the words 'even a penny will help' for some potential donors. With these words added, 50 per cent contributed to the cancer fund, with an average of $1.54 each; without the words, 29 per cent contributed, with an average of only $1.44 each. However, in a similar study, in Toronto, Doob and McLaughlin (1989) found that large requests to a Canadian Civil Liberties organisation produced no fewer donors, and larger gifts ($45.58) than smaller requests ($36.89). The ratio of the larger to the smaller options was less here than in the Weyant and Smith (1987) study. And this was a very different situation, in that there was a small success rate, of 5.5 per cent in both conditions, all those approached had given before or were members of the society, and when there were donations these were much bigger. It seems that small requests are more effective with the general public, because they legitimate small gifts, while large requests may produce 'reactance', a negative reaction to feelings of coercion. With those who are committed already, larger donations are expected, and can be asked for, but they should not be too large.

The 'foot-in-the-door' phenomenon – making a small request first

Freedman and Fraser (1966) showed that if people are given a small request first they are much more likely to agree to a larger one later. The research on this phenomenon has been about behaviour such as giving blood and voting, rather than giving money. However, Bell *et al.* (1994) studied its effects in raising money for a local AIDS organisation. The 845 subjects were visited at home and those who were asked to sign a petition first gave more money than those who were asked to contribute directly.

Cialdini (1984) sees this as an example of commitment as a source of influence, and gives other examples from brain washing to joining religious sects and initiation rites. We saw a financial example above in the large donations to a Canadian Civil Liberties organisation, by those who were members, or who had given before. And earlier in the chapter we saw that charitable donations in Britain were much larger when in the form of covenants, which reflect a commitment to keep paying for at least four years (Table 9.1).

The 'door in the face', or reciprocal concession

Cialdini *et al.* (1975) sent confederates to ask students to do a large amount of unpaid social work with underprivileged juveniles, and they all refused. They were then asked to do a very small amount of the same: 50 per cent agreed to this second request compared with 11 per cent of those who had not received the original request. This principle has been used with success with selling and negotiation. For example, Benton *et al.* (1972) found that subjects who initially made very high demands on how to divide up some money, and then made a concession, ended up with more of it than those who made a reasonable demand to start with. Cialdini (1984) quotes

Dennis the Menace, who first asks for a horse, then 'if I can't have a horse can I have a cookie', later reflecting 'Who would believe it – an invisible horse who's worth his weight in cookies'. A meta-analysis by Dilliard *et al.* (1984) of the door-in-the-face phenomenon found that making a large request first leads to 17 per cent more being given. Abrahams and Bell (1994) found that the effect was greatest when future interaction with the asker was expected. The explanation Cialdini offers is that the subject is repaying the other's concession, by giving something. However, the Abrahams and Bell result suggests that maintaining reputation may also be involved.

Putting people in a good mood

Many studies have found that individuals are more likely to provide help when they are in a good mood, and this includes giving money away. For example, Cunningham (1979) found that waitresses received larger tips when the sun was shining: later Cunningham *et al.* (1980) found that good moods produced more contributions, especially when combined with requests to 'keep the children smiling'. It works with children too. Isen *et al.* (1973) found that 8 year olds who had been allowed to win at bowling gave three times as much to poor children as those who had been made to fail. Baumann *et al.* (1981) found that children who had received positive mood induction were more generous to poor children, but also engaged in more self-gratification, in helping themselves to more candy. This suggests an explanation of the effect of good moods on generosity – that good moods enhance the desire for pleasure, and helping others is known to be a source of pleasure (Sabini, 1995).

Being in a bad mood

It might be expected that bad moods would have the opposite effect of good moods; however, bad moods too often enhance helping and generosity. Cialdini *et al.* (1987) proposed that helping produces 'negative state relief'. They found that subjects were more altruistic when in a bad mood if they were led to believe that their mood could change compared with when they had been told that it was fixed. The negative moods which have been used in this kind of research are typically loss of self-esteem or guilt. Harris *et al.* (1975) found that Catholics on their way to confession were much more likely to give money to a charity than after they had made their confession; it was assumed that they were feeling more guilty before than after. Cunningham *et al.* (1980) also found that guilt produced contributions, especially when combined with suggested obligations 'you owe it to the children'. Isen *et al.* (1973) found that 8-year-old children who had been caused to fail gave more than the control group, but only if the experimenter who saw them fail also saw them being generous, a clear case of trying to restore reputation in the eyes of another.

However, help and generosity do not seem to work so well for depression or grief; it has been suggested that this is because these moods produce a high level of self-concern (Myers, 1993). Generosity does not remove bad moods in children; evidently some kind of socialisation is needed. One theory is that helping and generosity are innately rewarding; however, this only works if attention is directed to the other, and children have to learn to do this (Sabini, 1995). On the other hand, they do not seem to need to learn this in relation to positive moods.

ATTITUDES TO CHARITABLE GIVING

Recently, Furnham (1995) developed a measure of attitudes to charitable giving which was administered to nearly 200 British adults. Table 9.6 shows the items.

Five factors seem to underly these attitudes. The first (items 1, 3, 9, 11, 17) reflects the inefficiency of giving and the second (items 5, 10, 14, 16) the precise opposite. A third factor seems deeply cynical about giving (items 13, 15, 19), while a fourth factor seems to be about altruism (items 2, 12). A final factor concerns the purpose of charity (items 4, 7, 8).

Furnham (1995) also devised a questionnaire that examined preferential charity giving (see Table 9.7).

Children, medical and animal charities clearly attracted most money and religious charities least.

Furnham's (1995) study showed that other attitudes were clearly linked to charitable giving. Thus the more people believe the world is just – people deserve their fate and are the primary architects of both their fortune and misfortune – the less they support charitable giving. Clearly, attitudes towards fate are important predictors of charitable giving.

The research in attitudes to charitable giving is of direct applied importance, yet currently neglected.

THE EXPLANATION OF CHARITABLE GIVING

What motivates charitable giving? What are the rewards, if any, economic, psychological or otherwise? Economists can retain the idea that people always make economically advantageous choices, if it is accepted that psychological satisfaction is worth buying – and that this can result from giving money to charity. A further step is to accept that there can be altruism, that person A can obtain some satisfaction from the benefits to B.

Economic rewards for giving

This is where economists look first to explain charitable giving. Sometimes there are such rewards. Those who win lotteries, or who hope to win

Table 9.6 Attitudes to charitable giving

Statements		Mean	SD
1	Far too much money is wasted in the administration of charities	3.48	(1.20)
2	Each of us has a (Christian) duty to help others through charitable giving	3.08	(1.32)
3	Too many charities do not distinguish between deserving and undeserving	2.82	(1.02)
4	Helping people to help themselves is the ultimate aim of the charities	3.66	(1.06)
5	Charity is an intelligent way of distributing money	3.09	(1.08)
6	Giving to charity is a personal form of thanks-giving	2.88	(1.14)
7	There should be no need for charity: the state should pay for the needy through money collected in taxes	3.67	(1.20)
8	Most people give to charity out of pure sympathy with the recipient	3.16	(1.11)
9	The trouble with charity is that it leads to dependency	2.83	(1.14)
10	Unlike taxation, through charitable giving people can target or control exactly where their money is going	3.18	(1.09)
11	There seems to be a lot of corruption in charity collection and distribution	3.32	(1.05)
12	People who give to charity, and work for, charity are genuinely altruistic	3.03	(0.96)
13	Many individuals (and large organisations) who donate sums of money to charity have ulterior motives	3.40	(1.09)
14	Charitable giving is the most efficient way of getting help to needy	2.88	(1.14)
15	For many, charity donation is simply a tax dodge	2.75	(1.04)
16	Charities have to exist to assist causes not covered by the state	3.83	(1.08)
17	Charities rely too much on sentimentality and not enough on realities	2.75	(1.03)
18	People give more money to causes they identify with	4.36	(0.79)
19	Many people try to solve their conscience by small gifts to charity	3.70	(0.95)
20	Too many organisations hide behind the mask (and tax advantages) of being a charity	3.11	(0.93)

Source: Furnham (1995)
Note: 5 = agree; 1 = disagree

lotteries, stand to win much more than they contributed. Perhaps their real reward is in entertaining pleasant fantasies of what they would do if they won. Much that has been counted as charity in Britain is spending in charity shops, which are generally cheaper than ordinary shops. We have

Table 9.7 Charities that aim to help

		Mean rank
1	Adults in this country (e.g. handicapped groups, the elderly, etc.)	5.66
2	Education in other countries (e.g. alleviating illiteracy in Third World countries)	8.06
3	Animal charities abroad (e.g. saving and protecting endangered species)	10.88
4	Religious charities in this country (e.g. furthering the message of a particular religion)	13.00
5	Environmental issues in this country	7.22
6	Children in other countries (e.g. sponsoring individual children or children's charities that work in the Third World)	4.88
7	Political charities at home (e.g. anti-nuclear, anti-military, prison reform)	10.79
8	Educational charities in this country (e.g. helping special-interest groups receive an education)	7.48
9	Children in this country (e.g. special hospitals, clinics or units that deal with sickly, handicapped or abused children)	2.79
10	Medical charities in this country (e.g. helping patients of particular disease like AIDS, cancer, etc.)	4.32
11	Political charities in other countries (e.g. helping democratic processes in other countries, supporting peaceful bodies)	12.23
12	Animal charities in this country (e.g. charities that help protect certain species (birds) or general monitory bodies)	8.83
13	Environmental charities in other countries (e.g. charities that help bio-diversity, protecting special zone or areas)	9.37
14	Religious charities in other countries (e.g. attempting to evangelise people not to one particular faith)	14.12
15	Adults abroad in other countries (e.g. special groups who are disadvantaged, discriminated against)	8.62
16	Medical charities in other countries (e.g. helping people with medical problems quite specific to that area)	7.18

'Above are 16 different types of charity. They refer to the recipient or object of the charitable donation and the country of the beneficiary. Please read all 16 then *rank order* them by putting a 1 next to the charity you would *most* probably support, a 2 next to the charity you would next most probably support, through to 16 indicating the charity you are least likely to support.'

Source: Furnham (1995)
Note: Text below table was the introduction to the questionnaire

seen that when there is tax relief for charity, giving is increased by about 17 per cent, according to some economists.

Giving money away can be good for business. A study of 249 individuals who each contributed over $100,000 to George Bush's election campaign in 1988 found that Bush consulted them, took their advice and that this benefited their companies (Denny *et al.*, 1993). Business people, politicians and others gain goodwill, exposure and reputation, and professional contacts (Johnson, 1982). As we saw earlier, being involved in the administration of charities can play an important part in business careers, and the same is true of political ones. Corporate giving by firms is certainly good for business, indeed, it is a major form of advertising, for example, by sponsoring sports events or competitors. It is also tax-deductible.

Numerous other rewards may be given in return for charity, falling under the headings of prestige and entertainment rather than economics. But for economics proper it seems that the rewards for giving are mainly confined to those in the upper ranks of business or politics; for others the rewards are small, certainly much less than the donations.

Economists have attempted to explain charity in terms of various rational models (Collard, 1978). Game theory would work if people could be assured that the other will co-operate, so there will be gains from helping the other; however, there is no prospect of co-operation in the case of charity. And giving can be rewarding if people can enjoy some fraction of the gains of the other; this would work if there was empathy, and we have seen that there is not. There might be other kinds of satisfaction, and these are described next.

Altruism

Animals give food and other help to one another. Can biological models of animal help explain charity? The best-confirmed of these models is the inclusive fitness or 'selfish gene' theory, that animals help those with similar genes in order to promote the survival of these genes. However, charity is mainly to quite different others, the poor, handicapped, those in the Third World. The only cases which would fit this model are donations to old schools and colleges, or similar in-groups. A second animal model is that of reciprocal altruism, where others are helped, provided they reciprocate. Again, there is rarely any reciprocation in the case of charitable giving.

The best-known theory of helping behaviour in social psychology is Batson's (1991) two-stage model where the arousal of empathy is needed for help to be given, but we have seen that empathy does not affect giving to charity.

However, pity has been found to affect donations. Posters showing a photograph of a handicapped child looking distressed and pathetic are successful. This is quite different from empathy, since the recipient is very different from the donor, and it has been found that such posters result in the recipient's being seen as more different, i.e. as inadequate. The pictures in these studies have always been of children, and this may be needed for the pity response to be elicited.

We have seen that people give more when they are in a good mood or in certain negative moods. The explanation of the effect of good moods seems to be that when in these moods people have an enhanced desire for pleasure, and they know that help and charity are enjoyable. It has been argued that those who give blood and say that this is altruistic are rationalising, and that they are really just feeling good (Hagen, 1982). The effect of certain bad moods like guilt and distress is probably different: those concerned need to have learned to direct attention to others and to know that generosity will have positive effects on mood. Another negative mood, loss of self-esteem, can be removed if relevant others see the actor being generous.

The effect of religion and morals

We have seen that religious people give more. This is partly through the belief that it will lead to heavenly rewards, or ward off evil, or the belief that the poor are blessed, or that it is part of one's religious duty, that religion without good works is hollow, or simply because churches are very persuasive in extracting contributions. The research on donations to Jewish causes found that giving to Jewish causes was a central part of Jewish identity (Rimor and Tobin, 1990).

Some people are motivated by other moral considerations. Radley and Kennedy (1992) found that a small sample of professionals were not motivated by pity or perception of need, as working-class people were, but by abstract principles of fairness or justice, and concern with longer-term changes in society. Emler and Rushton (1974) studied 7–13 year olds in a role-taking task; while generosity was not affected by empathy, it was affected by moral-judgement ability, assessed from the answers to two of Piaget's questions about distributive justice.

Looking at the different causes for which people give money, we see that individual values are important. Some people give money for animals, others for religion, poverty, medicine, education, the arts, others for the environment. These are all 'values', that is, ends or goals which individuals believe to be important. There are various measures of such individual values, such as the Vernon–Allport–Lindzey values questionnaire. This assessed the relative strength of scientific, economic, aesthetic, social or humanitarian, political and religious values (Allport *et al.*, 1951). Indeed, one of the items asks how a subject would divide up donations between these six kinds of goal.

Collective concern

Do people have a concern for other members of their society as a whole? In pre-literate societies, which were quite small, they accepted responsibility for all the members. In Third World cultures today, and in Asia, there is collectivism rather than individualism, but this does not extend to the wider society, only to the narrower circle of kin, neighbours and friends. We have seen that American Jews and blacks give to organisations for the welfare of Jews and blacks respectively.

Nevertheless, in modern industrial society there is some evidence of wider concerns. People are willing to pay out a substantial proportion of their incomes in tax, a lot of it going to poorer individuals. It has been found that when there are disasters, most people do not try to make a profit out of shortages, and may bring pressure to bear on those who do; the immediate concern is with kin, but then with the wider community, including strangers (Douty, 1972). Historians consider that during earlier periods donations to the poor were partly to keep them from revolting. Collard (1978) quotes the decision of British trade unions in 1974 to restrain their wage demands in order to keep old-age pensions up. And Titmuss (1970) notes the 2–5 per cent of individuals in Britain who donate their blood to strangers for nothing. In this and other surveys the donors say that one of the main reasons is altruistic concern, or a feeling of duty towards the community; those who do voluntary work say the same.

We saw earlier that conformity pressures and modelling affected giving in social-psychological experiments. The same is found in other studies, such as the motivation for giving blood; here it is difficult to refuse if asked, and parents and friends are influential models (Hagen, 1982). This is how concern for the community is passed on.

TIPPING

The term TIP supposedly stands for 'To Insure Promptness', which was derived from the eighteenth-century English tradition of giving coins with written words to publicans. It is now estimated that over $10 billion is given as tips in America to waiters/waitresses, porters, hairdressers, taxi-drivers, chambermaids and a host of other 'professionals'.

What is the meaning and function of tipping? Why does it exist? Why tip cabbies and hairdressers but not tailors? What are the determinants of tipping? And, most important, how does tipping affect the service-givers (e.g. waiters), the recipients (i.e. customers) and the relationship between the two parties? Furnham (1996a) has pointed out three disciplinary explanations.

Economists argue that tipping has a rational economic explanation. A tip is a payment for something extra (extra service or extra effort) beyond those specified as normal. Most people we tip provide services that are fairly difficult to measure, so his or her obligations and performance cannot be fully controlled. Hence the tip is the mechanism which complements the fixed market price where the sole commodity (i.e. service) contains non-standard or immeasurable components. But if this were true, there would be a direct relationship between the size of the tip and the degree to which the performed service extended beyond normal duties in terms of speed, politeness, etc. While this may occasionally be the case, any waiter/waitress will tell you that the size of the tip (if not a standard amount) is a function of such things as size of the dining party, the size of the bill, the need of the bill-payer to impress his/her friends. So much for an economic explanation which at any rate cannot account for the fact that some tipping is genuinely altruistic and, as far as I know, beyond economists, who always posit to self-interest.

Sociologists, on the other hand, see the tip as a gift. Because the recipient of a service feels gratitude or indebtedness to the provider, he or she leaves a tip as a gift supplementary to the bill. This free giving becomes a way of establishing and maintaining social status and power over somebody. It is significant that in several different languages the word 'gift' means poison. The recipients of a service (the customers) get more than they pay for (in terms of service), which motivates them to reciprocate or discharge obligations and thereby balance the account. If they fail to do so, they will be under pressure to repay with social approval or subordination (or a mixture). Further, if the customer tips more than the person deserves, this superiority is established beyond any doubt because the balance tips in the donor's favour. Thus, paradoxically, the tip is not an expression of gratitude but a defence against gratitude. Tipping is a form of social control.

But is it true that tipping can be a demonstration of dominance and superiority? In some languages (such as Dutch and German) the tip contains a derogatory element implying that the money will be used for drink or some other improper purpose. Frequently, waiters and cabbies talk of the humiliation involved in tipping, though I appear to have met an equally large number who are humiliated by the lack of a tip!

The trouble with both sociological and economic explanations is that they both assume an 'ongoing' as opposed to a 'one-off' encounter. Most frequently, one tips those one never sees again. Both assume that people tip as an investment in future service but studies have shown the opposite: regular repeat-trade customers tip *less* than irregulars. Also, tipping is not frequently done publicly as a display of rank and power; it is characterised by privacy and discretion. Many recipients deliberately don't look at the amount until well after the transaction.

Psychologists, on the other hand, agree that tipping is a form of ego massage calculated to enhance the self-image of the tipper. Also, by giving a tip – above and beyond the agreed set price – the tipper can demonstrate he/she is not fully trapped by market forces and can be capable of voluntary, discretionary action. The tip can sometimes be seen as a result of the customer's insecurity or anxiety. A maid or hairdresser deserves a tip through having access to the customer's private territory or articles that may just pose a threat to the customer's public face. The tip can buy their server's silence because it buys loyalty or indebtedness. Psychologists stress that tipping is intrinsically motivated rather than performed for the sake of the external material or social rewards.

Lynn and Grassman (1990) spelt out, in detail, the three 'rational' explanations for tipping:

1 Buying social approval with tips: following the social norms (i.e. 15 per cent tipping) is a desire for social approval or else a fear of disapproval.
2 Buying an equitable relationship with tips: tips buy peace of mind by helping maintain a more equitable relationship with servers.
3 Buying future service with tips: tips ensure better service in the future because the tit-for-tat works but only with regular customers.

In their study they found support for the first two, but not the third explanation.

Despite the number of people fairly dependent on tips for their income, little research has been done until recently into their curious and wide-spreading habit. Lynn and Latane (1984) summarised studies done in the 1970s which found:

1 Most tips are around the 15 per cent American norm.
2 The percentage of the tip to total cost is an inverse power function of the number of people at the table.
3 Physically attractive and/or attractively dressed waitresses receive greater tips than less attractive waitresses.
4 Tips are bigger when paid by credit cards, relative to cash payers.
5 Tips are not related to whether alcohol is consumed.
6 Tips increase with the number of non-task-oriented 'visits' by waiter and waitress, but unrelated to the customers' ratings of service.
7 Often, but not always, males tip more than females.

In the past two decades various other variables have been considered in this area. In two American studies, Lynn and Latane (1984) found the percentage tipped in restaurants was related to group size, customer's gender, the method of payment (cash vs. credit card) and size of bill; but it was not related to service quality, wait/waitresses, perceived effort or gender, or the restaurant atmosphere or food. It seems particularly surprising that tips seem unrelated to service, food or dining atmosphere, suggesting tips may be governed by other principles like custom, group diffusion or responsibility or factors associated with the waiter's appearance or non-task-related visits.

Lynn (1988) investigated very closely the effect of alcohol on tipping. He argued that alcohol has clear effects on pro-social behaviour in that mood is improved and judgement clouded. Hence he argued alcohol consumption with a meal should be positively related to tipping. He found, as predicted, alcohol was a significant predictor of a residual tip. He further pointed out two important findings in his study. First, that the size of the bill is nearly always the single most powerful predictor of the tip. Second, that one therefore needs to calculate a more independent measure of tip size using regression equations (residuals from a regression of bill size on tip amount).

Various explanations have been given for the group-size effect: bigger dining parties tip a smaller percentage of the total bill size than smaller parties. Three classic explanations have been given:

1 There is a diffusion of responsibility for the waiter or waitress. That is, the responsibility is psychologically divided by all people present. Yet this is a poor explanation, because most often only one person pays the bill.
2 There is an equitable adjustment for the smaller per-person service effort required to wait on larger tables. This service effort increases at a marginally decreasing rate as the group size goes up, but tipping seems only weakly related to service.
3 There is an adjustment for the larger bill sizes acquired by larger parties. Therefore, if the price is high, tips may be reduced.

However, in a careful reanalysis of earlier data, Lynn and Bond (1992) found that the group-size effect on the tip is a statistical artifact rather than a psychologically meaningful artifact. Lynn (1992) also found a statistical artifact in the literature in the various studies which suggested an equivocal relationship between tipping and the rated quality of service. In a meta-analysis of eleven studies he found a clear, unambiguous, but small relationship between customer evaluation of service and the tip.

More recent studies have focused on the server's behaviour. Rind and Bordia (1995) noted that server (waiter) – diner interactions were related to tip size. Research that they reviewed found the following behaviours positively related to tip size:

1 Whether the server touched the diner.
2 Whether the server initially squatted in their interaction with the diner as opposed to stood.
3 The size of their initial smile.
4 Whether the server introduced himself/herself by their first name.
5 The number of incidental (non-task-oriented) visits to the table.

In their study, Rind and Bordia (1995) had waiters/servers deliver the bill in one of three conditions: with no one else; with 'thank you' written on the back; with 'thank you' plus the name of the server. The effect of 'thank you' significantly increased tip percentages, but the addition of the name had no effect. It increased tips by 11 per cent over a week-long period. This simple impressive management technique appears to have significant positive consequences.

In a more recent study, Rind and Bordia (1996) predicted and found that if female (but not male) waiters drew a happy smiling face on the backs of bills before delivering them, they would get bigger tips because it increased perceptions of friendliness. They argued that the same behaviour would not be true of males, because such behaviour would be seen as gender-inappropriate.

Harris (1995) focused on the characteristics of customers and tipping. She found tips were larger when customers are male, they pay by credit card, and they patronise the restaurant regularly. In her study she investigated over 100 waiters on their views. She asked the waiters what affected tipping: they believed it was 'friendly service, good suggestions from the waiter, excellent food, quick service of the main course, prompt delivery of the check, an expensive restaurant, the customer's drinking, the waiter's introducing him or herself, and the customer paying by credit card, which led to significant larger tips. They also reported that taking a long time to get the beverage, being seated in a bad location, and being served by a waitress with a flower in her hair led to significantly smaller tips' (p. 731).

The beliefs of the waiters can be seen in Table 9.8. In fact, there is some empirical evidence that each of these factors may affect tipping.

In a second study, she compared the beliefs of waiters and customers, and found considerable agreement. Compared to customers more waiters believed good fast service was predictive of tips. Interestingly, and predictably, all respondents felt they were more generous tippers than the average individual and waiters indicated that they were more generous tippers than customers though this could obviously be explained as an attribution error.

Harris (1995) points out the important implications of the potential clash between managers and waiters in their attempt to maximise personal income:

Table 9.8 Percentages of waiters with different beliefs about the effects of service variables on tip size

Variable	Increase (%)	No effect (%)	Decrease (%)
Friendly service	88	12	0
Excellent food	80	20	0
Seated in bad location	0	33	67
Customer has been drinking	50	29	21
Waiter touches your hand	11	75	14
Waiter introduces self	32	59	9
Long time to get beverage	1	5	94
Main course comes quickly	71	29	1
Separate checks	26	53	21
Restaurant is expensive	61	32	7
Waiter makes good suggestions	85	15	0
Customer gets check promptly	61	39	0
Waitress wears flower in her hair	0	91	9
Payment by credit card	22	74	5
Weather is sunny	14	84	1

Source: Harris (1995)

Waiters may be more attuned than customers to relevant characteristics of the situation and of the individuals involved. If their beliefs lead waiters to provide better service to customers they think might be bigger tippers or to concentrate on those aspects of service they think have the largest impact on tip size, this might have some interesting implications for restaurant managers, as well as customers. If managers wish to maximize total income to the restaurant (perhaps by increasing the size of the check, speed of the visit, and frequency of visits), whereas waiters wish to maximize their tip size and customers wish to receive maximum service, it may be difficult to reconcile these three different points of view. Other service professionals who receive tips (e.g. hairdressers, taxi drivers, and hotel maids) may be in the same position of having financial incentives to please both an employer and a customer.

(p. 742)

CONCLUSION

The first point we have established is that the majority of people in the modern world do give money away to charity. They do not give very much away, about 1.4 per cent of salary in Britain, about twice as much in the USA, although a lot is given to beggars in Third World countries. The rich give more than the poor; in addition the proportion that they give away is a little greater.

There is no economic advantage in giving money away for most people, but this may be rewarding in some non-material way to the giver. There is tax relief for some, especially for the rich, and there may be the hope of gains in lotteries, though the majority do not receive these. There may be some material rewards for those managers who become involved in corporate giving, or the administration of charities, for whom organising giving is part of their career. Some politicians may gain votes from their connection with charities.

Social motivation is probably more important as a source of charitable giving. There is the desire to please, impress or not be rejected by the asker, with resultant gain in self-esteem. It is difficult to refuse when the asker is known personally, as in sponsoring. There are usually no such rewards from the recipient, who is usually anonymous, except in the case of beggars. There is little empathy with recipients, who are either unknown or totally different from the donor, though there may be arousal of pity. There are conformity pressures from neighbours or colleagues, who may know what has been donated, and there may be imitation of the generosity of others. Giving depends, too, on the social skills of the asker, how the request is made, and it is affected by strategies like foot in the door.

Altruism can be seen in the powerful effects of church membership, the effects of moral principles, or of the possession of values for which money may be given. This is a form of altruism which takes place without any empathy. Another kind of altruism can be seen in generosity to members of the in-group or community. Perhaps some degree of empathy extends to strangers simply because they belong to the wider community; or this could be explained by the principles of social-identity theory, that there is favouritism to members of the in-group, which is valued highly because our identity depends partly on the features of this group. In collectivist cultures it only extends to members of the immediate group of neighbours and kin.

The explanation of both kinds of altruism lies partly in the fact that helping behaviour and generosity are rewarding to the giver and have the effect of putting him or her in a good mood. This may be an in-built response, and is partly due to empathy, and partly due to socialisation to have concern for religious principles or for the community.

10 The very rich

For many men, the acquisition of wealth does not end their troubles, it only changes them.

Lucius Annaeus Seneca

Someone who's obsessed with making money to the exclusion of other goals in life has likely forgone the possibility of the acceptance of God's kingdom.

Jimmy Carter

Keep company with the very rich and you'll end up picking up the check.

Stanley Walker

I would not say any millionaires were mean. They simply have a healthy respect for money. I've noticed that people who don't respect money don't have any.

Paul Getty

Once you are past your first million pounds it doesn't make much difference. We're amused by it, it just seems slightly ridiculous.

Richard Branson

Time is money – says the vulgarest saw known to any age or people. Turn it round about and you get a precious truth – money is time.

George Gissing

Wealth is the product of man's capacity to think.

Ayn Rand

If you want to know what the Lord God thinks of money, you have only to look at those to whom he gives it.

Maurice Baring

INTRODUCTION

Nearly everyone wants to know who the rich are, how they became so rich, why they wanted to be rich, and what they do with it when they have got it.

There are also sociological questions, about whether they fulfil some useful social or economic function, or whether they should be taxed very highly.

Table 10.1 (p. 260) shows the pattern of consumption for the top 10 per cent of families, who were earning an average of £32,000 in 1994–5, which is 7.62 times what the lowest 10 per cent were earning. They were fairly rich, but not very rich. Wealth, like poverty, is a comparative issue. Or we could look at the members of social class I, as used for social survey purposes. These are individuals and their families where the main earner is in 'professional or higher managerial work', and about 5 per cent of the population fall into this category. On average, they earn about two to three times the national average (Reid, 1989). However, there are some occupations in this class which do a lot better than that. In 1995, when the national average was £17,000, 10 per cent of doctors got over £60,000 p. a., and over 10 per cent of underwriters, stockbrokers and other finance workers got over £77,000 (New Earnings Survey, 1995). In addition there are other rich individuals who would not normally be accepted as members of class I, that is by social scientists or by their neighbours. These are small businessmen, entrepreneurs who have done well out of building or manufacturing, for example, who were often originally skilled manual workers. There are now also lottery winners; a millionaire is now created every week in Britain.

So some of social class I are rich, but not all. We will now look more closely at the top 1 per cent, the top 0.1 per cent, and the few thousands who own and earn very large sums. There is more than one kind of person with a large income. There has been much public concern in Britain about the very large salaries paid to the heads of nationalised industries, though it is recognised that the heads of all big companies are paid similar large salaries, over £1 million a year in some cases. There has been a big increase in these salaries in Britain during recent years. There are others who have a large salary from commercial activities, such as buying and selling shares, or investing in new enterprises, and others who draw a large income from businesses which they have inherited or which they have created themselves.

The distribution of salaries is shown in Figure 10.1. This distribution is like the normal, bell-shaped, distributions familiar for intelligence and other human capacities and traits, except that it is not symmetrical – there is a long tail at the upper end. This distribution is skewed mainly because of the salaries of top executives, which form a long tail at the top, though a few lawyers and financiers also fall into this group; the top of the scale corresponds to a salary of £62,400 p. a. Figure 10.2 shows how top executives earn 8–32 times the lowest-paid group, farm labourers, that is, 5–21 times average income, £300,000 or more. However, a lot of these high incomes come from unearned income, 68 per cent of the incomes of the top 1 per cent in 1920, according to Wedgwood (1929).

These inequalities were even greater in the past: in 1688, the families of Lords who were not bishops earned £3,200 a year, while cottagers and

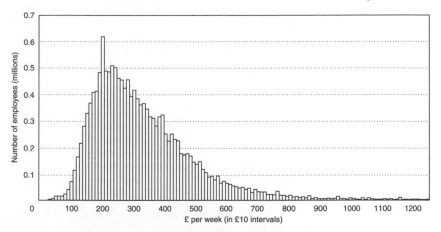

Figure 10.1 Distribution of gross weekly earnings (full-time employees on adult rates)
Source: HMSO (1996)

paupers earned £6.50, a ratio of 492: 1, and 'vagrants, beggars, gypsies, thieves and prostitutes' received £2 (Rubinstein, 1986). At an earlier period still, King Richard I and King John had incomes equivalent to those of 24,000 serfs, who were paid a penny a day (Lenski, 1966).

The inequality of wealth is greater than that of income. Townsend (1979) found that the top 1 per cent in terms of income received 6.2 per cent of total income in 1968–9 but the top 1 per cent in terms of wealth owned 26 per cent of the total. The top 1 per cent in 1989 owned 11 per cent of national wealth, when houses and pension rights are included. When only marketable wealth is counted they owned 18 per cent of it. They owned £190,000 each, compared with an average of £845 for the bottom 50 per cent of the population, that is, 225 times as much. If we look at a smaller and richer group, the top 0.1 per cent, they owned 7 per cent of national wealth, £740,000 each, 867 times the average for the bottom 50 per cent. As Galbraith said in *The Affluent Society* (1984), it may be desirable to have rich people but this is too much. It is this top 0.1 per cent in terms of wealth who constitute the 'business class' of individuals and their families who own and control the 1,000 largest companies (Scott, 1982).

Like differences in earnings, differences in wealth were also greater in the past. The richest 1 per cent owned 18 per cent of wealth in 1989 but it was 69 per cent in 1911–13 (Central Statistical Office, 1992). In 1858, a study of probate found that over 80 per cent of men and over 90 per cent of women left no property at all; this actually means less than £100. But 440 landowners left £53,000 each, and 13 of them left £5.7 million each (Rubinstein, 1986).

There is, of course, some redistribution of income. In Britain, in 1994–5, the best paid 20 per cent were paid £16,720 on average, and after taxes and

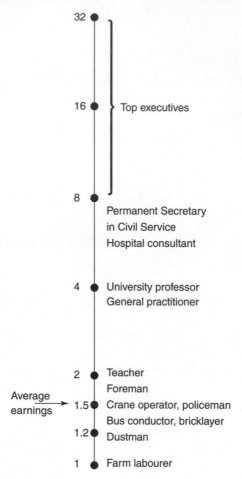

Figure 10.2 The earnings tree (men only)
Source: Atkinson (1983)

allowances this came to £15,570. The poorest 20 per cent on the other hand started at an average of £2,040 which was raised to £7,720. So the ratio of the final incomes of the richest to the poorest fifth of the population was only 2: 1. The redistribution has the effect of raising the poorest quite a lot and reducing the richest rather a little.

The question of whether this distribution is fair or healthy for any society is the subject of passionate political and economic debate. There are advocates on both sides, some believing that an inequitable distribution is inevitable and economically desirable, and others believing that governmental intervention should be used to prevent this unfair state of affairs continuing.

DIFFERENT ROUTES TO WEALTH

Rubinstein (1987) traced the development of three elite groups in recent English history. There was the traditional aristocracy, of titled families, whose wealth was in land. In the nineteenth century there was the rise of commercial fortunes, on the part of London-based financiers and the owners and managers of large companies, most of whom had themselves inherited money. And there were entrepreneurs, often in the north of England, the founders of smaller firms, many of them in manufacturing or textiles. There was more in common and there were more links between the aristocratic and the commercial groups, since they both lived in the south of England, tended to be Anglicans, and went to the same schools and universities. The self-made men were culturally different, though their children sometimes became educated and became country gentlemen, producing what has been called a 'haemorrhage of talent'. By 1914 these three elite groups had converged and formed a unified property class. Wealth had been linked to honours since the eighteenth century and there continued to be 'honours for sale'; the rich were also titled. But those who had inherited money often believed that 'old' money was somehow superior to money which had been earned by the 'nouveau riche'.

> The motive for entering trade was generally to accumulate the kind of wealth which would enable oneself or one's successors to enter landed society and to participate in the institutions of the landed class and its life style. Profit-seeking was a means rather than an end.
>
> (Scott, 1982, p. 61–2)

Harbury and Hitchens (1979) confirmed the distinction between the two kinds of new rich in Britain. The self-made men were mostly in metal extracting, construction, chemicals, clothing, printing, transport and finance – activities in which small firms could be successful. The inheritors were more often in agriculture, textiles, food and drink, metal manufacturing, distribution, public administration and the professions. The remaining aristocratic families of course still made their money from land. In this and other studies it has been found that inheritance is an important factor in becoming rich, and in this study it was found that about two-thirds of sons who left £100,000 or more in the period 1956–73 had themselves inherited at least £25,000 and a third of them had inherited £250,000.

Self-made men, who start their own businesses, become rich without inheriting anything. Examples are the founder of Green Shield stamps, the inventors of Xerox and of the Land camera, Ford and Lord Nuffield, who all became multi-millionaires. Studies of social mobility show that, for example, 7.1 per cent of individuals born into social class 7 in Britain end up in social class 1 (Goldthorpe *et al.*, 1987). Who are these successful, socially mobile people? Intelligence is one factor, but it works indirectly, via getting a good education (Heath, 1981, and see Figure 10.3). If intelligence, or other abilities are important, it would be expected that earnings would have the same kind of normal distribution that intelligence has; but, as we have seen, it does not, there is a long tail, for which economists have offered various explanations (Atkinson, 1983). Differences in wealth can be explained by the fact that money grows over time, so that inherited money has partly grown without any additional effort, other than shrewd investment. Large differences in income are harder to explain. If there is competition, as in business there usually is, the winner may take all. If there is a technical advance, the rivals will lose this particular race. If there is a commercial new idea, like Green Shield stamps, again, the inventor may get very rich. Or the sheer combination of factors – intelligence, social skills, motivation, education, and family help – put some individuals well ahead in the race.

Education is important, and it has been found that the cost of a degree, for example, is a good investment; in Britain, this is (or perhaps was) a major route to social mobility, for those clever enough to pass the exams. It is a familiar piece of British sociology to show that a majority of company chairmen, as well as top civil servants, bishops and vice-chancellors have been to public schools, very often to certain public schools like Eton and Harrow; they have also often been to Oxford or Cambridge, and to certain colleges, such as Christ Church and Trinity. But, as Rubinstein (1987) points out, many of these successful individuals had received scholarships, or their parents had saved up; they had often had fathers who were for example, clergymen or teachers, and thus had been socially mobile via education. The sons of the rich were at these schools and colleges, too, but as has often been pointed out 'there are two Oxfords'.

Motivation, such as achievement motivation, has been found to be as good a predictor of social mobility as intelligence, as was found in a longitudinal study by Cassidy and Lynn (1991), shown in Figure 10.3. This also shows the indirect effect of intelligence via education.

It has been proposed by Furnham and Rose (1987) that there is a motive to make money, which they called a 'wealth ethic'. They constructed a scale, which was found to have three factors – financial independence, wealth status (inherited money gives more respect), and wealth contentment (from avoiding the problems of not having it). Some of the items are about wanting money for its own sake; this may be part of the motivation of the very rich.

Entrepreneurs, who are the group most likely to become self-made rich, have been found to be high in achievement motivation and in the Protestant work ethic (McClelland *et al.*, 1953). In addition, they have been found to have somewhat unusual personalities. Case studies have found that they are often non-conformist, rebellious, distrust authority, are unwilling to work with others, and come from families where they were not appreciated, or were from marginal minority groups, giving them a great drive to succeed

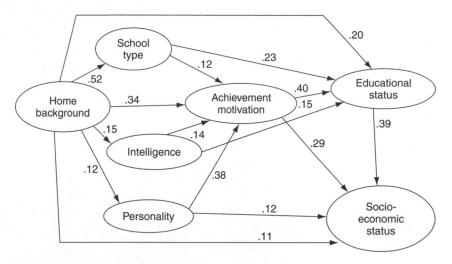

Figure 10.3 Path analysis of the effects of achievement motivation and other variables on social mobility
Source: Cassidy and Lynn (1991)

and establish a new identity (Kets de Vries, 1977). They seem to be high on the financial-independence part of the wealth-ethic scale.

Another way of becoming rich is by being successful in a profession or in management; we have seen that a few earn very large salaries in this way. However, they are unlikely to become owners of great wealth unless they also invest successfully. An individual on three times average earnings, who saved 25 per cent of his earnings from age 25–60, would join the top 0.1 per cent by that age – after a very frugal life (Atkinson, 1983). Runciman (1966) reports a bus driver who died in 1972 leaving £62,388; he had no children, had never taken a holiday and just bought the bare necessities.

There are further ways of becoming rich. Lottery winners do it by luck. Pop singers do it by developing the kind of voice and persona that the young like at a particular period. Tennis players, prize fighters and other sports players have developed a particular skill in a field where those who win are highly rewarded. Inventors can become very rich overnight, as can treasure hunters. Popular authors are very high earners, as are corrupt politicians. There are many ways to become rich, legal and illegal, socially acceptable or not.

HOW THEY SPEND IT

We have quantitative information about how the top 10 per cent of families in terms of income spend their money, but do not have the same information about the really rich. Table 10.1 shows the expenditure of the bottom,

Table 10.1 Household weekly expenditure by the bottom and top 10 per cent income groups, in Britain, 1994–5

	Bottom 10%	Average	Top 10%	Ratio top/ average
Housing	12.05	46.42	102.02	2.20
Fuel and power	8.96	12.95	18.51	1.43
Food, non-alcoholic drinks	20.89	50.43	89.36	1.77
Alcoholic drinks	3.11	12.32	26.54	2.15
Tobacco	3.78	5.61	6.10	1.09
Clothing and footwear	3.60	17.13	40.26	2.35
Household goods	6.92	22.66	52.89	2.33
Household services	4.65	15.08	35.46	2.35
Personal goods and services	2.86	10.78	22.60	2.10
Motoring	4.06	36.17	81.24	2.25
Fares and other travel	2.50	6.64	20.07	3.02
Leisure goods	3.06	13.89	33.64	2.42
Leisure services	5.35	31.20	90.11	2.89
Misc.	0.26	2.30	6.23	2.71
Total	82.05	283.58	625.03	2.22

Source: HMSO (1996)

average and top 10 per cent of income families, and ratios of top to average for each item.

The top 10 per cent spent over twice as much as average on housing, although many own their houses so their expenses should be less. They live in larger houses, in better areas; the really rich in country houses. The latter not only own their houses but usually own more than one. The top group also spend 2.33 as much as average on household goods, as they keep their houses better equipped, and spend a similar amount on 'household services', i.e. servants, such as nannies and gardeners, and over twice as much on 'personal goods and services', that is, other employees such as private doctors and hairdressers.

There is a large difference for 'leisure services', which will include restaurants, hotels and holidays, with a ratio of 2.89: 1. There is a ratio of 2.42: 1 for 'leisure goods', which will include boats, horses, caravans and electronic equipment. There is a ratio of 2.25 for 'motoring', and 3.02 for other travel, but this is partly because the rich drive further to work, as they live in distant suburbs or villages.

Education, for public school and university, is not included in this table, and is a major expense for many families in this group. Public-school fees in 1996 were about £14,000 per annum, and some families have several children at school at the same time.

All this provides a very simple answer to the question of why people, or some people, want to be rich. They can live in nicer houses, be looked after by servants, go to restaurants and hotels, and pay for leisure goods and services which will expand their life; buying a boat means you can go boating, buying a horse means you can go riding. Some rich people are too busy to spend it on holidays, horses or boating; some of them simply buy property, art or land.

THE EFFECTS OF MONEY ON PEOPLE'S LIVES

The pattern of expenditure described above tells part of the story. Studies of the very wealthy in Britain have shown how they form a distinct and closed social group, linked by kinship and marriage, who own shares in each other's firms with many interlocking directorships. It is difficult to join this group from outside, partly because the members groom their own children, by sending them to schools and colleges with children from other wealthy families, where they get to know each other and establish an old-boy network. This group has a distinctive and expensive culture and life-style, with elaborate balls and dinners, expensive sports (shooting and polo), and annual rituals (Ascot, Henley). Though different from the aristocratic upper class of an earlier period, many of them do live in country houses and own land, and some acquire titles through their connections with politics, industry or charitable organisations (Argyle, 1994). The position of the rich in America is very similar. The top 0.5 per cent belong to exclusive clubs, which others cannot afford or are not allowed to join, and are members of the Social Register, the young people go to debutante balls, and belong to the right fraternities and sororities (Kerbo, 1983).

What is the effect on well-being? Do riches make people healthy or happy? We shall see later (p. 267) that while larger incomes had no effect on happiness over the upper half of the income scale, there was a small rise for the very rich; this was confirmed by a study of millionaires, who said they were happier than members of a control group. The reason for the declining effect of income is probably that the things bought were of less benefit, for example, antiques compared with food. We still have to explain the effect of large incomes. This may be because self-esteem is greater for those of higher social class, either because they feel they are successful, or because of the deference and respect they may receive from others.

Income is generally found to have a positive effect on health (Argyle, 1994). However, one of the most extensive and careful studies in Britain, the *Health and Lifestyles* survey (Blaxter, 1990), found a reversal of this effect in 1984–5 for those earning over £250 a week at that time. This was mainly due to the poor health behaviour, especially drinking a lot, among young males, managers and owners of small businesses, not professional or technical people. There have been a number of cases in Britain of the children of rich and often aristocratic families taking to drink or drugs. This may be because of greater access to money, or because of the lack of incentives to work and compete, as well as being associated with others with the bored-rich experimental life-style.

THE PUBLIC VIEW OF INCOME AND WEALTH DIFFERENCES

British surveys find that a majority 71 per cent think that the existing differences are unfair, though about half thought that the gap was 'about right' (Marshall *et al.*, 1988), and 48 per cent thought that the rich did not deserve what they had (Gallie, 1983). Conservative voters are more satisfied with the present state of affairs than Labour supporters. Poorer individuals wanted more money for poor people, but Evans (1992) concluded that this represented instrumental self-interest rather than egalitarianism.

Surveys by Headey (1991) in Australia found that 80 per cent wanted more equality, but that they misperceived the actual distribution and thought it was more egalitarian than it really was. Errors were greater when there was a larger difference between incomes of perceiver and perceived, so that the poor underestimated the salaries of the rich. While most favoured more equality, the rich favoured large salaries for high-status jobs.

In the USA, Alves and Rossi (1978) asked subjects to judge the fair salaries for fifty individuals described in vignettes. From this it emerged that subjects thought that more skilled jobs should be paid more, $5,600 more for men, that education was worth $195 for each year, with a total range of $1,379, that those with children should be paid $325 more for each, and those with wives $1,700. From this and other studies it is clear that most people recognised the need to reward occupational status, and also to meet people's needs.

Mitchell *et al.* (1993) asked participants to choose between various income distributions. The results showed that a compromise was favoured between having a hierarchy of incomes, believed to benefit society economically, and the need to look after the disadvantaged, especially if the subjects were told that there was a meritocracy, where effort and talent were rewarded. But if they were told that there was little relation between rewards and effort, they preferred a policy which did the best for the least fortunate. In both cases they not did want to see the disadvantaged fall below the poverty line.

Some sociologists and most economists have defended the existence of large differences in wealth, on the grounds that this fulfils certain 'functions' in society. From an economic point of view the most important of these is that there need to be incentives to reward and encourage entrepreneurs to take risks, raise and invest money, and work hard, and this will have the effect of creating jobs and benefiting the whole economy. It is widely believed that the economic success of society depends on the existence of such incentives; the economic success of entrepreneurs is expected to trickle down to many others. This does not explain why those who have inherited money need to be rewarded, or why those who are successful in non-economic fields need these rewards. Incentives are needed in non-capitalist settings too. In communist Russia, Stalin introduced wage differentials in the 1930s, to motivate people to acquire the skills and accept the responsibilities of higher-administrative and technical jobs. Subsequently, technical staff earned about 50 per cent more than manual workers, and the top 10 per cent of white-collar intelligentsia more than this (Parkin, 1971). It has often been said that the growth of industry in Africa has been impeded by the custom of relatives' expecting to share any financial good fortune on the part of a member of the family (Herskovitz, 1952). The Protestant work ethic prescribed that those who are successful in business should not spend it on themselves, but plough it back into the business. This must surely happen in the early years of new firms, but how far it happens later, or to those who inherit the fortune, may be doubted.

Another supposed function of the rich is for an elite group of talented people to act as an independent source of leadership in the interest of society as a whole. While a number of American sociologists have argued that this happens, others think that the rich use their influence mainly to produce good outcomes for themselves, their families and their firms (Kerbo, 1983). It has also been argued that the rich exert a kind of cultural leadership, since they are first to have new things, such as cars, television, and other new products which might never have taken off without sales to those able to afford them and try them out (G. Richardson, personal communication). This has happened with new forms of leisure, such as foreign travel, skiing, yachting and several forms of sport such as rugby football and tennis. But while some of these filtered through society, others like polo and yachting are too expensive (Argyle, 1994). And other new products like TV and washing machines didn't need the rich to lead the way.

Another defence of the rich is that they are said to give to charities and to promote charities. In the USA, where charitable donations are tax deductible, those earning over $1 million a year give a median amount of $44,000, and the top quartile $132,000, which is over 10 per cent of their incomes. In Britain, giving is not tax-deductible, and giving rises from about 1.4 per cent of income for those on average incomes to a modest 1.75 per cent for the rich; the number who are tithing must be rather small. However, a few of the very rich set up foundations which did a great deal for education and health, such as the Wolfson, Nuffield and Rowntree. In the case of Rowntree this was in line with Quaker intentions. This has the benefit to the giver of keeping the fortune intact instead of dividing it all between heirs. The rich support charities in another way too, in taking a lead in charitable organisations, and going to 'charity balls', which are themselves part of upper-class symbolism. In the nineteenth century most voluntary work was done by ladies of leisure, who had servants. However, less was done by the Lady Bountiful of the manor than by the middle-class ladies who taught working-class children to read in Sunday School, tried to improve working-class leisure, and founded many charities (Argyle, 1994).

Some rich people in the past have been important in giving money to schools and colleges, and in recent British history, the Wolfson and Nuffield foundations have continued this tradition, also giving a lot to medical and other scientific research. However, the majority of rich people are not known for their interest in or contributions to education. Similarly, in the past rich people were important patrons of the arts, such as by financing court musicians, and paying for works of art. Sainsbury's has paid for two art galleries in recent years. They have also financed major building projects, including churches, castles, palaces and many country houses, without which our heritage would be the poorer. However, such projects today are mainly paid for by the state or large institutions.

CONCLUSION

It is generally agreed that financial rewards are needed as incentives, but most people think that the differences should be smaller, and many do not realise how rich the rich are. They become rich by different routes, most by career success leading to large salaries, or being successful entrepreneurs, or inheriting and investing money made by forbears. Two-thirds of millionaires inherited substantial sums. The money is spent in financing an expensive and superior way of life, with large houses, servants, expensive cars, holidays and social life. It is claimed that the rich are useful through their contributions to charity, good works and support for the arts and education; this seems to be true of a small minority. The main motivation to be rich appears to be to join or stay in this high-prestige group, but there may also be some who pursue money as an end in itself. Can any of this be regarded as irrational? If wealth is sought as a means to status this is not irrational, unless the pursuit of status is so regarded. It was generally regarded as rather comical in Oxford when a famous physicist was found seeking the company of duchesses in grand houses (rather than that of his colleagues, who were possibly wittier and certainly knew more about physics). The cost of social mobility may be to lose the company of those who were loved and of activities which were enjoyed, and to be despised and rejected by the members of a 'higher' stratum. On the other hand, we have seen that over half of the very rich have inherited a lot of money and some of them belonged to this superior group already; their motivation may be to stay in it.

11 The economic model

How far does money produce
happiness or motivate people?

*Money alone can't bring you happiness, but money alone has
not brought me unhappiness. I won't say my previous
husbands thought only of my money, but it had a certain
fascination for them.*

Barbara Hutton

*Money is human happiness in the abstract; he, then, who is
no longer capable of enjoying human happiness in the
concrete devotes himself utterly to money.*

Arthur Schopenhauer

*Nothing is a greater proof of a narrow and grovelling
disposition than to be fond of money, while nothing is more
noble and exalted than to despise it, if thou hast it not; and if
thou hast it, to employ it in beneficence and liberality.*

Cicero

*Money is a stupid measure of achievement, but unfortunately
it is the only universal measure we have.*

Charles Steinmetz

*For the love of money is the root of all evil: which while some
coveted after, they have erred from the faith, and pierced
themselves through with many sorrows.*

Bible: 1 Timothy

*Whenever money is the principle object of life with either
man or nation, it is both got ill, and spent ill; and does both
harm in the getting and spending.*

John Ruskin

*I have a rich neighbour that is always so busy that he has no
leisure to laugh; the whole business of his life is to get money,
more money, that he may still get more. He considers not that
it is not in the power of riches to make a man happy; for it
was wisely said that 'there be as many miseries beyond riches
as on this side of them'.*

Izaak Walton

> *If you do anything for just the money you don't succeed.*
>
> Barry Hearn

> *They say money can't buy happiness, but it can facilitate it. I thoroughly recommend having lots of it to anybody.*
>
> Malcolm Forbes

> *Money brings honor, friends, conquest and realms.*
>
> John Milton

INTRODUCTION

This chapter takes us to the heart of the relation between psychology and economics. It is widely assumed by economists and by governments that what people want are goods and services which will provide satisfaction, and that money is the measure of how much of these can be afforded; it follows that having a larger income should make people happier. In fact, the findings on these topics do not support these assumptions. While economists suppose that there is in a sense only one motivation, this is not listed by most psychologists in their lists of human motivation – with the exception of Freud.

We begin by considering whether money leads to happiness, and how far money can buy happiness. We then consider whether there is a psychological need for money, and if there is how it relates to other better-known motivational systems. Finally, we draw together the main findings of earlier chapters to see how far they fit the assumptions of economists, the concept of 'economic man'. We shall find that at many points they certainly do not.

DOES MONEY LEAD TO HAPPINESS?

Are rich people happier than poor people? To start with, what is the effect of pay on satisfaction? There have been a number of studies of this relationship, and they all come up with a correlation of about .25, for example,, in *The Quality of American Life* study by Campbell *et al.* (1976). Headey (1993) obtained a causal model in which family income predicted satisfaction with income (.36) and this in turn predicted well-being (.36), but there was little direct causal influence of income on well-being. Pay satisfaction is affected by other variables than pay, for example employees are more satisfied with their pay if they are satisfied in other ways (Weitzel *et al.*, 1977). The very small correlation between pay and satisfaction with pay has led many to suggest that relative pay is more important than absolute pay, which will be discussed later.

There are four good reasons why this is so:

- *Adaptation:* although everybody feels 'happier' after a pay rise, windfall or pools win, one soon adapts to this and the effect very rapidly disappears. Relatively quick adaptation to pay increases means that it can only be effective if done very regularly, which is particularly expensive.

- *Comparison:* people define themselves as rich/wealthy by comparing themselves with others. However, with increased wealth, people usually move in more 'up-market' circles where there is always someone wealthier than themselves.
- *Alternatives:* as economists say, the declining marginal utility of money means that as one has more of the stuff, other things such as freedom and true friendship seem much more valuable.
- *Worry:* an increased income is associated with a shifting of concern from money issues to the more uncontrollable elements of life (e.g. self-development), perhaps because money is associated with a sense of control over one's fate.

Economists argue that money does act as a work motivator, but to a large extent in the short term, for some workers more than others, and at a cost often to the morale of the organisation. Yet money is only one of many motivators of behaviour, and the power of money as a motivator is short-lived. Further, in countries with high taxation, it is often less attractive than tangible goods – though these may be taxed too, as with business cars. In addition, it has less effect the more comfortable people are. Yet it may be particularly important in times or places of political (even economic) instability, because it is highly portable.

What about the relation between income and happiness? There have been a number of large-scale surveys of national samples in which income and level of happiness or satisfaction have been measured. Most of these studies have found a small positive and significant correlation of about .15 to .20. In an early American survey, Bradburn (1969) found that income made more difference to positive than to negative affect. Recent studies have found that the effect of money is much stronger at the lower ranges of income, and that it makes much less difference at the upper end of the scale. Diener *et al.* (1993) reported an American survey carried out with 6,913 respondents in 1971–5 and 4,942 of them again in 1981–4 (Fig. 11a and b).

In both periods it can be seen that there is a strong relation between income and well-being for the poor, a levelling off for those better off, and a final rise for the very rich. In 1981–4 there was little increase of happiness beyond an income of $15,000. The finding about the very rich, however, was confirmed in another study of 49 individuals earning over $10 million a year; they reported being happy 77 per cent of the time, while a comparison group were happy only 62 per cent of the time (Diener *et al.*, 1988). While the effect of income in the USA levels off in the way shown in Figure 11.1, there is a much stronger relation with income in countries like India and Brazil, where most people are poorer, and where there are large differences in incomes (Cantril, 1965). In fact, economists have often

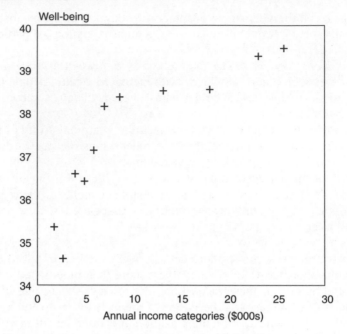

Figure 11.1a Income and well-being for US Time 1
Source: Diener *et al.* (1993)

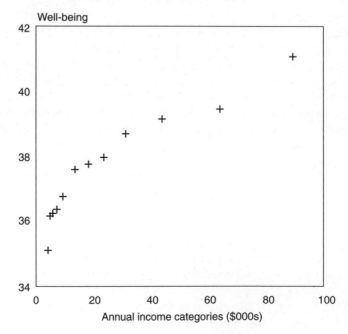

Figure 11.1b Income and well-being for US Time 2
Source: Diener *et al.* (1993)

assumed that there would be 'declining marginal utility of money', that is, it would make less difference at higher incomes.

However, there are two groups who do not fit this overall relationship. There are a lot of poor people who are perfectly happy and apparently satisfied with their lot, and who make no attempt to do anything about it – the so-called 'satisfaction paradox'. This has been interpreted as a state of adaptation and learned helplessness produced by long experience of being unable to control their situation (Olson and Schober, 1993). There are also unhappy rich people; this is no great surprise in view of the fairly weak relation between money and happiness (r = .15–.20), and the fact that there are several other and more important sources of happiness, which will be described later.

A similar pattern is found if the average happiness or satisfaction of whole countries is compared. Inkeles and Diamond (1986) compared individuals of the same occupational status, and found correlations of .60 between well-being and national economic growth. In the latest of a series of international studies, Diener, *et al.* (1995) used several measures of income and happiness for 55 countries. Income was measured by average GNP, and also by purchasing power, and there was a measure of satisfaction of basic physiological needs. Quite high correlations of .50 or above were found for all measures of income and happiness – considerably higher than the within-country correlations of .15 to .20 (Figure 11.2).

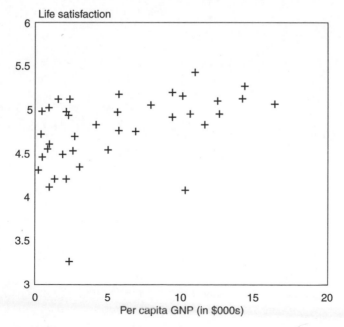

Figure 11.2. GNP per capita and life satisfaction in fifty-five countries
Source: Diener *et al.* (1995)

It would be expected that average national happiness would increase as overall prosperity rises, as it has done in many countries in recent decades. There have been repeated surveys of happiness and satisfaction in a number of countries. There have been fluctuations in those who said they were 'very happy', and there are certainly short-term effects of economic depression on happiness. In Belgium a striking fall in reported happiness was found in the years 1978–83, corresponding to a fall in national prosperity (Inglehart and Rabier, 1986). Veenhoven (1994) reports similar declines in average national happiness in Brazil, Ireland and Japan. The 1980–2 recession in Europe led to a small fall in happiness over one year. However, getting less than you have been used to is a different matter than simply having an income of a certain level; it is a form of frustration.

In the USA there have been repeated happiness surveys. Figure 11.3 shows the fluctuation in the percentage of people who said they were 'very happy', and also the average personal income between 1950 and 1990. It can be seen that happiness has fluctuated, while income has increased. The doubling of incomes has certainly not led to a doubling of happiness. The same is found in other countries, including Japan, where a fivefold increase in GNP between 1958 and 1987 had no effect on happiness, and in nine European countries between 1973 and 1989 (Easterlin, 1995). The lack of

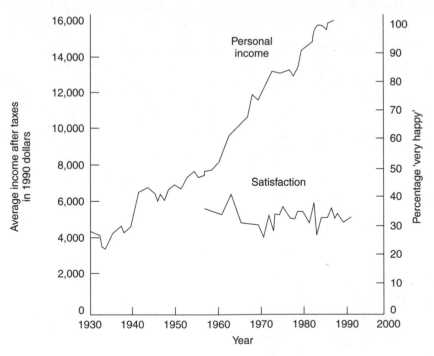

Figure 11.3 Income and happiness in the USA, 1950–90
Source: Myers and Dieners (1996)

long-term effects of economic changes on well-being may be due to *adaptation*, that is people become accustomed to a changed level of prosperity and no longer find it a source of increased satisfaction. In the USA there may be an additional factor of increasing expectations and an American optimistic belief that things will keep on improving. A further point is that if everyone is richer, there is no enhancement of *comparison* with others, which, as we shall see later, is an important source of happiness (Lane, 1991).

Wealth is a possible source of happiness, in addition to income. Mullis (1992) found that net worth makes an independent prediction of happiness, though it too is small. A better prediction of happiness or satisfaction can be made from a combined measure taking account of both wealth and income.

Another source of information about the possible effects of money on happiness comes from the study of lottery winners. A study of 191 British winners of football pools, all of whom had won £160,000 or more, found that many of them said they were a little happier than before (Smith and Razzell, 1975), and an American study of lottery winners found a quite small difference. These findings have been taken to support the idea that adaptation takes place, so that people very soon adjust to their new conditions, and the level of satisfaction returns to where it was before. However, in the British study some serious problems were reported: 70 per cent of winners gave up their work, thus losing job satisfaction and workmates, some moved to a larger house and were rejected by snobbish new neighbours, and some quarrelled with family and friends, who wanted a share in the winnings. Some had an identity problem – only 28 per cent were certain about which class they belonged to.

There have been numerous newspaper interviews with winners of the National Lottery. A rather sad one was with a woman of 24 who won £1,375,000. It had changed her life very little: she was still unemployed, had bought a car but couldn't drive, had bought a lot of clothes and had to put them into store, didn't like expensive food and preferred fish fingers. Her life sounded as if it was still empty and unsatisfying (*Sunday Telegraph*, 22 February 1997).

What is the explanation of these effects of money on happiness? There are obvious reasons for there being a positive effect – money buys the things we want, basic needs, leisure, possibly good health and social status, as we shall see later. In a comparison of 101 countries, Diener and Diener (1995) found that wealth correlated with 26 out of 32 possible indicators of quality of life, not only satisfaction of biological needs but also income equality, civil rights, protection of the environment, literacy and intellectual achievement. What needs explaining is why the effect of money is so weak, within countries at least, and in historical terms. It may be because comparative income is more important than absolute income, or because other causes of happiness are simply more important. We will look at both of these next.

COMPARISONS AND EXPECTATIONS

It has long been thought by economists that it is relative rather than absolute income which satisfies, that is income relative to that of others. Social-comparison theory has been revived to explain the very small apparent effects of income on happiness, particularly within countries, with correlations of the order of .15 to .20. There is no doubt that real income affects the material and other conditions of life; the interest now is whether with income held constant happiness varies with the comparison groups available. We saw in Chapter 9 that comparisons are important causes of pay satisfaction, and cited the studies by Runciman (1966) and Clark and Oswald (1993), and referred to the role of comparisons in wage bargaining.

Michalos (1985) developed the 'Michigan model', whereby happiness and satisfaction are a function of the 'goal–achievement gap': that is, the gap between present pay or other benefits and those which are wanted or expected. This gap in turn is due to two sets of comparisons, (1) with past life, and (2) with 'average folk'. This discrepancy is found to predict satisfaction better than satisfaction with different domains or resources, and 'financial security' is the domain with the strongest predictor of overall happiness. Part of the comparison here is with the past, and this has been found to work in other studies. For example, Strack *et al.* (1985) asked subjects to think about negative and unpleasant events in the past, and this had the effect of making them feel happier and more satisfied in the present, temporarily at least. Working within this framework, Harwood and Rice (1992) found that discrepancy with the salary wanted or expected was more strongly correlated with satisfaction than discrepancy between salary and that of co-workers. However, this study was done with students who would have limited experience of work. Smith *et al.* (1989) found that social comparisons correlated more strongly (av. 64) with satisfaction than did recent changes (.30). The strongest effects of recent changes were for courses and grades; since the subjects were students, income does not apply, but the effect of comparison on standard of living was .27 and for recent changes .06. However, Fox and Kahneman (1992) found that subjects rated recent changes more important than social comparisons, especially in private spheres; money is in the public sphere.

Diener *et al.* (1993) compared well-being in rich and poor areas of the USA for individuals of the same income; comparison theory predicts that people would be happier in poorer areas, but this was not found. Diener *et al.* (1995) similarly looked at the effect on national well-being of having richer or poorer neighbouring countries, but again found no difference. However, we do not know how far any of these comparisons were made. In several studies it has been found that poor people do not realise how rich the rich are, so presumably they will not make accurate comparisons (Headey, 1993). Comparisons are likely to be based on life-style, for example, size of house, date of car, domestic equipment, holidays, school fees, and other things that money is used to buy.

Social-comparison theory leads to the expectation that happiness will be greater if there is a smaller range of incomes within the country, and if people actually make these comparisons. Veenhoven (1994) had found that average happiness was greater in countries like Sweden where there was a smaller distribution of income (the gini index) – there was a correlation of $-.45$ between happiness and income inequality for 28 countries. Diener *et al.* (1995) also found that average national happiness was greater when there was a smaller income spread, with a correlation of $-.43$ for 55 countries, very similar to Veenhoven's figure. Another version of comparison theory is that people have expectations of what their income should be, and are satisfied if they get more than this, dissatisfied if they get less. Members of the public have very clear ideas of what different workers should be paid. Alves and Rossi (1978) used a vignette method in which subjects were asked whether the persons described were over- or under-paid. Occupation made a difference of $5,600 for men, education $195 for each year of education, and college added $779, children added $325 each and marriage $1,700.

Diener *et al.* (1993) carried out a study of the possible negative effects of education with their sample of 6,913 Americans. They expected that, as with the salary studies, with income held constant, education would have a negative effect, but in fact it had a small positive effect. They also expected that being black would have a positive effect, since expectations would be lower, but in fact it had a small negative effect. Both analyses show small differences in the opposite direction from those predicted by comparison theory.

Comparison theory has been most successful in British studies, perhaps because of the prominence of wage bargaining and trade unions. It has been less successful in American studies, and not at all in international ones. In the latter, actual income and real satisfactions are more important.

OTHER SOURCES OF HAPPINESS; CAN MONEY BUY THEM?

Money may have an effect on happiness and other aspects of well-being, but there are a number of other, and probably more important, causes of happiness. We will look at these and consider how far they in turn depend on money. The study in Australia by Headey and Wearing (1992) shows the correlations of some of them with life satisfaction, positive affect and two measures of unhappiness, anxiety and depression. The strongest correlations are with satisfaction with leisure, so we will start with this.

Table 11.1 Relationship of domain satisfactions with well-being and psychological distress: correlations

Domain satisfaction	Life satisfaction index	Positive affect	Anxiety	Depression
Leisure	.42	.28	−.29	−.29
Marriage	.39	.17	−.29	−.32
Work	.38	.26	−.27	−.36
Standard of living	.38	.20	−.18	−.26
Friendships	.37	.19	−.15	−.12
Sex life	.34	.17	−.19	−.33
Health	.25	.11	−.23	−.14

Source: Headey and Wearing (1992)

Leisure

This is an important source of happiness, and is the one which it is easiest to do something about. A number of studies have found that leisure satisfaction is one of the strongest predictors of overall life satisfaction (Argyle, 1996). In the study by Headey *et al.* (1994) it was found that enjoyable activities with friends, which would be nearly all leisure, predicted increases in happiness over two-year intervals. Different kinds of leisure have been studied from this point of view. Sport and exercise put people in a good mood very rapidly, and enhance happiness and reduce depression if done regularly (Biddle and Mutrie, 1991). Religion enhances happiness, especially for the elderly, partly through the social support of the church community, but also through feeling close to God, and the optimistic effect of beliefs, for example, that God will help us. Companionship and other aspects of social support from leisure groups are a major source of happiness. Watching soap operas seems to enhance happiness by providing a circle of imaginary friends, and holidays produce good moods from relaxation. However, the deepest satisfaction comes from more demanding activities, using skills, meeting challenges and tangible achievements (Argyle, 1996). Leisure is often good for health; sport affects many aspects of health, and members of strict churches which disallow smoking and drinking and make other demands may live four years longer; and, as we have seen, exercise is good for depression.

Lack of money can limit leisure, but much leisure is free or nearly so – church, evening classes, walking, the public library and voluntary work, for example. The effects on joy of some of these activities are shown in Figure 11.4.

Many sports and forms of exercise are very cheap, especially for the retired and unemployed. So is TV and radio. Much of this activity and satisfaction does not 'go through the market economy' as Scitovsky (1992) puts it. Some other kinds of leisure cost more, especially holidays and

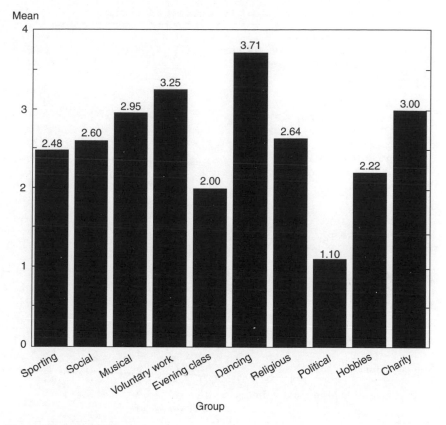

Figure 11.4. Joy by group
Source: Argyle (1996)

travel, meals out, theatre and opera, and sports like skiing, sailing and horse-riding, and some hobbies. In Britain, in 1994, people spent on average £45.04 per week on various kinds of leisure, 16.6 per cent of their budgets, and the largest items were meals out, and drink and holidays, see Table 11.2. A lot of these leisure activities are very cheap. Holidays are an obvious exception, they do cheer people up, and they are much indulged in by the very rich.

However, Riddick and Stewart (1994) studied a sample of retired people and found that their leisure satisfaction was not predicted by income, in fact, there was a correlation of $-.20$ for the black (Afro-American) subjects, though leisure satisfaction was predicted by health and leisure activities.

Social relationships

These are a second important source of happiness, though they are more difficult to do anything about than leisure. Being in love is the greatest

Table 11.2 Expenditure on leisure (£ per week per household)

1	TV purchases and rentals	7.59
2	Radios, music, cinema and theatre	1.62
3	Books, magazines and papers	3.84
4	Meals out, alcohol	13.89
5	Home repairs, etc.	3.96
	hobbies	0.07
	home computers	0.61
6	Sports	2.02
7	Spectator sports	0.24
8	Church (for attenders)	3.00
9	Voluntary work	–
10	Holidays	11.21
Total		£48.05

Source: Argyle (1996)
Note: As percentage of household expenditure total = 17.7

Table 11.3 Help by friends and relations

Type of help		Middle-class	White collar	Working-class
Advice on a personal matter	friends	64	67	39
	relatives	34	33	58
Source of financial loan	friends	26	23	9
	relatives	74	73	86
Main source of help in child's illness	friends	39	45	19
	relatives	56	55	77

Source: Willmott (1987)

source of joy, but being with friends also produces feelings of joy, partly through the enjoyable activities, and also from receiving smiles and other positive reactions from the others. Marriage and other close relationships produce happiness for most, especially when the marriage goes well; this is because of the social support given through companionship, emotional support and material help. Kin are often an important source of help, especially in times of crisis, and especially for working-class individuals, but middle-class people see much more of friends. The reason for this is that working-class individuals tend to stay in the same area, while middle-class people are much more geographically mobile – they go away for education and jobs, and they make more friends at work and in connection with leisure groups (Willmott, 1987).

Does money help with relationships? Middle-class, i.e. richer, couples stay married longer and have a much lower divorce rate. One reason for this is that they get married later than working-class couples, the bride is less likely to be pregnant at the time of marriage, and there is a longer interval between marriage and birth of first child. It follows that middle-class couples have a much easier start to their marriages, and probably choose more carefully. In addition, they have fewer money problems, and are more likely to have a place of their own instead of having to live with their parents, for example. Marriage is less stressful for those who do not have serious money problems, which are a common cause of marital conflict (Argyle and Henderson, 1985).

Money may help with friends too. Willmott (1987) carried out a regression equation to predict the number of friends people are likely to have, with the result shown in Table 11.4. Amazingly, owning a car leads to 2.36 more friends, and having another car does the same again. This may be because it is easier to get to see the friends or easier to go out with them, or perhaps because cars are a useful source of lifts. It may also be necessary to pay for drinks, meals or other entertainments. The unemployed complain that they can't afford to do things, but in fact they often drink a lot (Argyle, 1996). Money can't buy friendship or other relationships, but it makes them easier. However, having the right social skills is even more essential.

There are two relationships which the poor make more use of than do the rich. The poor see more of, and obtain more help from, kin. Working-class people also see a lot more of their neighbours, calling round for a chat daily, for example, while middle-class people ignore most of their actual neighbours, while recognising selected others who live further away (Argyle, 1994). So for kin and neighbours, money is not necessary at all, indeed it makes these relationships weaker.

Health

It is well known that happiness and good health are correlated, to some extent. Table 11.1 showed the correlation in a large study in Australia. A meta-analysis of many studies found an overall correlation of .32 (Okun *et al.*, 1984). This correlation was stronger for women, and when subjective measures of health were used – this is because unhappy people exaggerate their symptoms. But does health lead to happiness or vice versa? In fact, both directions of causation have been found to operate (Feist *et al.*, 1995).

Table 11.4 Number of friends from each source

Source	No. of friends
Basis number of friends	5.85
Further education adds	6.74
Middle-class job adds	4.59
One car adds	2.36
Second car adds	2.36

Source: Willmott (1987)

A number of studies have found that health is a good predictor of happiness, and that this holds up when other variables like age and social status have been controlled (Edwards and Klemmack, 1973). For old people health has often been found to be the strongest predictor of happiness (Willits and Crider, 1988).

The effects of health on happiness do not need much explanation. When people are in good health they are able to do more things, indeed, this is the basis of functional definitions of health; and they also simply feel better.

Do rich people have better health or live longer? There are difficulties about how to measure health, but mortality is clear enough. Those born in Britain in 1972 whose parents were in social class I had a life expectancy 7.2 years longer than those born into social class V. Much of the difference lay in different risks in childhood, and by age 15 the difference was only 4 years (Reid, 1989). There are greater working-class death rates from a number of causes, particularly male child deaths, mental disorders, injury and poisoning, infectious diseases, diseases of the respiratory system, and of the digestive system, heart disease and cancer (Occupational Mortality, 1990). Working-class people in Britain have higher death rates from most illnesses, except from skin cancer, polio and brain tumours (Black *et al.*, 1988). Another way of studying the problem is to survey population samples, with objective assessment of health. Blaxter's (1990) *Health and Lifestyle* survey did this, and some of the findings are shown in Figure 11.5. It can be seen that there were massive effects of income on two measures of health, but again with a reversal for the very rich. In this study health was affected by income more than by any other measure of class. These effects of class on income vary between different countries; in Sweden, for example, the ratio of the prevalence of long-standing illness for the bottom class to the top one is 1.52, while in Britain it is 2.65 (Vagero and Lundberg, 1989).

Subjective health, that is how well people say or feel they are, is something different, and not always very closely related to real health; for example, neurotic individuals exaggerate their symptoms, while some symptoms like high blood pressure are often unnoticed. However, there are class differences here too; 36 per cent of working-class people think their health is fair or poor, compared with 12 per cent for class I. This difference is greater for old people, and working-class individuals report higher rates for a wide range of symptoms.

What is the explanation of these differences? (1) The main reason lies in differences in life-style. Working-class people in Western cultures smoke more, take much less exercise, are more often obese, have higher blood pressure and cholesterol levels. This in turn is due to a whole working-class culture of poor diet, and the effects of stress and poor medical education. Marmot *et al.* (1984) studied 17,530 British civil servants, and found that those in the lower ranks had 3.6 times as many deaths from heart attacks as those in the highest grades. The investigators were able to explain 40 per

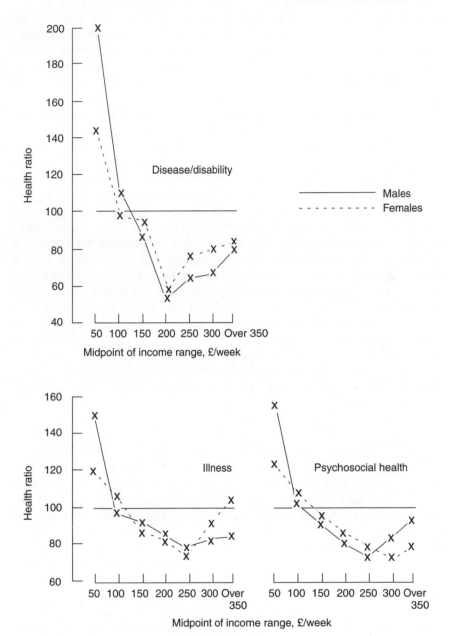

Figure 11.5 Income and health: age-standardised health ratios, illness and psychosocial health, in relation to weekly income, demonstrating the effect of £50/week increments in household income, males and females aged 40–59 (all of a given age and gender = 100)
Source: Blaxter (1990)

cent of the variance from finding that the lower ranks had higher blood pressure, smoked more, had higher blood sugar and cholesterol, and were shorter; they also had less active leisure, but this was not quantified or its effects examined. Forty per cent of the variance could be explained by these variables but 60 per cent remained to be explained. (2) Middle-class people have better medical care, both because of access to private medicine, but also by making more use of the National Health Service, such as going to check-ups and taking preventive measures; doctors even spend longer talking to them than to working-class patients. (3) Manual workers often have bad working conditions, with heat, noise, dust or other pollution, or other dangerous conditions, as in mining. (4) Working-class home conditions are often less favourable, with poor heating, poor air, damp, less cleanliness, lack of safe play areas for children, and difficulty of getting to the doctor. (5) Social support is important in health; in close relationships people not only look after one another, but in addition their immune systems are strengthened by the relationship. The high rate of broken marriages in the working-class, together with loss of job relations through unemployment, and lower attendance at church and leisure groups, would be expected to lead to poorer health (Williams, 1990). (6) We have seen that health behaviour only accounts for part of the class differences found. It seems possible that sheer status, or sheer wealth, have a further effect on health, via the feelings of self-esteem and self-confidence produced.

So, richer people are on average in better health, but this is less because they are able to buy something, but more as a result of a different and more healthy life-style.

Mental health

Does being better off lead to better mental health, or does being poor drive you crazy, as a result of the life-style or conditions for life of rich and poor people? In Britain there are many working-class patients in mental hospitals; a study in Aberdeen found that 20.5 per cent of psychotic patients were from class V, while in the population there are 9 per cent of people in this class. Similar differences were found for classes III and IV (Birtchnell, 1971). These classes were defined by occupation, for example, class V consists of unskilled workers and their families, but occupational class is closely correlated with income. If different mental disorders are examined, class differences are greatest for schizophrenia, where class V individuals have five times the expected rate, and for depression, where they have two to three times the expected rate.

Another way of tackling this issue is to carry out surveys of mental health in population samples. In the *Health and Lifestyles* study, Blaxter (1990) assessed the mental health of 7,414 British adults, and found that it was related to income, as shown in Figure 11.5. It can be seen that poorer people were in much worse mental health than richer ones, but that there was a reversal for the very rich; this was found to be due to excessive alcohol consumption in this group. She also found that the effect of income on mental health was greater for older people.

American studies have also found that mental health is worse for the poor. Kessler (1982) reanalysed the data from 8 national surveys carried out between 1967 and 1976, with a total of 16,000 respondents, and was able to separate different aspects of social status. He found that, for men, income, especially earned income, was the strongest predictor of good mental health, while for women education was stronger. For both sexes occupational status was a weaker predictor than income or education.

What is the explanation of these effects of income? To begin with, are they effects? In the first of four processes listed below the causation is in reverse, from ill-health to income, but the other three are assumed to be from income to mental health, and make more conceptual sense this way round. Several processes may be operating. (1) There may be a downward drift of the mentally disturbed, or a failure of upward drift, and this is most important in the case of schizophrenia; in other words, social status and income are consequences of mental disturbance. (2) Working-class, i.e. poorer, people report more stresses, such as unemployment, trouble with the law, bad housing, shortage of money, drunken husbands, or several young children at home. This has been found to be important for depression (Brown and Harris, 1978), and here lack of money is part of the explanation. (3) Working-class people are more vulnerable to stress, partly due to passive and ineffective styles of coping, which are in turn due to the experience of being unable to control events (Kohn and Schooler, 1983). (4) Richer people can afford private psychotherapy, and we will discuss the possible benefits of this in the next section.

As with health, richer people have better mental health, but this is mainly the result of greater stress in working-class life (partly due to lack of money) and less effective styles of coping.

Work

Work is an important source of happiness, and it is the major source of money. Traditional economic theory assumed that people had to be paid to work because they would prefer to be doing something else, i.e. nothing or leisure. Some jobs have to be paid because they are unpleasant or dangerous, and indeed such jobs have to be paid more. But as we saw in Chapter 9 there are other reasons for working apart from the pay – many enjoy their work. Job satisfaction is a major source of happiness, but it is not a form of satisfaction we pay for; paradoxically, it is one for which we are paid. At least, it is paradoxical in terms of the common assumptions of economists. For many people their work is the most important thing in life.

Job satisfaction is correlated with life satisfaction and happiness, though it is not entirely clear which causes which, and bi-directional causality has been demonstrated; perhaps they are both parts of the same underlying state (Near *et al.*, 1983). There are several separate components of job satisfaction. One is satisfaction with the pay, and we discussed this earlier. Another part of job satisfaction is 'intrinsic job satisfaction', that is, with the activities, skills and products of the work itself; the most satisfying jobs are those of scientists and professionals, the least satisfying are those of unskilled manual workers. There are large differences here; asked if they would choose the same job again, 91 per cent of mathematicians, 83 per cent of lawyers, and 82 per cent of journalists said that they would, but only 16 per cent of unskilled steel workers and 21 per cent of unskilled car workers said the same (Blauner, 1960). This is not just due to differences of pay, since the most highly paid, who are managers, are below scientists and professionals. Part of such satisfaction is the experience of achievement and success at work, and it is mainly at work that such experiences are found. Gecas and Seff (1990) found that work affected self-esteem, and therefore happiness, but it was job complexity and job control rather than pay or status which were most important.

Another aspect of job satisfaction is being with workmates, belonging to friendly and co-operative working groups, having immediate superiors who consult and look after their subordinates. There is often a lot of fun to be had at work, joking, teasing and gossip, and this strengthens the relations between workers (Argyle, 1989). Although people work primarily in order to be paid, in most cases this is not the only reason, and it is not the main reason that they enjoy the work.

Unemployment makes people very unhappy, as well as ill and in poor mental health. This is not entirely due to money, since these differences are still found when income has been held constant (Campbell *et al.*, 1976). The retired often say that they miss the work itself and they miss their workmates, as well as the pay (Parker, 1982).

Work affects health. If work is stressful there is a higher rate of heart attacks, ulcers and arthritis, but if job satisfaction is high health is good and workers live longer (e.g. Sales and House, 1971). The same applies to mental health; that of school-leavers who go to work improves, while that of those who are unemployed gets worse (Banks and Jackson, 1982). Mental health is made worse by stress, but this can be buffered by supportive relations with the work group.

There are those who work without pay. 'Voluntary' work is unpaid, by definition, and in Britain about 15 per cent of the population do some, on average for about five hours a month, though some do a lot more. Middle-class individuals do most, women a little more than men, and those between 35 and 44, though volunteers are drawn from all sections of the population. When asked why they do it, and why they enjoy it, there is evidence of a lot of real concern for others; about 40 per cent said that they 'wanted to improve things, or help people', about 28 per cent said 'there was a need in the community', and 50 per cent because 'someone asked me to help'. Furthermore, voluntary workers really enjoy it, at any rate 72 per cent of them do, mainly from the satisfaction of seeing the results (67 per cent), meeting people and making friends (48 per cent), and having a sense of personal achievement (47 per cent) (Lynn and Smith, 1991).

Others who work unpaid are housewives, children and students. While they are not actually paid, they do share the family income. Children and students are working partly to prepare themselves for paid employment later; they are not paid, and they, or their families, pay for them to do it.

Then there are people who do not need to work, but still do so. Of those who win lotteries, 17 per cent stay in full-time work afterwards (Smith and Razzell, 1975). Many people in good jobs now work longer hours than in the past, while average hours of work have declined. For some it is because they enjoy their work, as in the cases of scientists and other academics, but this is not the only reason. And there are a lot of people in full-time work who are already so rich that they do not need any more money, so presumably they are working for some other reason.

It is not usual to pay for the privilege of working, it is usual to be paid for working. However, some leisure is very like work. Voluntary work is done for no pay, and many hobbies, for example, gardening, involve hard and serious work, and to some extent have to be paid for.

The traditional economic model that work has to be done to earn money to pay for satisfactions is true only for those doing unpleasant or boring jobs with very low job satisfaction. Most jobs produce moderate or high job satisfaction, so that employees are rewarded twice, by money and by the other satisfactions of work. They do not pay for these satisfactions, they are themselves paid to receive them.

Perhaps this is recognised by those individuals who accept lower incomes than they could find in other jobs, because they enjoy the work they have chosen. This may apply to academics, clergy, nurses and farmers. These people have decided that they do not need to be rewarded twice.

Personality.

The same individuals, over quite long periods of time, tend to be happier than others, apart from fluctuations due to good and bad things happening to them. There is evidence that happiness is partly inherited (Diener and Lucas, in press), and that it correlates with general traits which are known to be partly innate. The strongest personality correlate is extraversion, which correlates with happiness at .40 or more. This can be explained by the superior social skills of extroverts, and their greater frequency of belonging to teams and clubs and going to parties and dances (Argyle and Lu 1990). Headey *et al.* (1984) found that extraversion predicted enjoyable events with friends. The general trait of neuroticism works in the opposite direction and predicts unhappiness.

Several cognitive aspects of personality are related to happiness. These include the 'Pollyanna effect', the tendency to look on the bright side, optimism, including unrealistic optimism, internal control, the belief that events are under one's control, positive attributional style, that is feeling responsibility for bringing about good events but not for bad ones, and not having a large gap between desires and attainments. These cognitive aspects of personality are all ways of looking at the world, and the fact that they are correlated with happiness makes possible various kinds of cognitive therapy for happiness, for example, persuading people not to blame themselves when things go wrong. Some of these aspects of personality are, as we have seen, partly inherited, but the remainder is due to environmental experiences.

Are the favourable (from the point of view of happiness) aspects of personality due to wealth? There may be something in this. Extroversion and social skills are greater in those in professional and managerial jobs, but probably because these jobs require and give much practice in dealing with people (Argyle, 1994). There are class differences in internal control, probably because middle-class people find by experience that they can control events.

Can money buy us a happier personality? Some people spend a great deal of money on psychoanalysis or other forms of therapy, in the hope that they can do this. Do they get the results they desire? There have been many investigations to find out. Smith and Glass (1977) reanalysed 375 controlled studies of the recovery rates of those treated and members of control groups who were not; they concluded that the treated patients improved on average somewhat more than the untreated controls, in terms of reduced anxiety, increased self-confidence, and adjustment and achievement at work. Some individuals, who are not patients, also pay for psychotherapy or counselling, but less is known about the benefits for non-patients. However, there are other, and much cheaper ways, of acquiring a happier personality. In their Australian study, Headey *et al.* (1984) found that positive experiences with friends and at work led to changes in personality, such as increased extroversion, which is the strongest correlate of happiness. It is likely that other social experiences, such as being married, may have a similar effect.

Self-esteem is an important source of happiness and is sometimes regarded as part of it. But does self-esteem depend on money? In children and students there is a rather small correlation between wealth and self-esteem, of the order of .15 to .20, and this can mainly be explained by the children from wealthier homes achieving more educational success. However, Rosenberg and Pearlin (1978) found with a sample of 2,300 adults in Chicago that for those for whom income was of central importance the correlation was .52, while for those who valued occupation more it was only .25.

Personality can affect happiness indirectly through leading to better health. For example, health is worse for the famous type A personalities (or at least those with the hostility part of it) who have heart attacks, for type C personalities (compliant and passive copers) who are more likely to have cancer, and for neurotic individuals, though they just think they are ill. Then there are those with strong affiliative tendencies which strengthen the immune system, and hardy individuals who can stand up to stress. But more important than any of these is having the right life-style, which includes exercise, not smoking, not drinking too much, having a good diet and not becoming obese. Again, these differences are really due to differences in life-style, and to parental styles of child-rearing than to any effects of money (Argyle, 1992).

Positive life events and mood induction

Happiness is enhanced by positive life events. It correlates with their frequency rather more than with their intensity (e.g. .33 and .25, Kanner *et al.* [1981], .50 and .25, Diener *et al.* [1991]). The events which people say produce the most positive moods are meetings with friends, sex, food and drink, leisure activities and success (Scherer *et al.*, 1986). In real life, success experiences are obtained most often at work, though also for some at leisure, for example, in winning sports events. Humour is another source, and is a regular ingredient of popular entertainment. Happiness is found to correlate with number of friends, frequency of sexual intercourse, going to parties, etc., and these correlations survive controls for age, education, etc. But are these effects causal, or could they be due to happy people choosing to spend more time with friends and so on? Laboratory experiments on mood induction show that positive moods can be produced by pleasant music, seeing funny films, 'succeeding' at laboratory tests or tasks, finding or winning small sums of money. However, the effects are often short-lived, lasting only ten to fifteen minutes. But, as we saw earlier, exercise can have longer-lasting effects, such as a brisk ten-minute walk enhancing mood for two hours. There is also evidence that people generate their own good and bad events. Headey *et al.* (1984) found that extroverts experienced more of such events with friends and at work.

Major life events are different. We saw the complex and often negative effects of winning lotteries. The same is true of other major positive events, such as having a baby or being promoted. There is an immediate positive effect which fades with time, and there may be further effects as the result of an inevitable change of life-style.

Positive life events have been used as a means of happiness enhancement. In 'pleasant-activities therapy' clients keep a diary for a month, recording the good things they did each day and their mood by the end of the day. Most of these activities turn out to be forms of leisure. Computing shows which activities each enjoys most, and they are encouraged to do them more often. This has been found to be successful both with depressed patients and with normals (Lewinsohn *et al.*, 1982).

Are positive life events made more possible by money? Some of them can be, if the favourite events are expensive, such as eating in restaurants or going to the opera. However, the great majority are not, and indeed are free – seeing friends, sex and most forms of leisure, as we have seen. The only laboratory form of mood induction involving money bas been 'finding' coins, but other methods, like cheerful music and funny films, do even better.

IS MONEY THE MAIN HUMAN MOTIVATION?

It is very odd that psychologists (apart from Freud) never include a need or desire for money in their long lists of human motivations, for example, the lists of Maslow (1970) and Kabanoff (1982). None of these lists mentions money as a form of human motivation. Nevertheless, there is evidence that for many people there is such a need. Economists suppose that people want more money in order to buy more sources of satisfaction. However, they also recognise that leisure is satisfying, and that this entails taking time off from earning money.

Most people say that they would like to earn more. In an early American survey those in the middle ranges said they would be satisfied with 60 per cent more, but poorer ones wanted more than this, 162 per cent more (Centers and Cantril, 1946). On the other hand, only 12 per cent of Americans thought of happiness in terms of 'money, sufficient money, good wages and wealth', though 52 per cent of a French sample did (Cantril, 1951). Rokeach (1974) found that Americans valued money below nine other values: top came peace, followed by security for the family, freedom and equality. Other surveys have found that very few people admit to having money as an important life goal (Lane, 1991). This may be because people are reluctant to admit to such a materialistic, politically incorrect way of thinking.

Of course, money enables other needs to be satisfied, at least some other needs, so perhaps money is more a route to a goal. Money-like incentives have been used with success in 'token' economies, but it is not supposed that the clients have any 'need' for the plastic tokens used. These are schemes for changing the behaviour, originally of patients who were mentally handicapped, or other patients with learning disabilities. They would be given a metal or plastic token if they behaved as desired, and the tokens could later be cashed for food, privileges or money. Any behaviour whatsoever could be rewarded in this way, and different behaviour could be targeted for individuals. Later the method has been used at work, for example, to discourage smoking or make people use the safety equipment. Many experiments have found that token economies are successful in influencing behaviour; the only exceptions have been with stopping drug use, and in one study 9–11-year-old boys were more affected by the immediate reward of breakfast. It has been found that there are also effects on non-target behaviour, especially social interaction and well-being. There has been less success with bringing about permanent changes in behaviour, however (Lea *et al.*, 1987). The need here is for breakfast, not tokens, but could a new need for the tokens not be created over time?

It is familiar in psychology that 'secondary needs' can arise out of primary, biological ones, if, for example, achievement is frequently rewarded with food or love. Could the same happen with money, so that money becomes a new need independent of what it can be used for?

Some individuals do value money, a lot. Furnham (1984) factor analysed attitudes to money in Britain and found six factors. The first factor most clearly assessed a need for money, or the valuation of money, and included items such as 'I worry about my finances most of the time', 'I firmly believe that money can solve all my problems', 'I would do practically anything for money if it were enough', and 'I put money ahead of pleasure'. Lynn (1991) used a shorter version of this scale in an international survey, and found that Britain had a low score (6.11) compared with the USA (10.69) and Japan (11.01). Poorer countries had higher scores (r = −.52 with GNP), and the economic growth rate was higher in countries which valued money more. Men scored higher than women, and other studies have found that need for money correlates with the Protestant work ethic.

However, seeking financial goals is found to have a negative effect on other goals. Kasser and Ryan (1993) found that those individuals who valued or expected financial success were lower in well-being and self-actualisation and higher in depression and anxiety than others. Those who were high in aspirations for self-acceptance, community feeling and affiliation had greater well-being. These authors argue that external goals like money give only superficial satisfaction and do not meet important needs or promote personal growth or well-being. We saw that the pursuit of possessions operates in a similar way, in Chapter 6.

It is also odd that for economists money is the only kind of motivation discussed. However, from the studies reviewed in this chapter, there is no doubt that there is a widespread desire for money, in the developed world at least; there is also widespread evidence that there are other needs, and that often they can be more important. And there is also evidence that money is not desired only for what it will buy.

SOME VARIATIONS IN THE WAY MONEY BEHAVES

Economists do not talk about the theory of 'economic man' nowadays; this theory has not been formulated very precisely, is hard to test, and is perhaps unfalsifiable (Sen, 1977). Nevertheless, economists clearly do operate with a set of working assumptions to the effect that they are dealing with the behaviour of 'rational economic man'. These assumptions seem to be that: (1) individuals, or families, pursue their own self-interest; (2) they are trying to maximise their utilities, that is, satisfaction, by paying for them; (3) they have good, if not perfect, information about how to realise their satisfactions; (4) money is the only way these utilities can be obtained, and so money is a basic form of motivation, (5) most people obtain money by working, and that is the reason that they work

These ideas have been much criticised in the past (see Furnham and Lewis, 1996), and those arguments will not be rehearsed here. In this book we have covered different areas of monetary behaviour, and described what happens in these fields of human activity. What we will do here is bring together the main findings from the point of view of rational economic man, to see how he fares.

1 The symbolic value of money

In Chapter 1 we looked at money itself, and saw that the meaning and value of money do not depend only on its monetary value. Coins, bank notes, cheques and gift vouchers operate quite differently and have different meanings. For example, cash is not generally acceptable as a present, whereas a gift voucher is. Money from different sources may be 'ear-marked', so that only certain individuals can spend it or only on certain kinds of expenditure.

2 Different attitudes to money

Statistical analysis of items about attitudes to money produced a number of factors, some reflecting the ideas of rational economic man, but most of them did not. Some people hold the attitude that money is evil, or that it is a symbol of success, some really enjoy spending it, some are very worried about it, some are obsessed by it, some spend it to impress other people. This is not what rational economic men should be doing.

3 Socialisation and money

Studies of how children learn about money show that there is a great deal to learn and understand, so that children are in no position to act as rational economic men. Since most adults are in a state of partial ignorance too on these topics, the same applies to them, for example, in the fields of investment, tax and pensions.

4 Saving, spending, gambling and taxation

Saving is partly rational preparation for the future – for retirement, to buy a house, etc., but is partly for its own sake, when it is pointless. Savers do not save more when interest rates are high, or less when inflation rates are high, as rational economic men should do. Gamblers are mostly going to lose their money; compulsive gamblers ruin their lives too. All most gamblers gain is the dream of winning.

5 The pathology of money

Surveys of what people feel about money have found that many are not at all rational. For example, one in three said that they bought things when they felt 'anxious, bored, upset, depressed or angry', and 19 per cent said they bought things they didn't really need because they were 'great bargains'. Several kinds of money pathology have been found, such as misers, spendthrifts, gamblers, 'tycoons' (absorbed with money-making) and 'bargainers' (who compulsively hunt bargains). There are some more rational people too.

6 Possessions

Some possessions obviously satisfy needs, for example, clothes, cars and houses. Other possessions extend life, for example, TV sets, and boats. Possessions are also symbolic, for example, of wealth and of being up to date, and this leads to constant changes of fashion – to other clothes which are no better than the previous ones. Some of the most valued objects, like family heirlooms and photographs, have no economic value. And those individuals who most value material objects are less satisfied with life.

7 Money in the family

Economists sometimes take the family as the basic unit of consumption, but there are further interesting features of money inside the family. Wives do most of the housework, but receive no wage. Children receive pocket money, but this is not in return for any work; they are often given board and lodging until their 20s. Old people may be similarly accommodated. The main earner's salary supports the family, but the others do not feel so free to spend it. However, the house and its contents are felt to be jointly owned, and are inherited by close kin. Presents at Christmas and birthdays are mainly to members of the family, especially children, whether they have done anything or even been seen or not. Presents carry meanings quite apart from their economic value, and money is often thought unsuitable as a present.

8 Giving to charities

People give away about 1.4 per cent of their incomes on average to charity in Britain, 2 per cent in the USA, while some in the USA give up to 10 per cent. This is mostly given to the major charities, anonymously. There is no economic return, though there is a tax concession in the USA, and there is no evidence of the satisfaction of empathy. Charitable giving seems to be based on altruistic concern for the disadvantaged, together with concern for members of the wider society, and it is also affected by relations with the person asking.

9 Work

Here the economic model works quite well up to a point: workers will work harder if they are paid by results, and they will stay in jobs longer if wages are increased. On the other hand, employees are more concerned with how their pay compares with that of other workers than with the absolute amount of it. Pay is a very minor factor in occupational choice, and there are various kinds of intrinsic motivation which are more important than money for many workers. Job satisfaction depends on use of skills, achievement and recognition, and workmates, more than on pay. Money is not the only reason that people work, and many work for nothing, like 'voluntary workers' and those who go on working after retirement.

10 The very rich

Some of the very rich inherited it, others worked very hard, and invested a large proportion of their earnings instead of spending it. They spend it on large houses, servants and other aspects of a lavish life-style, perhaps in the hope of being accepted by a higher stratum of society, but at the cost of abandoning former pursuits and social groups.

11 Money and happiness

At the lower end of the income scale the better-off are happier; there is no effect from the middle of the scale onwards. And there has been no historical effect of increased national prosperity on happiness. There is evidence that people are happier if they think they are doing better than other people, or than they did themselves previously. Other sources of happiness are much more important, such as leisure, job satisfaction, social relations and personality. Money has very little effect on these. Many people want to be rich or richer, and many take part in lotteries, no doubt in the belief that winning will make them happier.

CONCLUSION

Some people value money highly, and there is a need for money. This is not the only kind of human motivation, though it does lead to the satisfaction of other needs. On the other hand, those who value money most are less satisfied and in poorer mental health. This may be because money provides only superficial kinds of satisfaction. Money is not the only kind of human motivation, and other kinds of motivation affect behaviour at work, at play, in the family, and whether money will be given away.

The model of 'rational economic man' is only partly successful, and we have noted many points at which it fails. It fails because psychological and sociological factors as well as economic ones affect behaviour in relation to money. Economic behaviour is affected by sensible, rational, economic considerations, but also by personality, attitudes and beliefs, other motivations, relations with family and friends, social class, and sometimes by delusions and personality disorders. There are other economic systems apart from the market economy, such as the movement of money inside the family, where there is no buying or selling, and no wages, though the total sums of money involved may be very large.

Appendix A

Money, like language, facilitates social interaction. Both function as an abstraction. Further, money has both denotative and connotative aspects: emotionally toned connotative units are situation specific, often having more significance than underlying more general denotations.

NAMES FOR MONEY

Perhaps it says something about our obsession with money that we have, over time, invented so many names for it:

Bacon	Courage	Iron	Needful	Simoleans
Ballast	Crap	Ironman	Nonsense	Slippery
Bangers	Dibs	Jack	Nuggets	stuff
Beans	Dimes	Jake	Oil	Smuties
Bees and honey	Dinero	Juice	Ointment	Snow
Berries	Dingbats	Junglers	Oof	Specic
Blunt	Dirt	Junk	Pay dirt	Spondulicks
Boodle	Dots	Kale	Peanuts	Spoons
Brads	Dough	Kopecks	Pesos	Spuds
Brass	Ducats	Legal tender	Pieces	Stamps
Browns	Dues	Lettuce	Plush	Stuff
Bucks	Dumps	Lolly	Pony	Stumpy
Bullets	Fat	Long green	Pot of honey	Suds
Bunce	Filthy lucre	Loot	Powder	Sugar
Buttons	Fish	Lucre	Readies	Sugar and
Cabbage	Flour	Lump	Remedy	honey
Charms	Frozen work	Mammon	Rivets	Swag
Checks	Gelt	Manna	Rocks	Syrup
Cherries	Gilt	Mazuma	Roll	The doubloons
Chickenfeed	Gingerbread	Mica	Root of all	The evil
Chink	Glue	Mint drops	evil	The hard
Chips	Gravy	Mint sauce	Rubbish	Trash
Clink	Grease	Mon	Salt	Velvet
Coal	Greenbacks	Moolah	Sand	Wad
Coconuts	Grip	Mopus	Sauce	Washers
Coin of the	Groceries	Moss	Scads	
realm	Hardware	Muck	Scratch	
Collat	Honey	Necessary	Shekels	
Corn	Horse nails	evil	Shiner	

Appendix B

The sheer number and variety of idioms, slang terms, and everyday expressions associated with money have meant that whole books have been dedicated to the topic. Smithback (1990) has done an exhaustive study concerning the origin of many of these terms. To examine a few:

CASH

The word 'cash' comes from a Latin word meaning 'a box', where people kept their money: in a cashbox. In time the idea of a box was forgotten and we are left with *cash* meaning money.

There is *hard cash* and *cold cash*, for example, meaning money that is immediately available. Those requesting it don't wish to be paid later: they prefer it right away.

Another way of speaking of available cash is by calling it *ready cash* or *cash in hand*.

To have *cash on hand*, is very similar to the above except that *cash in hand* refers to a business transaction (buying and selling) whereas *cash on hand* refers to the amount of money that one has available.

Petty cash always refers to small amounts of money kept around the home or in an office to use when making minor purchases. Offices keep *petty cash* available to buy small items when it becomes necessary.

When a person is said to be *in* cash they have money. When they have no money they are *out of cash*. When they have very little money, they are *short of cash*.

When a person is *relieved of their cash* they either lose their money foolishly (when gambling, for instance) or someone tricks them out of their money.

The term *cash flow* is a business expression which has two meanings. The first is rather technical, referring to the worth of a company in terms of its common stock. That definition is very different from *cash flow* when it is used to indicate money that comes into a company and is, in turn, spent by it.

Money coming into a company is termed *cash inflow*, while that being spent or used to pay for goods or services is *cash outflow*. *Cash outlay* is money a company spends or invests.

When farmers or governments speak of *cash crop* they are speaking of produce which they specifically raise in order to sell rather than grow it for their own consumption or to feed their cattle.

Those who are lucky and have lots of money can be said to be *rolling in cash.*

A *cash and carry* store is one that does not grant credit to its customers. For that reason the merchandise is often sold at a cheaper price. Those who shop in such stores purchase goods and carry them away themselves, thus saving delivery expenses. This is described as buying on a *cash-and-carry* basis.

Shops or markets such as this – and many others as well – always demand that payments be made immediately. To pay immediately is described as paying *cash on the barrelhead, cash on the nailhead* or *cash on the nail*. All three terms mean the same thing.

Perhaps the reason that Joe is demanding immediate payment is because he prefers to *take the cash and let the credit go*. People who prefer doing business this way do not think it wise to have anyone owing them money. They'll accept cash only, never any promises or notes.

To cash in on something, meaning to take advantage of the profitability of something, is sometimes used in a non-money sense.

CAPITAL

Capital relates to profits, though not necessarily always in cash terms. In the business world, *capital* refers to wealth which is invested to produce more wealth. Therefore when people speak of a *capital expense* or a *capital expenditure* they are speaking of money invested in property or machinery or goods that will help them to make more money. In general, capital can also refer to money.

Fixed capital refers to the value of the machinery or property of a company, while *floating capital* refers to the value of their goods or products which they have on hand or in stock.

A *capital gain* refers to profits made by selling any or all of the goods, stock, equipment or investment shares in a company.

A *capital loss* is money lost in the course of selling any of the above.

Capital stock refers to the shares that are issued by a company and sold to individuals within the company or to the general public. Those owning *capital stock* own a share in the company.

An idiom derived from *capital* meaning invested wealth is *to make capital (out) of* something. It means to profit from or to be able to use something (such as a piece of information, a particular situation, etc.) to one's advantage. In doing so, one *capitalises on* the situation. This could also be expressed by saying that one is able *to make capital of* it.

MONEY

- *A fool and his money are soon parted* One who is foolish in the way he handles his money is likely to lose it.
- *A licence to print money* one spending too much money.
- *A ride for one's money* to give or receive satisfaction after much time and effort. Often expressed as to *give* or *get a good ride for one's money*. Can be used in a positive or negative sense.
- *A run for one's money* same as *a (good) ride for one's money.*
- *Bad money* in the most common sense, money that has been earned by evil or illegal means. In a modern sense (since about 1960) it can be used to indicate a great deal of money.
- *Bad money drives out good* investment from corrupt sources or from people of questionable character frightens away honest people.
- *Bags/Baskets/Bushels of money* lots of money.
- *Blood money* money obtained illegally. Often money a murderer receives for having killed a person.
- *Blow money* to spend money quickly and foolishly.
- *Bogus money* this refers to false (counterfeit) money.
- *Coin money* to earn money.
- *Come into money* to receive a considerable amount of money all at once, either by one's hard work or by inheriting it upon someone's death.
- *Conscience money* money paid or given because one has a guilty conscience and hopes to feel better by the act of paying or giving it.
- *Dirty money* money obtained illegally. The same as *bad money* in the common sense of the idiom.
- *Earn money hand over fist* earn lots of money, usually very easily or very quickly.
- *Earnest money* money paid to a person to prove one is serious about making a purchase from him.
- *Easy money* money obtained easily and by doing very little work.
- *Egg money* a small amount of money, usually kept at home for emergencies. This comes from farm days, when the woman or wife is the one who generally feeds and takes care of the chickens – including collecting and selling the eggs. The money from the sale of the eggs is considered hers. It would never be a large sum but it would be enough for her to buy an occasional treat or a necessity – and in an emergency be a welcome contribution to the family needs.
- *Even money* in betting or gambling, to say that the chances of anything happening are fifty-fifty.
- *Filthy money* either money gained illegally or a sarcastic reference to money made by someone who thinks it's all bad.
- *Filthy with money* describes someone who is very rich.
- *Finish out of the money* in horse racing, a horse that loses a race. Colloquially, to fail or to be defeated.

- *Fistful of money* a large sum of money.
- *Flush with money* to have a lot of money.
- *Folding money* paper currency, as opposed to coins. Often used humorously.
- *For love or money* used as a comparison indicating something done for love and something done for money. Most often used in the negative saying *not for love or (nor) money.*
- *For my money* an expression indicating or saying the same as 'In my opinion'.
- *Free and easy with one's money* the act of spending liberally with no concern about saving money.
- *Front money* (1) money paid in advance to purchase goods or services; (2) money provided by an unknown person or persons.
- *Funny money* a humorous way of referring to false (counterfeit) money.
- *Gate money* money received from the sale of tickets to an outdoor sporting event.
- *Get one's money's worth* to get good value for money one has spent.
- *Give someone a (good) ride/run for their money* the same as *a ride for one's money.*
- *Get through money like water* to spend money freely and quickly, as though it had no meaning or value.
- *Good money* (1) money recognised as being valuable because it's been earned by means of hard work; (2) a substantial amount of money.
- *Good money after bad* to waste money by investing it in (or spending it on) something that has proved to be bad.
- *Good money chasing bad* the same as *good money after bad.*
- *Happy money* personal savings one set aside to spend purely for enjoyment.
- *Hard-earned money* money earned by means of hard work.
- *Hard money* (1) on the international money markets, the currency of a nation which is in good financial shape and whose money has proved stable; (2) money that is difficult to borrow from banks during times of recession.
- *Hot money* (1) stolen money or money illegally obtained; (2) counterfeit (false) money.
- *Hush money* money paid or received in order to buy someone's silence, very similar to a bribe.
- *In the money* to have a considerable amount of money.
- *It's not the money, it's the principle* to have more regard for the ethics or morals of a situation than the money. The word 'principle' is a play on the word 'principal' leading to this expression being frequently used humorously Principle = rules of conduct, integrity; principal = a sum of money less the interest.
- *Judas money* money received for having violated an agreement of trust

or betraying a person or a cause. From the Bible, after Judas Iscariot, the apostle who betrayed Jesus.

- *Laundered money* money which, through various means, is transferred from banks and financial institutions so that its origin cannot be traced.
- *Like money in the bank* (1) an investment considered so secure that it's as though one had the money safely in a bank; (2) a simile used to describe anything about to be successfully achieved.
- *Luck money* a small sum of money a seller sometimes gives back to a buyer after a purchase.
- *Mad money* small amounts of money saved to spend on trivial things or personal luxuries.
- *Made of money* describes a person who is very rich. Often used in the negative by those who aren't rich.
- *Make money hand over fist* to make a lot of money.
- *Make nothing but money* describes one who is earning a great deal of money.
- *Marry money* to marry someone rich.
- *Minting money* to be earning great sums of money.
- *Money attracts/breeds/draws/makes money* those who are wealthy have no problem earning more money, often from the interest earned on their investments.
- *Money burning a hole in one's pocket* to spend money as quickly as one gets it.
- *Money class* describes the very rich class of people.
- *Money doesn't grow on trees* money must be earned; it is not so plentiful that one can pick it off trees like leaves.
- *Money doesn't stink* an old saying implying that few people would refuse accepting money, no matter how it's earned or where it comes from.
- *Money for jam/old rope* a British idiom referring to money that is easily earned.
- *Money goes to money* the same as *money attracts money* and *money breeds money*.
- *Money-grubber* one whose main interest is in making money.
- *Money is no object* regardless how much something costs, it does not matter.
- *Money is the root of all evil* a misquotation from the Bible ('The love of money is the root of all evil', I Timothy 6: 10) implying that money is the chief cause of all the world's problems.
- *Money makes the world go around* implies that money is the most important thing in the world; without it, life would be nothing. This contradicts the statement that *money is the root of all evil*.
- *Money of account* a very large sum of money.
- *Money rolling in* a continual supply or amount of money earned.
- *Money-spinner* a job or object that earns money.

- *Money squeeze* a condition arising when interest rates and inflation are high, making it difficult to borrow money from financial institutions.
- *Money talks* by having money, one can get or do most of what one desires.
- *Money to burn* having so much money that one has no concern about saving it. Therefore one spends what one has.
- *Money to money* another way of saying *money goes to money*. It means the same as *money attracts money*.
- *Money under the table* money paid secretly in order to obtain favours.
- *Moneybags* a slang term for a rich person.
- *Moneyed* describes a rich person, family, or company. Pronounced MON-eed or mon-EED.
- *Moneyed interests* describes the very rich class.
- *Moneyed person* a person who is very wealthy.
- *Muck and money go together* there are riches in dirty occupations.
- *New money* funds invested in a company, a programme or in the stock market from new sources.
- *New-money people* those who have become rich recently. You'll often hear or read of these people described in the French expression *nouveau riche*.
- *Newly moneyed* the same as *new-money people*.
- *Not for love nor money* refer to *for love or money*.
- *Not made of money* refer to *made of money*.
- *Old money* the opposite of *new money* (see above). That is, money from the same sources that is invested and reinvested.
- *Old money people* wealthy people whose money has been within the family for at least one generation but often longer. This is the opposite of *new money people*.
- *On the money* this idiom doesn't refer to money at all. It means to be exactly right or accurate.
- *One for someone's money* a person who, in the opinion of the speaker, is ideal for a particular job or position. Refer to *for my money*.
- *One's money's worth* to get good value for the money one spends.
- *Out of money* the same as *finish out of the money*.
- *Paper money* bank notes, but sometimes counterfeit money.
- *Pay money down* to pay for something with cash.
- *Pin money* a small amount of money.
- *Plastic money* plastic credit cards.
- *Play ducks and drakes with one's money* in almost all other uses, to *play drakes and ducks* with something or someone means to cause problems or to create confusion. Used with *money* the expression means to spend money in a careless manner.
- *Plunk (put) down one's money* pay one's money, sometimes in advance when buying on credit.
- *Pocket money* small amounts of money. Much the same as *pin money*.

- *Pots of money* a lot of money.
- *Protection money* (1) money paid to criminals who threaten to do a person harm unless they are paid; (2) bribes paid to policemen or politicians in order to continue an illegal business or activity without danger of arrest or interference.
- *Put money into* apart than the obvious definition (of placing money in a bank, in one's purse or wallet), this means to invest.
- *Put one's money on someone/something* (1) to make a bet in a gambling game or sport; (2) a statement used to indicate one's confidence concerning someone or something. No bets are actually made; merely an opinion being expressed.
- *Put one's money where one's mouth is* in (2) above, those who express great confidence are often requested to do this. This is a demand that a person supports their words by a willingness to actually make a bet of money or, at the least, produce evidence that what they say is true.
- *Queer money* false (counterfeit) money.
- *Raise money* to get money from a source or a variety of sources.
- *Rake in money* to make a great deal of money, often quite easily.
- *Ready money* money readily available or on hand.
- *Relieve someone of their money* this could mean to steal or rob someone of their money, but it's generally used humorously as accepting someone's money.
- *Rolling in money* very rich.
- *Scrounge around, scrounge for* and *scrounge up money* colloquialisms meaning to search or hunt for money.
- *See the colour of someone's money* a demand to see someone's money if a bet is to be made or a desire to see someone's money if it has been promised.
- *Seed money* a business term referring to initial funds.
- *Set money down* to make a payment of money.
- *Short of money* not having much money, lacking funds.
- *Skads of money* lots of money.
- *Smart money* in investment terms, the money of those who are informed, professional investors.
- *Sock money away/Sock away money* to put money away in savings.
- *Soft money* on international money markets, a currency considered weak or unstable.
- *Spend money as if it was going out of fashion/style* to spend freely and liberally with no thought of saving.
- *Spend money hand over fist* to spend a lot of money, usually in large amounts.
- *Spend money like water* essentially the same meaning as the above term except to spend it quickly.
- *Splash money about/around* to spend liberally.
- *Squeeze money* similar to *protection money* money paid under threat.

- *Stinks of money* said of something that appears very expensive.
- *Take the money and run* to have an interest or concern in something but not getting what money one can.
- *Tea money* an Asian idiom (primarily Chinese) meaning a bribe.
- *The best that money can buy* precisely what the expression says of the best quality; there is nothing better.
- *The stink of money* a situation which, from outside observation, gives the impression of being illegal or crooked.
- *Throw good money after bad* see *good money after bad.*
- *Throw one's money around* to spend liberally, particularly on unimportant and unnecessary things.
- *Tight money* money that is difficult to borrow from financial institutions in troublesome times; similar to *hard money* (2).
- *Time is money* an old saying, which means that time is as valuable as money and should be spent carefully and not wasted.
- *Token money* a small amount of money paid as evidence of someone's trust or faith. The same as *earnest money.*
- *Toss good money after bad* the same as *good money after bad.*
- *Toss money away* to waste money by spending it unwisely or foolishly.
- *Up-front money* the same as *front money.*
- *Value for money* getting excellent quality goods or services for one's money.
- *Wallowing in money* having a large amount of money.
- *Where there's muck there is money* a variation of an old British saying *where there's muck there is brass,* which means that though a job or a place of work is dirty there is still money to be earned there.
- *You pay your money and (you) take your chance* in many instances, someone spends money for goods or services and accepts the fact that they may not get good value for their money. There are risks involved.
- *You pays your money and (you) takes your chances/choices* a humorous, ungrammatical way of stating the above; to take a risk and trust to luck.
- *Your money or your life* a demand a robber might make of a person they are robbing, though sometimes used humorously by someone asking to be paid money due to them.

Source: Reprinted from J. Smithback (1990) *Money Talks*. Singapore: Federal Publications.

Bibliography

Abrahams, M. F. and Bell, R. A. (1994). Encouraging charitable contributions: an examination of three models of door-in-the-face compliance. *Communications Research*, *21*, 131–53.

Abramovitch, R., Freedman, J. and Pliner, P. (1991). Children and money: getting an allowance, credit versus cash, and knowledge of pricing. *Journal of Economic Psychology*, *12*, 27–46.

Adams, B. N. (1968). *Kinship in an Urban Setting*. Chicago: Markham.

Agnew, J.-C. (1993). Coming up for air: consumer culture in historical perspective. In J. Brewer and R. Porter (eds), *Consumption and the World of Goods* (pp. 19–39). London: Routledge.

Allingham, M. and Sandmo, A. (1972). Income tax evasion: a theoretical study. *Journal of Public Economics*, *1*, 323–8.

Allport, G. W., Vernon, P. E. and Lindzey, G. (1951). *Study of Values*. Boston, MA: Houghton Mifflin.

Alves, W. M. and Rossi, P. H. (1978). Who should get what? Fairness judgments of the distribution of earnings. *American Psychologist*, *84*, 541–64.

Anand, P. (1993). *Foundation of Rational Choice Under Risk*. Oxford: Oxford University Press.

Anderson, M. (1980). *Family Structure in Nineteenth Century Lancashire*. Cambridge: Cambridge University Press.

Anikeeff, A. (1957). The effect of parental income upon attitudes of business administrators and employees. *Journal of Social Psychology*, *46*, 35–9.

Argyle, M. (1987). *The Psychology of Happiness*. London: Methuen.

Argyle, M. (1988). *Bodily Communication* (second edn). London: Methuen.

Argyle, M. (1989). *The Social Psychology of Work* (second edn). London: Penguin.

Argyle, M. (1991). *Co-operation*. London: Routledge.

Argyle, M. (1992). *The Social Psychology of Everyday Life*, London: Routledge.

Argyle, M. (1994). *The Psychology of Social Class*. London: Routledge.

Argyle, M. (1996). *The Social Psychology of Leisure*. London: Penguin.

Argyle, M. and Henderson, M. (1985). *The Anatomy of Relationships*. Harmondsworth: Penguin.

Argyle, M. and Lu, L. (1990). The happiness of extraverts. *Personality and Individual Differences*, *11*, 1011–17.

Arocas, R., Pardo, I. and Diaz, R. (1995). *Psychology of Money: Attitudes and Perceptions within Young People*. Valencia, Spain: UPPEC.

Atkinson, A. B. (1983). *The Economics of Inequality*. Oxford: Clarendon Press.

Auten, G. and Rudney, G. (1990). The variability of individual charitable giving in the U.S. *Voluntas*, *1*, 80–97.

Ayllon, T. and Azrin, N. (1968). *The Token Economy*. New York: Appleton-Century-Crofts.

Aylton, T. and Roberts, M. (1974). Eliminating discipline problems by strengthening academic performance. *Journal of Applied Behaviour Analysis, 7*, 71–6.

Babin, B. and Darden, W. (1996). The good and bad shopping vibes: Spending and patronage satisfaction. *Journal of Business Research, 35*, 201–6.

Bailey, W. and Gustafson, W. (1991). An examination of the relationship between personality factors and attitudes to money. In R. Frantz, H. Singh and J. Gerber (eds), *Handbook of Behavioral Economics* pp. 271–85. Greenwich, CT: JAI Press.

Bailey, W. and Lown, J. (1993). A cross-cultural examination of the aetiology of attitudes toward money. *Journal of Consumer Studies and Home Economics, 17*, 391–402.

Bailey, W., Johnson, P., Adams, C., Lawson, R., Williams, P. and Lown, J. (1994). An exploratory study of money beliefs and behaviours scale using data from 3 nations. *Consumer Interests Annual* pp. 178–85. Columbia, MO: ACCZ.

Banks, M. H. and Jackson, P. R. (1982). Unemployment and risk of minor psychiatric disorder in young people: cross-sectional and longitudinal evidence. *Psychological Medicine, 12*, 789–98.

Batson, C. D. (1991). *The Altruism Question*. Hove: Erlbaum.

Baumann, D. J., Cialdini, R. B. and Kenrick, D. (1981). Altruism as hedonism: helping and self-gratification as equivalent responses. *Journal of Personality and Social Psychology, 40*, 1039–46.

Beaglehole, E. (1931). *Property: A Study in Social Psychology*. London: Allen & Unwin.

Beggan, J. K. (1991). Using what you own to get what you need: the role of possessions in satisfying control motivations. In *To Have Possessions: A Handbook on Ownership and Property, Special issue of Journal of Social Behavior and Personality, 6*, 129–46.

Behrend, H. (1988). The Wage–Work bargain. *Managerial and Decision Economics, 18*, 51–7.

Belk, R. W. (1984). Three scales to measure constructs related to materialism: reliability, validity, and relationships to measures of happiness. In T. C. Kinnear (ed.), *Advances in Consumer Research*, Vol. 11 (pp. 291–7). Provo, UT: Association for Consumer Research.

Belk, R.W. (1991). The ineluctable mysteries of possessions. In *To Have Possessions: A Handbook on Ownership and Property, Special issue of Journal of Social Behavior and Personality, 6*, 17–55.

Belk, R. and Wallendorf, M. (1990). The sacred meaning of money. *Journal of Economic Psychology, 11*, 35–67.

Bell, R. A., Cholerton, M., Fraczek, K. E. and Rohifs, G. S. (1994). Encouraging donations to charity: a field study of competing and complementary factors in tactic sequencing. *Western Journal of Communication, 58*, 98–115.

Bellack, A. and Hersen, M. (1980). *Introduction to Clinical Psychology*. Oxford: Oxford University Press.

Beloff, H. (1957). The structure and origin of the anal character. *Genetic Psychology Monograph, 55*, 141–72.

Benson, P. L. and Catt, V. L. (1978). Soliciting charity contributions: the parlance of asking for money. *Journal of Applied Social Psychology, 8*, 84–95.

Benton, A. A., Kelley, H. H. and Liebling, B. (1972). Effects of extremity of offers and concession rate on the outcome of bargaining. *Journal of Personality and Social Psychology, 24*, 73–82.

Berdyev, M.-S. and Il'yasov, F.-N. (1990). When a wedding partner is bought. *Sotsiologicheskie-Issledovaniya, 17*, 58–65.

Bergler, E. (1958). *The Psychology of Gambling*. London: Hanison.

Bergström, S. (1989). Economic phenomenology: Naive economics in the adult population in Sweden. Conference Paper.

Berkowitz, L., Fraser, C., Treasure, F. P. and Cochran, S. (1987). Pay, equity, job qualifications, and comparisons in pay satisfaction. *Journal of Applied Psychology, 72*, 544–51.

Bertaux, D. and Bertaux-Wiame, I. (1988). The family enterprise and its lineage: inheritance and social mobility over five generations. *Récits de Vie, 4*, 8–26.

Berti, A. and Bombi, A. (1979). Where does money come from? *Archivio di Psicologia, 40*, 53–77.

Berti, A. and Bombi, A. (1981). The development of the concept of money and its value: a longitudinal analysis. *Child Development, 82*, 1179–82.

Berti, A. and Bombi, A. (1988). *The Child's Construction of Economics*. Cambridge: Cambridge University Press.

Berti, A., Bombi, A. and Beni, R. (1986). Acquiring economic notions: profit. *International Journal of Behavioural Development, 9*, 15–29.

Berti, A., Bombi, A. and Lis, A. (1982). The child's conception about means of production and their owners. *European Journal of Social Psychology, 12*, 221–39.

Biddle, S. and Mutrie, N. (1991). *Psychology of Physical Activity and Exercise*. London: Springer-Verlag.

Binder, L. and Rohling, M. (1996). Money matters: a meta-analytic review of the effects of financial incentives on recovery after closed-head surgery. *American Journal of Psychiatry, 153*, 7–10.

Birdwell, A. E. (1968). A study of the influence of image congruence on consumer choice. *Journal of Business, 41*, 76–88.

Birtchnell, J. (1971). Social class, parental social class, and social mobility in psychiatric patients and general population controls. *Psychological Medicine, 1*, 209–21.

Black, D. (1976). *The Behaviour of Law*. New York: Academic Press.

Black, D. (1988). *Inequalities in Health*. Harmondsworth: Penguin.

Black, S. (1966). *Man and Motor Cars*. London: Secker & Warburg.

Blauner, R. (1960). Work satisfaction and industrial trends in modern society. In W. Galenson and S. M. Lipset (eds), *Labor and Trade Unions*. New York: Wiley.

Blaxter, M. (1990). *Health and Lifestyle*. London: Tavistock/Routledge.

Blood, R. O. (1995). *The Family* (fifth edn.). Fort Worth TX: Harcourt Brace.

Blood, R. O. and Wolfe, D. M. (1960). *Husbands and Wives: The Dynamics of Married Living*. Glencoe, Ill: The Free Press.

Blumberg, P. (1974). The decline and fall of the status symbol: some thoughts on status in a post-industrial society. *Social Problems, 21*, 490–8.

Borneman, E. (1973). *The Psychoanalysis of Money*. New York: Unrizen.

Bradburn, N. (1969). *The Structure of Psychological Well-being*. Chicago: Aldine.

Brenner, M. (1973). *Mental Illness and the Economy*. Cambridge, MA: Harvard University Press.

Brophy, M. and McQuillan, J. (1993). *Charity Trends 1003*. Tonbridge: Charities Aid Foundation.

Brown, G. W. and Harris, T. (1978). *Social Origins of Depression*. London: Tavistock.

Brown, R. (1978). Divided we fall: an analysis of relations between sections of a factory workforce. In H. Tajfel (ed.), *Differentiation between Social Groups*. London: Academic Press.

Bruce, V., Gilmore, D., Mason, L. and Mayhew, P. (1983a). Factors affecting the perceived value of coins. *Journal of Economic Psychology, 4*, 335–47.

Bruce, V., Howarth, C., Clark-Carter, D., Dodds, A. and Heyes, A. (1983b). All change for the pound: human performance tests with different versions of the proposed UK one pound coin. *Ergonometrics*, *26*, 215–21.

Bruner, J. and Goodman, C. (1947). Value and need as organizing factors in perception. *Journal of Abnormal and Social Psychology*, *42*, 33–44.

Bull, R. and Gibson-Robinson, E. (1981). The influences of eye-gaze, style of dress, and locality on the amounts of money donated to a charity. *Human Relations*, *34*, 895–905.

Bull, R. and Stevens, J. (1981). The effects of facial disfigurement on helping behaviour. *Italian Journal of Psychology*, *8*, 25–33.

Burgard, P., Cheyne, W. and Jahoda, G. (1989). Children's representations of economic inequality: a replication. *British Journal of Developmental Psychology*, *7*, 275–87.

Burgoyne, C. B. (1990). Money in marriage: how patterns of allocation both reflect and conceal power. *Sociological Review*, *38*, 634–65.

Burke, P. (1993). Conspicuous consumption in the early modern world. In J. Brewer and R. Porter (eds), *Consumption and the World of Goods* (pp. 140–61). London: Routledge.

Burris, V. (1983). Stages in the development of economic concepts. *Human Relations*, *36*, 791–812.

Burroughs, W. J., Drews, D. R. and Hallman, W. K. (1991). Predicting personality from personal possessions: a self-presentational analysis. In F. W. Rudmin (ed.), *To Have Possessions: A Handbook on Ownership and Property, Special Issue of Journal of Social Behavior and Personality*, *6*, 147–63.

Campbell, A., Converse, P. E. and Rogers, W. L. (1976). *The Quality of American Life*. New York: Sage.

Campbell, C. (1992). The desire for the new. In R. Silverstone and E. Hirsch (eds), *Consuming Technologies*. London: Routledge.

Canter, D. (1977). *The Psychology of Place*. London: Architectural Press.

Cantril, H. (ed.). (1951). *Public Opinion 1935–1946*. Princeton, NJ: Princeton University Press.

Cantril, H. (1965). *The Pattern of Human Concerns*. New Brunswick, NJ: Rutgers University Press.

Caplow, T. (1982). Christmas gifts and kin networks. *American Sociological Review*, *47*, 383–92.

Caplow, T. (1984). Rule enforcement without visible means: Christmas gift giving in Middletown. *American Psychologist*, *89*, 1306–23.

Carrier, J. G. (1995). *Gifts and Commodities*. London: Routledge.

Carruthers, B. and Babb, S. (1996). The colour of money and the nature of value: greenbacks and gold in post bellum America. *American Journal of Sociology*, *101*, 1556–91.

Carson, E. D. (1990). Patterns of giving in Black churches. In R. Wuthnow and V. A. Hodgkinson (eds), *Faith and Philanthropy in America*. San Francisco: Jossey-Bass.

Casey, J. (1989). *The History of the Family*. Oxford: Blackwell.

Cassidy, T. and Lynn, R. (1991). Achievement motivation, educational attainment, cycles of disadvantage and social competence: some longitudinal data. *British Journal of Educational Psychology*, *61*, 1–12.

Catt, V. and Benson, P. L. (1977). Effect of verbal modeling on contributions to charity. *Journal of Applied Psychology*, *62*, 81–5.

Centers, R. and Cantril, H. (1946). Income satisfaction and income aspiration. *Journal of Abnormal and Social Psychology*, *41*, 64–9.

Central Statistical Office (1984). *Social Trends*. London: HMSO.

Central Statistical Office (1987). *Social Trends*. London: HMSO.

Central Statistical Office (1992). *Social Trends*. London: HMSO.

Central Statistical Office (1993). *Family Spending*. London: HMSO.
Central Statistical Office (1994). *Family Expenditure Survey*. London: HMSO.
Central Statistical Office (1995). *Family Spending*. London: HMSO.
Central Statistical Office (1996). *Social Trends*. London: HMSO.
Certo, S. (1995). *Human Relations Today*. New York: Austen Press.
Charities Aid Foundation (1990). *International Giving and Volunteering*. Tonbridge: Charities Aid Foundation.
Charities Aid Foundation (1991). *Individual Giving Survey 1990–1*. Tonbridge: Charities Aid Foundation.
Charities Aid Foundation (1993). *Charity Trends 1993*. Tonbridge: Charities Aid Foundation.
Charities Aid Foundation (1994). *International Giving and Volunteering*. Tonbridge: Charities Aid Foundation.
Cheal, D. (1988). *The Gift Economy*. London: Routledge.
Chizmar, J. and Halinski, R. (1983). Performance in the Basic Economic Test (BET) and 'Trade-offs' *Journal of Economic Education*, *14*, 18–29.
Chown, J. (1994). *A History of Money*. London: Routledge.
Cialdini, R. B. (1984). *Influence*. New York: Quill.
Cialdini, R. B. and Schroeder, D.A. (1976). Increasing compliance by legitimizing paltry contributions: when a penny helps. *Journal of Personality and Social Psychology*, *34*, 599–604.
Cialdini, R. B., Houlihan, D., Arps, K., Fultz, J. and Beaman, A. L. (1987). Empathy-based helping: is it selflessly or selfishly motivated? *Journal of Personality and Social Psychology*, *52*, 749–58.
Cialdini, R. B., Vincent, J. E., Lewis, S. K., Catalan, J., Wheeler, D. and Danby, B. L. (1975). Reciprocal concessions procedure for inducing compliance: the door-in-the-face technique. *Journal of Personality and Social Psychology*, *31*, 206–15.
Clark, A. E. and Oswald, A. J. (1993). Satisfaction and comparison income, University of Essex, Dept of Economics Discussion Paper. Series No. 419.
Clark, M. S. (1986). Evidence for the effectiveness of manipulation of communal and exchange relationships. *Personality and Social Psychology Bulletin*, *12*, 414–25.
Clark, M. S. and Reis, H. T. (1988). Interpersonal processes in close relationships. *Annual Review of Psychology*, *39*, 609–72.
Clydesdale, T. T. (1990). Soul winning and social work: giving and caring in the evangelical tradition. In R. Wuthnow and V. A. Hodgkinson (eds), *Faith and Philanthropy in America*. San Francisco: Jossey-Bass.
Cohen, A. and Gattiker, U. E. (1994). Rewards and organisational commitment across structural characteristics: a meta-analysis. *Journal of Business*, *9*, 137–57.
Cohen, J. (1972). *Psychological Probability*. London: Allen & Unwin.
Collard, D. A. (1978). *Altruism and Economics*. Oxford: Martin Robertson.
Conger, R. D. Ge, X., Elder, G. H., Lorenz, F. O. and Simons, R. L. (1994). Economic stress, coercive family process, and developmental problems of adolescents. *Child Development*, *65*, 541–61.
Cordes, J., Galper, H. and Kirby, S. (1990). Causes of over-withholding: Forced saving, transaction costs? Unpublished paper. Economics Dept, George Washington University.
Cornish, D. (1978). *Gambling: A Review of the Literature*. London: HMSO.
Corrigan, P. (1989). Gender and the gift: the case of the family clothing economy. *American Journal of Sociology*, *23*, 513–34.
Coulborn, W. (1950). *A Discussion of Money*. London: Longmans, Green & Co.
Couper, M. and Brindley, T. (1975). Housing classes and housing values. *Sociological Review*, *23*, 563–76.

Cowell, F. (1990). *Cheating the Government*. Cambridge, MA: MIT Press.

Cox, C. and Cooper, C. (1990). *High Flyers*. Oxford: Blackwell.

Cram, F. and Ng, S. (1989). Children's endorsements of ownership attributes. *Journal of Economic Psychology, 10*, 63–75.

Croome, H. (1956). *Introduction to Money*. London: Methuen.

Crosbie-Burnett, M. and Giles-Sims, J. (1991). Marital power in stepfather families: a test of normative-resources theory. *Journal of Family Psychology, 4*, 484–96.

Crusco, A. H. and Wetzel, C. G. (1984). The Midas touch: the effects of interpersonal touch on restaurant tipping. *Personality and Social Psychology Bulletin, 10*, 512–17.

Csikszentmihalyi, M. and Csikszentmihalyi, I. S. (eds) (1988). *Optimal Experience*. Cambridge: Cambridge University Press.

Csikszentmihalyi, M. and Rochberg-Halton, E. (1981). *The Meaning of Things: Domestic Symbols and the Self*. Cambridge: Cambridge University Press.

Cummings, S. and Taebel, D. (1978). The economic socialization of children: A neo-Marxist analysis. *Social Problems, 26*, 198–210.

Cunningham, M. R. (1979). Weather, mood, and helping behavior: quasi-experiments with the sunshine Samaritan. *Journal of Personality and Social Psychology, 37*, 1947–56.

Cunningham, M. R., Steinberg, J. and Grev, R. (1980). Wanting and having to help: Separate motivations for positive mood and guilt-induced helping. *Journal of Personality and Social Psychology, 38*, 181–92.

Dahlbäck, O. (1991). Saving and risk taking. *Journal of Economic Psychology, 12*, 479–500.

Dalton, G. (1971). Economic theory and primitive society. *American Anthropologist, 63*, 1–25.

Daly, M. and Wilson, M. (1988). Evolutionary social psychology and family homicide. *Science, 242*, 519–24.

Danziger, K. (1958). Children's earliest conceptions of economic relationships. *Journal of Social Psychology, 47*, 231–40.

Davidson, O. and Kilgore, J. (1971). A model for evaluating the effectiveness of economic education in primary grades. *Journal of Economic Education, 3*, 17–25.

Davies, E. and Lea, S. (1995). Student attitudes to student debt. *Journal of Economic Psychology, 16*, 663–79.

Davis, J. (1972). Gifts and the UK economy. *Man, 7*, 408–29.

Davis, J. (1992). *Exchange*. Buckingham: Open University Press.

Davis, K. and Taylor, R. (1979). *Kids and Cash*. La Jolla, CA: Oak Tree.

Davison, J. P., Sargent Florence, P., Gray, B. and Ross, N. S. (1958). *Productivity and Economic Incentives*. London: Allen & Unwin.

Dawson, J. (1975). Socio-economic differences in size – judgements of discs and coins by Chinese Primary VI children in Hong Kong. *Perceptual and Motor Skills, 41*, 107–10.

Deci, E. L. (1980). *The Psychology of Self-determination*. Lexington, MA: D. C. Heath.

Deci, E. L. and Ryan, R. (1985). *Intrinsic Motivation and Self-determination in Human Behavior*. New York: Plenum Press.

Delphy, C. and Leonard, D. (1992). *Familiar Exploitation*. Cambridge: Polity Press.

Denny, J., Kemper, V., Novak, V., Overby, P. and Young, A. P. (1993). George Bush's ruling class. *International Journal of Health Services, 23*, 95–132.

Devereux, E. (1968). Gambling in psychological and sociological perspective. *International Encyclopedia of the Social Sciences, 6*, 53–62.

D'Hondt, W. and Vandewiele, M. (1984). Beggary in West Africa. *Journal of Adolescence*, 7, 59–72.

Dickins, D. and Ferguson, V. (1957). Practices and attitudes of rural white children concerning money. Technical report No. 43. Mississippi State College.

Dickinson, J. and Emler, N. (1996). Developing ideas about distribution of wealth. In P. Lunt and A. Furnham (eds), *Economic Socialization* (pp. 47–68). Cheltenham: Edward Elgar.

Diener, E. and Diener, C. (1995). The wealth of nations revisited: income and quality of life. *Social Indicators Research*, 36, 275–86.

Diener, E. and Lucas, R. E. (in press). Personality and subjective well-being. In D. Kahneman, E. Diener and N. Schwarz (eds), *Understanding Well-being: Scientific Perspectives on Enjoyment and Suffering*, New York, Russell Sage.

Diener, E., Diener, M. and Diener, C. (1995). Factors predicting the subjective well-being of nations. *Journal of Personality and Social Psychology*, 69, 851–64.

Diener, E., Horwitz, J. and Emmons, R.A. (1988). Happiness of the very wealthy. *Social Indicators Research*, 16, 263–74.

Diener, E., Sandvik, E. and Pavot, W. (1991). Happiness is the frequency, not the intensity, of positive versus negative effect. In F. Strack, M. Argyle and N. Schwarz (eds), *Subjective Well-being*, Oxford, Pergamon.

Diener, E., Sandvik, E., Seidlitz, L. and Diener, M. (1993). The relationship between income and subjective well-being: relative or absolute? *Social Indicators Research*, 28, 195–223.

Dilliard, J. P., Hunter, J. E. and Burgoon, M. (1984). Sequential request persuasive strategies: meta-analysis of foot-in-the-door and door-in-the-face. *Human Communication Research*, 10, 461–88.

Dismorr, B. (1902). Ought children to be paid for domestic services? *Studies in Education*, 2, 62–70.

Dittmar, H. (1992). *The Social Psychology of Material Possessions*. Hemel Hempstead: Harvester Wheatsheaf.

Dittmar, H. (1994). Material possessions as stereotypes: material images of different socio-economic groups. *Journal of Economic Psychology*, 15, 561–85.

Dittmar, H. and Pepper, L. (1994). To have is to be: materialism and person perception in working-class and middle-class British adolescents. *Journal of Economic Psychology*, 15, 233–51.

Dodd, N. (1994). *The Sociology of Money*. New York: Continuum.

Doob, A. N. and McLaughlin, D. S. (1989). Ask and you shall be given: request size and donations to a good cause. *Journal of Applied Social Psychology*, 19, 1049–56.

Dooley, D. and Catalano, R. (1977). Money and mental disorder: toward behavioral cost accounting for primary prevention. *American Journal of Community Psychology*, 5, 217–27.

Douglas, M. (1967). Primitive rationing. In R. Firth (ed.), *Themes in Economic Anthropology*. (pp. 119–46) London: Tavistock.

Douglas, M. and Isherwood, B. (1979). *The World of Goods: Towards an Anthropology of Consumption*. London: Allen Lane.

Douty, C. M. (1972). Disasters and charity: some aspects of cooperative economic behavior. *The American Economic Review*, 62, 580–90.

Downes, D., Davis, B., David, M. and Stone, P. (1976). *Gambling, Work and Leisure*. London: Routledge.

Duesenberry, J. (1949). *Income, Saving and the Theory of Consumer Behaviour*. Cambridge, MA: Harvard University Press.

Dunn, P. (1983). *The Book of Money Lists*. London: Arrow Books.

Easterlin, R. (1973). Does money buy happiness? *The Public Interest*, 30, 3–10.

Easterlin, R. A. (1974). Does economic growth improve the human lot? Some empirical evidence. In P. A. David and M. Abrovitz (eds), *Nations and Households in Economic Growth*. New York: Academic Press.

Easterlin, R. A. (1995). Will raising the incomes of all increase the happiness of all? *Journal of Economic Behavior and Organization*, 27, 35–47.

Eayrs, C. B. and Ellis, N. (1990). *British Journal of Social Psychology*, 29, 349–66.

Edgell, S. (1980). *Middle-class Couples*. London: Allen & Unwin.

Edgell, S. and Duke, V. (1982). Reactions to the public expenditure cuts: occupational class and part realignment. *Sociology*, 16, 431–5.

Edgell, S. and Duke, V. (1991). *A Message of Thatcherism*. London: Harper-Collins.

Edwards, W. (1953). Probability-preferences in gambling. *American Journal of Psychology*, 66, 349–64.

Edwards, J. N. and Klemmack, D. L. (1973). Correlates of life satisfaction: A re-examination. *Journal of Gerontology*, 28, 497–502.

Eisenberg, N., Haake, R. J. and Bartlett, K. (1981). The effects of possessions and ownership on the sharing and proprietary behaviors of preschool children. *Merrill-Palmer Quarterly*, 27, 61–8.

Eisenberger, R. (1992). Learned Industriousness. *Psychological Review*, 99, 248–67.

Ellis, L. (1985). On the rudiments of possessions and property. *Social Science Information*, 24, 113–43.

Elston, M. A. (1980). Medicine: half our future doctors? Cited in I. Reid and E. Stratta, *Sex Differences in Britain*. Aldershot: Gower.

Emler, N. and Anderson, J. (1985). Children's representation of economic inequality: the effects of social class. *British Journal of Developmental Psychology*, 3, 191–8.

Emler, N. and Dickinson, J. (1985). Children's representation of economic inequality. *British Journal of Developmental Psychology*, 3, 191–8.

Emler, N. P. and Rushton, J. P. (1974). Cognitive-developmental factors in children's generosity. *British Journal of Social and Clinical Psychology*, 13, 277–81.

Emswiller, T., Deaux, K. and Willits, J. E. (1971). Similarity, sex, and requests for small favours. *Journal of Applied Social Psychology*, 1, 284–91.

Evans, G. (1992). Is Britain a class-divided society? A reanalysis and extension of Marshall *et al.*'s study of class consciousness. *Sociology*, 26, 233–58.

Evans-Pritchard, E. E. (1940). *The Nuer*. Oxford: Clarendon Press.

Eysenck, H. (1976). The structure of social attitudes. *Psychological Reports*, 39, 463–6.

Eysenck, M. and Eysenck, M. (1982). Effects of incentive on cued recall. *Quarterly Journal of Experimental Psychology*, 34, 191–8.

Faber, R. and O'Guinn, T. (1988). Compulsive consumption and credit abuse. *Journal of Consumer Policy*, 11, 97–109.

Fank, M. (1994). The development of a money-handling inventory. *Personality and Individual Differences*, 17, 147–52.

Feather, N. (1991). Variables relating to the allocation of pocket money to children: Parental reasons and values. *British Journal of Social Psychology*, 30, 221–34.

Feist, G. J., Bodner, T. E., Jacobs, J. F. and Miles, M. (1995). Integrating top-down and bottom-up models of subjective well-being: a longitudinal investigation. *Journal of Personality and Social Psychology*, 68, 138–50.

Felson, M. (1978). Invidious distinctions among cars, clothes and suburbs. *Public Opinion Quarterly*, 42, 49–58.

Fenichel, O. (1947). The drive to amass wealth. In O. Fenichel and O. Rapoport (eds), *The Collected Papers of O. Fenichel*. New York: Norton.

Ferenczi, S. (1926). *Further Contributions to the Theory and Techniques of Psychoanalysis*. New York: Norton.

Fischer, L. (1983). Mothers and mothers-in-law. *Journal of Marriage and the Family*, *45*, 187–192.

Fischer, E. and Arnold, S. J. (1990). More than a labor of love: Gender roles and Christmas gift shopping. *Journal of Consumer Research*, *17*, 333–45.

Fletcher, R. (1966). *The Family and Marriage in Britain*. Harmondsworth: Penguin.

Foa, U. G., Converse, J., Tornblom, K.V. and Foa, E.B. (1993). *Resource Theory: Explorations and Applications*. San Diego: Harcourt Brace Jovanovich.

Forman, N. (1987). *Mind over Money: Curing your Financial Headaches with Money Sanity*. Toronto, Ontario: Doubleday.

Formanek, R. (1991). Why they collect: collectors reveal their motivations. In *To Have Possessions: A Handbook on Ownership and Property, Special Issue of Journal of Social Behavior and Personality*, *6*, 275–86.

Forsythe, S. M. N., Drake, M. F. and Hogan, J. H. (1985). Influence of clothing attributes on the perception of personal characteristics. In M. R. Solomon (ed.), *The Psychology of Fashion*. Lexington: Heath.

Fournier, S. and Richins, M.L. (1991). Some theoretical and popular notions concerning materialism. In *To Have Possessions: A Handbook on Ownership and Property, Special issue of Journal of Social Behavior and Personality*, *6*, 403–14.

Fox, C. R. and Kahneman, D. (1992). Correlations, causes and heuristics in surveys of life satisfaction. *Social Indicators Research*, *27*, 221–34.

Freedman, J. L. and Fraser, S. C. (1966). Compliance without pressure: the foot-in-the-door technique. *Journal of Personality and Social Psychology*, *4*, 195–202.

Freedman, R., Moots, B., Sun, T. -H. and Weinberger, M. B. (1978). Household composition and extended kinship in Taiwan. *Population Studies*, *32*, 65–80.

Freud, S. (1908). *Character and Anal Eroticism*. London: Hogarth.

Freud, S. (1928). Dostoevsky and parricide. In J. Strachey (ed.), *The Standard Edition of the Complete Psychological Works of Sigmund Freud*, *21*, 177–96. London: Hogarth.

Friedman, H. (1957). *A Theory of the Consumption Function*. Princeton, NJ: Princeton University Press.

Furby, L. (1978). Possessions: toward a theory of their meaning and functions throughout the life-cycle. In P. B. Baltes (ed.), *Life Span Development and Behavior* (pp. 297–336). New York: Academic Press.

Furby, L. (1980a). The origins and development of early possessive behaviour. *Political Psychology*, *1*, 3–23.

Furby, L. (1980b). Collective possession and ownership. *Social Behaviour and Personality*, *8*, 165–84.

Furnham, A. (1982). The perception of poverty among adolescents. *Journal of Adolescence*, *5*, 135–47.

Furnham, A. (1983). Inflation and the estimated sizes of notes. *Journal of Economic Psychology*, *4*, 349–52.

Furnham, A. (1984). Many sides of the coin: the psychology of money usage. *Personality and Individual Differences*, *5*, 95–103.

Furnham, A. (1985a). A short measure of economic beliefs. *Personality and Individual Differences*, *6*, 123–6.

Furnham, A. (1985b). The perceived value of small coins. *Journal of Social Psychology*, *125*, 571–5.

Furnham, A. (1985c). Why do people save? *Journal of Applied Social Psychology*, *15*, 354–73.

Furnham, A. (1990). *The Protestant Work Ethic*. London: Routledge.

Furnham, A. (1992). *Personality at Work*. London: Routledge.

Furnham, A. (1995). The just world, charitable giving and attitudes to disability. *Personality and Individual Differences*, *19*, 577–83.

Furnham, A. (1996a). *The Myths of Management*. London: Whurr.

Furnham, A. (1996b). Attitudinal correlates and demographic predictors of monetary beliefs and behaviours. *Journal of Organizational Behaviour*, *17*, 375–88.

Furnham, A. (1997). *The Psychology of Behaviour at Work*. London: Psychology Press.

Furnham, A. and Bochner, S. (1996). *Culture Shock*. London: Methuen.

Furnham, A. and Cleare, A. (1988). School children's conceptions of economics: prices, wages, investments and strikes. *Journal of Economic Psychology*, *9*, 467–79.

Furnham, A. and Jones, S. (1987). Children's views regarding possessions and their theft. *Journal of Moral Education*, *16*, 18–30.

Furnham, A. and Lewis, A. (1996). *The Economic Mind*. Brighton: Wheatsheaf.

Furnham, A. and Lunt, P. L. (1996). *Economic Socialization*. Cheltenham: Edward Elgar.

Furnham, A. and Rose, M. (1987). Alternative ethics. *Human Relations*, *40*, 561–74.

Furnham, A. and Stacey, B. (1991). *Young People's Understanding of Society*. London: Routledge.

Furnham, A. and Stringfield, P. (1994). Congruence of self and subordinate ratings of managerial practices as a correlate of supervisor evaluation. *Journal of Occupational and Organizational Psychology*, *67*, 57–67.

Furnham, A. and Thomas, P. (1984a). Adult perceptions of the economic socialization of children. *Journal of Adolescence*, *7*, 217–31.

Furnham, A. and Thomas, P. (1984b). Pocket-money: a study of economic education. *British Journal of Developmental Psychology*, *2*, 205–12.

Furnham, A. and Weissman, D. (1985). Children's perceptions of British coins. Unpublished paper.

Furth, H. (1980). *The World of Grown-ups*. New York: Elsevier.

Furth, H., Baur, M. and Smith, J. (1976). Children's conceptions of social institutions: A Piagetian framework. *Human Development*, *19*, 351–74.

Fussell, P. (1984). *Caste Marks: Style and Status in the USA*. London: Heinemann.

Galbraith, J. K. (1984). *The Affluent Society* (4th edn). Boston, MA: Houghton Mifflin.

Gallie, D. (1983). *Social Inequality and Class Radicalism in France and England*. Cambridge: Cambridge University Press.

Garner, T. I. and Wagner, J. (1991). Economic dimensions of household gift giving. *Journal of Consumer Research*, *18*, 368–79.

Gecas, V. and Seff, M. A. (1990). Social class and self-esteem: psychological centrality, compensation, and the relative effects of work and home. *Social Psychology Quarterly*, *53*, 165–73.

Gianotten, H. and van Raaij, W. (1982). Consumer credit and saving as a function of income and confidence. Paper at 7th Economic Psychology Conference.

Gibbins, K. (1969). Communication aspects of women's clothing and their relation to fashionability. *British Journal of Social and Clinical Psychology*, *8*, 301–12.

Gilovitch, T. (1983). Biased evaluation and persistence in gambling. *Journal of Personality and Social Psychology*, *6*, 1110–26.

Godfrey, N. (1995). *A Penny Saved: Teaching your Children the Values of Life Skills they will Need to Live in the Real World*. New York: Fireside.

Goffman, E. (1956). *The Presentation of Self in Everyday Life*. Edinburgh: Edinburgh University Press.

Goffman, E. (1961). *Asylums*. Garden City, NY: Doubleday Anchor.

Goldberg, H. and Lewis, R. (1978). *Money Madness: The Psychology of Saving, Spending, Loving and Hating Money*. London: Springwood.

Goldthorpe, J. H., Llewellyn, C. and Payne, C. (1987). *Social Mobility and Class Structure in Modern Britain*. Oxford: Clarendon Press.

Gouldner, A. W. (1960). The norm of reciprocity: a preliminary statement. *American Sociological Review*, 25, 161–78.

Graham, H. (1987). Being poor: perception and coping strategies of lone mothers. In J. Brannen and G. Wilson (eds), *Give and Take in Families: Studies in Resource Distribution*. London: Allen & Unwin.

Gresham, A. and Fontenot, G. (1989). The different attitudes of the sexes toward money: an application of the money attitude scale. *Advances in Marketing*, 8, 380–4.

Grusec, J. E., Kuczynksi, L., Rushton, J.-P. and Simutis, Z. M. (1978). Modelling, direct instruction, and attributions: Effects on altruism. *Developmental Psychology*, 14, 51–7.

Grygier, T. (1961). *The Dynamic Personality Inventory*. Windsor: NFER.

Gulerce, A. (1991). Transitional objects: a reconsideration of the phenomenon. In F. W. Rudmin (ed.), *To Have Possessions: A Handbook on Ownership and Property. Special Issue of Journal of Social Behavior and Personality*, 6, 187–208.

Guzzo, R., Jette, R. D. and Katzell, R. A. (1985). The effects of psychologically based interventions programs on worker productivity: a meta analysis. *Personnel Psychology*, 38, 275–91.

Hackman, J. R. and Oldham, G. R. (1980). *Work Redesign*. Reading, MA: Addison-Wesley.

Hagen, P. J. (1982). *Blood: Gift or Merchandise*. New York: Alan R. Liss.

Haines, W. (1986). Inflation and the real rate of interest. *Journal of Economic Psychology*, 7, 351–7.

Halfpenny, P. and Lowe, D. (1994). *Individual Giving and Volunteering in Britain* (7th ed). Tonbridge: Charities Aid Foundation.

Halfpenny, P. and Petipher, C. (1994). *Individual Giving and Volunteering in Britain* (7th edn). Tonbridge, Kent: Charities Aid Foundation.

Hamid, P. N. (1968). Style of dress as a perceptual cue in impression formation. *Perceptual and Motor Skills*, 26, 904–6.

Hanf, C. and von Wersebe, B. (1994). Price quality and consumers' behaviour. *Journal of Consumer Policy*, 17, 335–48.

Hanley, A. and Wilhelm, M. (1992). Compulsive buying: An exploration into self-esteem and money attitudes. *Journal of Economic Psychology*, 13, 5–18.

Hansen, H. (1985). The economics of early childhood education in Minnesota. *Journal of Economic Education*, 16, 219–24.

Hanson, J. (1964). *Money*. London: English Universities Press.

Harbury, C. D. and Hitchens, D. M. W. M. (1979). *Inheritance and Wealth Inequality in Britain*. London: Allen & Unwin.

Harp, S. S., Stretch, S. M. and Harp, D. A. (1985). The influence of apparel on responses to television news anchor women. In M. R. Solomon (ed.), *The Psychology of Fashion*. Lexington: Heath.

Harris, M. (1995). Waiters, customers and service: some tips about tipping. *Journal of Applied Social Psychology*, 25, 725–44.

Harris, M. B., Benson, S. M. and Hall, C. L. (1975). The effects of confession on altruism. *Journal of Social Psychology*, 96, 187–92.

Harwood, M. K. and Rice, R. W. (1992). An examination of referent selection processes underlying job satisfaction. *Social Indicators Research*, 27, 1–39.

Haste, H. and Torney-Purta, J. (1992). *The Development of Political Understanding*. San Francisco: Jossey-Bass.

Haynes, J. and Wiener, J. (1996). The analyst in the counting house: money as a symbol and reality in analysis. *British Journal of Psychotherapy*, *13*, 14–25.

Headey, B. (1991). Distributive justice and occupational incomes: perceptions of justice determine perceptions of fact. *British Journal of Sociology*, *42*, 581–96.

Headey, B. (1993). An economic model of subjective well-being: integrating economic and psychological theories. *Social Indicators Research*, *28*, 97–116.

Headey, B. and Wearing, A. (1992). *Understanding Happiness*. Melbourne: Longman Cheshire.

Headey, B. W., Holmstrom, E. L. and Wearing, A. (1984). Models of well-being and ill-being. *Social Indicators Research*, *17*, 211–34.

Heath, A. (1976). *Rational Choice and Social Exchange*. Cambridge: Cambridge University Press.

Heath, A. (1981). *Social Mobility*. London: Fontana.

Heer, D. M. (1963). The measurement and bases of family power: an overview. *Marriage and Family Living*, *25*, 133–9.

Henley Centre for Forecasting (1985). *Leisure Futures*, London: Quarterly.

Henry, H. (1958). *Motivation Research*. London: Lockwood.

Herskovitz, M. J. (1952). *Human Problems in Changing Africa*. New York: Knopf.

Herzberg, F., Mausner, B. and Snyderman, B. B. (1959). *The Motivation to Work*. New York: Wiley.

Hill, A. (1976). Methodological problems in the use of factor analysis. *British Journal of Medical Psychology*, *49*, 145–59.

Hill, R. (1970). *Family Development in Three Generations*. Cambridge, MA: Schenkman.

Hinchcliffe, T. (1992). *North Oxford*. New Haven, CT: Yale University Press.

Hitchcock, J., Munroe, R. and Munroe, R. (1976). Coins and countries: the value-size hypothesis. *Journal of Social Psychology*, *100*, 307–08.

HMSO (1996). Labour market trends. *Employment Gazette*, November, 480.

Hobhouse, L., Wheeler, G. and Ginsberg, M. (1915). *The Material Culture and Social Institutions of the Simpler Peoples: An Essay in Correlation*. London: Chapman & Hall.

Hoffman, S. W. and Manis, J. D. (1982). The value of children in the United States. In F. I. Nye (ed.), *Family Relationships*. Beverly Hills, CA: Sage.

Homans, G. (1961). *Social Behaviour: its Elementary Forms*. New York: Harcourt Brace Jovanovitch.

Horrell, S. (1994). Household time allocation and women's labour force participation. In M. Anderson, F. Bechhofer and J. Gershuny (eds), *The Social and Political Economy of the Household*, (pp. 198–224). Oxford: Oxford University Press.

Howarth, E. (1980). A test of some old concepts by means of some new scales: Anality or psychoticism, oral optimism or extraversion, oral pessimism or neuroticism. *Psychological Reports*, *47*, 1039–42.

Howarth, E. (1982). Factor analytic examination of Kline's scales for psychoanalytic concepts. *Personality and Individual Differences*, *3*, 89–92.

Hui, C. H. and Triandis, H. C. (1986). Individualism-collectivism: a study of cross-cultural researchers. *Journal of Cross-Cultural Psychology*, *17*, 225–48.

Hurlock, E. B. (1929). Motivation in fashion. *Archives of Psychology*, *3*, 18–27

Hyman, H. (1942). The psychology of status. *Archives of Psychology*, *269*, 147–65.

Inglehart, R. and Rabier, J.-R. (1986). Aspirations adapt to situation – but why are the Belgians so much happier than the French? A cross-cultural analysis of the subjective quality of life. In F. M. Andrews (ed.), *Research on the Quality of*

Life, (pp. 45–6). Ann Arbor, MI: Institute for Social Research, University of Michigan.

Inkeles, A. and Diamond, L. (1986). Personal development and national development: a cross-cultural perspective. In A. Szalai and F.M. Andrews (eds), *The Quality of Life: Comparative Studies,* (pp. 73–109). Ann Arbor, MI: Institute for Social Research, University of Michigan.

Isen, A. M. and Noonberg, A. (1979). The effect of photographs of the handicapped on donations to charity: when a thousand words may be too much. *Journal of Applied Social Psychology, 9,* 426–31.

Isen, A. M., Horn, N. and Rosenhan, D. L. (1973). Effects of success and failure on children's generosity. *Journal of Personality and Social Psychology, 27,* 239–47.

Jackson, K. (ed.) (1995). *The Oxford Book of Money.* Oxford: Oxford University Press.

Jackson, L. A. (1989). Relative deprivation and the gender wage gap. *Journal of Social Issues, 45,* 117–33.

Jahoda, G. (1979). The construction of economic reality by some Glaswegian children. *European Journal of Social Psychology, 9,* 115–27.

Jahoda, G. (1981). The development of thinking about economic institutions: The bank. *Cashiers de Psychologic Cognitive, 1,* 55–73.

Jencks, C. (1987). Who gives to what? In W.W. Powell (ed.), *The Nonprofit Sector.* New Haven: Yale University Press.

Johns, G. (1991). *Organizational Behavior: Understanding Life at Work.* New York: HarperCollins.

Johnson, D. B. (1982). The free-rider principle, the charity market and the economics of blood. *British Journal of Social Psychology, 21,* 93–106.

Joshi, H. (1992). The cost of caring. In C. Glendinning and C. Millar (eds), *Women and Poverty in Britain: The 1990s* (pp. 110–25). London: Harvester Wheatsheaf.

Judge, D. S. and Hardy, S. B. (1992). Allocation of accumulated resources among close kin: inheritance in Sacramento, California, 1890–1984. *Ethology and Sociobiology, 13,* 495–522.

Kabanoff, B. (1982). Occupational and sex differences in leisure needs and leisure satisfaction. *Journal of Occupational Behaviour, 3,* 233–45.

Kaiser, S. B. (1990). *The Social Psychology of Clothing and Personal Adornment* (second edn). London: Macmillan.

Kamptner, N.L. (1991). Personal possessions and their meanings: a life-span perspective. In F. W. Rudmin (ed.), *To Have Possessions: A Handbook on Ownership and Property. Special Issue of Journal of Social Behavior and Personality, 6,* 209–28.

Kanfer, R. (1990). Motivation theory and industrial and organisational psychology. In M. D. Dunnette and L. M. Hough (eds), *Handbook of Industrial and Organizational Psychology,* (pp. vol 1, 75–170). Palo Alto, CA: Consulting Psychologists Press.

Kanner, A. D., Coyne, J. C. and Lazarus, R. S. (1981). Comparison of two methods of stress measurement: hassles and uplifts versus major life events. *Journal of Behavioural Medicine, 4,* 1–39.

Kasser, T. and Ryan, R. M. (1993). A dark side of the American dream: correlates of financial success as a central life aspiration. *Journal of Personality and Social Psychology, 65,* 410–22.

Katona, G. (1960). *The Powerful Consumer.* New York: McGraw-Hill.

Katona, G. (1975). *Psychological Economics.* New York: Elsevier.

Kelman, H. (1965). Manipulation of human behavior: An ethical dilemma for the social scientist. *Journal of Social Issues, 21,* 31–46.

Kemp, S. (1987). Estimates of past prices. *Journal of Economic Psychology, 8,* 181–9.

Kemp, S. (1991). Remembering and dating past prices? *Journal of Economic Psychology*, *12*, 431–45.

Kennedy, L. (1991). Farm succession in modern Ireland: elements of a theory of inheritance. *Economic History Review*, *44*, 477–99.

Kerbo, H. R. (1983). *Social Stratification and Inequality*. New York: McGraw-Hill.

Kessler, R. C. (1982). A disaggregation of the relationship between socioeconomic status and psychological distress. *American Sociological Review*, *47*, 752–64.

Kets de Vries, M. (1977). The entrepreneurial personality: a person at the crossroads. *Journal of Management Studies*, *14*, 34–57.

Keynes, J. (1936). *The General Theory of Employment, Interest and Money*. London: Macmillan.

Kinsey, A. C., Pomeroy, W. B. and Martin, C. E. (1953). *Sexual Behavior in the Human Female*. London: Saunders.

Kirton, M. (1978). Wilson and Patterson's Conservatism Scale. *British Journal of Social and Clinical Psychology*, *12*, 428–30.

Kline, P. (1967). *An investigation into the Freudian concept of the anal character*. Unpublished Phd, University of Manchester.

Kline, P. (1971). *Ai3Q Test*. Windsor: NFER.

Kline, P. (1972). *Fact and Fantasy in Freudian Theory*. London: Methuen.

Kohler, A. (1897). Children's sense of money. *Studies in Education*, *1*, 323–31.

Kohler, W. (1925). *The Mentality of Apes*. London: Kegan Paul, Trench & Trubner.

Kohn, M. L. and Schooler, C. (1983). *Work and Personality*. Norwood, NJ: Ablex.

Kourilsky, M. (1977). The kinder-economy: A case of kindergarten pupils' acquisition of economic concepts. *The Elementary School Journal*, *77*, 182–91.

Kourilsky, M. and Campbell, M. (1984). Sex differences in a smaller classroom economy. *Sex Roles*, *10*, 53–66.

Kraut, R. E. (1973). Effects of social labelling on giving to charity. *Journal of Experimental Social Psychology*, *9*, 551–62.

Lambert, W., Soloman, R. and Watson, P. (1949). Reinforcement and extinction as factors in size estimation. *Journal of Experimental Psychology*, *39*, 637–71.

Lane, R. E. (1991). *The Market Experience*. Cambridge: Cambridge University Press.

Langford, P. (1984). The eighteenth century. In K. O. Morgan (ed.), *The Oxford Illustrated History of Britain*. Oxford: Oxford University Press.

Laslett, P. (1983). *The World We Have Lost; Further Explored* (third edn). London: Methuen.

Lassarres, D. (1996). Consumer education in French families and schools. In P. Lunt and A. Furnham (eds), *Economic Socialization* pp. 130–48. Cheltenham: Edward Elgar,

Lawler, E. (1981). *Pay and Organization Development*. Reading, MA: Addison-Wesley.

Lea, S. (1981). Inflation, decimalization and the estimated size of coins. *Journal of Economic Psychology*, *1*, 79–81.

Lea, S. and Webley, P. (1981). Théorie psychologique de la Monnaie. Paper presented at 6th International Symposium on economic psychology. Paris.

Lea, S., Webley, P. and Walker, C. (1995). Psychological factors in consumer debt: money management, economic socialization, and credit use. *Journal of Economic Psychology*, *16*, 681–701.

Lea, S. E. G., Tarpy, R. M. and Webley, P. (1987). *The Individual in the Economy*. Cambridge: Cambridge University Press.

Leahy, R. (1981). The development of the conception of economic inequality. *Child Development*, *52*, 523–32.

Lee, N. (ed.) (1989). *Sources of Charity Finance*. Tonbridge: Charities Aid Foundation.

Lee, N., Halfpenny, P., Jones, A. and Elliot, H. (1995). Data sources and estimates of charitable giving in Britain. *Voluntas, 6*, 39–66.

Legal and General (1987). *The Price of a Wife*. London: Legal & General Press Office.

Leicht, K. T. and Shepelak, N. (1994). Organizational justice and satisfaction with economic rewards. *Research in Social Stratification and Mobility, 13*, 175–202.

Leiser, D. (1983). Children's conceptions of economics – the constitution of the cognitive domain. *Journal of Economic Psychology, 4*, 297–317.

Leiser, D. and Ganin, M. (1996). Economic participation and economic socialization. In P. Lunt and A. Furnham (eds), *Economic Socialization* pp. 93–109. Cheltenham: Edward Elgar,

Leiser, D., Sevón, G. and Lévy, D. (1990). Children's economic socialization: summarizing the cross-cultural comparison of ten countries. *Journal of Social Psychology, 12*, 221–39.

Lenski, G. E. (1966). *Power and Privilege: A Theory of Social Stratification*. New York: McGraw-Hill.

Leonard, D. (1980). *Sex and Generation*. London: Tavistock.

Lewinsohn, P. M., Sullivan, J. M. and Grosscup, S. J. (1982). Behavioral therapy: clinical applications. In A. J. Rush (ed.), *Short-term Therapies for Depression*. New York: Guildford.

Lewis, A. (1982). *The Psychology of Taxation*. Oxford: Martin Robertson.

Lewis, A., Webley, P. and Furnham, A. (1995). *The New Economic Mind*. London: Harvester.

Lindgren, H. (1991). *The Psychology of Money*. Odessa, FL: Krieger.

Linquist, A. (1981). A note on determinants of household saving behaviour. *Journal of Economic Psychology, 1*, 39–57.

Livingstone, S. (1992). The meaning of domestic technologies: a personal construct analysis of familial gender relation. In R. Silverstone and E. Hirsch (eds), *Consuming Technologies* (pp. 113–30). London: Routledge.

Livingstone, S. and Lunt, P. (1993). Savers and borrowers: strategies of personal financial management. *Human Relations , 46*, 963–85.

Loscocco, K. A. and Spitze, G. (1991). The organizational context of women's and men's pay satisfaction. *Social Science Quarterly, 72*, 3–19.

Lozkowski, T. (1977). *Win or Lose: A Social History of Gambling in America*. New York: Bobbs Merril.

Luft, J. (1957). Monetary value and the perceptions of persons. *Journal of Social Psychology, 46*, 245–51.

Luna, R. and Quintanilla, I. (1996). *Attitudes towards money: influence in consumption patterns*. Research Paper. University of Valencia, Spain.

Lunt, P. (1996). Introduction: Social aspects of young people's understanding of the economy. In P. Lunt and A. Furnham (eds), *Economic Socialization* (pp. 1–10). Cheltenham: Edward Elgar.

Lunt, P. and Furnham, A. (eds) (1996). *Economic Socialization: The Economic Beliefs and Behaviours of Young People*. Cheltenham: Edward Elgar.

Lunt, P. and Livingstone, S. (1991a). Everyday explanations for personal debt: a network approach. *British Journal of Social Psychology, 30*, 309–23.

Lunt, P. and Livingstone, S. (1991b). Psychological, social and economic determinants of saving. *Journal of Economic Psychology, 12*, 621–41.

Lunt, P. K. and Livingstone, S. L. (1992). *Mass Consumption and Personal Identity*. Buckingham: Open University Press.

Lynn, M. (1988). The effects of alcohol consumption on restaurant tipping. *Personality and Social Psychology Bulletin, 14*, 87–91.

Lynn, M. (1991). Restaurant tipping: A reflection of customers' evaluations of a service? *Journal of Consumer Research, 18*, 438–48.

Lynn, M. and Bond, C. (1992). The group size effect on tipping. *Journal of Applied Social Psychology*, *22*, 327–41.

Lynn, M. and Grassman, A. (1990). Restaurant tipping: an examination of three 'rational' explanations. *Journal of Economic Psychology*, *11*, 169–81.

Lynn, M. and Latane, B. (1984). The psychology of restaurant tipping. *Journal of Applied Social Psychology*, *14*, 551–63.

Lynn, M. and Grassman, A. (1990). Restaurant tipping: an examination of three 'rational' explanations. *Journal of Economic Psychology*, *11*, 169–81.

Lynn, P. and Smith, J. D. (1991). *Voluntary Action Research*. London: The Volunteer Centre.

Lynn, R. (1994). *The Secret of the Miracle Economy*. London: Social Affairs Unit.

McClelland, D. C. (1987). *Human Motivation*. Cambridge: Cambridge University Press.

McClelland, D., Atkinson, J., Clark, R. and Lowell, E. (1953). *The Achievement Motive*. New York: Appleton-Century-Crofts.

McClure, R. (1984). The relationship between money attitudes and overall pathology. *Psychology*, *21*, 4–6.

McCracken, A. (1987). Emotional impact of possession loss. *Journal of Gerontological Nursing*, *13*, 14–19.

McCracken, G. (1988). *Culture and Consumption*. Indianapolis: Indiana University Press.

McCracken, G. (1990). *Culture and Consumption*. Indianapolis: Indianapolis University Press.

McCurdy, H. (1956). Coin perception studies in the concept of schemata. *Psychological Review*, *63*, 160–8.

McDonald, W. (1994). Psychological associations with shopping. *Psychology and Marketing*, *11*, 549–68.

McKenzie, R. (1971). An exploratory study of the economic understanding of elementary school children. *Journal of Economic Education*, *3*, 26–31.

McLuhan, M. (1964). *Understanding Media*. New York: Barton Books.

Machlowitz, M. (1980). *Workaholics*. Reading, MA: Addison-Wesley.

Marmot, M. G., Shipley, M. J. and Rose, G. (1984). Inequalities in death – specific explanations of a general pattern. *The Lancet*, *1*, 1003–6.

Marriott, R. (1968). *Incentive Payment Systems*. London: Staples.

Marsh, P. and Collett, P. (1986). *Driving Passion*. London: Cape.

Marshall, G., Newby, H., Rose, D. and Vogler, C. (1988). *Social Class in Modern Britain*. London: Hutchinson.

Marshall, H. (1964). The relation of giving children an allowance to children's money knowledge and responsibility, and to other practices of parents. *Journal of Genetic Psychology*, *104*, 35–51.

Marshall, H. and Magruder, L. (1960). Relations between parent money education practices and children's knowledge and use of money. *Child Development*, *31*, 253–84.

Marx, K. (1977). *Selected Writings*. Oxford: Oxford University Press.

Maslow, A. H. (1970). *Motivation and Personality*. New York: Harper.

Maton, K. I. (1987). Patterns and psychological correlates of material support within a religious setting: the bidirectional support hypthesis. *Journal of Community Psychology*, *15*, 185–207.

Matthaei, J. (1982). *An Economic History of Women in America*. New York: Schocken.

Matthews, A. (1991). *If I Think about Money so much, Why Can't I Figure it out*. New York: Summit Books.

Mauss, M. (1954). *The Gift*. New York: W. W. Norton.

Mead, M. (ed.). (1937). *Cooperation and Competition among Primitive Peoples*. New York: McGraw-Hill.

Medina, J., Saegert, J. and Gresham, A. (1996). Comparison of Mexican–American and Anglo–American attitudes towards money. *Journal of Consumer Affairs*, *30*, 124–45.

Merton, R. and Rossi, A. (1968). Contributions to the theory of reference group behaviour. In K. Merton (ed.), *Social Theory and Social Structure*. New York: Free Press.

Michalos, A. C. (1985). Multiple discrepancies theory. *Social Indicators Research*, *16*, 347–414.

Micromegas, N. (1993). *Money*. Paris: Micromegas.

Millenson, J. S. (1985). Psychosocial strategies for fashion advertising. In M. R. Solomon (ed.), *The Psychology of Fashion*. Lexington: Heath.

Miller, J. and Yung, S. (1990). The role of allowances in adolescent socialization. *Youth and Society*, *22*, 137–59.

Miner, J. (1993). *Industrial–Organizational Psychology*. New York: McGraw-Hill.

Mitchell, G., Tetlock, P. E., Mellers, B. S. and Ordonez, L. D. (1993). Judgements of social justice: compromises between equality and efficiency. *Journal of Personality and Social Psychology*, *65*, 629–39.

Modigliani, F. and Brumberg, R. (1954). Utility analysis and the consumption factor: an interpretation of the data. In K. Kurihara (ed.), *Post-Keynesian Economics*. New Brunswick, NJ: Rutgers University Press.

Morgan, E. (1969). *A History of Money*. Harmondsworth: Penguin.

Morris, L. (1990). *The Working of the Household*. Oxford: Polity Press.

Morsbach, H. (1977). The psychological importance of ritualized gift exchange in modern Japan. *Annals of the New York Academy of Science*, *293*, 98–113.

Mortimer, J. and Shanahan, M. (1994). Adolescent experience and family relationships. *Work and Occupation*, *21*, 369–84.

Mortimer, J. T. and Lorence, J. (1989). Satisfaction and involvement: disentangling a deceptively simple relationship. *Social Psychology Quarterly*, *52*, 249–65.

Mullis, R. J. (1992). Models of economic well-being as predictors of psychological well-being. *Social Indicators Research*, *6*, 119–35.

Munro, M. (1988). Housing wealth and inheritance. *Journal of Social Policy*, *17*, 417–36.

Murdoch, G.P. (1949). *Social Structure*. New York: Macmillan.

Myers, D.G. (1992). *The Pursuit of Happiness*. New York: Morrow.

Myers, D.G. (1993). *Social Psychology* (fourth edn). New York: McGraw-Hill.

Myers, D.G. and Diener, E. (1996). The pursuit of happiness. *Scientific American*, May, 54–6.

Near, J. P., Smith, C., Rice, R. W. and Hunt, R.G. (1983). Job satisfaction and nonwork satisfaction as components of life satisfaction. *Journal of Applied Psychology*, *13*, 126–44.

New Earnings Survey (1995). London: HMSO.

Newlyn, W. and Bootle, R. (1978). *Theory of Money*. Oxford: Clarendon Press.

Newson, J. and Newson, E. (1976). *Seven Year Olds in the Home Environment*. London: Allen & Unwin.

Ng, S. (1983). Children's ideas about the bank and shop profit. *Journal of Economic Psychology*, *4*, 209–21.

Ng, S. (1985). Children's ideas about the bank: a New Zealand replication. *European Journal of Social Psychology*, *15*, 121–3.

Nightingale, B. (1973). *Charities*. London: Allen Lane.

Nimkoff, M. F. and Middleton, R. (1960). Types of family and types of economy. *American Psychologist*, *66*, 215–25.

Oakley, A. (1974). *The Sociology of Housework*. Oxford: Martin Robertson.

O'Brien, M. and Ingels, S. (1987). The economic inventory. *Research in Economic Education*, *18*, 7–18.

O'Neill, R. (1984). Anality and Type A coronary-prone behaviour patterns. *Journal of Personality Assessment*, *48*, 627–8.

O'Neill, R., Greenberg, R. and Fisher, S. (1992). Humour and anality. *Humour: International Journal of Human Research*, *5*, 283–91.

Occupational Mortality. (1990). *The Registrar General's Centennial Supplement*. London: HMSO.

Offer, A. (in press). Between the gift and the market: The economy of regard.

Okun, M. A., Stock, W. A., Haring, M. J. and Witten, R. A. (1984). Health and subjective well-being. *International Journal of Aging and Human Development*, *19*, 111–32.

Olmsted, A.D. (1991). Collecting: leisure, investment or obsession? In F. W. Rudmin (ed.), *To Have Possessions: A Handbook on Ownership and Property. Special issue of Journal of Social Behavior and Personality*, *6*, 287–306.

Olson, G. I. and Schober, B. I. (1993). The satisfied poor. *Social Indicators Research*, *28*, 173–93.

OPCS (1996). *Living in Britain*. London: HMSO.

Oropesa, R. S. (1995). Consumer possessions, consumer passions, and subjective well-being. *Sociological Forum*, *10*, 215–44.

Osborne, K. and Nichol, C. (1996) Patterns of pay: results of the 1996 New Earnings Survey. *Employment Gazette*, *104*, 477–85.

Pahl, J. (1984). *Divisions of Labour*. Oxford: Blackwell.

Pahl, J. (1989). *Money and Marriage*. London: Macmillan.

Pahl, J. (1995). His money, her money: Recent research on financial organisation in marriage. *Journal of Economic Psychology*, *16*, 361–76.

Pahl, R. E. (1984). *Divisions of Labour*. Oxford: Blackwell.

Parker, S. (1982). *Work and Retirement*. London: Allen & Unwin.

Parkin, F. (1971). *Class Inequality and Political Order*. London: MacGibbon and Kee.

Pearce, J. L. (1993). *Volunteers*. London: Routledge.

Petipher, C. and Halfpenny, P. (1991). The 1990/91 individual giving survey. In S. K. E. Saxon-Harrold and J. Kendall (eds), *Researching the Voluntary Sector*. Tonbridge: Charities Aid Foundation.

Phelan, J. (1994). The paradox of the contented female worker: an assessment of alternative explanations. *Social Psychology Quarterly*, *57*, 95–107.

Pierce, A. (1967). The economic cycle and the social suicide rate. *American Sociological Review*, *32*, 457–62.

Pieters, R. G. M. and Robben, H. S. J. (1992). Receiving a gift: evaluating who gives what when. In S. E. G. Lea, P. Webley and E. M. Young (eds), *New Directions in Economic Psychology*. Aldershot: Elgar.

Pliner, P., Freedman, J., Abramovitch, R. and Darke, P. (1996). Children as consumers: in the laboratory and beyond. In P. Lunt and A. Furnham (eds), *Economic Socialization*. Cheltenham: Edward Elgar, pp. 35–46.

Poduska, B. E. and Allred, G. (1990). The missing link in MFT training. *American Journal of Family Therapy*, *18*, 161–8.

Pollio, H. and Gray, T. (1973). Change-making strategies in children and adults. *Journal of Psychology*, *84*, 173–9.

Prentice, D. A. (1987). Psychological correspondence of possessions, attitudes and values. *Journal of Personality and Social Psychology*, *53*, 993–1003.

Prevey, E. (1945). A quantitative study of family practices in training children in the use of money. *Journal of Educational Psychology*, *36*, 411–28.

Price, M. (1993). Women, men and money styles. *Journal of Economic Psychology*, *14*, 175–82.

Pritchard, R. D., Dunnette, M. D. and Jorgenson, D. O. (1972). Effects of perception of equity and inequity on worker performance and satisfaction. *Organizational Behavior and Human Performance*, *10*, 75–94.

Quinn, R., Tabor, J. and Gordon, L. (1968). *The Decision to Discriminate*. Ann Arbor, MI: Survey Research Center, University of Michigan.

Radley, A. and Kennedy, M. (1992). Reflections upon charitable giving: a comparison of individuals from business, manual and professional backgrounds. *Journal of Community and Applied Social Psychology*, *2*, 113–29.

Raiddick, C. C. and Stewart, D. G. (1994). An examination of the life satisfaction and importance of leisure in the lives of older female retirees: a comparison of blacks to whites. *Journal of Leisure Research*, *26*, 75–87.

Ramsett, D. (1972). Toward improving economic education in the elementary grades. *Journal of Economic Education*, *4*, 30–5.

Randall, M. (1996). *The Price You Pay: The Hidden Cost of Women's Relationship to Money*. London: Routledge.

Regan, D. T. (1971). Effects of a favour and liking on compliance. *Journal of Experimental Social Psychology*, *7*, 627–39.

Reid, I. (1989). *Social Class Differences in Britain* (third edn). London: Fontana.

Reid, I. and Stratta, E. (1989). *Sex Differences in Britain*. Aldershot: Gower.

Reingen, P. H. (1982). Test of a list procedure for inducing compliance with a request to donate money. *Journal of Applied Psychology*, *67*, 110–18.

Rendon, M. and Kranz, R. (1992). *Straight Talk about Money*. New York: Facts on File.

Rex, J. and Moore, R. (1967). *Race, Community and Conflict*. London: Oxford University Press.

Richardson, J. and Kroeber, A. L. (1940). Three centuries of women's dress fashions: a quantitative analysis. *Anthropological Records*, *5*, 111–53.

Richins, M. and Dawson, S. (1992). Materialism as a consumer value: measure, development and validation. *Journal of Consumer Research*, *19*, 303–16.

Richins, M. and Rudrin, F. (1994). Materialism and economic psychology. *Journal of Economic Psychology*, *15*, 217–31.

Riddick, C. C. and Stewart, D. G. (1994). An examination of the life satisfaction and importance of leisure in the lives of older female retirees: a comparison of Blacks and Whites. *Journal of Leisure Research*, *26*, 75–87.

Rim, Y. (1982). Personality and attitudes connected with money. Paper given at Economic Psychology Conference, Edinburgh.

Rimor, M. and Tobin, G. A. (1990). Jewish giving patterns to Jewish and non-Jewish philanthropy. In R. Wuthnow and V. A. Hodgkinson (eds), *Faith and Philanthropy in America*. San Francisco: Jossey-Bass.

Rind, B. and Bordia, P. (1995). Effect of server's 'thank you' and personalization on restaurant tipping. *Journal of Applied Social Psychology*, *25*, 745–51.

Rind, B. and Bordia, P. (1996). Effect of restaurant tipping of male and female servers drawing a happy, smiling face on the backs of customers' checks. *Journal of Applied Social Psychology*, *26*, 218–25.

Robben, H. and Verhaller, T. (1994). Behavioral costs as determinants of cost perception and preference formation for gifts to receive and gifts to give. *Journal of Economic Psychology*, *15*, 333–50.

Robertson, A. and Cochrane, R. (1973). The Wilson–Patterson Conservatism scale: a reappraisal. *British Journal of Social and Clinical Psychology*, *12*, 428–30.

Robinson, J. P. (1977). *How Americans Use Time*. New York: Praeger.

Rohling, M., Binder, L. and Langhinmchsen-Rohling, J. (1995). Money matters. *Health Psychology*, *14*, 537–47.

Rokeach, M. (1974). Change and stability in American value systems, 1968–1971. *Public Opinion Quarterly*, *38*, 222–38.

Roland-Levy, C. (1990). Economic socialization: basis for international comparisons. *Journal of Economic Psychology*, *11*, 469–82.

Rosenberg, M. (1957). *Occupations and Values*. Glencoe, Ill: Free Press.

Rosenberg, M. and Pearlin, L. L. (1978). Social class and self-esteem among children and adults. *American Psychologist*, *84*, 53–77.

Ross, A.D. (1968). Philanthropy. *Encyclopedia of the Social Sciences*, *12*, 72–80.

Rubinstein, W. D. (1981). Survey report on money. *Psychology Today*, *5*, 24–44.

Rubinstein, W. D. (1986). *Wealth and Inequality in Britain*. London: Faber & Faber.

Rubinstein, W. D. (1987). *Elites and the Wealthy in Modern British History*. Brighton: Harvester.

Rudmin, F. W. (1990). Cross-cultural correlates of the ownership of private property. Unpublished MS, cited by Dittmar (1992).

Runciman, W. G. (1966). *Relative Deprivation and Social Justice*. London: Routledge & Kegan Paul.

Rusbult, C. E. (1983). A longitudinal test of the investment model: the development (and deterioration) of satisfaction and commitment in heterosexual involvement. *Journal of Personality and Social Psychology*, *45*, 101–17.

Sabini, J. (1995). *Social Psychology*, (second edn). New York: W. W. Norton.

Sales, S. M. and House, J. (1971). Job dissatisfaction as a possible risk factor in coronary heart disease. *Journal of Chronic Diseases*, *23*, 861–73.

Scanzoni, J. (1979). Social exchange and behavioral interdependence. In R. L. Burgess and T. L. Huston (eds), *Social Exchange in Developing Relationships*. New York: Academic Press.

Scherer, K. R., Walbott, H. G. and Summerfield, A. B. (1986). *Experiencing Emotion*. Cambridge: Cambridge University Press.

Scherhorn, G. (1990). The addiction trait in buying behaviour. *Journal of Consumer Policy*, *13*, 33–51.

Schoemaker, P. (1979). The role of statistical knowledge in gambling decisions. *Organizational Behaviour and Human Performance*, *24*, 1–17.

Schug, M. and Birkey, C. (1985). The development of children's economic reasoning. Paper given at American Educational Research Association, Chicago.

Schverish, P. G. and Havens, J. J. (1995). Explaining the curve in the U-shaped curve. *Voluntas*, *6*, 203–25.

Scitovsky, T. (1992). *The Joyless Economy*, (revised edn). New York: Oxford University Press.

Scott, J. (1982). *The Upper Classes*. London: Macmillan.

Scott, J. W. and Tilly, L. A. (1975). Women's work and the family in nineteenth century Europe. *Comparative Studies in Society and History*, *17*, 36–64.

Scott, W.D., Clothier, R.C. and Spriegel, W.R. (1960). *Personnel Management*. New York: McGraw-Hill.

Seeley, J., Kajura, E., Bachengana, C., Okongo, M., Wagner, U. and Mulder, D. (1993). The extended family and support for people with AIDS in a rural population in South West Uganda: A safety net with holes? *AIDS-Care*, *5*, 117–22.

Sen, A. (1977). Rational fools: A critique of the behavioral foundations of economic theory. *Philosophy and Public Affairs*, *6*, 317–44.

Sevon, G. and Weckstrom, S. (1989). The development of reasoning about economic events: A study of Finnish children. *Journal of Economic Psychology*, *10*, 495–514.

Shefrin, H. and Thaler, R. (1988). The behavioural life-cycle hypothesis. *Economic Inquiry*, *26*, 609–43.

Sherman, E., and Newman, E.S. (1977–8). The meaning of cherished personal possessions for the elderly. *International Journal of Aging and Human Development*, 8, 181–92.

Simmel, G. (1957). Fashion. *American Journal of Sociology*, 62, 541–58.

Simmel, G. (1978). *The Philosophy of Money*. London: Routledge & Kegan Paul.

Smelser, N. (1963). *The Sociology of Economic Life*. Englewood Cliffs, NJ: Prentice-Hall.

Smith, A. (1975). *An Inquiry into the Nature and Causes of the Wealth of Nations*. New York: Modern Libras.

Smith, H., Fuller, R. and Forrest, D. (1975). Coin value and perceived size: a longitudinal study. *Perceptual and Motor Skills*, 41, 227–32.

Smith, K. and Kinsey, K. (1987). Understanding tax paying behaviour. *Law and Society Review*, 21, 639–63.

Smith, P. M. and Glass, G. V. (1977). Meta-analysis of psychotherapy outcome studies. *American Psychologist*, 32, 752–60.

Smith, R. H., Diener, E. and Wedell, D. H. (1989). Intrapersonal and social comparison determinants of happiness: a range–frequency analysis. *Journal of Personality and Social Psychology*, 56, 317–25.

Smith, S. and Razzell, P. (1975). *The Pools Winners*. London: Caliban Books.

Smithback, J. (1990). *Money Talks: A Glossary of Idioms, Terms and Standard Expressions on Money*. Singapore: Federal Publications.

Snelders, H., Hussein, G., Lea, S. and Webley, P. (1992). The polymorphous concept of money. *Journal of Economic Psychology*, 13, 71–92.

Sonuga-Barke, E. and Webley, P. (1993). *Children's Saving: A Study in the Development of Economic Behaviour*. Hove: Lawrence Erlbaum Associates.

Stacey, B. (1982). Economic socialization in the pre-adult years. *British Journal of Social Psychology*, 21, 159–73.

Stacey, B. and Singer, M. (1985). The perception of poverty and wealth among teenagers. *Journal of Adolescence*, 8, 231–41.

Stanley, T. (1994). Silly bubbles and the insensitivity of rationality testing: an experimental illustration. *Journal of Economic Psychology*, 15, 601–20.

Staub, E. and Noerenberg, H. (1981). Property rights, deservingness, reciprocity, friendship: the transactional character of children's sharing behavior. *Journal of Personality and Social Psychology*, 40, 271–89.

Steers, R. M. and Rhodes, S. R. (1984). Knowledge and speculation about absenteeism. In P. S. Goodman, R. S. Atkin and associates (eds), *Absenteeism*. San Francisco: Jossey-Bass.

Stokvis, R. (1993). Entrepreneurs, markets and environment: The fate of the Model T Ford. *Sociologishe-Gids*, 40, 34–48.

Stone, E. and Gottheil, E. (1975). Factor analysis of orality and anality in selected patient groups. *Journal of Nervous and Mental Diseases*, 160, 311–23.

Strack, F., Schwarz, N. and Gschneidinger, E. (1985). Happiness and reminiscing: the role of time perspective, affect, and mode of thinking. *Journal of Personality and Social Psychology*, 49, 1460–9.

Strauss, A. (1952). The development and transformation of monetary meaning in the child. *American Sociological Review*, 53, 275–86.

Strickland, L., Lewichi, R. and Katz, A. (1966). Temporal orientation and perceived control as determinants of risk-taking. *Journal of Experimental Social Psychology*, 2, 143–51.

Summers, T. P. and Hendrix, W. H. (1991). Modelling the role of pay equity perceptions: a field study. *Journal of Occupational Psychology*, 64, 145–57.

Sutton, R. (1962). Behavior in the attainment of economic concepts. *Journal of Psychology*, 53, 37–46.

Swift, A., Marshall, G. and Burgoyne, C. (1992). Which road to social justice. *Sociology Review*, 2, 28–31.

Tajfel, H. (1977). Value and the perceptual judgement of magnitude. *Psychological Review*, 64, 192–204.

Takahashi, K. and Hatano, G. (1989). Conceptions of the Bank: A Developmental Study. JCSS Technical Report No. 11.

Tang, T. (1992). The meaning of money revisited. *Journal of Organizational Behaviour*, 13, 197–202.

Tang, T. (1993). The meaning of money: extension and exploration of the money ethic scale in a sample of University students in Taiwan. *Journal of Organizational Behaviour*, 14, 93–9.

Tang, T. (1995). The development of a short money ethic scale: attitudes toward money and pay satisfaction revisited. *Personality and Individual Differences*. ' 19, 809–16.

Tang, T. (1996). Pay differentials as a function of rater's sex, money, ethnic, and job incumbent sex: a test of the Matthew effect. *Journal of Economic Psychology*, 17, 127–44.

Tang, T. and Gilbert, P. (1995). Attitudes towards money as related to intrinsic and extrinsic job satisfaction, stress and work-related attitudes. *Personality and Individual Differences*, 19, 327–32.

Tang, T., Furnham, A. and Davis, G. (1997). A cross-cultural comparison of the money ethic, the Protestant Work Ethic and job satisfaction. Unpublished paper.

Thaler, R. (1990). Saving, fungibility and mental accounts. *Journal of Economic Perspectives*, 4, 193–205.

Thibaut, J. W. and Kelley, H. H. (1959). *The Social Psychology of Groups*. New York: Wiley.

Thornton, B., Kirchner, G. and Jacobs, J. (1991). The influence of a photograph on a charitable appeal: a picture may be worth a thousand words when it has to speak for itself. *Journal of Applied Social Psychology*, 21, 433–45.

Thurnwald, A. (1932). *Money*. London: Methuen.

Titmuss, R. M. (1970). *The Gift Relationship*, London: Allen & Unwin

Townsend, P. (1979). *Poverty in the United Kingdom*. Harmondsworth: Penguin.

Turkle, S. (1984). *The Second Self: Computers and the Human Spirit*. New York: Simon & Schuster.

Vagero, D. and Lundberg, O. (1989). Health inequalities in Britain and Sweden. *The Lancet*, July 1st, 35–6.

van Raaij, W. and Gianotten, H. (1990). Consumer confidence, expenditure, saving and credit. *Journal of Economic Psychology*, 11, 269–90.

Veblen, T. (1899). *The Theory of the Leisure Class*. New York: Viking.

Veenhoven, R. (1994). Is happiness a trait? Tests of the theory that a better society does not make people any happier. *Social Indicators Research*, 32, 101–60.

Veenhoven, R. (1996). Developments in satisfaction research. *Social Indicators Research*, 37, 1–46.

Veenhoven, R. and co-workers (1994). *World DataBase on Happiness*. Rotterdam: Rotterdam University Press.

Vlek, C. (1973). A fair betting game as an admissible procedure for assessment of subjective probabilities. *British Journal of Mathematical and Statistical Psychology*, 26, 18–30.

Vogel, J. (1974). Taxation and public opinion in Sweden. *National Tax Journal*, 27, 499–513.

Vogler, C. (1994). Money in the household. In M. Anderson, F. Bechhofer and J. Gershuny (eds), *The Social and Political Economy of the Household*, (pp. 225–66). Oxford: Oxford University Press.

Vogler, C. and Pahl, J. (1994). Money, power and inequality within marriage. *Sociological Review*, *42*, 263–88.

Waite, P. (1988). Economic awareness: context, issues and concepts. *Theory and Practice*, *4*, 16–29.

Walker, M. (1995). *The Psychology of Gambling*. London: Butterworth-Heinemann.

Walls (1991). *Pocket-money Monitor*. Walton-on-Thames: Bird's Eye Walls.

Walstad, W. (1979). Effectiveness of a USMES in service economic education programme for elementary school teachers. *Journal of Economic Education*, *11*, 1–20.

Walstad, W. and Watts, M. (1985). Teaching economics in the schools: a review of survey findings. *Journal of Economic Psychology*, *16*, 135–46.

Wapner, S., Demick, J. and Redondo, J. P. (1990). Cherished possessions and adaptation of older people into nursing homes. *International Journal of Aging and Human Development*, *31*, 219–35.

Ward, S., Wackman, D. and Wartella, E. (1977). *How Children Learn to Buy*. London: Sage.

Warren, P. E. and Walker, I. (1991). Empathy, effectiveness and donations to charity: social psychology's contribution. *British Journal of Social Psychology*, *30*, 325–37.

Weatherill, L. (1993). The meaning of consumer behaviour in late seventeenth and early eighteenth century England. In J. Brewer and R. Porter (eds), *Consumption and the World of Goods*. London: Routledge.

Webley, P. (1983). Growing up in the modern economy. Paper at 6th International Conference on Political Psychology.

Webley, P. (1996). Playing the market: the autonomous economic world of children. In P. Lunt and A. Furnham (eds), *Economic Socialization* (pp. 149–60). Cheltenham: Edward Elgar.

Webley, S. E. G. and Lea, S. (1993). The partial unacceptability of money as repayment for neighbourly help. *Human Relations*, *46*, 65–76.

Webley, P. and Wilson, R. (1989). Social relationships and the unacceptability of money as a gift. *Journal of Social Psychology*, *129*, 85–91.

Webley, P., Lea, S. E. G. and Portalska, R. (1983). The unacceptability of money as a gift. *Journal of Economic Psychology*, *4*, 223–38.

Webley, P., Levine, M. and Lewis, A. (1991). A study in economic psychology: children's saving in a play economy. *Human Relations*, *44*, 127–46.

Wedgwood, J. (1929). *The Economics of Inheritance*, London: Routledge.

Weigel, R., Hessing, D. and Elffers, H. (1987). Tax evasion research. *Journal of Economic Psychology*, *8*, 215–35.

Weitzel, W., Harpaz, I. and Weiner, N. (1977). Predicting pay satisfaction from non pay work variables. *Industrial Relations*, *16*, 323–34.

Wells, W. D., Andriuli, F. J., Goi, F. J. and Seader, S. (1957). An adjective check list for the study of 'product personality'. *Journal of Applied Psychology*, *41*, 317–19.

Wernimont, P. and Fitzpatrick, S. (1972). The meaning of money. *Journal of Applied Psychology*, *56*, 248–61.

Weyant, J. H. (1978). Effect of mood states, costs, and benefits of helping. *Journal of Personality and Social Psychology*, *36*, 1169–76.

Weyant, J. M. (1984). Applying social psychology to induce charitable donations. *Journal of Applied Social Psychology*, *14*, 441–7.

Weyant, J. M. and Smith, S. L. (1987). Getting more by asking for less: the effects of request size on donations. *Journal of Applied Social Psychology*, *17*, 392–400.

Whitehead, D. (1986). Students' attitudes to economic issues. *Economics*, *4*, 24–32.

Wicklund, R. A. and Gollwitzer, P. M. (1982). *Symbolic Self-Completion.* Hillsdale, NJ: Erlbaum.

Wiesenthal, D. L., Austrom, D. and Silverman, I. (1983). Diffusion of responsibility in charitable donations. *Basic and Applied Social Psychology,* 4, 17–27.

Williams, D. R. (1990). Socioeconomic differentials in health: a review and redirection. *Social Psychology Quarterly, 53,* 81–99.

Willits, F. K. and Crider, D. M. (1988). Health rating and life satisfaction in the later middle years. *Journal of Gerontology, 43,* 172–S176.

Willmott, P. (1987). *Friendship Networks and Social Support.* London: Policy Studies Institute.

Willmott, P. and Young, M. (1960). *Family and Class in a London Suburb.* London: Routledge & Kegan Paul.

Wilson, E. O. (1975). *Sociobiology: The New Synthesis.* Cambridge, MA: Harvard University Press.

Wilson, G. (1973). *The Psychology of Conservation.* London: Academic Press.

Wilson, G. and Patterson, J. (1968). A new measure of conservatism. *British Journal of Social and Clinical Psychology, 7,* 264–8.

Winocur, S. and Siegal, M. (1982). Adolescents' judgement of economic arguments. *International Journal of Behavioral Development, 5,* 357–65.

Wiseman, T. (1974). *The Money Motive.* London: Hodder & Stoughton.

Witryol, S. and Wentworth, N. (1983). A paired comparisons scale of children's preference for monetary and material rewards used in investigations of incentive effects. *Journal of Genetic Psychology, 142,* 17–23.

Wolfe, J. (1936). Effectiveness of token-rewards for chimpanzees. *Comparative Psychological Monographs, 12,* No.5.

Wosinski, M. and Pietras, M. (1990). Economic socialization of Polish children in different macro-economic conditions. *Journal of Economic Psychology, 11,* 515–29.

Wyatt, E. and Hinden, S. (1991). *The Money Book: A Smart Kid's Guide to Savvy Saving and Spending.* New York: Somerville House.

Yamauchi, K. and Templer, D. (1982). The development of a money attitude scale. *Journal of Personality Assessment, 46,* 522–8.

Yang, H. and Chandler, D. (1992). Intergenerational grievances of the elderly in rural China. *Journal of Comparative Family Studies, 23,* 431–53.

Young, M. and Willmott, P. (1973). *The Symmetrical Family.* London: Routledge & Kegan Paul.

Zabukovec, V. and Polic, M. (1990). Yugoslavian children in a situation of rapid economic changes. *Journal of Economic Psychology, 11,* 529–43.

Zelizer, V. (1985). *Pricing the Priceless Child: The Changing Social Value of Children.* New York: Basic Books.

Zelizer, V. (1989). The social meaning of money: 'Special monies'. *American Journal of Sociology, 95,* 342–77.

Zinser, O., Perry, S. and Edgar, R. (1975). Affluence of the recipient, value of donations, and sharing behaviour in pre-school children. *Journal of Psychology, 89,* 301–5.

Zweig, F. (1961). *The Worker in an Affluent Society.* London: Heinemann.

Index

Roland-Levy, C. 77
role play study 65
Rose, M. 258
Rosenberg, M. 218, 284
Ross, A. D. 221, 222
Rossi, P. H. 262, 273
Rothschild, Baron Guy de (quoted) 203
Rothschild, Lord (quoted) 62
Rubinstein, W. D. 45–6, 47, 49, 52, 255,
    257, 258
Rudney, G. 227, 229
Runciman, W. G. 259, 272
Rushton, J. P. 236, 245
Ruskin, John (quoted) 265
Russia, wage differential 263
Rutherford, Lord (quoted) 101
Ryan, R. 215
Ryan, R. M. 165, 287

Sabini, J. 236, 240, 241
Santayana, George (quoted) 1
satisfaction paradox 269–70
saving 101, 107, 130, 138, 288; age factors
    111–12; and borrowing 113; children
    75–6, 82–3, 90–1; household 111–13;
    income-saving theory 109; Protestant
    work ethic 148; social comparisons 108;
    theories 107–11; USA 105–6
Schooler, C. 219, 281
Schopenhauer, Arthur (quoted) 265
Schroeder, D. A. 238
Schug, M. 65
Scitovsky, T. 164, 274
Scotland, study 77
Scott, J. 255, 257
security 5, 137–9, 209
self-denial 136, 138
self-employment 179
self-esteem 45, 52, 103, 143, 261, 282, 284
self-image 157
self-interest 119, 220, 287–8
Seneca, Lucius Annaeus (quoted) 253
Sevon, G. 65, 74
Shefrin, H. 110
Shenstone, William (quoted) 203
shopping 25, 49, 101, 103–4
Sickert, Walter Richard (quoted) 203
similarity, social influence 235, 237
Simmel, G. 102, 173
Singer, M. 75
situationalists, gambling 121
Slater, Jim (quoted) 101
Smelser, N. 21, 34
Smith, Adam 10, 21
Smith, S. 217, 271, 283
Smith, S. L. 238, 239
Smith, Sydney (quoted) 1
Social Change and Economic Life Initiative
    182–3
social class: children and money 67, 77;

clothes 173; gambling 119–20; health
    278; help from kin 189–90; houses 170;
    jobs 219; life-style 278–80; mental health
    280–1; mobility 257–8, 264; pocket
    money 83, 86; possessions 157, 163–4,
    167–8; sacred meaning of money 40;
    social relationships 276–7
social comparison 29, 108, 211, 271, 272–3
social control 221, 246, 247
social dilemma 127
social influence 234, 235–6, 237
social psychology 28–30, 244
social relationships 21–2, 198–9, 275–7
Social Trends 171, 181
socialisation: charity 241; children 143, 288;
    economic 63, 64, 78–86, 143; family
    income allocation 183–4, 185; money
    values 102
socialism 92–3, 221
sociolobiology 157, 158
sociology of: money 21–4, 101–2; tipping
    247
Sonuga-Barke, E. 75, 76, 82, 106
Sophocles (quoted) 129
spending 101, 104–5, 109, 130, 288;
    children 91; family 36, 155, 182–6, 260;
    life-cycle hypothesis 109, 110;
    psychology of 103–13; styles 49; wealthy
    259–61
spendthrifts 45, 134, 144, 145
sponsorship 232, 244
Stacey, B. 64, 75, 78
status symbols 4, 161–2, 171–2
Stein, Gertrude (quoted) 220
Steinmetz, Charles (quoted) 265
stereotyping 24–5, 78, 182
Stevens, J. 235
Stockdale, Sir Edmund (quoted) 37
Stratta, E. 180, 183
Strauss, A. 64, 66, 69
Stringfield, P. 207
sumptuary laws 163
Sunday Telegraph 271
Swedish studies 102, 124
symbolism: money 20–1, 31, 32, 151, 288;
    possessions 36, 159, 160–2; values 288

taboo, money 3, 130, 131
Taebel, D. 66
Taiwan 42, 191
Tang, T. 42, 43, 54, 55, 148
tax avoidance/evasion 124–5, 126
tax relief, charity 243, 263, 289–90
taxation: economic understanding 95;
    indirect 124; political allegiance 125;
    progressive 124; as social contract 123;
    typology of taxpayers 126–7; US 125–6
Taylor, R. 93–6
Templer, D. 46, 52–3, 54
territory 158, 169